Commendations

This work on Spirit-empowered evangelists is a strategic reference for reaching the unreached in our complex, interconnected world. By re-personalizing the Great Commission through Spirit-empowered strategies, it equips believers for holistic transformation. This volume is a clarion call, masterfully mobilizing the global church toward radical obedience in this defining *kairos* moment.

Peter Oyugi
Movement for African National Initiatives

This essential resource inspires and equips scholars, church leaders, and missionaries to pursue effective, Spirit-led engagement with the world. Through its compelling narratives, scholarly analysis, and strategic guidance, the book highlights the vital role of healing, empowerment, adaptability, and technology in fulfilling the Great Commission. It is with great pleasure that I recommend this book.

Victor John
Global Mission Strategist,
Catalyst for CPM/DMM

Everyone Reaching EveryONE is both a reference work and a handbook for this pivotal hour. Edited with care and global breadth, it offers strong biblical foundations, Spirit-empowered theological reflection, and compelling case studies that demonstrate how the Holy Spirit continues to advance the gospel through men and women in every context, including the digital world and the most difficult mission fields. As co-chair of the Global Evangelist Alliance and a member of the Empowered21 council, I am sincerely grateful for the outstanding scholarship and the practical missional insight represented in these pages. I recommend this book to evangelists, pastors, students, and leaders who want to see EveryONE reached, and to help finish the Great Commission Jesus entrusted to His Church.

Jean-Luc Traschel
Co-Chair, Global Evangelist Alliance
President of the International Association
of Healing Ministries
President and founder of Europe Shall Be Saved

Foreword

"The supreme task of the church is the evangelization of the world." First articulated by missionary-statesman Oswald J. Smith, this assertion powerfully echoes the commission of Jesus Christ, who sent his followers to proclaim the gospel to the ends of the earth. Its simplicity and force capture both the urgency and the universality of the church's mission.

This declaration deeply influenced my own family's ministry trajectory. As a young couple, my parents, Drs. T. L. and Daisy Osborn, traveled to Canada and attended The People's Church in Toronto. Upon entering the sanctuary, they were confronted by a large banner bearing Dr. Smith's bold proclamation. That moment served not merely as a visual impression but as a defining affirmation of the church's highest priority: to take the message of Jesus Christ to the whole world. They proceeded to labor as evangelists in over a hundred nations, in cooperation with local churches, to fulfill this mandate.

Today, God is doing historic things through the leadership of Dr. William Wilson and the global Empowered21 movement. Its EveryONE Vision is mobilizing, training, and sending Spirit-empowered evangelists to every region of the world. The overarching aim of Empowered21— to see every person on earth experience an authentic encounter with Jesus Christ through the Holy Spirit by Pentecost 2033—has emerged as a unifying call that resonates deeply within the global evangelistic community. From the first century, the Holy Spirit has consistently compelled God's people toward the fulfillment of the Master's global assignment. Today, the wind of the Spirit continues to stir believers across continents to engage in intentional and comprehensive evangelism.

The urgency of this task can never be overstated. Amid growing global instability, moral fragmentation, and widespread spiritual hunger, the gospel of Jesus Christ remains humanity's only enduring hope. While the needs of the world have intensified, the transforming power of God's love has not diminished; indeed, it continues to demonstrate its efficacy in changing individuals, communities, and nations. Throughout more than fifty-five years of global evangelism, I have witnessed firsthand the power of the gospel—proclaimed in the authority of the Holy Spirit—to call people from every persuasion to faith in Jesus Christ. Christianity is not merely another world religion; it is the life of the resurrected Jesus made available to all who believe in him. Sharing his life with people is the sacred calling of the Spirit-empowered evangelist, who stands as a unique gift to the body of Christ.

This publication examines the urgency of evangelism within today's global context, articulates the biblical mandate that undergirds evangelistic engagement, and demonstrates the indispensability of Holy Spirit's empowerment in the life and ministry of an evangelist. Many case studies show how the work of the Spirit-empowered evangelist is fulfilling the EveryONE Vision in diverse and effective ways. Spirit-empowered evangelism is not optional but essential for faithful completion of the church's mission in this generation. Now is the time.

LaDonna C. Osborn
Osborn Ministries International
International Gospel Fellowship
Global Evangelists Alliance, Empowered21

Everyone Reaching EveryONE

Portraits of Spirit-Empowered Evangelists

Everyone Reaching EveryONE

Portraits of Spirit-Empowered Evangelists

Edited by

Wonsuk Ma and Opoku Onyinah

with Jaime L. Riddle, Associate Editor

Tulsa, Oklahoma, USA
2026

Everyone Reaching EveryONE: Portraits of Spirit-Empowered Evangelists
Copyright ©2026 Oral Roberts University and Contributors

Published by ORU Press
7777 S. Lewis Ave., Tulsa, OK 74171 USA

https://orupress.org/

ORU Press is the book and journal publishing division of Oral Roberts University.

Published in the United States of America with permission from Empowered21. https://empowered21.com. Empowered21 aims to help shape the future of the global Spirit-empowered movement throughout the world. This kingdom initiative is served by Oral Roberts University in Tulsa, Oklahoma, www.oru.edu.

Cover design by Jiwon Kim
Editorial Assistant: Shiloah Matic Ma
Interior Designer and Compositor: Sandra Kimbell

ISBN: 978-1-950971-41-1 (paperback)
ISBN: 978-1-950971-42-8 (e-book)

Printed in the United States of America

Contents

Acknowledgments

The editorial team wishes to express its gratitude to many who made this book possible. The first are the presenters to the 2023 Amsterdam Empowered21 Scholars Consultation and contributors whom the editors recruited subsequently. Their valuable studies, both foundational and contextual, make this book a rich resource for Spirit-empowered evangelism across the globe. The second group is the international church and ministry leaders who provided the Foreword and Commendations gracing the book. The third is the leadership of Empowered21 for their strong commitment to Spirit-empowered scholarship through the Consultation and publishing process. Additional thanks go to Oral Roberts University and ORU Press for its commitment to the ongoing publication of the GNSES series. Also the Center for Spirit-Empowered Research, which managed the editorial work, Professor Jiwon Kim for creating the cover, Polly Tjihenuna for creating the index, and Sandra Kimbell who composed the text. Special thanks to Shiloah Matic Ma, who undertook the copyediting, and Jaime Riddle who managed the project.

This book is another showcase for Spirit-empowered scholarship, for which both academics and practitioners explored the transformative work of the Holy Spirit in evangelism through Spirit-empowered evangelists, both known and less known. As their lives brought millions to the saving knowledge of Christ, so do we offer this book to the cause of the EveryONE initiative.

The Editors
New Year, 2026

Introduction

Opoku Onyinah and Wonsuk Ma

The twenty-first century marks an era of intensified global challenges and vast opportunities for gospel proclamation. In an age of rapid technological advances, complex inter-cultural migration, and economic globalization, the church is challenged to confront a world that is both complex and rapidly evolving. As societies become more interconnected, issues such as the recognition of gender equity, forced migration as a result of war or climate change, disability inclusion, and the increasing reality of cultural and religious pluralism demand a missiological response that is biblically grounded, Spirit-empowered, and contextually relevant.

Originally, evangelism was, in a way, confined to the verbal proclamation of the gospel to those who were not yet converted; but now it takes on many forms and platforms, from preaching the word on the streets of busy urban centers to walking alongside displaced persons in refugee camps, from digital evangelism to evangelistic crusades with power encounters. It is in this dynamic theater that the figure of the "Spirit-empowered Evangelist" emerges as a potentially rich and timely model for Christian witness. These are people of God—men and women—whose ministry is grounded in the Word of God, fueled by the presence and power of the Holy Spirit, and expressed through love, compassion, boldness, and cross-cultural sensitivity. They disciple not just through proclamation but also through holistic transformation—meeting spiritual, physical, emotional, and societal needs as the Spirit leads.

2023 Scholars Consultation

The 2023 Empowered21 Scholars Consultation was held from June 19-20, 2023, in Amsterdam, Netherlands. To support and align with the Empowered21's EveryONE launch, based on the commitment of two dozen Christian leaders who met in December 2022 in New York, the consultation's theme was "Spirit-empowered evangelists." The program also included the launch of the Global Network of Spirit-Empowered Scholars (GNSES).

This volume is based on that first GNSES consultation held under the theme "Spirit-Empowered Evangelists." It is packed with contributions from missiologists, historians, theologians, and ministry practitioners from across the globe that offer Spirit-driven perspectives for understanding evangelism. The consultation included seven substantive studies that reckoned with the deeper and wider implications of what it means to be a Spirit-empowered witness in our time. These studies offered biblical, theological, historical, and missiological frameworks alongside dynamic portraits of evangelists whose Spirit-empowered ministries have engaged, converted, and transformed cultures, ethnicities, and continents.

The consultation also featured five studies examining the ministries of key evangelists with regional or continental reach. Among them were Reinhard Bonnke, who through power evangelism by the Holy Ghost saw mass conversions in Africa, and the effect of a warm friendship between Oral Roberts and Bill Graham, which enriched each other's evangelistic work, while crossing ecclesial boundaries and cultural expectations. A case study on evangelism among refugees was equally remarkable, communicating the suffering of displaced persons and their potential as both receivers and bearers of the gospel. This presentation highlighted the necessity of contextual strategies to honor trauma, cultural identity, and human dignity, but also to develop hope through the Spirit.[1]

Ultimately, the consultation reflected a wide-ranging vision of evangelism demonstrating that Spirit-empowered evangelists are not limited to stadiums or pulpits; they also consist of laypeople, women, refugees, persons with disabilities, and digital missionaries—all filled with the same Spirit to engage every sector of human life. In this manner, Spirit-empowered evangelism develops into convergence with the holistic mission of God.[2]

The Book Project

Following the Amsterdam consultation, we engaged several individuals to write on particular topics. The result of the consultation and the engagement of other writers is the content presented in this book. The volume is divided into two sections (twenty chapters in total) that work together to provide a robust exploration of Spirit-empowered evangelism.

The first section, Foundations, contains seven chapters laying down the biblical, theological, and strategic framework for understanding and engaging in Spirit-led evangelistic ministry. The second section, Cases in Context, provides thirteen enlightening case studies on how Spirit-empowered evangelists function in different global contexts. Together, Foundations and Cases in Context reflect the breadth and depth of the Spirit's contemporary action in global evangelism.

Part I: Foundations opens with a keynote chapter on the task of Spirit-filled scholarship in fulfilling the mandate of reaching "EveryONE" for Christ. The next study explores the biblical mandate for evangelism by examining its necessity, the call to proclamation, the qualifications required, and the various methods used. Another biblical study examines a Johannine case for Spirit-empowered witnessing, demonstrating the importance of the Holy Spirit in the Gospel of John. Next, the role that spiritual gifts play is analyzed through the lens of the fivefold ministry of Ephesians 4:11–12. Another chapter provides future-oriented perspective on the EveryONE initiative, looking ahead to 2033, alongside a strategic white paper from the Global Evangelists Alliance of Empowered21. A concluding round-table engagement highlights prophetic evangelism, drawing attention to the Spirit's revelatory and time-sensitive guidance in mission. Part one has firmly established that when we speak of Spirit-led evangelism, we are not just talking about proclamation but also the transformation of people, communities, and nations.[3]

Part II: Cases in Context shifts gears from theory to practice, providing real-life examples of Spirit-empowered evangelism. These include historical and contemporary figures such as Reinhard Bonnke, T. L. and Daisy Osborn, Niilo Yli-Vainio, and Oral Roberts in the context of his friendship with Billy Graham. Contexts across the globe—from Africa to Asia, Europe to Latin America—reflect the dynamic nature of Spirit-driven evangelism. The case studies range from digital evangelism in Africa to Greek evangelism with Muslim refugees, Spirit-empowered women in Japan, Spirit-empowered evangelists in Korea, and female Catholic missionaries. The section also looks at unique contexts such as Spirit-empowered Anglican-Pentecostalism in Chile, rural Indian Pentecostalism, and internet evangelism in our hyper-individualistic age.

The global diversity of presenters contributing to this volume attests to the international nature of Spirit-empowered mission. With coverage of all the continents, and historically marginalized groups of all kinds, this book provides a panoramic vision of the continuing work of the Holy Spirit in all kinds of settings. It reminds us that Spirit-led evangelism is not a ten-step program but a trans-dimensional movement grounded in divine agency and human volition. In addition, tellingly, five of the contributors are women; their perspectives add to the volume's planetary and gender-inclusive reach. The book sends a clear message that every believer empowered by the Spirit is an "evangelist" to reach everyONE!

In summary, this is a reference work and a handbook combined for Spirit-empowered evangelists who desire to engage the world for Christ in the power of the Spirit faithfully and effectively. This volume hopes to be a guide for the scholar, church leader, missionary, and student who want to know the character and calling of Spirit-empowered evangelists today. Each chapter shows rigorous study with implications for the church's mission. The themes of the original Amsterdam consultation— global diversity, biblical foundations, historical reflection, theological depth, and missional praxis— are reflected in the structure of this book. As you read these chapters, I hope you are motivated not just to believe in the manifold expressions of Spirit-empowered evangelism but also to discover your place in this Spirit-driven movement that knows no time, geography, or cultural boundaries.

Notes

1 Paul G. Hiebert, *Gospel in Human Contexts: Anthropological Exploration for Contemporary Missions* (Grand Rapids, MI: Baker Academic, 2009), 201–204.

2 As articulated by theologians, including Bosch and Walls. See D. J. Bosch, *Transforming Mission: Paradigm Shifts in Theology of Mission* (Maryknoll, NY: Orbis Books, 1991), 390–393; Andrew F. Walls, *The Cross-Cultural Process in Christian History: Studies in the Transmission and Appropriation of Faith* (Maryknoll, NY: Orbis Books, 2002), 67–71.

3 Michael Green, *Evangelism in the Primitive Church* (Grand Rapids: Eerdmans, 2004), 19.

Part I

Foundations

1   The Task of Spirit-Empowered Scholarship in Reaching EveryONE for Christ: Keynote Address

William M. Wilson

The Roots of GNSES

The role of the Global Network of Spirit-Empowered Scholars (GNSES), of Empowered21, is to ensure scholarship that would serve the church, help guide the Spirit-empowered movement forward, and address real needs within global Christianity. The Empowered21 emphasis on Spirit-empowered scholarship began with the Azusa Street Centennial Celebration in 2006. To highlight its significance, scholars contributed papers reflecting on the Azusa Street Revival's national and global impact. The integration of Spirit-empowered research with revival demonstrated the critical role of scholarship in understanding and advancing the movement.

This centennial event brought together over fifty thousand attendees from 114 nations, serving as a global homecoming for diverse Pentecostal and Charismatic communities. Following the event, the newly acquired database of Spirit-empowered leaders inspired the creation of a global network. Together with Dr. Vinson Synan and others, we launched Empowered21, a Spirit-empowered relational network focused on the future of Spirit-empowered Christianity to engage a new generation with the power of the Holy Spirit.

The term "Spirit-empowered Christianity" was chosen intentionally. Dr. Synan, myself, and others traveled the world holding a series of conversation events about Spirit baptism and terminology. These insightful conversations convened on five continents, with over five hundred people from fifty-four nations and more than fifteen different universities participating in seventeen unique conversations. Wherever we went, we asked the same questions: What does it mean to be Spirit-empowered in the twenty-first century? "What does it mean to be Spirit-empowered in the twenty-first century?" and "What steps can we take to engage new generations in the Spirit-empowered experience." Also, "What do you see as the movement's greatest needs, and the greatest needs in your context?"

Out of these conversations, Oral Roberts University held a Global Congress on Holy Spirit Empowerment in 2010. During the congress, we conducted surveys that revealed that young adults favored the term "Spirit-empowered" over alternatives like "Pentecostal" or "Charismatic." "Spirit-empowered" resonated as a unifying term encompassing Pentecostals, Charismatics, neo-Pentecostals, Third Wave Charismatics, Charismatic Catholics, and others connected to Azusa's spiritual heritage.

Early conversations around the future of the Spirit-empowered movement included three key groups: new generation voices, spiritual parents, and scholars. New generation voices are essential for connecting future leaders with the movement's history and wisdom. Spiritual parents—pastors and leaders with deep integrity—provide intergenerational mentoring and connectivity. Scholars contribute theological depth and insights to address unique challenges within Spirit-empowered contexts across the globe.

Through these discussions, eight primary needs of the movement were identified:

1) Leadership Character
2) Greater Biblical Literacy
3) Desire for Spiritual Fathers and Mothers
4) Resources for Ministry
5) Education
6) Contextualization
7) Transition of Leadership
8) Rise of Islam

These needs remain critical today as the Spirit-empowered church navigates a generational leadership transition. The twenty-first-century church is in a supernaturally expanded passing zone in which one generation is passing the baton of leadership to another. This is especially true in the global Spirit-empowered movement. Since the launch of Empowered21, our annual Scholars Consultations organized by the Global Network of Spirit-Empowered Scholars have served the movement by compiling papers and research on unique subjects and publishing books that emerge from that research.

I am honored to serve and provide guidance as we build such an amazing network where scholarship is serving the church and, ultimately, the world. There are four pillars that I pray will characterize and set a precedent for the task of Spirit-empowered scholarship in the twenty-first century.

1. Scholarship that Builds the Spirit-Empowered Movement

Spirit-empowered scholarship must prioritize the growth and maturation of the movement. Scholars should ask: "What should we study in our present circumstances that will help Spirit-empowered Christianity expand in the future?" and "How can we study, encourage, edify, deepen, and widen the Spirit-empowered movement?" In 2013, we discovered that only Europe and North America had solidified networks for Pentecostal leaders to unite. Other continents, including Asia, had some of the largest ministries in the world, but many of them had never met each other. We began to convene these leaders in the same room, and the energy around networking and getting to know one another was exciting and unity-provoking.

We recognized in early conversations that the Spirit-empowered movement had expanded globally; it was no longer a predominantly Western phenomenon. The predominance of the movement had shifted to the Global South and Global East. It was articulated in these early meetings that we needed a robust theology that would work around the world, whether in Africa, Asia, or Latin America. We needed to develop language that Christians in these areas could understand and resonate with, and recognize that scholars have played a vital role in this effort.

The Global Network of Spirit-Empowered Scholars still meets annually, and ultimately, the purpose of these meetings is to foster the power and move of the Holy Spirit and to reignite a commitment to the Great Commission. Spirit-empowered scholars must continue working together and exploring how to advance the gospel in unreached areas of Asia and the Middle East, addressing unique cultural and theological challenges. There are great historical works written on past missions movements, but I believe it is time for new work by scholars and practitioners regarding contemporary Great Commission efforts and strategies that have been informed by Spirit-empowered pastors, missionaries, theologians, and leaders worldwide.

2. Scholarship that Helps the World Understand the Movement

Spirit-empowered scholars have a unique opportunity to communicate the movement's identity to the world. We need vocabulary and concepts to characterize and clarify Spirit-empowered Christianity's global presence.

The Apostle Paul said in Acts 22:3 that he studied "at the feet of Gamaliel" (KJV). God used Paul to stand in Ephesus, Athens, Corinth, and Rome—all the cultural, educational, economic, and political capitals of the ancient world—and explain the message of Jesus to Greco-Roman audiences. Like Paul, who adapted his message to be understood, we need vocabulary and frameworks that resonate globally. My hope is that the Global Network of Spirit-Empowered Scholars will give itself to helping the world understand who we are by finding vocabulary and bridges that communicate the movement's purpose around the world. The Spirit-empowered church now finds itself at cultural, educational, economic, and political crossroads, and we need language and clarity to make our concepts understood. For example, in a post-pandemic world, Spirit-empowered research can offer insights into addressing depression, anxiety, and other societal challenges. Such scholarship can bridge gaps between the church and the world, demonstrating the relevance and transformative power of Spirit-empowered Christianity.

One of the most resounding societal challenges in today's world is justice. "What is justice?" and, more importantly, "What is biblical justice?" are topics that need to be explored. The Holy Spirit has placed on my heart that the greatest injustice in the twenty-first century is that the church has the means, the money, the mechanisms, the technology, and the power to share the Good News of Jesus with every person on earth, yet many still have never heard about Christ and are on their way to an eternity separated from God. Spirit-empowered scholarship must address this imbalance, emphasizing the urgency of fulfilling the Great Commission and helping the church return to its main mission. William Seymour, a prominent leader of the Azusa Street Revival, often emphasized that the power of the Holy Spirit equips us for evangelism, not just speaking in tongues. During and following the Azusa Street Revival, the Holy Spirit empowered the church for unparalleled evangelistic effectiveness. Spirit-empowered scholarship can help us refocus our efforts today to keep the mission central.

3. Scholarship that Connects Generations and Helps Us Reach EveryONE

In 2013, the Global Council adopted the Empowered21 vision to answer the question, "What will keep our network going?" The answer that arose was to try to do something so big that no one group could do it by themselves.

As we prayed, we felt the urging of the Holy Spirit to orient around our core values and launch a strong initiative to bring the Good News to every single person on earth. We adopted the following vision: "That every person on earth would have an authentic encounter with Jesus Christ through the power and presence of the Holy Spirit...by Pentecost 2033."

We chose Pentecost 2033 as our target date because it marks the two-thousand-year anniversary of the outpouring of the Holy Spirit, as recorded in Acts 2, and because it gives us the greatest opportunity to fulfill the vision. Some discussion ensued as to whether the two thousandth anniversary of Jesus' death, burial, resurrection, the giving of the Great Commission, Christ's ascension, and the birth of the church at Pentecost was the year 2033 or 2030, or an even earlier date. Pragmatically, the group chose 2033, which was the date farthest away, to give us as much time as possible to pursue the goal.

We recognized that reaching everyone is a task that no one can do alone—not a single church, nation, network, or ministry. There is a lot of energy in the kingdom of God that has created a *kairos* moment leading up to 2033, and several movements across Christianity have initiatives to reach the world by 2033. We saw similar momentum at the turn of the last millennium, in AD 2000. We now have this moment in time that I believe could propel us to advance the Great Commission further than ever before, and we have the opportunity in the coming years to put forth the most significant effort at Great Commission fulfillment in the history of the Christian church. The Spirit-empowered perspective is a vital contribution to this, and we must fan a flame around this vision that activates collaboration across generations. Reaching everyone will require "everyONE." Spirit-empowered scholars are uniquely equipped to ignite this passion in the church because they have studied their areas and know what the challenges and opportunities are.

I believe the method God has given us to reach everyone on earth is "one person at a time." As we re-personalize the Great Commission and focus on winning individual souls for Christ, God will unlock the multitudes. While great research has been done in the past surrounding unreached people groups, scholars continue to contribute understanding by exploring God's heart for unreached individuals in their communities. Scholars are also vital in addressing theological misconceptions that salvation is limited to a select few. Through books, papers, and other academic work, scholars contribute to an understanding that Jesus died for each person, making a way for everyone to know him and be filled with his Spirit: "[The Lord] is patient with you, not wanting anyone to perish, but everyone to come to repentance" (2 Pet 3:9, NIV). Jesus died for everyone, and he desires everyone to know him. Scholars can explore and communicate the heart of God in a fresh way.

4. Scholarship that Flows from Service and Love

Finally, Spirit-empowered scholarship must bring unity rooted in service and love. We know that "knowledge puffs up while love builds up" (1 Cor 8:1, NIV). Knowledge alone can lead to pride, but knowledge with love builds unity and strengthens the church. The Spirit-empowered movement is here to serve the world and our brothers and sisters who need fellowship and encouragement. Our network provides a place for fellowship, to bring divine unity and encouragement, and equips us to reach everyone on earth. By embodying Christ's self-sacrificial love, Spirit-empowered scholars can inspire and equip the church to fulfill its mission.

Conclusion

The task of Spirit-empowered scholarship is both profound and practical. It requires building the movement, communicating its identity, connecting generations, and serving with love. As scholars, we are called to contribute research that empowers the church to reach every person on earth with the Good News of Jesus. Through collaboration, theological insight, and Spirit-empowered research and publications, we can fulfill this mission. I pray that Jesus' mission in your work will become your passion and that you will find ways to serve the church and world in your research. May we unite across the globe and serve our movement to the glory of God.

2   Biblical Bases for Spirit-Empowered Evangelism

Opoku Onyinah

Abstract

Two thousand years ago, our Lord Jesus Christ commissioned his disciples to make disciples of all nations. In obedience to this clarion call, his disciples turned their world upside down by breaking down satanic kingdoms and winning their world for Christ. Following the disciples, there have been many attempts by church denominations, para-church organizations, and mission agencies to complete this commission. However, there still appears to be many unreached areas to be covered. Amsterdam 2023, a conference organized by Empowered21, looks forward to 2033, two thousand years after the death and resurrection of Jesus, and two thousand years after Pentecost. The conference aims to reactivate a new era of evangelism. This study attempts to find out the biblical mandate for evangelism by digging into the need for evangelism and the necessitation for proclamation. It also seeks to inquire about the qualifications for evangelism. Finally, it concludes by exploring the various methods of evangelism.

The Need for Evangelism

The Fall of Man and God's Promise of a Redeemer

The Bible clearly shows that human beings were created in the image of God: "Then God said, 'Let us make mankind in our image, in our likeness, so that they may rule over the fish in the sea and the birds in the sky, over the livestock and all the wild animals, and over all the creatures that move along the ground.' So God created mankind in his *own* image, in the image of God he created them; male and female he created them" (Gen 1:26–27, italics mine; see also Gen 5:1–2).[1] Although the Bible uses the male pronoun "he" in the presentation, yet the fact that God created male and female means that he created humankind. The first man created was called Adam and the first woman was Eve.

Basically, the image of God in humankind means human beings are like God in character and represent God on earth. It can be extended to mean God wanted human beings to make moral decisions or choices, exhibit moral purity, and possess intellectual ability or reasoning. God wanted human beings to take dominion over the earth, have a spiritual nature, and possess the capacity for immortality.

Unfortunately, we do not see human beings exhibiting this full image of God. The reason is that Adam sinned by disobeying God and that marred that image. That sin also resulted in human beings' separation from God, their death, and the decline of creation. The sin of "man" and its consequences is termed as "the Fall." Once Adam surrendered to sin, the human race was subjected to the fallen nature, not by its own choice, but by birth through the fall of the first man (Gen 3:1–19).

In the midst of the Fall, the Lord also promised a deliverer through the seed of the woman. While the serpent will strike the feet of the woman, the seed would crush the head of the serpent (Gen 3:15).

The Call of Abraham and Israel

God called Abraham and promised a nation would come from him (Gen 12:1–3), through which the redeemer would come to bless the world. God confirmed to Abraham that his descendants would become evangelists through whom he would bring to pass what he had promised. He said:

> Abraham will surely become a great and powerful nation, and all nations on earth will be blessed through him. For I have chosen him, so that he will direct his children and his household after him to keep the way of the Lord by doing what is right and just, so that the Lord will bring about for Abraham what he has promised him" (Gen 18:18–19).

By this, the Lord set an order through which his promise would be fulfilled. Abraham was to direct his children, and his children were to do the same. This is an evangelistic approach.

The descendants of Abraham, Isaac, Jacob (Gen 24:2–6), and eventually the nation of Israel continued until they became slaves in Egypt. The Lord delivered them from slavery, an act that became a picture of how the Lord would deliver his people from sin. When the nation of Israel was formed, the Lord called them to be an "evangelist" to the world: "'Now if you obey me fully and keep my covenant, then out of all nations you will be my treasured possession. Although the whole earth is mine, you will be for me a kingdom of priests and a holy nation.' These are the words you are to speak to the Israelites" (Exod

19:5–6). In the course of time, Israel became a strong nation with kings ruling over them.

During the times of the rule of the kings in Israel, the concept of the Messiah seemed self-evident. Sometimes, the king was described as someone whose rule of peace and justice included all nations; all nations would be blessed through him (Ps 72:1–20). Several such passages pointed to the Messiah as the perfect king who would redeem the world (Isa 32:1; Ps 2:1–12; 22:22–27; 67:1–7; 96:1–13).[2]

Israel could not fully obey the Lord and the contents of the covenant given to them. Israel's disobedience caused them to be sent into captivity, first by the Assyrians and then by the Babylonians (2 Kgs 17:1–23; 25:1–26). Close to the exile and after the return of the Babylonian exile, the messianic concept became more pronounced. The prophets predicted a period of perfect liberty where the kingdom of God would be established on earth.

The beginning of the restoration and the coming of the kingdom of God were to begin with the coming of the servant of the Lord, who would bring salvation to the world (Isa 4:2–6; 42:1–25; 49:1–7; 52:1–15). The servant of the Lord was to redeem the world through his death (Isa 53:1–12; Zech 3:8–10; 14:20–21). Some of the prophets vividly predicted the time when all who call on the name of the Lord would be saved, the time that Israel would be a blessing to the nations (Isa 56:1–8; Joel 2:32; Zech 8:13).

The Old Testament does not mention the word evangelism directly. However, the promise given to Abraham,[3] the command to direct his children to follow him, and the promise of blessing of the nations by the servant of the Lord in the prophetic books imply evangelism. The New Testament brings into focus the beginning of the fulfillment of the Old Testament hopes: the Messiah comes and dies to redeem humanity. This is the background of evangelism.

The Need to Announce the Good News

Beginning from Jesus

Jesus the Messiah is the focus of the gospels. After his death and resurrection, we find him present at the end of Luke in his interactions with the disciples, whom he encountered on the Emmaus Road. This is recorded in Luke 24:46–49:

> He told them, "This is what is written: The Messiah will suffer and rise from the dead on the third day, and repentance for the forgiveness of sins *will be preached* in his name to all nations, beginning at Jerusalem. You are witnesses of these things. I am going to send you what *my Father has promised*; but stay in the city until you have been clothed with power from on high" (Luke 24:44–49, emphases mine).

Here, Jesus tells the disciples that the gospel would be preached to all nations. As the disciples were witnesses to what had happened, Jesus would have to carry out that duty, and they would have to wait until he sent them what his Father promised.

Luke continues to further explain in Acts what Jesus had promised. The disciples would only be qualified to continue Jesus' ministry after they had received what the Father promised (Acts 1:5). Luke says it well in the passage that follows:

> … Do not leave Jerusalem, but wait for the gift my Father promised, which you have heard me speak about … He said to them: "It is not for you to know the times or dates the Father has set by his own authority. But you will receive power when the Holy Spirit comes on you; and you will be my witnesses in Jerusalem, and in all Judea and Samaria, and to the ends of the earth" (Acts 1:4–9).

The critical verse here, of course, is verse 8: "But you will receive power when the Holy Spirit comes on you; and you will be my witnesses in Jerusalem, and in all Judea and Samaria, and to the ends of the earth." A witness testifies to what he has heard, seen, and understood.

Jesus had told them that they would do their witnessing through preaching (Luke 24:47). The Greek term used, *kerysso*, means to proclaim. The noun form *kerygma* denotes a message, that is, "the substance of what is preached."[4] The book of Acts and the rest of the New Testament tell us the different ways in which the bearing of this witness was done. These include proclamation (*kerygma*), teaching (*didache*), defense (*apologia*), and service (*diakonia*).[5]

The rest of the Book of Acts bears witness to Acts 1:8, from the beginning of its fulfillment. The end of Acts is also a beginning, another beginning. It is the rest of the story of which we ourselves, among the nations, are a part—a story that has been nearly two thousand years in the making.

At Pentecost: The Holy Spirit and the Nations

The promise of the Father is fulfilled on the day of Pentecost (Acts 2:1–9). The Holy Spirit has fallen on all flesh, which is to say that it is the task of evangelizing the nations that makes the giving of the Spirit necessary. The many geographical areas present in Jerusalem at Pentecost that day is essential. Part of its importance is that many languages were spoken when everyone there all heard the gospel message in their own language. God's visitation in the form of the Holy Spirit came to declare the gospel is for all nations.

It is as if the whole world was present in Jerusalem that day. The Spirit is the Spirit of many languages and peoples. The Spirit of the proclamation of the gospel is for all nations. The giving of the Spirit at Pentecost is unintelligible without the calling of the nations.

Peter and the Content of the Gospel

On the day of Pentecost, when Peter was filled with the Holy Spirit, he gave the first gospel message. The gospel is about Jesus. Peter provided the main contents of the gospel, that is, the death (Acts 2:23–24, 36) of Jesus the Christ (Acts 2:31, 36, 38), his burial (Acts 2:27, 31), and his resurrection (Acts 2:24, 31–32); the cause of his death, which is the sin of humanity (Acts 2:23, 38, 40), and the witnesses to his resurrection (Acts 2:22, 32, 40). He also spoke of his exaltation and the sending of the Holy Spirit (Acts 2:33). In addition, he provided the opportunity for people to repent and respond (Acts 2:21, 38, 41). Take notice here that the promised Holy Spirit is for all who would respond (Acts 2:38). Evangelism, therefore, can be understood as defined by the Lausanne Movement, "the proclamation of the historical, biblical Christ as Savior and Lord, with a view to persuading people to come to him personally and so be reconciled to God."[6] This is the message of the evangelist. The promised Holy Spirit is the foundation of our witness about Christ.

The Spirit in Other Gospels

The importance of the Spirit is shown in the other Gospels beside Luke (and Acts). The other Gospels—Matthew, Mark, and John—suggest that the Spirit will lead us into all truth; the Spirit is our advocate, our helper, and our comforter. However, these attributes and characteristics make sense only insofar as the Lord of the harvest wishes to save the nations.

Consequently, Matthew 28:19 tells us about the Great Commission, the discipling of all nations. Mark also mentions the Holy Spirit in anticipation of the ministry of Jesus (Mark 1:7–8, also Matt 3:11–12). On his part, John mentions the comforter/advocate in that memorable passage in John 14:16–30. John also shows a lot about testifying to who Jesus is, right from the opening verse, John 1:1. Again, John gives an indication that Jesus did not only come to die for the Jewish nation but for the whole world (John 3:16–18; 11:51–52). This suggests that proclamation is still important. People should proclaim the good news. This will draw us back to the Old Testament.

The Proclamation of the Gospel to Abraham as a Foreshadowing of Evangelism

When the Lord called Abraham, he used Abraham's life to demonstrate how he was going to redeem the world through the substitutionary death of his son Jesus Christ instead of through the death of human beings. God provided a ram to die in the place of Abraham's son Isaac as an example of how God would offer the life of his son Christ Jesus as a ransom for people. God spoke to Abraham as he was ready to kill his son (Gen 22:11–14); then, God repeated the promise given to Abraham, blessing the nations through him (Gen 22:15–18).

In Galatians 3:1–2, when Paul was dealing with the Galatians concerning their reception of the Spirit, he brought to light that the gospel was first preached to Abraham (Gal 3:8).[7] He uses the term *proeuangelizomia*. It is a compound of *"pro"* and *"euangelizomia." Euangelizomia* can be interpreted as "I preach the gospel." The root word for *euangelizomia* is the same as for the term "evangelist." Paul then established the fact that the evidence of the promise given to Abraham was the presence of the Spirit whom the Gentiles had also received by faith in Christ. Thus, Paul makes it clear that by believing in Christ, we receive the promised Spirit through faith and, thus, inherit the blessings given to Abraham (Gal 3:13–14).[8] For Paul to conclude that the gospel was preached to Abraham was to insist on the need to preach the gospel. Linking the Spirit to the fulfilment of the blessing of Abraham shows that the preaching of the gospel goes along with the power of the Spirit. This is to say that the bad news inherited through Adam is reversed through Christ Jesus through the promise given to Abraham. Paul lays emphasis that this good news must be proclaimed.

The Emphasis on Proclamation

In dealing with the solution of the rejection of Christ among the Jewish people, Paul insists on the importance of proclaiming the gospel for sinners to hear. He shows that messengers need to be sent; the word must be proclaimed; sinners must hear the word; sinners must believe the word and call upon the Lord to be saved (Rom 10:13–17). Paul then quotes from Isaiah 52:7, to acknowledge those who preach the gospel, "How beautiful on the mountains are the feet of those who bring good news, who proclaim peace, who bring good tidings, who proclaim salvation, who say to Zion, 'Your God reigns!'" Bringing good news in this sense is always around the proclamation of the victory won during a war. No wonder after Isaiah 52, which is a strong messianic chapter, Isaiah followed it with the strongest passage on the substitutionary death of the Messiah in the Old Testament (Isa 53). The "beautiful feet" of the good news bearer may signify the glorious nature (that is, the good news) the person announces; it also implies the satisfaction that goes with the fulfillment of the king's assignment. The bringer of good news is like the evangelist who carries the message of the victory of Christ to the people.

Qualification to Evangelize

The question then is who qualifies someone to evangelize? The New Testament testifies that the purpose of the coming of the Spirit is for believers to receive power on high to witness about Christ. By implication, this says that all who have been baptized in the Holy Spirit are qualified to testify about Christ (Acts 1:8). However, there are some Christians who believe that evangelism is reserved for the apostles, prophets, pastors, and teachers. One of the reasons given for this line of thought is that "Paul makes no explicit command that individual Christians should evangelize."[9] It goes further to postulate that "to think that missions and evangelism is merely a spontaneous work of the laity alone is wrong-headed."[10]

However, the New Testament is quite clear that the believers who were scattered spread the gospel wherever they went (Acts 11:20–21). Green points out that one understanding mark of the early church was that evangelism was not the prerogative of the officially designated evangelist or "professionals." Every member of the church, including bishops, presbyters, and ordinary members, considers evangelism as their job and concern.[11] Consequently, Onyinah Gyamfi, a pastor of the Church of Pentecost, in his research on evangelism practices in the Church of Pentecost, asserts, "It is worth affirming that the early church grew in leaps and bounds through lay believers who shared the Good News."[12]

The Lausanne Movement, in a joint publication with the World Evangelical Fellowship, encourages the churches to continue to call some of its members to ministry in all kinds of offices for evangelism. In addition, they call upon the church to give its members the opportunity to exercise their evangelistic ministry in all areas including house-to-house, Sunday school teaching, and youth ministry. Moreover, they feel:

> There is an urgent need to encourage more of our Christian young people to respond to God's call into the professions, into industry and commerce, into public office in the political arena, and into the mass media, in order that they may penetrate these strongholds of influence for Christ. And whatever our church members' vocations are, we need both to help train them to serve there as Christians and to support them in their service.[13]

This does not mean that there is no specific gift as the gift of evangelist. The New Testament makes it clear that believers are endowed with diverse gifts such as apostles, prophets, teachers, workers of miracles, and evangelists (1 Cor 12:27–30; Eph 4:11). "The evangelist is the person who is given the ability by the Lord to present the gospel message so clearly and simply that people usually respond."[14] The evangelist also trains and prepares God's people for the work of the ministry (Eph 4:11–12). Thus, a major work of the evangelist is to train the believers and release them for evangelization.

The Methods of Evangelism

In the New Testament, preaching the gospel is done by some disciples such as Peter, Stephen, and Philip. However, Paul is the one who really championed evangelism. Paul's exclusive focus was proclamation; his concern was to proclaim the gospel through every possible means and win as many people as possible (1 Cor 2:1–5; 9:19–23; 1 Thess 2:1–12). Consequently, he was flexible; as indicated already, his diverse methods of approach included preaching, defending, and teaching. This section discusses the various methods used in evangelism, especially those applied by Paul.

Preaching in Cities and Provinces

Reading Acts and the Pauline letters gives the impression that Paul was proclaiming the gospels in cities, regions, and provinces. He preached in many cities, including Damascus (Acts 9:19–25) and Jerusalem (Acts 9:26–29).

Some of the provinces that he intentionally targeted and ministered to included Galatia, Achaia, and Macedonia (Acts 16:9–10). In Galatia, he preached in Pisidian Antioch in Phrygia, and then Iconium, Lystra, and Derbe in Lycaonia (Acts 13:14–14–23). Eckhard Schnabel, a German theologian, shows that "Pisidian Antioch was certainly an important city—the principal Roman colony in Greek East, divided into seven districts in analogy to the city of Rome and thus evidently established as 'a new Rome' in the border areas of Phrygia and Pisidia."[15] In Antioch, Paul and Barnabas taught a large number of people (Acts 11:26). In Achaia, Paul preached in Athens, and Corinth (Acts 17:16–18:17). Corinth, which was described as greater Corinth, was considered a striving and economic center.[16] Thus, proclaiming the gospel in Antioch and Corinth was strategic. Apparently, Paul wanted to reach the cities where he could get both human and physical resources to reach the villages. This does not mean that Paul was not preaching in the villages. It was quite possible that Paul might have been preaching in the villages, but Luke, who recorded Paul's evangelistic and mission activities, concentrated on the work in the cities to suit the aim of his presentation.[17]

Paul had wanted to go to Asia but was prevented by the Spirit (Acts 16:6). Rather, the Spirit directed him to go to Macedonia (Acts 16:9). In Macedonia, Paul's first contact was Philippi, but later went to Thessalonica. Thessalonica was said to be the most populous city in Macedonia.[18] Here, we see divinity and humanity at work. Paul plans to do the evangelistic work; he is strategic. His strategy appears to be planting churches in the cities or metropolitan centers. As he plans, we also see the directive from the Holy Spirit. The Holy Spirit leads, but the Spirit expects Paul to use his human reasoning to work with him. God has always sought to collaborate with human beings in his work. While God convicts, he expects the human being to follow his own convictions and directives. Contemporary evangelistic activities need to follow this line—the combination of the Spirit and humanity.

On the one hand, Jesus' ministry cut across both the villages and the cities. He visited small villages and towns (Mark 6:6; Luke 8:1). He sent the apostles to go and preach in the villages and towns around (Matt 10:5–11; Luke 9:1–6). On the other hand, too, Jesus was portrayed as an evangelist who spoke in front of big audiences, over five thousand in number (Matt 14:13–21; 15:29–39). The passion of Jesus as portrayed in the Gospels shows that he wanted to reach people of all calibers. Evangelists must target all fronts.

Public Preaching

Paul's preaching was mostly done in public places, but also in private homes. At least three places served as avenues for public preaching: synagogues, open-air venues such as marketplaces, and lecture halls.

Synagogues

As a Jew, the synagogues provided the first contact point for Paul to reach out to other Jews. Some examples of Paul's preaching in the synagogues are found in Damascus (Acts 9:20); Pisidian Antioch (Acts 13:4), Thessalonica (Acts 17:1–4), and Athens (Acts 17:17). In both Thessalonica and Athens, Paul reasoned with the Jews from scripture, explaining that Jesus is the Christ, and that the Christ needed to suffer (Acts 17:1–4). In Athens, this type of approach attracted a group of Epicurean and Stoic philosophers, who began to dispute with him. Eventually, this opened the door for Paul to preach in the meeting of Areopagus, where the Athenians and the foreigners alike wanted to know more about the new teaching (Acts 17:18–23). This type of approach is apologetic. It is important to note that with both Jews and Gentiles (Athenians and foreigners), Paul started with what they knew, before coming in with what they did not know or did not understand. The proclamation can begin with any type of approach that will lead to Christ, "the Evangel."

Open-Air Venues

Open air preaching was also common in Paul's ministry. In Athens, Paul preached in the marketplace (Acts 17:17) and in the meeting place of

Areopagus (Acts 17:19–22). Peter's preaching on the day of Pentecost, Philip's preaching in Samaria, and Paul's preaching in Lystra might have been done in an open-air venue (Acts 2:14–41; 8:5–8; 14:8–14).

Lecture Halls

One of the places where Paul did his preaching and teaching was in lecture halls. In Ephesus, he taught the disciples at a Tyrannus lecture hall daily for two years (Acts 19:9–10). The outcome was the performance of extraordinary miracles that took place through the ministry of Paul, such as handkerchiefs and aprons that had touched him being taken to heal the sick and to cast out an evil spirit. Peter's preaching after the healing of the cripple was done at Solomon's Colonnade (Acts 3:11–13). Thus, teaching is part of the proclamation of the gospel.

Household Evangelism

Private homes were a common place for sharing the gospel. Peter preached the gospel at Cornelius' house (Acts 10:34–45) and the whole household turned to Christ. In Acts and 1 Corinthians, some who were identified as believers were said to have received Christ in the household of Lydia (Acts 16:14–15, 32–34), the household of Crispus the synagogue ruler (Acts 8:8), and the household of Stephanas (1 Cor 1:16; 16:15). One of the best outcomes of preaching in private homes is that it is more likely that you can have the whole household acknowledging Jesus as their Lord and savior. Preaching the gospel in private homes is part of our evangelistic duties.

Personal Evangelism

Personal evangelism is one of the biblical ways of evangelism. The best example of personal evangelism is the Lord Jesus himself. Jesus uses it in his approach to Nicodemus (John 3:1–10), the Samaritan woman (John 4), and Philip of Bethsaida (John 1:43–46). In Acts, a good example is seen in the ministry of Philip to the Ethiopian eunuch (Acts 8:26–40). Green says it all, when he tells us about the importance of personal evangelism: "The first chapter of St. John gives us the pattern. From the moment each man finds the truth about Jesus, he is constrained to pass it on. It was through the personal witness of John the Baptist that the two disciples [Andrew and Peter] found Jesus.[19] Personal evangelism is the duty of every believer.

Literature Evangelism

One of the methods that the New Testament church used in evangelism was literature. This method of evangelism has preserved the gospel as we know it today. Those with the gift or ability to write authored the Gospels and the epistles to carry out their evangelistic message. John purposely wrote, "But these are written that you may believe that Jesus is Christ, the Son of God, and that by believing you may have eternal life (John 20:31). Similarly, Paul said in Galatians, "As we have already said, so now I say again: If anybody is preaching to you a gospel other than what you accepted, let him be eternally condemned!" (Gal 1:9). Evangelism was on the heart of the human authors of the New Testament. Scholars within Pentecostal-Charismatic circles may be one of the persecuted groups within their own circles; however, Spirit-empowered scholars must not give up, since this is no doubt one of their ministries for sharing the gospel.

Social Services Evangelism

One of the means through which the gospel spread was through helping the needy (Acts 6:1–7). When the apostles deemed it unworthy to neglect the ministry of the word of God in order to serve tables, they chose seven men who were full of the Holy Spirit and gave them this responsibility. The product of this decision was the spread of the gospel. Luke records in Acts, "So the word of God spread. The number of disciples in Jerusalem increased rapidly, and a large number of priests became obedient to the faith" (Acts 6:7). Thus, social services (*diaconia*) can be another effective way of sharing the gospel.

The Lausanne Movement, whose sole aim is evangelism, sees social services from three perspectives. First, that "social activity is a *consequence* of evangelism."[20] This is meant to refer to what happens after a person is brought to a new birth; the new life must manifest itself in social service (Gal 2:10; 5:6; Jas 2:18). Second, "social activity can be a *bridge* to evangelism."[21] In other words, social services open the door for a person to present the gospel. Third, social services accompany evangelism "as its *partner*."[22] Put another way, social activities must not stop after evangelism but must follow evangelism as its consequences. The role of the Spirit must not be overlooked; it is the Spirit who urges people to contribute to supplying the needs of others (Rom 12:8). This is done for the common good of people.

Partnership Evangelism

Paul remarks how some people and churches partnered with him in the course of his evangelical ministry, including financially (Phil 4:14–19; 2 Cor 8:3; 11:8–9). The Philippians, for example, were able to support Paul through finance. They sent a message to encourage him and take care of his needs (Phil 2:25). No doubt they would also pray for him. Throughout Jesus' ministry, some people, including women, were supporting him. Luke is very specific here: "After this, Jesus traveled about from one town and village to another, proclaiming the good news of the kingdom of God. The Twelve were with him, and also some women … Joanna the wife of Cuza, the manager of Herod's household; Susanna; and many others. These women were helping to support them out of their own means" (Luke 8:1–3).

Partnership is reflected in Jesus' saying concerning how you would receive a prophet's reward if you receive a prophet:

> Anyone who receives a prophet because he is a prophet will receive a prophet's reward, and anyone who receives a righteous man because he is a righteous man will receive a righteous man's reward. And if anyone gives even a cup of cold water to one of these little ones because he is my disciple, I tell you the truth, he will certainly not lose his reward (Matt 10:41–42).

From this perspective, individual, local churches, and denominations can all seek to develop partnership in evangelism. Individuals and churches need to budget to partner with others for evangelism.

Power Evangelism and Persecutions in Evangelism

There is no doubt that in the ministry of Jesus, one thing that drew people to him was the unprecedented signs and wonders that followed him. The miracles authenticated him as the unique Son of God, the Messiah (John 10:37–38; 14:10; Acts 10:38). He promised the disciples that they should wait for this power from on high before witnessing about him. Certainly after the day of Pentecost, the next main evangelistic activity carried out was the message preached, when Peter and John, through the power in the name of Jesus, raised the lame. However, miracles, including healing the sick, raising the dead, and releasing prisoners from prison, though they did not always lead to faith, were one of the greatest attractions in evangelism (Acts 3:12–15; 5:12–15; 8:4–8; 9:33–36; 13:6–12; Acts 14:8–13; 16:25–38; 19:11–12). A miraculous sign is one of the ways the Lord confirms the gospel preached by his servants (Acts 14:3). Yet, miracles take place at the sovereign will of God (Acts 4:23–31).

In all the various methods of preaching, it is the Spirit who enables us. While some are given "miraculous powers" by the Spirit, others have the "gifts of healing," still others are given the ability "to help others" and "show mercy" (1 Cor 12:9, 10, 28; Rom 12:8). Speaking about the anointing of Jesus with the Holy Spirit and power, Peter says that "[Jesus] went around doing good and healing all who were under the power of the devil" (Acts 10:38). Notice that, for Peter, in this passage, the first thing that showed that Jesus was anointed with the Holy Spirit and power was the "doing good" aspect of his ministry.

Nevertheless, the New Testament also gives us the picture that suffering and death threats are associated with evangelism, though sometimes God delivers his people miraculously. For example, Stephen and James were killed (Acts 7; 12:1–2); Peter, John (and the apostles), Paul, and Silas were beaten and imprisoned (Acts 4:1–4; 5:40; 16:22–29). Paul was stoned and beaten up several times (2 Cor 11:23–32). Paul spoke of sometimes going without money and food (2 Cor 11:27; Phil 4:10–14). He also spoke of fighting against spiritual powers in the heavenly realms (Eph 6:1–12). In the midst of all this, the people of God still stood firm, felt the presence of the Holy Spirit (Matt 28:20), and proclaimed the gospel. All these manifestations authenticate the gospel and draw unbelievers to Jesus, the Messiah. The Holy Spirit manifests himself through various spiritual gifts to meet social, emotional, physical, and spiritual needs of people. They are all the works of the one Holy Spirit.

Conclusion

This study sought to find out the biblical mandate for evangelism. It was shown that evangelism becomes necessary because of the fall of human beings. The fall of humanity meant that, although God created human beings in his own image, the image was distorted through sin, and humanity was separated from God. The love of God caused him to promise a deliverer, who would be a ransom for humankind.

God called Abraham, made a covenant with him, and made him aware that he would be one of the instruments through whom the redeemer would come; a nation was to be formed through his descendants. He was to direct his children through generations to bring about what the Lord had promised. This was considered an evangelistic approach. Consequently, the nation of Israel was formed through a descendant of Abraham, and God confirmed his covenant with them. When the nation of Israel was fully developed and kings were ruling, the concept of the redeemer further developed to an expectation of a perfect king who would rule the kingdom of God in justice. Yet, Israel could not fully obey the Lord and the obligations of the covenant given them. Hence, they were taken into captivity. The messianic agenda was further advanced when some of the Israelites returned from captivity and the prophets predicted a time of liberty and freedom to be preceded by the servant of the Lord. The coming of Jesus fulfilled the Old Testament's prediction of the Messiah; he was authenticated with extraordinary signs and wonders. He is the gospel.

After his death and resurrection, he ordered his disciples to proclaim the good news to all nations, after they had received the promised Holy Spirit. The promise of the Father was fulfilled on the day of Pentecost (Acts 2:1–9) in the presence of many people from different nations. This was a sign that the Spirit had begun its work on the evangelization of the nations. Peter, who took leadership on the day of Pentecost, proclaimed the gospel; it was all about Jesus, his person, his ministry, his death, his resurrection, and the response he needed from the people. The Acts of the Apostles and the New Testament tell us how the disciples proclaimed the gospel. Diverse approaches were used to preach Christ. These included proclamation, teaching, defense, and service. Preaching could be done in any convenient place, such as public places, open-air venues, households, marketplaces, or workplaces. Social services could be used as part of evangelism. Writing and dissemination of literature were considered biblical ways of evangelism. The Holy Spirit was seen as the source of all Spirit-empowered evangelism with its challenges.

Notes

1   Unless otherwise indicated, all scripture quotations come from the New International Version (NIV).

2   Kitan Petreski, "A Project for Evangelism by the Churches in the Post-Communist Republic of Macedonia," (Ph.D. diss, Asbury Theological Seminary, 2009), 24.

3   We shall return to it in the New Testament.

4   W. E. Vine, *An Expository Dictionary of New Testament Words* (Old Tappan: Fleming H. Revell Company), 201–202.

5   Eric Tosi, "Evangelism in the Early Church," in *Patristics, Early Church, Evangelism, Mission, Academia*, 2011, 36–37, https://www.academia.edu/1949066/Evangelism_in_the_Early_Church, accessed June 5, 2023. Some scholars add witness (*martyria*) and confession (*homologia*). These two will not be dealt with in this chapter. For reading on them, refer to the study cited here.

6   Lausanne Movement, "Evangelism and Social Responsibility: An Evangelical Commitment," A Joint Publication of the Lausanne Committee for World Evangelization and the World Evangelical Fellowship, https://lausanne.org/content/lop/lop-21, accessed June 6, 2023.

7   F. B. A. Asiedu, *Paul and His Letters: Thinking with Josephus* (Minneapolis: Academic Fortress, 2019), 211–16.

8   Gordon Fee, *God's Empowering Presence: The Holy Spirit in the Letters of Paul* (Carlisle: Paternoster, 1994), 391.

9   Jason Piland, "Paul's Theology of Evangelism: Gospel-Proclaimers and Gospel-Promoters Today," Reformed Theological Seminary, 2018, 23, https://cdn.rts.edu/wp-content/uploads/2019/01/Piland-Pauline-Epistles.pdf/, accessed September 12, 2024. For discussion on this, read Piland's article cited here and Eckhard J. Schnabel, *Early Christian Mission: Jesus and the Twelve–Paul and the Early Church*, 2 volumes (Leicester: InterVarsity Press, 2004), 1452.

10 Piland, "Paul's Theology of Evangelism," 24.

11 Michael Green, *Evangelism in the Early Church* (Crowborough: Highland Books, 1969), 270, 209.

12 Onyinah Gyamfi, "Evangelism Practices of the Church of Pentecost in the Afigya Kwabre District, Ghana (1962 to 2016): Towards Designing a New Missional Strategy," (Ph.D. diss, South African Theological Seminary, 2021), 248.

13 Lausanne Movement, "Evangelism and Social Responsibility."

14 Opoku Onyinah, *Apostles and Prophets: The Ministry of Apostles and Prophets throughout the Generations* (Eugene, OR: Wipf & Stock, 2022), 184.

15 Eckhard J. Schnabel, *Paul the Missionary: Realities and Strategies and Methods* (Downers Grove: InterVarsity Press Academic), 265.

16 Schnabel, *Paul the Missionary*, 275.

17 For those interested in a discussion on Paul's ministry in villages and personal evangelism, see Schnabel, *Paul the Missionary*, 285; William M. Ramsay, *St Paul the Traveller and the Roman Citizen* (London: Hodder & Stoughton, 1896), 305; Piland, "Paul's Theology of Evangelism," 3–10.

18 Schnabel, *Paul the Missionary*, 272.

19 Green, *Evangelism in the Early Church*, 270.

20 Lausanne Movement, "Evangelism and Social Responsibility," emphasis in original.

21 Lausanne Movement, "Evangelism and Social Responsibility," emphasis in original.

22 Lausanne Movement, "Evangelism and Social Responsibility" emphasis in original.

3   A Johannine Case for Spirit-Empowered Witness

Dongsoo Kim

Abstract

This chapter concerns Jesus' command to receive the Holy Spirit in John 20:22. The symbolic interpretation is not persuasive because it fails to see the significance of the technical term "ἐμφυσάω" for the new creation. The interpretation of the so-called "Johannine Pentecost" is helpful as it attempts to contextualize the command within the Johannine narrative and Johannine theology. However, it overlooks the background of the Spirit in the first century. In early Judaism, there were two distinct roles of the Spirit: as Keener notes, one is "the Spirit of purification," and the other is "the Spirit of prophecy." The theory of two-track fulfillment proposed by Robert P. Menzies is preferable to the above two theories because it divides the roles of the Spirit into two, as in early Judaism. However, it has a flaw in that it fails to reconcile the promises of the Spirit within John's narrative. My arguments in this chapter are as follows: first, John intentionally divides the roles of the Spirit into two, mirroring early Judaism; second, each role of the Spirit is promised to the disciples; third, both promises are fulfilled simultaneously in 20:22. This is unique to John's Gospel. In Luke, receiving the Spirit refers to receiving the Spirit of prophecy; in Paul, the Spirit of purification; but in John, both occur in a single event. This thesis can be a biblical foundation for Spirit-empowered witnessing concerning the Gospel of John. In addition, it can encourage diverse modern church movements seeking Spirit-empowered witness.[1]

Introduction

When seeking theological grounds for Spirit-empowered witness in the New Testament, we first think of Luke-Acts. Here, not only does Acts 1:8 directly mention Spirit-empowered witness, but also references to baptism in the Spirit, being filled with the Spirit, or experiencing the Spirit all point in this direction. The following documents we turn to are the Pauline Epistles. Paul speaks not only of the fruit of the Spirit and sanctification but also of the direct manifestations of the spiritual gifts. The significant purpose of the gifts of the Spirit is to empower the church through their manifestations (1 Cor 12:7).

What about the Johannine literature regarding this matter? Is it true that we cannot find grounds for Spirit-empowered witness in the Johannine literature? Many scholars think so. They argue that in Johannine literature, it is hard to find passages like in Luke-Acts where receiving the power of the Spirit for witness or for the function of proclaiming the gospel through the spiritual gifts, as in Paul's letters, are mentioned. However, we can find theological grounds for Spirit-empowered witness in the Johannine literature. Notably, we can find this in the command Jesus gave to his disciples after the resurrection: "Receive the Holy Spirit" (John 20:22).

One of the longstanding puzzles in Johannine pneumatology is related to this command by Jesus to receive the Holy Spirit.[2] Any interpreter of this verse needs to explain the relationship between this event and the Pentecost event in Acts 2:1–4. Additionally, the relationship between this verse and the prophecy of the disciples receiving the Spirit in the pre-Johannine narrative (7:39; 14:16) must be elucidated.

Raymond Johnson distinguishes five interpretations presented by scholars in a recent article on this matter. Firstly, the interpretation that the Spirit bestowal in John 20:22 and Acts 2:4 differs in "quality," i.e., content. Secondly, an interpretation that sees the difference between them merely as a matter of "quantity" in the bestowal of the Spirit. Thirdly, the doctrinal interpretation that suggests that John 20:22 supports the notion in the *filioque* controversy that the Spirit proceeds not only from the Father but also from the Son. Fourthly, a fulfillment interpretation that sees John 20:22 as the fulfillment of Spirit bestowal anticipated in the Old Testament eschatological context (e.g., Joel 2:28–29; Isa 44:3) or as the fulfillment of promises of Spirit bestowal within the Gospel of John (7:39; 14:26). Fifthly, an interpretation viewing this symbolically.[3]

As a proponent who sees the need to resolve this issue from the perspective of John, the following three interpretations seem most significant. First, the symbolic interpretation suggests that what John expresses as "Receive the Holy Spirit" symbolically refers not to the actual experience but to the symbolic anticipation of the Spirit experience that will occur on Pentecost. Second, the so-called "Johannine Pentecost" interpretation suggests that this event in John 20:22 is the actual fulfillment of all promises regarding the Spirit within the narrative of the Gospel of John. Third, the separate fulfillment interpretation suggests that, in the Gospel of John, the ministry of the Spirit comes in two phases, each historically separate and accomplished.

What I intend to argue in this chapter is that, in the Gospel of John, two distinct ministries of the Spirit are delineated, and each of these ministries is anticipated to be fulfilled in one event (John 20:22). Thus, the promises of both ministries of the Spirit were accomplished simultaneously. If we were to label this, it would be termed as integrated fulfillment. In the Old Testament and Judaism, the ministry of the Spirit can be divided into the ministry of purifying the heart and leading his agents with powerful abilities. Craig S. Keener identifies the former as the ministry of the "Spirit of purification" and the latter as the ministry of the "Spirit of prophecy."[4] In this chapter, we will follow Keener's distinction.

To make this argument, first, we will evaluate the three claims mentioned above and point out the issues with those claims. Then, we will demonstrate that my argument is more persuasive than previous interpretations. Thus, I will come to the following conclusions. Firstly, Jesus' bestowal of the Spirit in John 20:22 is not merely symbolic but an actual event of Spirit bestowal independent of the Pentecost event in Acts. Secondly, it represents a combination of the two elements of the Spirit's ministry: the Spirit of purification and the Spirit of prophecy, or the simultaneous fulfillment of the promises regarding the salvific ministry of the Spirit and the missionary ministry.[5]

History of Interpretations

Symbolic Interpretation

One of the most prominent advocates of the symbolic interpretation today is D. A. Carson.[6] In essence, the symbolic interpretation suggests that when Jesus commands the disciples to receive the Holy Spirit in John 20:22, it is not an actual bestowal of the Spirit but a symbolic representation of the Spirit's bestowal that would occur on the day of Pentecost, as described in Acts 2. The crux of this argument can be summarized as follows. Firstly, since there is no direct object for the verb ἐμφυσάω in 20:22, it implies no specific target. Therefore, the word here does not mean "breathe into someone," but simply, "breathe." Secondly, just as Jesus used the terminology of being "glorified" even before his crucifixion (12:23; 17:1, 5), "Receive the Holy Spirit" also indicates the imminent bestowal of the

Spirit rather than an actual bestowal at that moment. Thirdly, there is no evidence in the post–resurrection narratives in the Gospel of John that this bestowal of the Spirit transformed the disciples' lives. The disciples were still fearful, locking doors (20:26), and returned to fishing rather than engaging in missionary activities (21:1–13).[7] Fourthly, a commonly raised issue is that if the bestowal of the Holy Spirit is an actual event, it disrupts the chronological sequence of Jesus' crucifixion, resurrection, ascension, and the bestowal of the Holy Spirit, as Jesus had not yet ascended.

This argument acknowledges historical facts of the account in John 20:22 and the Pentecost event described in Acts 2, alleviating commentators' concerns about historical facts. However, there are several difficulties with this interpretation. Contrary to Carson's assertion, most commentators recognize that the verb ἐμφυσάω in 20:22 does not simply denote breathing for the sake of respiration but carries the specialized sense of breathing new life into someone, akin to a new creation, as also seen in the Septuagint (e.g., Gen 2:7; Ezek 37:9–10). It would be natural to interpret it as the risen Jesus breathing the breath of new creation into the disciples.

It is also problematic to interpret "receive [the Spirit]" in John 20:22 as a present imperative used to denote future action. While there are instances in John's Gospel where present tense verbs are used to indicate future events, they are usually verbs that imply motion or occurrence (e.g., come, go, happen) (3:8; 4:35; 8:14).[8] Most present tense verbs denote actions happening at the present moment (15:4; 20:27). Furthermore, the disciples "receiving" the Spirit had already been prophesied (7:39; 14:16–17), so interpreting "receive" in connection with that prophecy seems more natural. Therefore, the command "receive the Spirit" here likely denotes the actual bestowal of the Spirit.

The post-bestowal behavior of the disciples in the Gospel of John also differs somewhat from that of the disciples after the Pentecost event in Acts. In the narrative following the bestowal of the Spirit, the disciples in the Gospel of John do not immediately become bold witnesses or perform miracles while preaching. However, John does not regard their behavior as cowardice or a lack of mission. Instead, he records the incident of Jesus appearing to the disciples at the Sea of Tiberias (John 21:1–13) not as a sign of the disciples' failure or lack of calling but as Jesus giving Peter a new commission after the resurrection.

Lastly, a perennial problem with the symbolic interpretation is the issue of Jesus' chronology. If, as in John 20:22, the Spirit was bestowed on the day of Jesus' resurrection, it disrupts the traditional chronological sequence of Jesus' life, death, resurrection, ascension, and Spirit bestowal found in the synoptic Gospels and Acts. Carson also acknowledges this point. Considering that John or his audience likely knew the Pentecost narrative from Acts, there was no pressing need for him to specify the timing of the Spirit's bestowal here, especially if it conflicted with that narrative.[9] While chronological issues might be problematic for historians, they are less significant for theologians like John, who view Jesus' passion and resurrection as glory, incorporating ascension and Spirit bestowal into the same theological framework.

The Johannine Pentecost

The Johannine Pentecost theory, notably championed by R. E. Brown, suggests that the bestowal of the Holy Spirit by Jesus in John 20:22 signifies a unique event within John's theology, distinct from the Pentecost event described in Acts 2.[10] According to Brown, John either did not know about the Pentecost event or, if he did, did not consider it relevant, instead emphasizing a distinct bestowal of the Holy Spirit within the narrative of the Gospel of John.

Brown's main points are as follows. Firstly, this event represents the fulfillment of the ongoing promise of the Holy Spirit's outpouring in the Gospel of John (John 7:37–39; 14:16, 26; 15:26; 16:7, 13). Secondly, within the Gospel of John, Jesus' death, resurrection, and ascension are portrayed as a unified event of glory. Before the event of the bestowal of the Holy Spirit, Jesus tells Mary Magdalene not to touch him because he had not yet ascended (John 20:17). However, shortly after, he invites Thomas to touch his body (John 20:27), indicating that his ascension had been completed in between these events.[11] Thirdly, John 20:22 and Acts 2:1–4 should describe the same event from a functional perspective.[12] Therefore, according to this view, the bestowal of the Holy Spirit by Jesus in John 20:22 is an actual event, which can be referred to as the Johannine Pentecost.

This theory receives broader support than the symbolic interpretation. Moreover, it aligns with the suggestion by James D. G. Dunn that John's theology should be interpreted within the framework of John's theological system.[13] However, the main issue with Brown's argument lies in his assertion that the bestowal of the Holy Spirit by Jesus in John's Gospel and the outpouring of the Holy Spirit in Acts 2 functionally describe the same event. While it is true that each event records the fulfillment of the promise of the outpouring of the Holy Spirit in the messianic age as foretold in the Old Testament (Ezek 39:26-27; Joel 2:28–29), it is premature to claim that these two events serve the same function. A thorough analysis of each event's narrative is necessary before making such a claim, as the promises concerning each event were fulfilled in different aspects, making it difficult to assert that the functions of the two events are identical.

The Two-Track Fulfillment

One prominent scholar advocating this view is Robert P. Menzies. He perceives John's pneumatology as the pinnacle of development in the historical progression of early church pneumatology. Whereas pneumatology in the Synoptic Gospels, including Luke, is limited to the role of the Spirit as the Spirit of prophecy following the Old Testament and Jewish pneumatology, John integrates both the Spirit of purification and the Spirit of prophecy, including Paul's concept of the Spirit of sanctification. John describes the role of the Spirit as the Spirit of purification in the pneumatological passages in chapters 1–12 and as the Spirit of prophecy in the farewell discourses in chapters 14–16. He argues that the promise of the Spirit's bestowal, especially in the first part as the Spirit of purification (c.f. 7:37–39), was fulfilled in 20:22. In contrast, the promise of the Paraclete's bestowal as the Spirit of prophecy was fulfilled in the Pentecost event described in Acts 2.[14]

I agree with Menzies' perspective on dividing the role of the Spirit in John's pneumatology into two categories. However, Menzies argues that the bestowal of the two aspects of the Spirit's role, namely the Spirit of purification and the Spirit of prophecy, occurred separately, with the bestowal of the Spirit of prophecy happening at Pentecost as described in Acts. I see this as an external, rather than an internal, solution to the issue. Thus, I believe that while the two roles of the Spirit are indeed present in the Gospel of John, they are integrated and fulfilled in one event in John 20:22. Whereas Menzies views John's pneumatology as the integration of two separate pneumatological events, I see it as the integration of the two promises of the Spirit's bestowal.[15]

As discussed above, while the theory of symbolic action presents more problems than any other argument and John's Pentecost theory has fewer problems, it still fails to account for the interaction between different pneumatologies within the early church or between authors. Menzies' Separate Fulfillment Theory has many merits as well; however, it also falls short of addressing the entirety of Johannine theology internally. Therefore, I want to present my solution to these challenges in the following discussion.

The Background of Johannine Pneumatology

John's pneumatology did not arise in a vacuum. It is rooted in the understanding of the Spirit in the Old Testament and Judaism and indirectly related to pneumatology in New Testament writings prior to John's literature. To distinguish the two pneumatological occurrences in the Gospel of John, it is necessary to examine the understanding of the Spirit in early Judaism and in the writings of Paul and Luke.

The Spirit of Purification and the Spirit of Prophecy in Judaism

Did the Spirit in early Judaism primarily have an ethical or salvific role? Scholarly opinions on this matter are divided. H. Gunkel, E. Schweizer, and Menzies argue that the role of the Spirit at this time was mainly revelatory, involving the disclosure of divine wisdom. Therefore, it did not have an ethical function.[16] Conversely, Max Turner suggests that the role of the Spirit at this time included aspects that exert "life-transforming or directing ethical influences."[17] To resolve this issue, further in-depth research is necessary. However, I agree with Keener that the roles of the Spirit in early Judaism can be divided into the Spirit of purification and the Spirit of prophecy, representing the ethical and ministerial functions of the Spirit, respectively. Of course, in early Judaism, the function of the Spirit of prophecy overwhelmingly dominated.[18]

The Experience of the Spirit of Prophecy in Luke-Acts

So, how does New Testament pneumatology relate to early Jewish pneumatology? Initially, Dunn argues that, in the New Testament, the Spirit is related to believing in Jesus and becoming the covenant people, regardless of whether this pneumatology is in the writings of Paul, Luke, or John.[19] Conversely, Menzies suggests that the pneumatology of each New Testament author is different, and he sees Luke as the author who owes the most to early Judaism in terms of pneumatology. Menzies contends that Luke limits the role of the Spirit solely to the function of the Spirit of prophecy, bestowing power upon believers to become witnesses to the resurrection of Jesus.[20]

Turner, taking the middle ground, interprets the Spirit's experience at the Jordan River baptism of Jesus (Luke 3:21–22) not as leading to "covenantal life" or "eschatological sonship" but as empowering for a mission, contrary to Dunn's view.[21] Turner also argues that the occurrences of the Spirit in Acts cannot be regarded merely as incidental gifts unrelated to salvation.[22] In Luke, the role of the Spirit is primarily seen as that of the Spirit of prophecy (Luke 24:49; Acts 1:8; 2:4), but it cannot be said that there is no aspect of the Spirit of salvation or Spirit of purification (Acts 5:3, 9; 15:8–9). I believe Turner's moderate stance provides the fairest treatment of Luke's pneumatology.

The Experience of the Spirit of Salvation in Paul

In dealing with the gifts of the Spirit as the role of the Spirit (1 Cor 12–14), there is an aspect of the Spirit's role in Paul's writings that emphasizes the Spirit of prophecy. However, unlike in early Judaism, in Paul's understanding, the aspect of the Spirit of purification or the Spirit of salvation is significantly expanded. For Paul, the Spirit is deeply related to the salvation and sanctification of believers.[23] As Menzies aptly summarizes, for Paul, the Spirit is the source of purification (1 Cor 6:11; Rom 15:16), righteousness (Gal 5:5; Rom 2:29; 8:1–17; 14:17; Gal 5:16–26), intimate fellowship with God (Gal 4:6; Rom 8:14–17), knowledge of God (1 Cor 2:6–16; 2 Cor 3:3–18), and ultimately, eternal life through resurrection (Rom 8:11; 1 Cor 15:44–45; Gal 6:8).[24] In short, the Spirit in Paul's writings is the giver of these blessings as the Spirit of salvation.

**Unified Bestowal Event of the Spirit of Purification
and the Spirit of Prophecy in the Gospel of John**

Similar to Luke's and Paul's understanding of the Spirit, John also encompasses both aspects of the Spirit's role: the aspect of the Spirit of purification and the aspect of the Spirit of prophecy. What is unique about John is that he clearly distinguishes and addresses these two roles of the

Spirit within the narrative structure of the Gospel of John. In the various mentions of the Spirit in chapters 1–12 of the Gospel of John, the Spirit is primarily associated with the Spirit of purification (1:33; 3:5–8, 34; 4:23–24; 6:63; 7:37–39). This point is most evident in verse 3:5, which mentions "water and the Spirit." Additionally, in the passages concerning the Advocate in chapters 14–16, the role of the Spirit is associated with the Spirit of prophecy.

The Spirit of Purification (John 1–12)

In Ezekiel 36:25–27, the Spirit is symbolized by water, signifying the Spirit's work of cleansing the human spirit. John presupposes or describes a similar aspect of the Spirit's work in the Gospel of John. In John 1:33, John the Baptist baptizes with water, but Jesus is introduced as the one who baptizes with the Spirit. Here, it is implied that if John's baptism with water has the function of cleansing people's hearts, then Jesus' baptism with the Spirit can do this even more. The role of the Spirit in purifying hearts is most prominent in John 3:5 and 7:37–39.

When Jesus speaks of being born again to Nicodemus, who does not understand, Jesus explains it as being born "of water and the Spirit" (John 3:5). The question arises as to what is signified by "water" and "Spirit," either individually or together as "water and the Spirit." Initially, interpreting water as Christian baptism or the word does not seem appropriate in the context of the conversation with Nicodemus, who is a Jew. Also, interpreting water as the word, although plausible in the entire Scripture, does not fit well in this context. Alternatively, linking water to some Jewish ritual does not align with John's thought.[25]

John now sees the temple as unnecessary as a place of worship (2:22; 4:24). Water signifies natural birth, while the Spirit signifies birth from above, or "water and Spirit" refer to the Spirit. The idea that water signifies natural birth aligns with 3:6, "What is born of the flesh is flesh, and what is born of the Spirit is spirit." Here, water represents the flesh and Spirit represents the Spirit. Viewing both water and Spirit as being born of the Spirit fits well with the view of water as representing the Spirit in the Old Testament and in John's writings.

What is essential for us is that John attributes the work of purifying hearts to the Spirit. This work of purifying hearts is well illustrated in Ezekiel 36:25–27 and the Qumran texts (1QS 3.8–9, 4.21). This is also evident in Paul's writings (Gal 4:29). John introduces this traditional work of purification as the work of the Spirit.

In John 3:5, the Spirit is symbolized by water, whereas in 7:37–39, "living water" directly represents the Spirit. During the Feast of Tabernacles in Jesus' time, there was a ritual of drawing water from the Siloam pool and pouring it onto the altar in the temple. Regarding this custom, Jesus tells believers that those who believe in him will receive a blessing of "living water" overflowing from "their belly," which is none other than the Spirit. This Spirit will be received only by those who believe in Jesus. However, this was already predicted in the Old Testament.

For many scholars, their main concern is identifying which Old Testament verse Jesus was referring to. Indeed, various Old Testament verses were proposed as candidates. Among them, looking at the feast of Tabernacles and water-related verses, we can select Zechariah 14 and Ezekiel 47. If we expand the blessings God's covenant people will receive, we can enumerate many more verses.[26]

Scholars have shown interest, more importantly for our study, in whether "his belly" in verse 38 refers to the believer's belly (so-called ecclesiological interpretation) or Christ's (so-called Christological interpretation). So far, there has been sufficient discussion on this issue, and each argument has merit. Whether it refers to the believer's belly or to Christ matters little for our study. Regardless of the interpretation, it is agreed that the source of living water is Jesus and that this experience of overflowing water refers directly to the experience of the Spirit. The only difference is whether this water comes directly from Jesus' belly or the believer's belly, originating from Jesus.

The Spirit experienced here by believers does not seem to be related to any charismatic abilities to perform tasks. It is something like the joy that believers receive that overflows from within, as in John 3:5, renewing and purifying people. Jesus indicates that the moment of purification is when Jesus is glorified, that is, at the time of his death and resurrection. Therefore, disciples tasting such an experience of the Spirit naturally is in the future; it is prophesied, and it is expressed by the word "receive" (λαμβάνειν).

The Spirit of Prophecy (John 14–16)

In the Farewell Discourse of Jesus, the Holy Spirit is introduced as the Paraclete (14:16–17, 25–26; 15:26–27; 16:7–11, 12–15). However, the role of the Paraclete, or Advocate, presented here differs somewhat from the mentions of the Spirit in the prelude to the Gospel of John. Scholarly research has extensively explored the Advocate's linguistic, religious, and contextual background. In our study, it is crucial to understand how the function of the Advocate aligns with Keener's classification.

Menzies has effectively shown that the Paraclete (παράκλητος) is essentially a legal term, and the function described here emphasizes testifying in a legal context. Particularly in John 15:26, this function is explicitly stated: "...he will testify (μαρτυρήσει) on my behalf." Additionally, the discourse on sin, righteousness, and judgment in John 16:7–11 also depicts a legal scenario.[27]

Furthermore, even in situations where legal terminology is not explicitly used, the Advocate is presented as someone who will act as a defense attorney for the disciples in the absence of Jesus. When Jesus promises to send another advocate like himself in John 14:16, it implies that in the context of the world's accusations, Jesus will not leave his disciples alone but will send an advocate who will perform the same role. Helping the disciples remember accurately in John 14:25–26 is also a supportive function, teaching them how to respond correctly amidst persecution. Moreover, the function of guiding "into all truth" and revealing "things to come" in John 16:12–15 can also be seen as a function of helping the disciples cope appropriately with persecution (John 16:1–4).

In summary, the function of the Advocate in the Farewell Discourse is to assist the disciples in dealing correctly with the persecution and accusations they will face in the church age. This differs from the role of the Spirit in chapters 1–12, where the Spirit's role is primarily to make someone a disciple of Jesus through the ministry of purifying the heart. On the other hand, in the Advocate passages, the Spirit's role is to help those who are already disciples of Jesus bear the responsibilities given by Jesus during the church age. The context then is persecution and accusations, and the Advocate helps the disciples overcome these accusations (John 14:16–17), interpret Jesus' words correctly (John 14:25–26), testify for them in legal proceedings (John 15:26; 16:7–11), and guide them in interpreting future events (John 16:12–15).

It is important to note that the disciples do not yet receive this function of the Advocate when Jesus teaches them. It is something for the future.

The world will not receive (λαβεῖν) the Advocate; only the disciples will (John 14:17). In the Advocate passages, without exception, the time of the Advocate's activity does not overlap with the time of Jesus' activity, and it is seen as the church age after Jesus has departed.[28] One crucial point is that John expresses experiencing the Holy Spirit with the verb "receive." Although this word is not used with the disciples in John 14:17, it is implied that the disciples will receive it through the statement that the world cannot receive it.

Bestowal of the Spirit of Purification and the Spirit of Prophecy in One Event (John 20:22)

After the resurrection, Jesus appears to his disciples and instructs them to receive the Holy Spirit (John 20:22). It is clearly about fulfilling what was previously promised within the narrative of the Gospel of John. So, what does this accomplishment of Jesus' words entail? Menzies argues that it is the fulfillment of the promise of bestowing the Spirit of purification, precisely the accomplishment of Jesus' words mentioned in John 7:39.[29] At first glance, this argument seems quite convincing. Primarily, since the Greek verb ἐμφυσάω, used here when Jesus breathed on them before bestowing the Spirit, was a technical term used in the Old Testament to signify creation (Gen 2:7) or new creation (Ezek 37:9), it is natural to see the role of the Spirit of purification—making disciples of Jesus—being fulfilled here.

However, there is a problem with Menzies' argument in the context of Jesus' bestowal of the Spirit. In the commissioning context, Jesus says, "As the Father has sent me, I send you" (John 20:21). This context of commissioning is directly reflected in the Farewell Discourse, where the promise of the Advocate is located (17:18). As previously seen, one of the functions of the Advocate is to testify in favor of the disciples in the world they are sent to (John 15:26; 16:7–11), implying its connection to the fulfillment of the promise of commissioning.

Furthermore, before bestowing the Spirit, Jesus says, "Peace be with you! As the Father has sent me, I send you," and this phrase, "when he said this" (20:22) is noteworthy. This phrase is used in John's gospel to link events together. Just before, in the narrative of Jesus' passion, after entrusting his mother and beloved disciple to each other (19:25–27), he says a significant statement: "It is finished" (19:30). He says this just before concluding that event with the phrase "after this" (μετὰ τοῦτο), which in essence is the same as "having said this." Thus, John indicates through 20:22 that Jesus' bestowal of the Spirit is deeply connected to Jesus sending the disciples.

The following verse, 20:23, is also related to the function of the Advocate. One of the Advocate's functions is to speak about sin, righteousness, and judgment to the world, revealing what they are (John 16:7–11). The Advocate reveals to the disciples what they are, and there will be a response from the world to their ministry—the part about forgiving sins ties directly to Jesus granting authority to the disciples to forgive sins. Jesus has delegated the authority to forgive sins to the disciples. Just as not listening to the words sent by God in John's gospel (3:36; 5:23) is not listening to the one sent by God, not listening to the disciples sent by Jesus is not listening to Jesus who sent them. So, whoever listens to the words of the disciples sent by Jesus receives forgiveness of sins, and whoever does not listen to them does not. Since forgiveness of sins is like being born again through the Spirit, one can also interpret this in connection with the role of the Spirit of purification. However, here, it speaks about the disciples performing such a ministry, thus speaking about the help of the Advocate Spirit in performing such a ministry; this is related to 21:21, the commissioning.

So, is Jesus' bestowal of the Spirit both the fulfillment of the promise of the Spirit of purification (7:39) and the promise of the Advocate, the Spirit of prophecy? Yes. As described earlier, while the content of the bestowal of the Spirit itself is described concerning the bestowal of the Spirit of purification, at the same time, John indicates that it is also the bestowal of the Spirit of prophecy, the Advocate. This claim is supported by the fact that John uses the verb "to receive" (λαμβάνειν) for the disciples receiving the Spirit. The role of the Spirit, mentioned in John 7:39 as the Spirit of purification, is expressed as something the disciples will "receive" after Jesus is glorified. Likewise, in 14:17, the Advocate Spirit is the one who performs the function of prophecy, and it is expressed as something they "cannot receive" (λαβεῖν) by the world but will dwell with them and be in them if they receive it. The same word is used for both the bestowal of the Spirit of purification and the bestowal of the Advocate and the actual bestowal of Jesus' Spirit. This fact is reinforced by the fact that John uses the verb "to receive" (λαμβάνειν) to mean to experience the anointing of the Advocate mentioned in 1 John 2:27.[30]

Through this, we can say that while John distinguishes between two roles of the Spirit, he also sees them as being bestowed simultaneously. As Keener says, "The two major aspects of John's pneumatology (rebirth and prophetic empowerment) are fulfilled together in Jesus' 'return' to give the disciples the Holy Spirit."[31] John saw the disciples becoming pure by receiving the Spirit and receiving the power of the Spirit to fulfill the mission of preaching as being bestowed at the same time. The pneumatology of each book of the New Testament is indebted to the understanding of the Spirit in the Old Testament and Judaism. Luke, Paul, and John all base their pneumatology on the background of early Judaism. Luke, Paul, and John each acknowledged that the role of the Spirit, according to Keener's classification, is the Spirit of purification and the Spirit of prophecy. Moreover, each acknowledged the two roles of the Spirit. However, they differ in importance and priority, which is the uniqueness of each one's pneumatology.

What we should pay attention to is the phrase commonly used in the early church for the believer's experience of the Spirit, "receive the Spirit" (λαμβάνειν τὸ Πνεῦμα). Each book uses this phrase differently.[32] Paul uses this phrase in connection with believing in Jesus (1 Cor 2:12; 2 Cor 11:4; Gal 3:2, 14). Paul says that receiving the Spirit is experiencing the Spirit of purification when believing in Jesus. In contrast, Luke uses this phrase in connection with experiencing the power of the Spirit after believing in Jesus (Acts 2:38; 8:15–19; 10:47; 19:2). So, Luke uses the term "receiving the Spirit" in connection with receiving the Spirit of prophecy. In contrast, John uniquely sees receiving the Spirit as receiving an integration (20:22) of both the promise of the Spirit of purification (7:39) and the promise of the Spirit of prophecy (14:16–17). In other words, for John, receiving the Spirit entails the simultaneous fulfillment of two aspects of the Spirit's work. This fact demonstrates where Paul, Luke, and John emphasize the role of the Spirit. Paul focuses on the salvific aspect of the Spirit, Luke on the missionary ministry of the Spirit, and John on their integration.

Conclusion

This chapter has examined the meaning, actualization, and significance of Jesus' command to bestow the Holy Spirit in John 20:22. Several points have been elucidated through this study. First of all, this command is not symbolic but an actual directive. It also represents the integrated fulfillment of the promises to send both the Spirit of purification and the Spirit of prophecy, as delineated in the Gospel of John. While John distinguishes between the roles of purification and prophecy, he uniquely sees them as experienced together rather than separately. This aspect highlights the uniqueness of John's pneumatology. Both symbolic interpretations and traditional Pentecostal interpretations fail to distinguish these two roles as John does. Asserting the integrated fulfillment of the two promises of Spirit bestowal as a single event demonstrates the distinctiveness of John's pneumatology compared to that of Luke and Paul.

This study reveals insights into John's understanding of Spirit-empowered witness. Johannine literature portrays this role of the Holy Spirit as the *Paraclete* in the Gospel of John and as the anointing in the Johannine epistles. John, like Luke and Paul, distinguishes between the ministry of the Spirit of purification and the ministry of the Spirit of prophecy. However, John uniquely presents the simultaneous experience of "receiving the Spirit."

While classical Pentecostalism associates receiving the Spirit with experiencing the Spirit of prophecy, and non-Pentecostalism associates it with experiencing the Spirit of purification, John speaks of experiencing both conceptually distinct roles simultaneously. This Johannine theology can be seen as an integration of Luke's and Paul's theologies regarding the experience of the Spirit at the end of the first century.[33] This Johannine theology of Spirit experience demonstrates the diversity of experiences in the New Testament's understanding of Spirit experience, thereby providing a foundation for diversity and unity of experience and theology for Spirit-empowered witness in the contemporary church.

Notes

1 This chapter is a slightly adapted and translated version of the author's article published in Korean. Dongsoo Kim, "'Receive the Holy Spirit' (John 20:22): Fulfillment of the Two Distinct Promises of the Holy Spirit in One Event," *Korean New Testament Studies* 26 (2019): 981–1010.

2 Gary M. Burge, *The Anointed Community: The Holy Spirit in the Johannine Tradition* (Grand Rapids: Eerdmans, 1987), 114–49; Tobias Hägerland,

"The Power of Prophecy: A Septuagintal Echo in John 20:19–23," *Catholic Biblical Quarterly* 71 (2009): 84–103; George Johnston, *The Spirit-Paraclete in the Gospel of John* (New York: Cambridge University Press, 1970), 49–51; John Pretlove, "John 20:22: Help from Dry Bones," *Criswell Theological Review* 3 (2005): 93–101; Joost van Rossum, "The 'Johannine Pentecost': John 20:22 in Modern Exegesis and in Orthodox Theology," *St. Vladimir's Theological Quarterly* 35 (1991): 149–67; Max Turner, "The Concept of Receiving the Spirit in John's Gospel," *Vox Evangelica* 10 (1977): 24–42.

3   R. Johnson, "The Church's Mission: John 20:19–23 Reconsidered," *Currents in Theology and Mission* 43 (2016): 22–28.

4   Craig S. Keener, *The Spirit in the Gospels and the Acts: Divine Purity and Power* (Peabody, MA: Hendrickson, 1997), 6. Menzies also makes this distinction, labeling the former as the ministry of the "life-giving Spirit" or the soteriological ministry of the Spirit, and the latter as the role of the Paraclete. Robert P. Menzies, "John's Place in the Development of Early Christian Pneumatology," *The Spirit and Spirituality: Essays in Honor of Russel P. Spittler* (London: T & T Clark, 2004), 41–52. Turner views the entirety of the early Jewish history of the Spirit from the aspect of "the Spirit of prophecy." Indeed, Jewish literature refers to the ministry of the Spirit as "the spirit of prophecy" (e.g., Jubilees 31:12), encompassing the two ministries distinguished by Keener. Max Turner, *The Holy Spirit and Spiritual Gifts: In the New Testament Church and Today* (Peabody, MA: Hendrickson, 1998), 5.

5   Keener has already made this argument in his doctoral dissertation. However, his paper focused on the function of Johannine pneumatology in the context of early Judaism rather than explicitly addressing this issue, and he acknowledges that he only "briefly" examined this issue. Craig S. Keener, "The Function of Johannine Pneumatology in the Context of Late First-Century," (PhD. diss, Duke University, 1991), 317.

6   The originator of such an interpretation is Theodore of Mopsuestia (c. 350–428).

7   Carson provides seven arguments in favor of the symbolic interpretation in his commentary, with the three mentioned above being the core arguments. D. A. Carson, *The Gospel According to John* (Grand Rapids: Eerdmans, 1991), 651–55.

8   F. Blass and A. Debrunner, *A Greek Grammar of the New Testament and Other Early Christian Literature* (Chicago: The University of Chicago Press, 1961), 168, §323.

9   Carson, *The Gospel According to John*, 653–54.

10 Raymond E. Brown states that the term "Johannine Pentecost" was first
used by Cassien. Raymond E. Brown, *The Gospel According to John (xiii–
xxi)* (Garden City, NY: Doubleday & Company, 1970), 1039. For further
insights into Cassian's assertion and the usage of this term, one can refer
to the following article: Joost van Rossum, "The 'Pentecost': John 20:22 in
Modern Exegesis and in Orthodox Theology," *St. Vladimir's Theological
Quarterly* 35, no. 2–3: 149–67.

11 Brown, *The Gospel According to John (XIII–XXI)*, 1036–39.

12 Brown, *The Gospel According to John (XIII–XXI)*, 1038.

13 James D. G. Dunn, "Let John be John: A Gospel of its Time," *Das
Evangelium und die Evangelisten*, ed. P. Stuhlmacher (Tübingen: J. C. B.
Mohr, 1983), 309–15.

14 Menzies, "John's Place in the Development of Early Christian
Pneumatology," 41–52.

15 Cf. Craig S. Keener, *The Gospel of John: A Commentary*, vol. 2 (Peabody,
MA: Hendrickson, 2003), 1196–1208.

16 Menzies, "John's Place in the Development of Early Christian
Pneumatology," 41–52.

17 Max Turner, *Power from on High: The Spirit in Israel's Restoration and
Witness in Luke-Acts* (Sheffield: Sheffield Academic Press, 2000), 136.
These aspects are found in various Jewish writings such as the Dead Sea
Scrolls, the Qumran tradition, Philo, Wisdom literature, the Testament of
the Twelve Patriarchs, the Testament of Job, Rabbinic Jewish teachings,
and 1 Enoch.

18 Keener, *The Spirit in the Gospels and the Acts: Divine Purity and Power*, 6.

19 James D. G. Dunn, *Jesus and the Spirit: A Study of the Religious and
Charismatic Experience of Jesus and the First Christians as Reflected in the
New Testament* (London: SCM Press, 1975).

20 Robert P. Menzies, *Empowered for Witness: The Spirit in Luke-Acts*
(Sheffield: Sheffield Academic Press, 1994).

21 Turner, *The Holy Spirit and Spiritual Gifts*, 36–56.

22 Turner, *The Holy Spirit and Spiritual Gifts*, 46.

23 Turner, *The Holy Spirit and Spiritual Gifts*, 114–35.

24 Menzies, *Empowered for Witness*, 17.

25 Keener suggests that when Jesus speaks of being born again to Nicodemus,
Nicodemus' misunderstanding might lie in the fact that baptism with water
was for Gentile converts to Judaism, whereas Jesus demanded it for Jews,

meaning that Jesus referred to "baptism by the Spirit." In other words, this means spiritual purification. Keener, *The Spirit in the Gospels and the Acts*, 151.

26 Carson lists Isaiah 12:3; 44:3; 49:10; Ezekiel 36:25–27; 47:1; Joel 3:18; Amos 9:11–15; and Zechariah 13:1 as such candidates. Instead of quoting a specific verse of the Old Testament as the basis for Jesus' words, John uses the term "scripture" with various verses in mind. Carson, *The Gospel According to John*, 328.

27 Menzies, "John's Place in the Development of Early Christian Pneumatology," 41–52.

28 Dongsoo Kim, "The Church in the Gospel of John," (unpublished Ph.D. diss., University of Cambridge, 1999), 127–30.

29 Menzies, "John's Place in the Development of Early Christian Pneumatology," 41–52.

30 Cf. Johannes C. Coetzee, "The Holy Spirit in 1 John," *Neotestamentica* 13 (1981): 43–67.

31 Keener, *The Gospel of John: A Commentary*, 1196, 1204.

32 Contra James D. G. Dunn, *The Epistle to the Galatians* (Peabody, MA: Hendrickson, 1993), 152–53. Dunn says this expression is a technical term related to becoming a believer.

33 Menzies views this as a historical development. Menzies, "John's Place in the Development of Early Christian Pneumatology," 41–52.

4   Empowered and Equipped: An Analysis and Application of the Fivefold Giftings of Ephesians 4:11–12

Scott Adams

Abstract

A key theme of Lukan theology is the power of the Holy Spirit for missions and evangelism (cf. Luke 24:49; Acts 1:8). While this emphasis has been rightly celebrated by Pentecostals for well over a century, this chapter seeks to expand the discussion concerning how Paul's presentation of the so-called fivefold gifts of Ephesians 4:11 also relate to and serve this missional agenda. In addition to exploring the background of Paul's letter to the Ephesians and examining the nature of his argument in 4:7-12, this chapter also provides practical steps toward the application of the fivefold gifts in the local church. In the final analysis, this present work highlights the Christ-appointed means by which the saints are equipped, the church is built up, and the gospel is carried forth into the world with missional success.

Introduction

Over time, Pentecostals have rightly focused a significant amount of attention on the Lukan portrayal of the Spirit for power in evangelism and bearing witness to Jesus (Luke 24:49; Acts 1:8, etc.). As noted by Luke, the gift of the Holy Spirit was given on the day of Pentecost after Jesus' departure from the Mount of Olives into heaven (Acts 1:9–12; 2:1–4). However, according to Paul's letter to the Ephesians (4:7–12), the ascended Christ also provided gifts that directly relate to the growth of the church and the advancement of the gospel in the world, most notably, the gifts of apostles, prophets, evangelists, shepherds, and teachers (4:11). After Jesus' ascent to the Father, he gave gifts to his people, creating a gifted people, so that the mission of the heavenly Christ would continue through the church. By examining Ephesians 4:7–12, this chapter will seek first to bring fresh scriptural awareness concerning the nature and necessity of the fivefold giftings and then to provide practical steps that believers can take toward recognizing and utilizing these giftings in the local church and beyond.

The Background of Paul's Letter

It is widely believed that the apostle Paul wrote to the Ephesian church community around AD 62 while under house arrest in Rome (Acts 28:16–31).[1] But how did this church begin? What are the key features of this city that help us understand the nature of Paul's address to this ancient community? In the book of Acts, Luke provides key details concerning Paul's ministry in Ephesus that took place before the apostle addressed the Ephesian believers by letter (Acts 19:1–20:1). As such, Luke highlights Paul's three-year ministry in Ephesus (Acts 20:31), a city on the west coast of Asia that was home to the Temple of Artemis, one of the Seven Wonders of the Ancient World. Artemis was associated with the Roman goddess Diana, the goddess of protection and power.[2] Over time a religious cult of sorcery developed around her that may provide the background for understanding Paul's concept of "powers."[3] Additionally, the city of Ephesus was known for emperor worship, particularly the worship of Augustus. The fact that Ephesus contained three temples dedicated to this imperial cult underscores the importance of emperor worship in this ancient city.[4]

With this background in mind, Luke is careful to record the supernatural nature of Paul's missionary work in Ephesus. For example, we are told that upon ministering to some "disciples" in this city, "the Holy Spirit came on them, and they began speaking in tongues and prophesying" (Acts 19:6).[5] Accordingly, we are told that Paul spoke boldly in the synagogue (19:8) and proclaimed the word of the Lord in Asia to Jews and Greeks for two years (19:9–10). This ability is undoubtedly the result of the power of the Holy Spirit at work in Paul that enables him to bear witness to Jesus (1:8). Furthermore, Luke highlights the supernatural authority over evil spirits at work in Paul's ministry. He writes:

> And God was doing extraordinary miracles by the hands of Paul, so that even handkerchiefs or aprons that had touched his skin were carried away to the sick, and their diseases left them and the evil spirits came out of them. Then some of the itinerant Jewish exorcists undertook to invoke the name of the Lord Jesus over those who had evil spirits, saying, "I adjure you by the Jesus whom Paul proclaims." Seven sons of a Jewish high priest named Sceva were doing this. But the evil spirit answered them, "Jesus I know, and Paul I recognize, but who are you?" And the man in whom was the evil spirit leaped

on them, mastered all of them and overpowered them, so that they fled out of that house naked and wounded (Acts 19:11–16).

It is important to point out that Luke was both a historian and a theologian.[6] As such, he not only provides an accurate report of specific events that occurred in the progress of the Gospel, but he also reports these events with a theological purpose. For example, Clinton Arnold notes, "Luke is concerned to show that the gospel of the Lord Jesus and the power of God are indeed mightier than any opposition... In all these instances the work of the devil through these people hindered the progress of the gospel. The power of God working through his messengers needed to confront and overcome Satanic opposition."[7] As will be discussed in more detail below, Paul wrote to the Ephesians, in part, to remind them of the victory of the risen and ascended Christ, who exercises his heavenly rule and authority through his body, the church. His heavenly rule provides the basis for the church's advancement and success in a fallen and darkened world.[8]

From the "Ascended One" to the "Gifted Ones"

Paul provides and unpacks numerous themes throughout his letter. After providing a brief greeting (Eph 1:1–2), the apostle outlines the spiritual benefits of being "in Christ" with theological precision (1:3–14). He then recalls his heartfelt thanksgiving and prayer for the Ephesians (1:15–23), explains to them the nature of salvation and its benefits by grace through faith (2:1–10), underscores the unity of Jews and Gentiles and the Gentiles' nearness to God through Christ (2:11–22), addresses the so-called "mystery" of the gospel (3:1–13), and prays for them to be granted spiritual power and knowledge (3:14–21).[9] Then, after offering practical instruction concerning how to walk—with humility, gentleness, etc. (4:1–3)—Paul stresses their unity in Christ by his repetitious use of the term "one." He says, "There is one body and one Spirit—just as you were called to the one hope that belongs to your call—one Lord, one faith, one baptism, one God and Father of all, who is over all and through all and in all" (4:4–6). Although the Ephesian believers previously had "many" things to be divided over, they are now "one" in Christ. But ecclesiastical oneness, by itself, does not guarantee missional effectiveness. More is required. Therefore, Paul goes on to describe how the body becomes equipped, mature, and ultimately effective for Jesus' mission in the world. Paul says,

> But grace was given to each one of us according to the measure of Christ's gift. Therefore it says, "When he ascended on high he led a host of captives, and he gave gifts to men." (In saying, "He ascended," what does it mean but that he had also descended into the lower regions, the earth? He who descended is the one who also ascended far above all the heavens, that he might fill all things (Ephesians 4:7–10).

In the first case, Paul notes that "grace was given to each" of the Ephesian believers "according to the measure of Christ's gift" (4:7). In other words, the oneness of the body does not preclude the uniqueness of the individuals in it and God's call on their lives. As such, "grace" is not given to some, but to "each one" in the church. Paul then goes on to appropriate a summary of Psalm 68, which portrays God "ascending" to Mount Zion after defeating Israel's enemies. The psalmist says in verse 18, "You ascended on high, leading a host of captives in your train and receiving gifts among men, even among the rebellious, that the LORD God may dwell there." A cursory reading of these passages reveals that Psalm 68:18 and Ephesians 4:8 differ in certain respects. Specifically, the psalmist speaks of God "receiving gifts among men," whereas Paul says that Christ "gave gifts to men." Frank Thielman highlights the differences by saying, "In its original form, Ps. 68:18 tells God that after triumphing over his enemies, he has led them in a triumphal procession to a mountaintop (probably Zion) and taken booty from them. Paul's text speaks quite differently of a triumphant Christ distributing gifts to each of his human subjects."[10] Thus, in one case, God "receives"; in the other case, Christ "gives." While it may seem strange that the wording has changed in Ephesians 4:8, this alteration is likely the result of Paul's desire to summarize the whole of Psalm 68 in a modified manner.[11] But this change ("he gave gifts," Eph 4:8) accords well with the psalmist's declaration that God "gives power and strength to his people" (Ps 68:35).[12]

Paul goes on to describe the giving of such gifts as a response to Christ's descent and ascent. The former is likely a reference to Christ's death on the cross and his defeat of the forces and spirits of the underworld (hence, "the lower regions," Eph 4:9). In this reading, Paul is saying that Christ descended into the underworld and proclaimed the victory he achieved over hostile powers (see also Col 2:15). The latter refers to his resurrection from the dead and ascension "far above all the heavens, that he might fill all things" (Eph 4:10; Acts 2:33). In other words, Christ went low and declared victory and then went high above all powers and principalities as demonstrative proof of his authority over "all things" (Eph 1:21, 23). Accordingly, although Christ is physically (or bodily) absent from the world, he is spiritually present through the power of the Spirit. John Calvin says it well by noting,

> When we hear of the ascension of Christ, it instantly strikes our minds that he is removed to a great distance from us; and so he actually is, with respect to his body and human presence. But Paul reminds us, that, while he is removed from us in bodily presence, he *fills all things* by the power of his Spirit. Wherever the right hand of God, which embraces heaven and earth, is displayed, Christ is spiritually present by his boundless power; although, as respects his body, the saying of Peter holds true, that "the heaven must receive him until the times of restitution of all things, which God hath spoken by the mouth of all his holy prophets since the world began." (Acts iii. 21.).[13]

As such, in addition to the authority of the ascended Christ being perpetuated on earth through the Spirit, so likewise the ministry of the ascended Christ continues through those whom he appointed for the equipping of his body, namely, "the apostles, the prophets, the evangelists, the shepherds and teachers…" (Eph 4:11).[14] This list is not exhaustive but is rather indicative of the gifts in Paul's thinking that are essential for equipping the church in the present context of his address to the Ephesians (and wider readership).

The first gift Paul mentions is "the apostles" ("the sent ones"). Of course, Jesus was the One sent from the Father par excellence who came to do the will of God and proclaim the gospel of the kingdom (Heb 3:1). But the risen Christ also appointed apostles (in addition to the twelve, Matt 10:2–4; Luke 6:13–16)[15] like Barnabas (Acts 14:14), Andronicus, and Junias (Rom 16:7), who served as authorized messengers to carry forth the gospel and establish churches.

The second gift Paul mentions is "the prophets." Simply, prophets are those who speak by the Spirit of God in various situations and circumstances. In the truest sense, Jesus spoke for God, but he did so as the incarnate Son of God. However, upon his ascent, the risen Christ gave the gift of prophets to the church for her edification. Therefore, "the prophets" of Ephesians 4:11 are not Old Testament prophets but are those like Judas and Silas who spoke by the Spirit in a manner that provided encouragement and strength for the brothers (Acts 15:32).[16] Paul says elsewhere that those who prophesy provide edification and encouragement for believers (1 Cor 14:3), as well as conviction for the outsider and unbeliever (14:24–25).

The third gift Paul mentions is "the evangelists." As noted above, Jesus was the One sent from the Father who preached the good news of the kingdom (Matt 4:17; Mark 1:14–15). But the risen Christ gave the gift of evangelists to the church so that the ministry of proclaiming this message would continue in His physical absence. The evangelists of the early church were individuals like Philip and Timothy who went on mission to proclaim the Good News of Jesus (Acts 8:4–5, 35, 40; 21:8; 2 Tim 4:5).

The fourth gift Paul mentions is "the shepherds" (or "pastors," NIV), who are individuals like the Ephesian elders who provided oversight and care for the church (Acts 20:28-30; 1 Pet 5:1–2). Various Old Testament passages portray God as a shepherd who takes care of his people (Ps 23:1–4; Isa 40:11; 49:9–10; etc.).[17] Of course, the Gospel of John presents Jesus as the "Good Shepherd" who lays down his life for his sheep (10:11–15). As such, the risen "Chief Shepherd" (1 Pet 5:4) gave the gift of shepherds to his church so that his sheep will be tended to in his physical absence (John 21:15–17).

Closely related to "the shepherds" is the fifth and final gift of "the teachers." Such individuals are those who teach sound doctrine and provide instruction for the church (1 Tim 1:10; 2 Tim 4:3). Paul is likely thinking of elders who labor in this manner (1 Tim 5:17). Certainly, teaching is one of the primary ways by which teachers tend to the flock and provide doctrinal guidance for the sheep. This gift combats false teaching and promotes doctrinal integrity in the church.

Moreover, Paul says that Christ gave the fivefold giftings "to equip the saints for the work of ministry…" (Eph 4:12). Grant Osborne notes,

> The leaders of the church are primarily responsible to "equip the saints" (NIV, "his people") for service. The verb means to train or prepare people. It is also a medical term for the setting of broken bones and thus can be understood as restoring people to their God-given task in the body of Christ.[18]

The idea that Paul wants to get across is that Christ gave these gifts to prepare or train the saints for the works of ministry that Christ will perform through them. But it must be pointed out that each gift contributes to the growth of the body in unique ways. For example, the apostles equip the saints with the skills that are required for advancing the gospel and establishing new churches. They are the "sent ones" who prepare the saints for the work of apostolic ministry as they venture into unevangelized areas to proclaim the supremacy of Christ over the powers of darkness. The prophets equip the saints for the work of speaking words of edification and encouragement by the Spirit of God. The evangelists prepare the saints for the work of proclaiming the gospel in a bold and authoritative manner. The shepherds/pastors prepare the saints for the work of caring for one another and for those who have been reached by the apostles and evangelists. Finally, the teachers equip the saints to do the work of promoting sound doctrine and instruction in the established churches.

However, it is important to note that the aim is not necessarily for the saints to be uniquely gifted as those listed in Ephesians 4:11. Rather the aim is for them to be beneficiaries of these giftings in a manner that equips them for both the general and specific works of ministry that God has called them to perform.[19] Osborne points out,

> Gifted leaders are not just hired or appointed but are sovereignly bestowed, and the church should consider its staff and volunteer leaders to be gifts from God. Their purpose is not just to do the work of the Lord but to train and involve every member in that work. In other words, gifted leaders help all members to develop and use their gifts.[20]

The diversity of spiritual giftings reflects the multiplicity of spiritual needs within the body. If every saint were equipped to evangelize then the church would grow in number, but not in spiritual maturity. However, if every saint were equipped to teach then the church would grow in theological depth but not in numerical size. If every saint were equipped to establish new churches then who would be responsible for providing care for those in the established churches? Once again, every gift has a purpose and a place. Therefore, believers do not have to choose one gift over another. They do not have to pick one leader over another. Instead, they have access to the wide variety of gifts that serve to equip and strengthen them in their ministerial calling. And when every gift is in operation, the church will grow in numerical size and spiritual maturity.

Moreover, Paul doesn't spell out how such equipping takes place. Instead, he emphasizes the reason why they are given, namely, "...for building up the body of Christ, until we all attain to the unity of the faith and of the knowledge of the Son of God, to mature manhood, to the measure of the stature of the fullness of Christ" (Eph 4:12–13). In short, Paul indicates that the gifts are given so that the body of Christ can "grow up." As parents expect their children to grow in physical size and emotional maturity, so the risen Christ expects his body, the Church, to grow "to the measure of the stature of the fullness of Christ" (4:13). A balanced reading of Jesus and Paul suggests that the saints must be childlike in their posture (Matt 18:3–4; Mark 10:14–15; Luke 18:17) but not childish in their attitudes and actions (1 Cor 13:11). They are called to grow up, but this process involves becoming more dependent on God and less focused on self. Although the saints understandably begin with "milk," those who are mature move on to "solid food" (Heb 5:11–14). Just as the physical body grows and becomes healthy through the nourishment of food, so also the body of Christ grows and becomes healthy through the nourishment provided by the shepherds and teachers appointed by the risen Christ.

However, growing up also involves the process of learning how to properly communicate. This takes place in the early years of child development through imitation and instruction. Similarly, for the saints, they also must grow in their ability to communicate the truth of the Word of God. As such, they not only learn sound doctrine from the scriptures, but they also learn to proclaim the scriptures with the help of the prophets and evangelists. The aim, then, is to "no longer be children tossed to and fro by the waves and carried about by every wind of doctrine, by human cunning, by craftiness in deceitful schemes" (Eph 4:14). Instead, "speaking the truth in love, we are to grow up in every way into him who is the head, into Christ, from whom the whole body, joined and held together by every joint with which it is equipped, when each part is working properly, makes the body grow so that it builds itself up in love" (Eph 4:15–16).

Accordingly, growing up involves the process of learning how to walk. Saints also go through the process of learning how to walk out their faith as they take the gospel into places where it has not been preached.

Finally, growing up involves the process of learning how to take care of oneself. A similar process occurs for the saints as they take personal responsibility for their spiritual growth. Growing up also involves the process of learning how to care for one another with the help and influence of the shepherds in the church.

Practical Steps for Believers in the Local Church

Over the years a great deal of controversy has surrounded the nature of the fivefold gifts and the validity of their modern-day operation. Since much attention has been given to this controversy elsewhere,[21] I will simply proceed with my conviction that the gifts discussed above are distributed to the body of Christ throughout the church age until Jesus returns. As such, my aim centers on discussing three steps that believers can take toward recognizing and utilizing the fivefold giftings in their local church. Of course, there are many other steps that one can take, but the ones provided below are, in my view, foundational and indispensable.

The first step involves obtaining a biblical education concerning the nature and practice of spiritual gifts in the local church. David Lim insightfully notes that the "church is a school to prepare us... Ephesians 4 and the parallels in 1 Corinthians 14 and Romans 12 picture the church as a school of the Messiah.[22] He says further, "...the church is not the primary place where the work of God is done; the church is the primary place where the work of God is learned. We learn about the exercise of spiritual gifts."[23] If Lim is correct, then "the fivefold gifts" (and those discussed elsewhere in the New Testament) must be one of the core subjects that is taught on a regular basis. Such teaching should occur in sermons, Sunday school gatherings, small groups, and in any other suitable context where biblical instruction can be offered. Further, it may be helpful to offer a spiritual gifts assessment that provides clarity concerning the nature and purpose of the gifts. How believers practically equip and empower others for ministry will be discussed in more detail below.

The second step involves receiving a real-life impartation from other spiritually gifted believers in the local church. While books and various forms of literature provide valuable written instruction, impartation often takes place through our face-to-face interaction with one another as we impart and utilize spiritual gifts. Alan Hirsch insightfully notes,

> Embodiment is an important factor in the healthy leadership of all human organizations, but it is absolutely crucial to the viability and witness of the Christian movement and therefore to both discipleship and missional leadership. And this cannot be passed on through mere writing and books; it is always communicated through life itself, by the leader to the community, from teacher to disciple, and from believer to believer.[24]

Although Hirsch is not directly addressing the topic of spiritual gifts in this quotation, his insight reminds us of the necessity and indispensability of person-to-person impartation in real-life scenarios. In simple terms, it is one thing to learn about the gift of apostleship in a classroom setting; it is another thing altogether to see this gift embodied "on the go," and to have this gift "imparted" through personal contact such as the laying on of hands. Furthermore, embodying one's gift provides an example that others can learn from and practically imitate (cf. 1 Cor 11:1; 1 Thess 1:6–7; 2 Thess 3:9).[25] I am not suggesting that believers can operate in a spiritual gift simply by mimicking others. However, believers will do well by serving in close, relational proximity with others wherein they can see the gifts in action, which may provide an example for them to use their gifts in a similar way.

This sort of closeness was modeled by Jesus in his earthly ministry. For example, Mark says in his gospel, "And he [Jesus] appointed twelve (whom he also named apostles) so that they might be with him and he might send them out to preach and have authority to cast out demons" (3:14–15). Opoku Onyinah asks, "What is the purpose of 'being with him'?" He answers by noting, "He was to train and equip them. They were to be with him so that they would constantly hear him, know and understand his teaching, manner of life, give an account of his ministry and life, and be qualified to equip others. The ultimate purpose was to know him and be like him in order for them to carry on his ministry after his death."[26]

Accordingly, such closeness is also seen in Timothy's interaction with the leaders in his ecclesiastical community. Paul writes to Timothy saying, "Do not neglect the gift [χάρισμα] you have, which was given you by prophecy when the council of elders laid their hands on you" (1 Tim 4:14). Osvaldo Padilla notes, "The laying on of hands was common in the OT and NT for the conferring of an office, the invoking of God's blessing, for healing, and for the giving of the Holy Spirit (see Exod 29:10; Deut 34:9; Acts 8:17). Here the laying on of hands by the council of elders and Paul was a recognition of God's antecedent calling and gifting of Timothy."[27] Paul says to Timothy elsewhere, "For this reason I remind you to fan into flame the gift [χάρισμα] of God, which is in you through the laying on of my hands, for God gave us a spirit not of fear but of power and love and self-control" (2 Tim 1:6–7). George Knight says, "Paul knows that Timothy has the gift within him (ἐν σοὶ) because he was one of the instruments through which God bestowed it, and therefore he can rightly call on him to stir it up."[28] These passages highlight the importance of impartation in the ministry of Paul, but they also remind us of the need for face-to-face encounters in the contemporary church.

The third step involves publicly recognizing and celebrating all the spiritual gifts within the local church. Oftentimes the public expression of ministry is built upon the gifting of one or a few charismatic leaders instead of the collective, empowered gifting of the whole. Sadly, in certain cases, the giftedness of some within the body of Christ is maximized to the point where the giftings of others are minimized or overlooked. Inevitably, as this occurs, some believers will become discouraged to the point where they no longer appreciate the unique way by which the Spirit has gifted them and, in some cases, stop using their gifts altogether. Therefore, it is vitally important that every local church establish a culture where all the gifts are esteemed and its members are actively encouraged and equipped to minister with them. In addition to investing in those who lead the church (senior and associate pastors, elders, etc.), churches should also invest time, energy, and resources into the development and training of all its members so that the body will grow proportionately and function properly. In short, churches must teach the gifts, preach the gifts, promote the gifts, practice the gifts, and share as many testimonies as possible about believers who are using their gifts for the good of the body and the glory of God.

Moreover, some believers are gifted in unique, awe-inspiring ways that set them apart in ministry settings. For example, some gifted preachers and teachers draw crowds of hundreds and even thousands, and no one should apologize for having such widespread influence. Nor should anyone seek to minimize his or her gifting in fear that people might be drawn to it. However, a word of caution is necessary: believers must be careful not to have an exaggerated sense of self-importance. Paul's words to the church in Rome serve as a timely reminder of this important point. He writes,

> For by the grace given to me I say to everyone among you not to think of himself more highly than he ought to think, but to think with sober judgment, each according to the measure of faith that God has assigned. For as in one body we have many members, and the members do not all have the same

function, so we, though many, are one body in Christ, and individually members one of another (Rom 12:3–5).

Furthermore, it has been said that the fight against pride is not a war that we win but a battle that every believer fights. Thus, one's motivation should center on serving others with his or her gifts, rather than on being seen and served by others (Phil 2:3–4; 1 Pet 4:10–11). As such, celebrating the usefulness of all the gifts inevitably promotes unity amid the church's Spirit-empowered diversity.

Conclusion

In this chapter, I have examined the nature of Jesus' descent and ascent, determined the nature and purpose of the fivefold giftings listed in Ephesians 4:11, and provided steps that believers can take toward recognizing and utilizing these gifts in their local churches. This analysis was performed to remind believers that the heavenly Christ continues to minister to the world through his body, the church. While the church will continue to face great moral and spiritual opposition, the apostle Paul reminds us that Jesus Christ is our victorious warrior (Eph 4:8–10) who is seated in the heavenly places "far above all rule and authority and power and dominion, and above every name that is named, not only in this age but also in the one to come" (Eph 1:21). And from this place, the ascended Christ distributes gifts to the church for the ultimate good of the church until he descends a final time at the *parousia*.

Adhering to this theological truth does not exempt us from experiencing real-life challenges. Embracing this victorious point of view does not guarantee overnight evangelistic success. Recovering the fivefold giftings does not preclude the necessity of ongoing ecclesiastical reformation. But it does serve to highlight the Christ-appointed means by which the saints are equipped, the church is built up, and the gospel is carried forth into the world with eschatological urgency and missional success. While additional work needs to be performed concerning the nature and application of the fivefold ministry, I pray that this chapter provides believers with a clearer understanding of and a greater appreciation for the gifts distributed to us by our victorious Lord.

Notes

1 However, David deSilva helpfully supplies: "[I]t is quite possible that this letter was intended for a broader readership than the Christ-followers in Ephesus proper. It may have been circulated—by the author's design—to Christian assemblies outside Ephesus, perhaps in cities as far away as Laodicea and Colossae." David A. deSilva, *Ephesians*, New Cambridge Bible Commentary (Cambridge: Cambridge University Press, 2022), 11. Also, for an overview of authorship and dating of Ephesians, see Darrell L. Bock, *Ephesians*, Tyndale New Testament Commentaries (Downers Grove: InterVarsity Press, 2019), 10–23.

2 See Grant R. Osborne, *Ephesians Verse by Verse* (Bellingham, WA: Lexham Press, 2017), 11, Kindle.

3 Osborne, *Ephesians*, 11.

4 See Clinton E. Arnold, *Ephesians*, Zondervan Exegetical Commentary on the New Testament (Grand Rapids: Zondervan Academic, 2010), 51, Kindle.

5 Unless otherwise referenced, all scripture quotations are taken from the English Standard Version (ESV).

6 See Roger Stronstad, *The Charismatic Theology of St. Luke* (Peabody: Hendrickson Publishers, 1984), 9–12; and William W. and Robert P. Menzies, *Spirit and Power: Foundations of Pentecostal Experience* (Grand Rapids: Zondervan, 2000), 37–44.

7 Clinton E. Arnold, *Powers of Darkness: Principalities & Powers in Paul's Letters* (Downers Grove: InterVarsity Press, 1992), 290–292, Kindle.

8 Michael Gorman is right to point out, "Although the church as Christ's (universal) body is currently the 'fullness of him [Christ]' (1:23), God's plan does not end in the church, for all creation will eventually be 'gather[ed] up' in Christ (1:10; cf. Rom 8:18–25)." Michael J. Gorman, *Apostle of the Crucified Lord: A Theological Introduction to Paul and His Letters* (Grand Rapids: Eerdmans, 2017), 582, Kindle.

9 This outline draws from and follows the textual arrangement provided in the ESV.

10 Frank Thielman, *Ephesians*, Baker Exegetical Commentary on the New Testament (Grand Rapids: Baker Academic, 2010), 265.

11 For a full discussion of the differences between these passages, see Harold W. Hoehner, *Ephesians: An Exegetical Commentary* (Grand Rapids: Baker Academic, 2002), 526–530. He concludes by saying, "[I]t is quite possible that instead of trying to quote Ps 68:18 specifically, Paul is summarizing Ps 68 with words that resemble verse 18. It is similar, perhaps, to the way

a news reporter summarizes a thirty-minute speech in just two or three sentences. It is possible that one sentence by the reporter is very close to a sentence in the speech. Some could accuse the reporter of inaccuracy because it was not identical. However, the reporter's purpose is not direct citation on any one sentence but a summary of the whole speech." Hoehner, *Ephesians*, 528.

12 As noted by Arnold, *Ephesians*, 416. He says, further, "After defeating his enemies and ascending to his throne, Christ 'gave gifts to his people' (ἔδωκεν δόματα τοῖς ἀνθρώποις). The well-known difficulty here is that the text of the MT and LXX has precisely the opposite, that is, 'you received (ἔλαβες) gifts from men'" Arnold, *Ephesians*, 420–421. But he is most likely right in suggesting that "it is likely that the apostle Paul would have been familiar with a form of the OT text of the Psalms that actually read 'he gave.' But the question remains why Paul would choose this form of the text over the LXX (which was widely known and used in Asia Minor) and the MT (which Paul assuredly knew). The answer to this is that he was probably seeking to bring out the full meaning of the text of Psalm 68 by not simply citing it verbatim from the MT (or LXX), but by explaining the sense of it" (Arnold, *Ephesians*, 422).

13 John Calvin, *Commentaries on the Epistles of Paul to the Galatians and Ephesians*, trans. William Pringle (Grand Rapids: Baker Books, 2003), 276.

14 I depend heavily on Arnold's position in this paragraph. See Arnold, *Ephesians*, 420–426.

15 Grant Osborne remarks, "While the apostolic office as held by the Twelve and Paul did not continue, 'apostles' continued both in the first century and afterward, referring to those 'sent' to establish churches and proclaim the gospel. In the second-century document the Didache (also called the Teaching of the Twelve Apostles), prophets were the primary church leaders, and 'apostles' referred to missionaries sent out to distant lands." Osborne, *Ephesians*, 127.

16 See Acts 11:27–28; 13:1; 21:9–10. See also, Osborne, *Ephesians*, 126.

17 As noted by Thielman, *Ephesians*, 277.

18 Osborne, *Ephesians*, 129.

19 Arnold notes, "Ministry should here be understood in its broadest sense and not just what apostles, prophets, evangelists, pastors, and teachers (or 'deacons') do." Arnold, *Ephesians*, 442.

20 Osborne, *Ephesians*, 125–126.

21 For an overview, see Wayne Grudem, ed., *Are Miraculous Gifts for Today: Four Views* (Grand Rapids: Zondervan, 1996).

22 David Lim, *Spiritual Gifts: A Fresh Look* (Springfield: Gospel Publishing House, 1991), 267.

23 Lim, *Spiritual Gifts*, 268.

24 Alan Hirsch, *The Forgotten Ways: Reactivating Apostolic Movements* (Grand Rapids: Brazos Press, 2016), 122.

25 Hirsch, *The Forgotten Ways*, 122–123.

26 Opoku Onyinah, *Apostles and Prophets: The Ministry of Apostles and Prophets Throughout the Generations* (Eugene, OR: Wipf & Stock, 2022), 191–192.

27 Osvaldo Padilla, *The Pastoral Epistles*, Tyndale New Testament Commentaries (Downers Grove: InterVarsity Press, 2022), 123.

28 George W. Knight III, *The Pastoral Epistles*, The New International Greek New Testament Commentary (Grand Rapids: Eerdmans, 1992), 371.

5 The EveryONE Initiative: Precedents and Prospects for 2033

Jay Gary

Abstract

Across four days in June 2023, Empowered21 convened Amsterdam2023—a global conference to launch EveryONE—a campaign to inspire the Spirit-empowered community to reach everyone on earth with the good news of Jesus Christ by the year 2033. As we enter this decade leading up to Pentecost 2033—the two-thousandth anniversary of the Church's birth—this chapter asks: How should we position the EveryONE 2033 initiative in the historical line of previous generations that aspired to fulfill the Great Commission? What are the prospects that EveryONE 2033 will fulfill its calling?

Introduction

Can anything worthwhile be accomplished in ten years? On May 25, 1961, President John F. Kennedy addressed a joint session of Congress to challenge the United States to commit to landing a man on the moon before the end of the decade. Neil Armstrong and Buzz Aldrin achieved that dream on July 21, 1969. Today, when we hear about a plan that seems impossible to achieve, we call it a "moonshot." Should moonshot thinking be applied to the Great Commission? According to Empowered21 (E21) leaders, the answer is yes. This chapter explores E21's "EveryONE 2033" initiative—launched at Amsterdam 2023—via three questions: "What events preceded the EveryONE initiative?," "What lessons can EveryONE draw from history?" and "Why is EveryONE 2033 important?"

What Is EveryONE 2033?

In late 2022, two dozen global Christian network leaders led by Dr. Billy Wilson of Empowered21 and Dr. Rick Warren met in New York City to unite their efforts to fulfill the Great Commission by 2033. Representatives from various denominations developed a "2033 Commitment"[1]: We dedicate our lives to obeying Christ's command and call for the global

Church to unite with us in making the next ten years the greatest decade of Great Commission effort in history."[2]

The origins of the EveryONE initiative can be traced to the "sweeping story of the work of the Holy Spirit over the past 120 years."[3] Starting in 1901, "the first day of the twentieth century," it began in a small Bible school in Topeka, Kansas, where students experienced a revival marked by speaking in tongues. From there, the Azusa Revival broke out in Los Angeles in 1906, which led to the formation of numerous Pentecostal denominations over the next fifty years, along with the Charismatic Renewal among Protestants and Catholics. This period, known as the century of the Holy Spirit, made the Spirit-empowered movement the fastest-growing segment of Christianity as it entered the twenty-first century, marked by healings, tongues, and prophecies. By 2001, the Pentecostal-Charismatic tradition had "grown from a handful to a global force of more than 600 million people."

In 2003, the Church of God in Cleveland, Tennessee, felt called to host a centennial celebration to mark the work of the Holy Spirit throughout the twentieth century. Wilson stepped in to lead the congress nine months before the centennial. In April 2006, some fifty thousand participants from 114 nations flocked to Los Angeles for the Azusa Street Centennial for a week of ministry, celebration, and impartation.

After the centennial, Oral Roberts University invited Wilson to join their Board of Trustees to form a Commission on the Holy Spirit Empowerment in the Twenty-First Century. "With more than 100 years behind them and a new century before them," it was felt that "the time is now for a serious conversation" on the movement's future. The Commission conducted three conversations on Spirit-empowered life and ministry in the following months among top-tier leaders, scholars, and next-generation students.[4] It found that there had been a dramatic growth in Spirit-empowered Christianity from 1970 to 2000, but after 2001, its growth leveled off in various regions, from North America to East Asia.[5] It recognized that a fresh move of the Holy Spirit was needed, marked by repentance combined with an openness to new generations.

In this context, E21 was formed in 2009 by Dr. Billy Wilson and Dr. Jack Hayford to become the largest global network of Spirit-empowered leaders in history. To actualize its work in 2013 across a twenty-year horizon, the E21 Global Council met in Honolulu, Hawaii, to adopt a vision "that every person on Earth would have an authentic encounter with Jesus Christ through the power and presence of the Holy Spirit . . . by Pentecost 2033."[6] E21 chose Pentecost 2033 as their target date because it marks the 2,000th anniversary of the outpouring of the Holy Spirit, as recorded in Acts 2. E21 did not mean that every person on Earth would become Christian, but that everyone would have "an authentic opportunity to intimately know Christ...to develop a personal...relationship with the one true God." According to E21, "reaching everyone will require everyone," as "we *all* unite to evangelize and disciple people...with an acute awareness that *nothing* can change without the supernatural power of God and the empowering of His Holy Spirit."[7]

In June of 2023, E21 convened Amsterdam 2023—a global conference to launch the EveryONE initiative to mobilize the Spirit-empowered community to reach everyone on earth with the good news of Jesus Christ by 2033. They formed an EveryONE fund to support strategic frontline ministry partners in Africa, Asia, Latin America, and Europe. By year's end, people had pledged $15 million, and $7 million had been received to fund sixty-five projects in more than seventy countries.[8]

While EveryONE 2033 collaborates with an external global strategy group that constitute the "2033 Commitment," E21 itself is comprised of a global council, regional cabinets, and various work groups, including a Discipleship Commission, a NextGen Network, a Global Evangelist Alliance, a Women's Alliance, and a Scholars Network.

What does EveryONE 2033 bring to the church as it moves through this decade of evangelism? Wilson responds that it is "the re-personalization of the Great Commission." He notes that the world has changed since the Billy Graham era when mass approaches defined outreach. Since the release of the iPhone in 2007, total strangers rarely talk to one another face to face. Generation Z turns to social media to seek affirmation while maintaining personal autonomy and self-expression. In this quest for individuality, Wilson sees new generations crying out to be noticed. They are questioning their peers, determined to stand against injustices. "So, how do we reach an introverted world?" Wilson proposes: "One person at a time."[9]

At its core, EveryONE 2033 is a call to a new generation to *experience* the Holy Spirit, to be *inspired* with a more excellent vision of God's heart, to *innovate* ways to reach more people, and to *collaborate* toward the fulfillment of the Great Commission.[10]

What Came Before EveryONE?

Numerous scholars have traced the spread of Pentecostalism and its impact on the growing ministry efforts from the Global South.[11] Fewer scholars have focused on how Pentecostal missions have focused on fulfilling the Great Commission by specific milestones. Evangelistic time targets set by leaders for AD 2033 are different from the typical "end-time" dates proclaimed by prophecy advocates. Date-setting by Bible prophecy often ties a given year to the end of the world: "It will be 1988, and I have 88 reasons why!" In contrast, global mission leaders have employed target dates as motivation,[12] often related to a century's end.[13] This chapter documents two movements that set target dates to fulfill the Great Commission.

Nineteenth-Century Protestants

While the Pentecostal movement dates to January 1, 1901, few people know that 1900 was a target date for the Protestant missionary movement. In his book "Countdown to 1900: World Evangelization at the End of the Nineteenth Century," Todd Johnson describes how pastors and missionaries on both sides of the Atlantic mobilized men and women through print and rhetoric to preach the gospel to every person by the turn of the century.

It started in 1881, with an article published in the year-end *Missionary Review* entitled "Can the World Be Evangelized in the Present Century?" The champion of this campaign was A.T. Pierson, a well-known pastor and mission advocate from Philadelphia. He wrote, "Why not! These are days of giant enterprises in the interests of commerce, science, art, and literature . . . . I wish to set forth a practical business proposition, *namely that before the year 1900, the gospel shall be preached to every living soul!*"[14] Pierson laid down three conditions that needed to be met to make the evangelization of the world a reality: "First, the whole Church had to be involved in evangelization. Second, evangelistic zeal was needed in the lives of all believers. And lastly, a baptism of the power of the Holy Spirit was needed. Only then was the goal realistic and reachable."[15]

Pierson's rallying cry to evangelize the world stirred a debate of support and caution in books, magazines, and missionary conferences throughout the 1880s. In 1885, D.L. Moody, the most prominent evangelist of the day, embraced Pierson's call at his Annual Northfield conference. In 1889, J. Hudson Taylor, the founder of the China Inland Mission, endorsed Pierson's call with an article entitled "To Every Creature," calling for "intelligent co-operation and such division and sub-division of the field that one part have not an undue share of workers while other parts are neglected."[16] However, by 1894, very few people spoke of the feasibility of reaching the world for Christ by 1900. Younger leaders began to look beyond the year 1900 into the new century.

John R. Mott was one of those emerging leaders in the 1890's. As a Cornell University sophomore, he had sat under the ministry of Moody and Pierson at a Mt. Hermon summer Bible conference in 1886, sponsored by the Young Men's Christian Association (YMCA). From the start, a handful of students began to host an afternoon missionary prayer meeting. Their numbers grew from four to fourteen, then to twenty-one. Each signed a declaration that read, "We, the undersigned, declare ourselves willing and desirous, God permitting, to go to the unevangelized portions of the world." Once they signed the declaration, they started challenging others to join them.

Mott described the mood of the conference in a letter to his parents: "The Holy Spirit is working here with mighty power. He has brought about the greatest missionary revival the world has ever known. Up to this noon, over 80 of the students have consecrated themselves to foreign missionary work and I know by Sunday night they will number 100. It thrills me through and through to record this fact. Here I have received a far richer anointing of the Spirit than I had dared to ask for before I came."[17] On the last day of the conference, ninety-nine students had signed the missionary declaration. As they knelt in prayer during a farewell meeting, one more person opened the door and slipped in, filling the ranks of what came to be known as the "Mount Hermon 100." Following graduation, Mott helped organize the Student Volunteer Movement for Foreign Missions, serving the YMCA and YWCA campus departments.

After the missionary enthusiasm toward the century's end had faded, in 1900, Mott, then thirty-five years old, wrote a pivotal book entitled "The Evangelization of the World in this Generation."[18] This became the watchword that "summed up the hope, zeal, breath, and urgency of the nineteenth-century missionary movement."[19] To extend the horizon of a time-dated evangelism effort, Mott redefined evangelism in perennial terms.

> If the Gospel is to be preached to all men it obviously must be done while they are living. The evangelization of the world in this generation, therefore, means the preaching of the Gospel to those who are now living. To us who are responsible for preaching the Gospel it means in our lifetime; to those to whom it is to be preached it means in their lifetime.[20]

In defending the watchword, Mott explained what it did *not* mean:

- It did not mean the conversion of the world within the generation.
- It did not imply the hasty or superficial preaching of the gospel.
- It did not signify the Christianization of the world.
- It did not involve the entertaining or supporting of any special theory of eschatology.
- It was not to be regarded as a prophecy. Stress is placed on what may be done.
- The evangelization of the world in this generation should not be regarded as an end to itself.
- It should be seen as enthroning Christ in individual life, family life, social life, national life, international relations, and every relationship of mankind.
- And, to this end, it should focus on planting and developing self-supporting, self-directing, and self-propagating churches in all non-Christian lands.[21]

From this platform, Mott became the leading apostle of Christian outreach and unity across the twentieth century. He circled the globe to form national associations of students, laypeople, and churches. He chaired the Edinburgh Missionary Conference in 1910 to foster cooperation among various denominations in world missions. This cooperation extended into relief work, before, during, and after World War I and II. The Edinburgh's continuation committees established the International Missionary Council to promote cooperation between mission-sending and receiving countries. As general secretary of the International Committee of the YMCA, he criticized the oppression of colonial peoples and struggled against racial discrimination. He was awarded the Nobel Peace Prize in

1946 for promoting peace and brotherhood across national boundaries.[22] Mott's pattern of drafting representative leadership from all continents led to the founding of the World Council of Churches in 1948.[23] In 1954, at age ninety, in his last public appearance among world church leaders, he said, "While life lasts, I am an evangelist."

The Twentieth-Century Evangelicals

"If you can't sleep at night and you wonder why, maybe God is trying to tell you something right now," so goes the Negro Spiritual. On the night of February 26, 1987, in Charlotte, North Carolina, God was trying to get the attention of Reverend Thomas Wang, a sixty-two-year-old Chinese evangelist. Three months earlier, Wang had been appointed international director of the Lausanne Committee for World Evangelization, an evangelical movement launched by Billy Graham in 1974. On that night, Wang was working late, trying to write an article for the June issue of Lausanne's bi-monthly magazine. At three o'clock in the morning, he paused and asked himself, "My, what is the Lord doing? So many groups are simultaneously beginning to talk about the year 2000. What is happening? What is God trying to say?"[24]

Like John Mott before him, Wang had become a diplomat of the kingdom of God, conducting major evangelism movements. In the 1970s, he founded the Chinese Coordination Center for World Evangelism in Hong Kong to serve five thousand Chinese churches outside mainland China. As he took up his role with the Lausanne movement in 1987, most of Christianity's largest denominations had proclaimed that 1991–2000 would be focused on world evangelism. The Assemblies of God termed it "a decade of harvest." The Anglican Communion refers to it as "the decade of evangelism." The Catholic church called it "a decade of worldwide evangelization." Others, such as Southern Baptists, or mega ministries such as Campus Crusade for Christ, referred to AD 2000 by program names such as Bold Mission Thrust or New Life 2000. In his article, Wang highlighted eight well-known denominations and mission agencies that had created plans for evangelism on a global scale. He entitled it "By the Year 2000: Is God Trying to Tell Us Something?" Wang wrote: "I think if only one or two of them succeed in all their objectives, they would truly turn the world upside-down."[25]

Throughout the summer and fall of 1987, thousands of Christian leaders worldwide read Wang's article. By April of 1988, Wang felt compelled to act. He formed a steering committee to convene a three-day "Global Consultation on World Evangelization by AD 2000 and Beyond," or GCOWE '89, in Singapore, January 5–9, 1989. A June 15 *Baptist Press* release heralded the meeting this way: "More than 400 plans exist among Christians to evangelize the world by the end of this century, and the authors of many of them will meet next January in southeast Asia to find ways to cooperate."[26] GCOWE 2000 gathered more than 300 mission leaders from some fifty countries, with more than one-half from the Global South.

Following the consultation, Dr. Vinson Synan, a network leader of Pentecostal-Charismatic movements in North America, wrote:

> This consultation was truly a historic moment for the church. Churches and ministries that had never talked together pledged cooperation in completing the task of world evangelization by the end of the century. There was a dynamic coming together of AD 2000 movements from diverse groups, including Southern Baptist, Catholic, and Pentecostal groups. The vision, data, and resources shared in Singapore will set the agenda for the church till the end of the century. It was a "kairos moment."[27]

Six months after GCOWE 2000, in July 1989, Wang presided over the Lausanne II in Manila Congress under the banner "Proclaim Christ Until He Comes." Some 4,300 were in attendance from 173 countries, including the Soviet Union and Eastern Europe. Wang sounded the vision of AD 2000 evangelism in a breakout track and in one of the evening programs. Yet the closing "Manila Manifesto" viewed 2000 as more of a challenge than a certainty.

After the Congress, Wang stepped down as Lausanne's international director to form an "AD 2000 Movement." As chairman of AD 2000, he turned to Luis Bush, a 43-year-old Argentina missionary and pastor, to serve as its International Director. From 1984 to 1987, Bush had worked to turn Latin America from a mission field to a mission-sending base by organizing dozens of missionary conferences among Spanish and Portuguese Evangelicals throughout Latin America.[28]

Capturing much of the energy emerging from Lausanne II, Bush led the "AD 2000 & Beyond" movement. According to Bush, the purpose of the movement was to be "servant-catalysts, seeking to encourage, motivate and network men and women church leaders by inspiring them with the vision of reaching the unreached by the year 2000 through consultations, prayer efforts, and communication materials."[29] Bush recruited a core group of twelve to represent ten world regions. Their task became to mobilize prayer for the "unreached peoples" and recruit two representatives from each country in their area to form national initiatives targeting the year 2000. By September 1992, 100 countries held AD 2000 vision meetings to foster cooperation among churches and ministries to reach their country for Christ by 2000. Heading up their "AD 2000 United Prayer Track" was C. Peter Wagner, a pioneer of the church growth movement and later advocate of spiritual warfare.

The watchword of the AD 2000 movement became "a church for every people and the gospel for every person by the year 2000." Before the 1990s, Wang and Bush were influenced by Ralph Winter, a maverick mission advocate,[30] who had given an influential address at the 1974 Lausanne Congress on frontier missions. At that time, he claimed, "there are still 2.4 billion people beyond the range of present efforts of any existing church or mission." By 1976, Winter formed the U.S. Center for World Mission in Pasadena, California, to champion unreached peoples. Four years later, in 1980, Winter convened the "World Consultation on Frontier Missions" in Edinburgh to mobilize mission agencies to establish a "church for every people by the year 2000."[31]

In line with Winter's aim, Bush promoted church planting movements among two thousand unreached people groups, who could then evangelize their populations through local church outreach. In 1989, Bush coined the term "the 10/40 Window" to popularize Winter's watchword as an imaginary box between ten- and forty-degree latitude north of the equator stretching across North Africa, the Middle East, India, Central Asia, and Japan. This window depicted a zone containing the greatest degrees of poverty, illiteracy, disease, and suffering. According to David Barrett, editor of the *World Christian Encyclopedia*, these were 2.3 billion people who make up 25 percent of the world's population and live in 3,030 segments, constituting two thousand ethnolinguistic peoples, one thousand urban centers, and thirty countries. They receive 0.1 percent of all Christian literature, and 0.01 percent of all missionaries, all Christian TV, and all missionary dollars.[32] To reverse this imbalance, the AD 2000

Movement launched four "Praying through the Window" campaigns throughout the 1990s involving millions of believers worldwide. Youth With a Mission (YWAM) published a book by Luis Bush and Beverly Pegues entitled, "The Move of the Holy Spirit in the 10/40 Window," featuring manifestations of how God was supernaturally revealing himself in this prayed-for part of the world.[33]

From May 17–25, 1995 in Seoul, Korea, the AD 2000 Movement scheduled GCOWE '95 for a "mid-decadal check-up."[34] Nearly 3,400 Evangelical leaders attended, representing 186 countries. Its purpose was to quicken the pace of the world evangelization race, if possible, to reach its year 2000 goals. There appeared to be a shift in the strategy during the congress, if not by its top leaders, at least by its running coaches. When asked if the AD 2000 movement had scaled back its goals or merely refocused them, track leader Patrick Johnstone replied, "I have been part of the attempts to make goals realistic yet within the spirit of the movement." Rather than see "a church for every people by the year 2000," Johnstone, the British author of *Operation World*, claimed that the AD 2000 movement aimed "to have missionaries working at discipling every significant people by 2001." Johnstone encouraged the movement to track the unfinished task as "12 affinity blocs," containing 130–161 strategic or "gateway" peoples. The movement named this "Joshua Project 2000," to scout the terrain and establish footholds among the least reached peoples.

Some felt that even if the AD 2000 movement were to take a silver medal through a more limited "team for every people" approach rather than "a church for every people," time would run out nonetheless. At GCOWE '95, Jeff Fountain, a leader of YWAM in Europe, felt that AD 2000 had said much about what should happen by the end of the decade, but it was strangely silent about the role of God's people in the third millennium. When asked what GCOWE '95 left undone, he said, "Their exclusive focus on the end of the millennium may leave the church unprepared for the challenges of the twenty-first century." Realizing its own "shelf-life" on the world mission scene, the AD 2000 Movement announced at GCOWE '95 that it would dissolve on December 31, 2000.

A year later, Bush began to see the AD 2000 movement as a bridge to a new century. At a North-East Asia consultation in Seoul, he stated: "The year 2000 can serve as a milestone to mark the advance of the Gospel, both as a focal point for intensified evangelistic work and a transition to a new century of missionary outreach."[35] The final AD 2000 congress was GCOWE '97, June 30 to July 5, hosted by South Africans in Pretoria for four thousand participants from 130 countries. By 1998, the crowing jewel of AD 2000 was announced as "Celebrate Messiah 2000"[36] in Jerusalem in December 2000. The congress, however, was canceled six weeks out due to terrorist threats.

In a final statement of the AD 2000 movement, Thomas Wang wrote in June 2001:

> God has put you and me into this crucial hour before the return of His Son, Jesus Christ, with a definite purpose, the fulfillment of His Great Commission. ...God in history has raised up various movements as His instrument for various purposes. When the purpose is fulfilled, the instrument must have the wisdom and the courage to die. ...Unless a kernel of wheat falls to the ground and dies, it remains only a single seed. But if it dies, it produces many seeds (John 12:24).[37]

What Can EveryONE Learn from History?

What can EveryONE 2033 learn from nineteenth-century Protestants or twentieth-century Evangelicals? How should E21, which has risen from Pentecostal-Charismatic traditions, emulate those who came before them? How should they avoid the pitfalls that Protestants and Evangelicals encountered in their calling to evangelize the world?

Embracing the Remaining Task

The first lesson from history for EveryONE 2033 from the nineteenth- and twentieth-centuries is that any Great Commission movement needs to focus on "the last, the least, and the lost" of society. As Jesus said, "the *last* will be first," or "whatever you did for one of the *least*...you did it for me," and "for the Son of Man came to seek and to save the *lost*."[38]

From the perspective of the nineteenth and twentieth centuries, the task of world evangelization today could be segmented into a three-tier oval. The first is World C or those who profess to be Christians. As of mid-2024, this is estimated to be 32 percent of the world's population. The second segment is World B, 40 percent of the world's population. This segment has adequate access to the Christian gospel, whether or not they have chosen to respond to it. The third segment is World A, 28 percent of the world's population. They have no gospel access from their friends or neighbors.[39] No church exists within their language or culture. As of mid-2024, the World Christian Database reports that World A—or this unreached world—comprises 2.3 billion people.[40]

If 28 percent of the world is unreached in 2024, the glass is more than half full with 72 percent being reached. If we were to visualize the Great Commission movement as a football gridiron, the gospel team would almost be in the red zone. In Asia, the ball has moved from 18 percent evangelized in 1900 to 40 percent evangelized today. Likewise, progress has been historically made in world evangelization, from 46 percent to 52 percent to 71 percent to 72 percent, from 1900, 1970, 2000, and 2024, respectively. The 1 percent increase in gospel access in World A, from 71 percent to 72 percent from 2000 to 2024, means the odds of fulfilling the Great Commission by 2050 are a long shot. Even if every Christian would share the gospel with their neighbor, it would still leave one of four persons on the planet unreached, as they have no witnessing church in their ethnolinguistic culture. Johnson and Wu caution, "We perceive a growing tendency in Christian circles to overestimate what can be done and underestimate how long it will take."[41] E21 must grapple with this often-overlooked cross-cultural challenge of the remaining task.

Catalyzing a Movement

The second lesson from history for EveryONE 2033 is that they must catalyze a movement from all traditions of Christianity, far more comprehensive than the coordination witnessed in the 1990s. Following the dissolving of the AD 2000 movement in 2000, Bush, at 53 years old, conducted a "World Inquiry" survey to connect with leaders in Africa, Asia, and Latin America from both church and mission organizations. By interpreting their responses through the lenses of scripture, theology, and missiology, Bush identified five catalysts from the history of the Christian movement that, when brought together, create brief transformational seasons that advance the Great Commission.[42]

1) God-given purpose: The mission to praise and glorify God gives purpose to drive evangelistic efforts.
2) Spiritual renewals: Revivals inspire and mobilize Christian communities for mission work.

3) Global conferences: International gatherings like Edinburgh 1910 or GCOWE 1989 facilitate collaborative and strategic mission innovation through relationships.
4) Visionary leaders: Global, network, and track leaders are crucial to catalyze and network movements, along with bottom-up grassroots, national, and regional leaders.
5) Inquiry and reflection: Ongoing analysis and adaptation ensure that mission strategies remain relevant in a changing world.

The AD 2000 movement is an exemplar worth studying.[43] Yet, it was not without shortcomings.[44] Following the GGOWE consultation in January 1989, Thomas Wang excluded Catholic Charismatic evangelists from participating in AD 2000, even though he invited them to share the platform in Singapore. They represented "Evangelization 2000," the largest AD 2000 program constituting the Decade of Evangelization, announced by Pope John Paul II.[45] In doing so, the AD 2000 movement overlooked a historic opportunity to join Catholics[46] in commemorating Jesus' two-thousandth jubilee, as a bimillennial season from 1999 to 2001.[47] After the 1989 Lausanne II Congress in Manila, AD 2000 broke from the network that Billy Graham launched. This caused a continuity crisis in 2001 as the new millennium began with "the evangelical global missions movement weakened, fragmented, and without a clear voice."[48]

Resetting the Horizon

The third lesson from history that the EveryONE initiative could take away as it looks to Pentecost 2033 is that it must reset the horizon to cast a vision for the twenty-first century; the call to preach the gospel must always be balanced with the task to prepare a new generation.

John Mott displayed this wisdom within the Protestant missions movement of the 1890s. As 1900 approached, he stopped claiming that "the work that centuries might have done must crowd the hour of setting sun."[49] Instead, he embraced the watchword "The Evangelization of the World in this Generation." Likewise, the period from 1999 to 2019 marked a season when various consultations[50] grappled with how to unite the Evangelical movement under a holistic banner of "The Whole Church taking the Whole Gospel to the Whole World"[51] while not losing focus on the 300 largest, least-reached people groups, comprising 11 percent of humanity.[52]

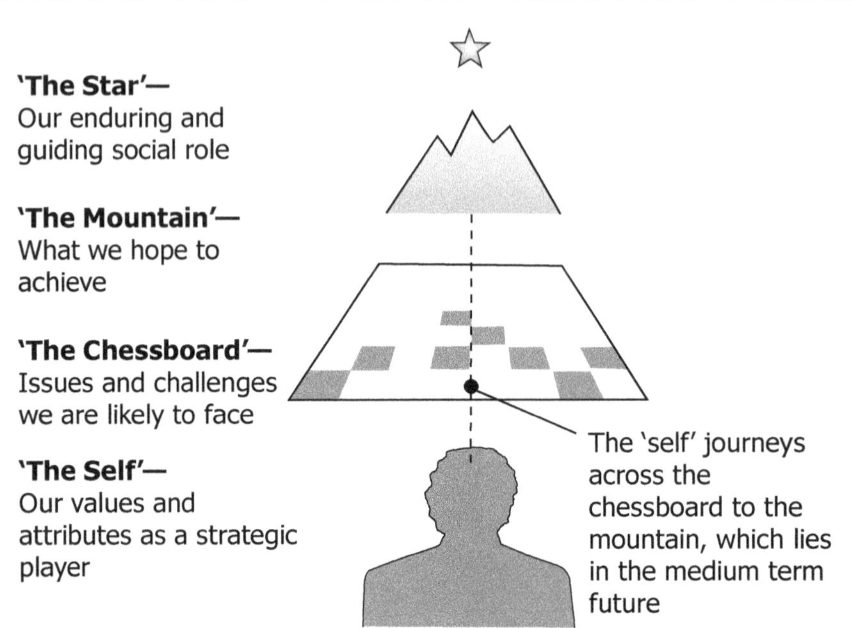

The purpose of the organization
- A 'future-focused role image'
- Not completed or 'used up'

The strategic objective:
- A compelling, relevant future
- BHAG—
  "Big Hairy Audacious Goal"
- A concrete, specific goal
- A challenge, but achievable

The strategic environment:
- Strategic implementation and tactics
- Threats and opportunities
- Actions of other strategic actors
- Driving forces
- Mapped and understood using scenarios

Strategic identity:
- Current reality
- Self-knowledge
- Strengths and weaknesses
- Values
- Preferences and experience

'Star, mountain, chessboard, self' image © Hardin Tibbs 1999

Figure 1: The Future as a Strategic Landscape, Tibbs, 2021

Perhaps the 2033 horizon of the EveryONE initiative and the role of E21 in the twenty-first century could best be understood as a landscape where the Spirit-empowered movement both looks toward 2033 and 2050. Tibbs portrays the future (see figure 1), individually or generationally, as a landscape comprised of the Self, the Chessboard, the Mountain, and the Star.[53]

We might mark the Self as 2001, representing the heritage and spiritual identity this generation of Pentecostals brought into the twenty-first century, celebrated at the Azusa Street Centennial. The Chessboard represents how Pentecostals size up the challenges and opportunities before them as a strategic environment, as well as other actors' counter moves.[54] We might mark 2033 as the Mountain, representing a compelling vision of an achievable objective by the Spirit-empowered movement. The Star, from 2033 into the twenty-second century, represents the church's faithful presence with a view to the coming of God.[55]

An open view of the twenty-first century might also help E21 overcome the tension that the AD 2000 movement experienced between its "by 2000" target and its undeveloped "beyond 2000" vision. It could leave room for Lausanne or the World Evangelical Alliance to support the 2033 Commitment with a focus on "closing the gaps" facing world evangelization by 2050, rather than completing the Great Commission by 2033.[56] Seeing 2033 as a horizon rather than a target date could open E21 evangelists to a larger vision and praxis for Christian mission in a post-colonial, postmodern, post-Christendom, post-Enlightenment, and post-Western world.[57]

Why is EveryONE 2033 Significant?

Like the starting gun in a 100-meter race, Amsterdam 2023 that was convened by E21, marked the start of the Spirit-empowered movement's race toward Pentecost 2033. It drew more than 7,500 individuals from over 125 nations, with an online presence presenting 150 countries. Its purpose was to hear together what the Holy Spirit was doing to help the world encounter Jesus Christ over the next ten years. Its achievements included the launch of the Global Network of Spirit-Empowered Scholars (GNSES) and the EveryONE Initiative Fund to support creative strategies for digital evangelism, church planting, and mass evangelism. It launched a Global

Evangelist Alliance (GEA) focused on training believers in evangelism and inspiring new evangelists for global mission work. And it launched a NextGen initiative to mobilize younger generations for evangelism, and a Global Worship Alliance to restore worship as a ministry of integrity and excellence within the kingdom.

Five Reasons Why

What is the significance of EveryONE 2033? For one, E21 is the world's largest relational ministry network, representing more than 650 million Spirit-empowered Christians who believe in the power of the Holy Spirit to do in the twenty-first century what was done in the book of Acts. Second, EveryONE 2033 has forged a partnership with Dr. Rick Warren of Finishing the Task, a network of evangelical ministries and mission agencies that developed out of Lausanne and AD 2000 with a laser focus on unreached peoples. The 2033 Commitment, launched by Wilson and Warren, welcomes all Christians. At the most, it asks, "How can we do this together?" or at the least, "How can we be aware of what we're each doing to avoid duplication?"[58] Unlike previous evangelical movements that excluded Catholics, EveryONE 2033 builds on a fifty-year tradition of Christian unity, pioneered by Vinson Synan and Kevin Ranaghan to join traditional Pentecostals, mainline Charismatics, and Catholic Charismatics together for spiritual renewal and evangelization.[59] Third, Dr. Billy Wilson, President of Oral Roberts University and Chair of Pentecostal World Fellowship, leads EveryONE 2033. Wilson brings educational and ecclesial leadership to this new era of evangelism at an institutional level not seen since John Mott's work as a twentieth-century missionary statesman. Fourth, EveryONE 2033 is significant because it points to Pentecost 2033, which will mark the two-thousandth anniversary of the original Pentecost described in the book of Acts, where the Holy Spirit descended upon the apostles and birthed the global church. E21 views the months leading up to this milestone as a prophetic moment to galvanize global evangelism efforts to reach every person on earth with the message of Jesus Christ.

The Power of One

Ultimately, the EveryONE initiative is unique because it brings a renewed focus on the potential of everyone to reach everyone—because every person is valuable, lovable, and forgivable. In an interview with Todd

Johnson, co-editor of the third edition of the *World Christian Encyclopedia*, when asked about the "Power of One" related to world evangelization, he reframed it as the role of hospitality to others.[60] He noted that one of the critical reasons Muslims, Buddhists, or Hindus have never had an authentic opportunity to hear the gospel is that they have no Christian friends who speak their language and live in their community. Over 87 percent of the world's unevangelized individuals live in the Global South. As Johnson sees it, the opportunity is that 67 percent of the world's Spirit-empowered Christians also live in the Global South. Christians can touch the lives of the unreached by practicing hospitality and opening their living rooms and dinner tables to their neighbors and co-workers. This is particularly true for Spirit-empowered women, who have historically engaged in ministry to people experiencing poverty through health, education, and justice work. In addition to women, Johnson sees young people as the other gift of the Spirit-empowered movement. Youth are more comfortable with diversity and well-suited to be friends with those from different religions and ethnicities.

EveryONE 2033 represents a modern-day moonshot, aiming to fulfill the Great Commission by reaching every person on earth with the message of Jesus Christ by 2033. What are its prospects? Perhaps Nelson Mandela said it best when working to end apartheid in South Africa: "It always seems impossible until it is done."

Notes

1   Empowered21, "Ministry Leaders Unite on Fulfilling the Great Commission by 2033," news release (Dec. 14, 2022), info@empowered21.com.

2   The 2033 Commitment, https://2033.earth.

3   Vinson Synan, *Spirit-Empowered Christianity in the Twenty-First Century* (Lake Mary, FL: Charisma House, 2011), 21.

4   ORU Library, Holy Spirit Research Center, "ORU Commission on Holy Spirit Empowerment in the 21st Century" (2008), Empowered21 Archive, 2, https://digitalshowcase.oru.edu/e21archive/2.

5   Todd M. Johnson and Gina A. Zurlo, *Introducing Spirit-Empowered Christianity: The Global Pentecostal and Charismatic Movement in the 21st Century* (Tulsa, OK: ORU Press, 2020). As of 2020, there were 664 million Spirit-empowered Christians in the world, or about 26 percent of

all Christians. That equals 8 percent of the world's population or one out of every twelve people on earth. Furthermore, 86 percent of all Spirit-empowered Christians live in the Global South (Asia, Africa, and Latin America), and it is projected that this group will grow twice as fast as Christianity as a whole by 2050.

6 Vinson Synan and Billy Wilson, *As the Waters Cover the Sea: The Story of Empowered21 and the Movement It Serves* (Tulsa, OK: ORU Press, 2020), 50.

7 Synan and Wilson, *As the Waters Cover the Sea*, 36–52.

8 EveryONE Annual Report 2023, https://everyone.earth/.

9 Billy Wilson, *The Power of One: Reaching Every Person on Earth* (Tulsa, OK: Empowered-ORU Press, 2023).

10 "Can We Reach the World for Jesus This Decade? #Amsterdam2023 || He chose YOU," Empowered21, October 25, 2022, https://vimeo.com/763797817.

11 Wonsuk Ma, Veli-Matti Kärkkäinen, and J. Kwabena Asamoah-Gyadu, *Pentecostal Mission and Global Christianity* (Minneapolis: Fortress Press, 2020).

12 Jay Gary, "AD 2000: Prophetic or Target Date?," May 20, 1995, www.christianfutures.com/ev95targ.

13 Hillel Schwartz, *Century's End: A Cultural History of the Fin de Siècle—From the 990s Through the 1990s* (New York: Doubleday, 1990).

14 Todd M. Johnson, *Countdown to 1900: World Evangelization at the End of the Nineteenth Century* (Birmingham, AL: New Hope, 1988), 1, 7.

15 Johnson, *Countdown to 1900*, 10.

16 Johnson, *Countdown to 1900*, 70.

17 C. Howard Hopkins and John R. Mott, *1865–1955: A Biography* (Grand Rapids: Eerdmans, 1979), 27.

18 John R. Mott, *The Evangelization of the World in This Generation* (New York: Student Volunteer Movement for Foreign Missions, 1900).

19 Denton Lotz, "The Watchword for World Evangelization," *International Review of Mission* 68, no. 270 (April 1979): 177.

20 Mott, *The Evangelization of the World in This Generation*, 6.

21 Mott, *The Evangelization of the World in This Generation*, 7–9, 16.

22 "John R. Mott – Facts," The Nobel Prize, NobelPrize.org, updated April 5, 2025, https://www.nobelprize.org/prizes/peace/1946/mott/facts/.

23 William Richey Hogg, *Ecumenical Foundations: A History of the International Missionary Council and its Nineteenth-Century Background* (New York: Harper, 1952).

24 Jay Gary and Olgy Gary, *The Countdown Has Begun: The Story of the Global Consultation on AD 2000* (Rockville, VA: AD 2000 Global Service Office, 1989), 21–22.

25 Luis Bush, Jay Gary, and Mike Roberts, *Toward AD 2000 and Beyond* (Rockville, VA: GCOWE 2000, 1989), 1–2.

26 Gary and Gary, *The Countdown Has Begun*, 218.

27 Gary and Gary, *The Countdown Has Begun*, 64–65.

28 Roberta H. Winter, "Luis Bush, Latin America, and the End of History," *Mission Frontiers: Bulletin of the U.S. Center for World Mission* 8, no. 3 (March 1, 1986): 3, 5, https://rdwrc.wciu.edu/mission-frontiers-archive/.

29 Luis Bush, "A Brief Historical Overview of the AD2000 & Beyond Movement and Joshua Project 2000" (Northeast Asia AD2000/Joshua Project 2000 Consultation; Seoul, Korea, 1996).

30 Harold Fickett, *The Ralph D. Winter Story* (Pasadena, CA: William Carey, 2012).

31 Alan Starling, *Seeds of Promise: World Consultation on Frontier Missions, Edinburgh '80* (Pasadena, CA: William Carey Library, 1981).

32 Luis Bush, "How Can All Peoples Be Reached by the Year 2000?," *International Society of Frontier Missions* (Kansas City, Missouri, September 17, 1992), https://luisbushpapers.com/ad2000/1992/08/11/how-can-all-peoples-be-reached-by-the-year-2000.

33 Luis Bush and Beverly Pegues, *The Move of the Holy Spirit in the 10/40 Window* (Seattle: YWAM, 1999).

34 Jay Gary, "AD 2000 Gets a Millennial Check-up," News Release, Bimillennial Press, last updated May 26, 1995, https://www.christianfutures.com/ev95chku/.

35 Bush, "A Brief Historical Overview."

36 Rick Wood, "Passing the Baton," *Mission Frontiers: Bulletin of the U.S. Center for World Mission* 23, no. 2 (June 1, 2001): 32–35.

37 Wood, "Passing the Baton," 32–33.

38 Matthew 20:16, Matthew 25:40, Matthew 18:11 (NIV); emphases mine.

39 The term "gospel access" is increasingly being used to describe the opportunity for people to hear the gospel. This is the flip side of whether the gospel has "reached" a person or their people group.

40 The percentages (rounded) and definitions are from the World Christian Database, as published in Gina A Zurlo, Todd M. Johnson and Peter F. Crossing, "Status of Global Christianity, 2024, in the Context of 1900–2050" in "World Christianity 2024: Fragmentation and Unity," *International Bulletin of Missionary Research* 48, no. 1 (2024).

41 Todd M. Johnson and Cindy M. Wu, *Our Global Families: Christians Embracing Common Identity in a Changing World* (Grand Rapids, MI: Baker Academic, 2015), 156.

42 Luis Bush, "Catalysts of World Evangelization," (Ph.D. diss., School of World Mission, Fuller Theological Seminary, 2002).

43 Luis Bush, "The AD2000 Movement—A Catalytic Case Study," Luis Bush Papers, 2002, https://luisbushpapers.com/assets/pdf/2002/05/22/The-AD2000-Movement-A-Catalytic-Case-Study-by-Luis-Bush.pdf.

44 Robert T. Coote, "'AD 2000' and the '10/40 Window': A Preliminary Assessment," *International Bulletin of Missionary Research* 24, no. 4 (Oct. 2000): 160–162,164–166.

45 Gary and Gary, *The Countdown Has Begun*, 50–53, 146–158.

46 His Holiness John Paul II, "Tertio Millennio Adveniente," 1994.

47 Jay E. Gary, *The Star of 2000: Our Journey Toward Hope* (Colorado Springs: Bimillennial, 1994).

48 Doug Birdsall, *Friends in the Mission of God: Relationships in Four Stories of Evangelical Mission History* (Oxford, UK: Regnum, 2019).

49 Attributed to Alexander Duff (1806–1878), a Scottish missionary in India.

50 See Jay E. Gary and Todd M. Johnson, "The Watchword in World Missions," *International Journal of Frontier Missions* 16, no. 3 (Fall 1999): 161–4; Ralph D. Winter, "The Rise and Fall of the IMC--and Today: Some Observations on the Gravest Transition in Mission Cooperative Structure in the 20th Century," *International Journal of Frontier Missions* 20, no. 1 (Spring 2003): 18–9.

51 Lausanne Theology Working Group, "The Whole Church Taking the Whole Gospel to the Whole World," Lausanne Movement, June 10, 2010, https://lausanne.org/content/twg-three-wholes.

52 R. W. Lewis, "Needed: A Strategy for the 300 Largest Frontier People Groups," *Mission Frontiers: A Magazine of Frontier Ventures* 46, no. 2 (April 1, 2024): 8–14.

53 Hardin Tibbs, "Making the Future Visible: Psychology, Scenarios, and Strategy," *World Futures Review* 13, no. 1 (Spring 2021): 8–13.

54 Wonsuk Ma, Opoku Onyinah, and Rebekah Bled, eds., *The Remaining Task of the Great Commission & the Spirit-Empowered Movement* (Tulsa, OK: ORU Press, 2023).

55 Jay E. Gary, "Outlook for 2020: Results from a Real-Time Delphi Survey of Global Pentecostal Leaders," *Pneuma* 34, no. 3 (Fall 2012): 383–414.

56 For the past fifty years, global NGOs associated with the United Nations have reset their horizons to reach global goals across decades and then the century's end. Millennium Development Goals for the year 2000 were tracked by indicators and transformed into 17 Sustainable Development Goals and 169 targets for 2030. See https://sdgs.un.org/.

57 Amos Yong, *The Missiological Spirit: Christian Mission Theology in the Third Millennium Global Context* (Eugene, OR: Cascade, 2014).

58 Interview, July 24, 2024, with Max Barroso, Global Assistant Director for E21 and Chair of the Pentecostal World Fellowship's World Missions Commission.

59 Synan and Wilson, *As the Waters Cover the Sea*, 30–35.

60 "E21 Leadership Podcast with Ashley Wilson & Todd Johnson," Empowered21, May 7, 2020, https://youtu.be/V2HAAsj0idI.

6 Strategies for Spirit-Empowered Evangelism: White Paper for the Global Evangelists Alliance of Empowered21[1]

Daniel King

Abstract

The Global Evangelist Alliance (GEA) is a network of Spirit-empowered evangelists who have a passion for evangelism. Below is the story of the origin of the GEA, a look at the GEA mandate to reach EveryONE on earth with the gospel, and an excerpt from a white paper that details four primary strategies the GEA uses for global evangelism. These strategies include advocacy for Spirit-empowered evangelism; equipping and training of evangelists, churches, and movements for Spirit-empowered evangelism; collaborating and coordinating evangelism outreaches; and activation and mobilization of Spirit-empowered evangelists. Desired outcomes and specific tactics are discussed for each of these strategic areas of focus.

Introduction

The Birth of the Global Evangelist Alliance

The Global Evangelist Alliance (GEA) was birthed at an Empowered21 (E21) meeting in Johannesburg, South Africa, in 2018. Daniel Kolenda, president of Christ for All Nations and the successor to Reinhard Bonnke, was asked by the Global Council of E21 to organize a gathering of evangelists. At Kolenda's invitation, nearly two dozen leading evangelists from around the world came together and prayerfully decided to launch the GEA.[2] Daniel Kolenda and Jean Luc Trachsel (from Europe Shall Be Saved) were nominated to co-chair the GEA. The evangelists gathered again in Bogota, Colombia, in 2020; in Dubai in 2021; in Seoul, South Korea, in 2022; and in Amsterdam in 2023. In 2022, Daniel Kolenda stepped down as co-chair and Nathan Morris (Shake the Nations) stepped up to lend his visionary leadership to the movement.

Working together, the GEA built a network of Spirit-empowered evangelists around the world, created an online video training course for evangelists, and published two books on evangelism. This led up to their historic meeting in Amsterdam in 2023.

Amsterdam 2023

Reinhard Bonnke, Billy Graham, Oral Roberts, and countless others revolutionized the work of evangelists in the twentieth century. In 1983, in Amsterdam, Billy Graham sponsored the first International Conference for Itinerant Evangelists. Forty years later, in 2023, evangelists, missionaries, and Great Commission-focused ministries converged on Amsterdam again for the dawn of a new era of evangelism. We gathered with a new vision: taking the gospel to every person in the next decade.

At the 2023 EveryONE conference in Amsterdam, Dr. Billy Wilson, the chairman of E21, announced that the Spirit-empowered movement had agreed to focus on evangelism for the ten-year period leading up to 2033, the two-thousand-year anniversary of the day of Pentecost. The GEA wholeheartedly endorsed this effort and set in motion plans to evangelize every person on earth within a decade.

At this Amsterdam meeting, evangelists collaborated with believers from around the world about the Great Commission, innovated new ways to reach more people with the gospel, experienced the power of the Holy Spirit, and were inspired to have a greater vision of God's heart for the world. All rallied around the one audacious goal to take the news of Jesus to every person on earth.

The EveryONE Vision

The goal of Empowered21 and the GEA is that every person on earth would have an authentic encounter with Jesus Christ through the power and presence of the Holy Spirit by Pentecost 2033. Billy Wilson asked God, "How are we going to reach everyone?" to which he felt the Holy Spirit reply, "One at a time." By focusing on the one, God will help us to ultimately reach everyone. We want to re-personalize the Great Commission and put the focus on the individual.

Repeatedly in scripture, we see both God's heart for everyone as well as the ability of God to use one person to change a city, a nation, or even a continent: In Mark 16, Jesus told us to "go and preach the gospel to every*one*" (Mark 16:15).[3] Paul tells us that "God our Savior wants every*one* to be saved" (1 Tim 2:4). The Shepherd leaves the ninety-nine sheep to go and find the *one* (Matt 18). Jesus meets with *one* Samaritan woman at the well, and her town is changed (John 4). Philip meets with *one* Ethiopian on the road, and Africa is opened to the gospel (Acts 8). Lastly, Peter visits the house of *one* Roman centurion, and the Holy Spirit is poured out on Gentiles (Acts 10).

Jesus died for every one of the eight billion people on earth—and it is going to take *every one* of us to reach them with the gospel. We need everyone to help reach everyone for the glory of God. The GEA is calling everyone in the church to get involved with sharing their faith, loving people, and praying for the lost.

We believe God wants to accelerate evangelism over the next decade. The world population is accelerating, knowledge is accelerating, technology is accelerating, and the Holy Spirit can accelerate us and help us get this task done. With this acceleration, the generation alive today can complete the Great Commission to reach our generation. E21 and the GEA are calling together Spirit-empowered believers from around the world to unite in an effort to lead people to Jesus. We are dedicated to spreading the gospel to everyone around the world. We are driven by the question: what can we do to take the gospel to the whole earth?

The Role of the GEA in E21

- The GEA works in conjunction with other initiatives of E21, including Next Gen, the Discipleship Commission, and the Scholars Consultation.
- The GEA considers itself to be the "tip of the spear" of E21.
- The GEA provides and trains frontline troops for accomplishing the vision to reach "EveryONE" on earth.
- The GEA plans and leads collaborative evangelistic efforts in countries around the world.
- The GEA champions the gift of the evangelist in the church.
- The GEA inspires and trains believers to engage in personal evangelism.

GEA Strategies for Effective Evangelism

On January 19–20, 2023, Rob Hoskins, the president of One Hope, and his staff, spent two days with the GEA working on a strategic plan for worldwide evangelism. From this time of strategic planning, the GEA developed a plan to focus its efforts on four primary areas: advocacy, equipping and training, collaborating and coordinating, and activation and mobilization. Let's examine these strategic areas in more detail and look at some specific tactics the GEA uses to achieve these strategic goals.

Advocacy

We advocate for Spirit-empowered evangelism in the following ways:

* We increase awareness about the need for evangelism across the body of Christ.
* We communicate the urgency of the Great Commission.
* We champion those who are called to be evangelists.
* We emphasize the role the Holy Spirit plays in evangelism.
* We bring evangelism to the forefront of church consciousness.
* We want a seat at every table so we can remind the church about the importance of evangelism.
* We help the church to think about and be involved in evangelism.
* We ignite a passion for evangelism in local churches around the world.

The Need for the GEA to be a Voice for Evangelism

The Great Commission is a monumental task that requires a united effort by the church. It is important to have a network of evangelists like the GEA because they play a critical role in reaching the world for Christ. The GEA currently provides a platform for evangelists in which to collaborate, receive training and resources, and gain support for their evangelistic efforts. With the rise of globalization and the increasing complexity of the world, evangelism requires a strategic approach and a deep understanding of the diverse cultures and languages of the people being reached. The GEA brings together a diverse group of evangelists with different backgrounds and experiences, allowing for a more comprehensive and effective strategy for evangelism.

The GEA also provides a network of prayer support and encouragement to evangelists, who may often feel isolated and unsupported in their work. The GEA has a vital part to play in completing the Great Commission and bringing people from every nation, tribe, and language into the kingdom of God.

Statistics about Attitudes towards Evangelism

When looking at statistics about the attitudes of believers towards evangelism, there is a clear need for an organization like the GEA to advocate for evangelism. According to Barna's research, young people in the United States are less likely to evangelize than previous generations: "Nearly half of Millennial practicing Christians say it is wrong to evangelize (47%). At the same time, two out of three Millennials believe being a witness about Jesus is part of their faith (65%)."[4]

Barna also reports: "Just 1 in 10 Christians in 1993 who had a conversation about faith believed evangelism was the job of the local church (10%). Twenty-five years later, 3 in 10 said so (29%). Nine out of 10 agreed in 1993 that "every Christian has a responsibility to share their faith" (89%). Only two-thirds said so in 2017 (64%)."[5]

This data indicates a downward trend in evangelism among younger generations, which may have significant implications for the future of the church. There are several reasons why today's generation may not like to evangelize. One possible reason is the fear of rejection or criticism, as sharing one's faith can be a vulnerable and intimidating experience. Additionally, there may be a lack of knowledge or confidence in how to effectively share the gospel message. Other factors may include cultural pressures and the desire to avoid uncomfortable or controversial topics. In some cases, individuals may also struggle with doubts or questions about their own faith, which can make evangelism challenging. However, with proper training, support, and a strong sense of purpose, believers can overcome these barriers and engage in effective evangelism.

Desired Advocacy Outcomes

As advocates for evangelism, we have the following goals:

1) Increase of awareness in churches about the importance of evangelism
2) Increase in the number of individuals who hear the gospel message
3) Increase in the number of individuals who respond to the gospel message and make a commitment to follow Christ
4) Increase in the number of individuals who are healed or experience other miraculous signs and wonders, which could potentially lead to further conversions
5) Increase in the growth of the church, particularly in regions where Spirit-empowered Christianity is already strong, such as the Global South
6) Increase in the number of Spirit-empowered evangelists and missionaries, who may be particularly effective in reaching those in unreached people groups or in difficult-to-reach urban areas

7) Increase in the use of technology and social media for evangelism, particularly among younger generations who are more likely to be reached through these channels

8) Decrease in resistance to the gospel message, particularly in regions where there is strong opposition to Christianity

9) Decrease in the prevalence of harmful cultural practices, such as witchcraft or spiritualism, as individuals come to embrace the power of the Holy Spirit in their lives

10) Decrease in spiritual and emotional distress, as individuals encounter the hope and love of Christ through Spirit-empowered evangelism

Tactics for Advocacy

First, we research the most recent trends in evangelism. The GEA is committed to identifying the regions of the world where the gospel is most needed. To achieve this, we utilize research initiatives that identify and highlight the people groups around the world with the least access to the gospel. We collaborate with other organizations that focus on the goal of world evangelization. We work closely with institutions such as Oral Roberts University to develop in-depth missions research, case studies of successful evangelism projects, and analysis of evangelism best practices.

Second, the GEA develops strategies for evangelism. In communicating our strategic plan for reaching the world for Jesus, we develop and articulate a clear and compelling vision that is both inspiring and realistic. Our vision seeks to be grounded in a comprehensive understanding of the needs of the people groups we seek to reach, and we aim to work collaboratively with other ministries and organizations to achieve our goals. Our goal is to see every person on earth have access to the message of salvation through Jesus Christ, and we believe that our strategic plan will help make this vision a reality.

Third, we desire to communicate about evangelism. The GEA is committed to increasing awareness across the body of Christ about the need for evangelism. We aim to communicate the urgency of the Great Commission and inspire a renewed passion for sharing the gospel message. As a network of evangelists, we are dedicated to championing those who are called to be evangelists and emphasizing the critical role the Holy Spirit plays in evangelism.

Our goal is to bring evangelism to the forefront of church consciousness over the next ten years, and to encourage believers to boldly proclaim the gospel to every nation, tribe, and tongue. We believe that through a united effort, we can make a significant impact for the kingdom of God and see countless lives transformed by the power of the gospel.

Responding to the Call for Evangelism

Equipping and Training Believers and Evangelists

We equip evangelists, churches, and movements for Spirit-empowered evangelism in the following ways:

- We provide practical tools and methods for training people to share their faith.
- We inspire young people to reach out to their peers.
- We move congregations "from their seats to the streets" to be a witness.
- We provide resources and support for the infrastructure of evangelism.
- We develop tools and media that promote evangelism and train believers to evangelize.
- We challenge evangelists to be people of character and integrity.

Desired Equipping and Training Outcomes:

As equippers of evangelists, we have the following goals:

1) Increase in the number of Spirit-empowered evangelists, who are equipped to effectively share the gospel and lead others to Christ
2) Increase in the number of churches that embrace Spirit-empowered evangelism as a core part of their mission, leading to greater effectiveness in reaching their communities
3) Increase in the number of believers who actively share their faith with others
4) Increase in knowledge among believers about effective methods for sharing their faith
5) Increase in the number of movements focused on Spirit-empowered evangelism, which could have a ripple effect and lead to greater growth and transformation in multiple regions
6) Increase in the number of churches and evangelists who are able to integrate technology and social media into their evangelism

strategies, leading to greater reach and impact, particularly among younger generations

7) Increase in the number of people who experience physical and emotional healing as a result of Spirit-empowered evangelism, leading to greater openness to the gospel and a deeper understanding of the power of the Holy Spirit

8) Increase in the number of people from unreached people groups who are effectively reached with the gospel, leading to greater diversity in the global church and greater opportunities for cross-cultural evangelism

9) Decrease in opposition to the gospel message, as Spirit-empowered evangelists are equipped to effectively address cultural and societal barriers to the gospel.

10) Decrease in spiritual warfare and attacks on evangelists and churches engaged in Spirit-empowered evangelism, as they are equipped with spiritual tools and resources to navigate these challenges

11) Increase in the number of people who are transformed by the power of the Holy Spirit, leading to a greater sense of spiritual revival and renewal, both locally and globally

Tactics for Equipping and Training Believers to Evangelize

Training and equipping the laity to share their faith is essential for effective evangelism in the world today. According to one survey, 62 percent of believers who want to evangelize have never undergone any formal evangelism training.[6] Many believers feel intimidated or ill-equipped to share their faith with others, but with the right training and tools, they can become confident and effective at leading people to Jesus.

Here are some ways GEA plans to train people in evangelism: First, we are conducting evangelism courses and seminars. These can be carried out by churches, parachurch organizations, or individual evangelists. These courses cover topics such as the biblical basis for evangelism, the power of the Holy Spirit, effective communication, and practical tips for sharing the gospel in various contexts. Churches can use these courses in a Sunday school setting for training their members in how to share their faith.

Second, GEA creates resources and tools for evangelism. These tools are helpful in equipping believers to share their faith, and include books, tracts, and other materials that provide a clear presentation of the gospel and practical guidance for sharing it with others. Online resources and training videos are also available for reaching a wider audience and providing ongoing support and training for evangelism. We partner with church movements that encourage believers to share their faith. We create evangelism resources that pastors can use to promote evangelism in their congregations.

Tactics for Training and Equipping Evangelists

Training and equipping evangelists is a critical aspect of spreading the gospel. There are several ways to train and equip evangelists. One way is to provide them with a solid biblical foundation by teaching them the doctrines of the Christian faith. This helps them understand the gospel message and communicate it effectively to others.

Evangelists need to be trained in various evangelism methods, such as street evangelism, door-to-door evangelism, and evangelism through social media. They also need to learn how to build relationships with people, listen to their needs and concerns, and effectively communicate the message of Christ's love and salvation. But most importantly, we need to train evangelists to follow the leading of the Holy Spirit. We like what Leonard Ravenhill wrote: "Any method of evangelism will work if God is in it."

Training and equipping evangelists is being done through formal training programs, mentorship, and apprenticeship programs. These programs also provide opportunities for evangelists to practice and apply what they have learned in real-life situations. In addition, evangelists are provided with ongoing support, feedback, and accountability to help them continue to grow and develop in their ministry.

It is also important to equip evangelists with practical resources such as Bibles, tracts, and other materials that they can use to share the gospel. Providing them with access to technology, such as audio and video equipment, is useful in enhancing their evangelistic efforts. Finally, evangelists are encouraged to network and collaborate with other evangelists and ministries to learn from each other, share resources, and work together to reach the lost.

GEA has developed the following resources to aid evangelists. The first are training courses. The GEA created two online courses called

Evangelism Masterclass for training evangelists. The first Evangelism Masterclass, titled "How to Lead People to Jesus," is a course designed to train every believer to be bold in sharing their faith with the lost. People learn how to share their faith in one-on-one settings. We are offering this course free of charge because we believe every Christian should be a soul winner! The second Evangelism Masterclass, titled "The Office of the Evangelist," is full of specialized knowledge for those in the body of Christ who are specifically called to be evangelists. In the body of Christ there are many resources available for those called to be pastors, but now for the first time, a high-level course is available for anyone who feels called to be an evangelist. Anyone can learn how to clearly communicate the gospel to masses of people.

The GEA has also released two evangelism training books at Amsterdam 2023: *The Spirit Empowered Evangelist* and *Spirit-Empowered Witnessing*. These books contain contributions from many of the members of the GEA. We are conducting evangelism conferences (El Salvador, 2024; Thailand, 2025) to equip, empower and inspire believers to engage in evangelism. Lastly, we offer mentorship and discipleship: experienced evangelists come alongside beginning evangelists to help them develop their evangelistic skills and build their confidence.

Tactics for Providing Resources for the Infrastructure of Sustainable Evangelism

Providing resources and support for the infrastructure of evangelism is a vital aspect of effective evangelistic efforts. This includes a wide range of tangible and intangible resources that can help to facilitate the sharing of the gospel in a clear, compelling, and accessible way.

One critical area of focus for supporting the infrastructure of evangelism is in the area of technology and sound systems. In many contexts, particularly in urban or large-scale events, having access to quality sound systems and audiovisual equipment is crucial to ensuring that the message of the gospel is heard and understood. Providing technical assistance and resources in these areas can help to remove barriers to effective communication and ensure that the message of the gospel is presented in a clear and compelling way.

For a church, the majority of the ministry occurs inside the church building. This is why churches do capital campaigns to raise money for the church building. For evangelism, most of the ministry occurs outside the doors of the church in the streets, soccer fields, and stadiums of the world. But a huge amount of resources is used each year to rent sound systems from secular sources. In order to do a large number of ongoing crusades, money needs to be raised specifically for the infrastructure of evangelism. By investing in large sound systems (Ethiopia), evangelism trucks (Thailand), and small sound systems, we are substantially cuting down on the overall cost of doing evangelism. We are strategically positioning sound systems in various locations around the world that are being used by evangelists for evangelism. These sound systems could be large enough to do a city-wide crusade, or the size of an evangelism truck that can be taken into neighborhoods in America, or into the marketplaces of Africa, or small portable sound systems that can be given to indigenous evangelists so we can empower them to go preach from village to village.

Developing technology for evangelists can also significantly increase the spread of the gospel. With the advent of the internet and the rise of Web 3.0, there are now more ways to equip evangelists and spread the gospel than ever before. Apps and online training courses can be created to teach evangelists how to engage with people in a digital age and how to use social media and other online platforms to share their faith. Other Web 3.0 tech such as virtual and augmented reality can be used to create immersive and engaging experiences that help people understand the gospel message. By leveraging these technologies, we can create new ways for people to connect with the gospel and make it easier for evangelists to reach people wherever they are.

Follow-up materials and resources are also critical in supporting the infrastructure of evangelism. After people hear the message of the gospel, it is important to provide them with resources and support to help them understand and apply what they have heard. This includes follow-up materials like discipleship resources, Bibles, and other resources to help new believers grow in their faith and become active members of a church. We work to connect new believers to local churches. We want to provide Bibles to new believers to help them deepen their understanding of scripture and build a strong foundation of faith. Witnessing tools, such as evangelistic tracts or digital resources, assist in equipping new believers to share their faith with others. Together, these three resources support the follow-up of new believers and help them grow in their faith, while also equipping them to share the gospel message with others.

In addition to providing resources and support, connections to denominations and churches help with the infrastructure of evangelism by providing access to a network of believers who have a passion for evangelism. Denominations and churches can offer training and support to evangelists, helping to develop and hone their skills for effective outreach. They can also provide funding and assistance in organizing events and programs for evangelism. Through these connections, evangelists can gain access to the expertise and knowledge of experienced church leaders and pastors, who can offer guidance and mentorship in their evangelistic efforts.

Lastly, funding supports the infrastructure of evangelism. This includes both the financial resources needed to organize and execute large-scale evangelistic events and the ongoing support and sustainability of evangelistic efforts. Providing financial resources and support through the Everyone Fund[7] help to ensure that evangelistic initiatives continue and grow over time, reaching more and more people with the message of the gospel.

Providing resources and support for the infrastructure of evangelism is a critical component of effective evangelistic efforts. By investing in technology, sound systems, funding, and follow-up materials, we help ensure that the message of the gospel is presented in a clear, compelling, and accessible way, and that those who respond to the message have the resources and support they need to grow in their faith and become active members of the church.

In these ways, the GEA aims to target resources at the areas where there is the most need for evangelism. According to Peter Youngren, of finances given to foreign missions, 87 percent goes for work among Christians, 12 percent for work among already evangelized, a mere 1 percent of all money given to foreign missions is used for work among unreached people. Only 0.1 percent of all Christian giving is used for mission efforts in the 38 least evangelized countries. Christians spend 95.4 percent of offerings on home-based ministry, 4.5 percent on cross-cultural efforts among already reached groups, and 0.1 percent to evangelize the unreached.[8] There is a need for Christians to target more resources towards reaching the unreached.

Collaborating and Coordinating

Another area of focus for the GEA is coordinating evangelism outreaches and collaborating with evangelistic efforts. To that end, we do the following:

- We use large evangelistic events as a catalyst for evangelism.
- We bring together ministries who have a passion for evangelism.
- We call evangelists and missions organizations together to focus on specific regions and nations.
- We send people out into the harvest fields to evangelize.
- We partner with evangelistic initiatives from other networks and organizations.

The Importance of a United Effort

Having a united effort for evangelism across various church denominations, ministry networks, and Great Commission movements is crucial because it allows for a greater impact and effectiveness in reaching people with the gospel. When different groups work together, they can pool their resources, talents, and strategies to better reach those who have not yet heard the gospel (Eccl 4:9-12, Prov 27:17). A united effort can lead to greater diversity and cultural sensitivity in evangelism, which can help bridge divides and build relationships with people of different backgrounds. A united effort for evangelism can demonstrate the unity and love of Christ to the world, serving as a powerful witness to the transformative power of the gospel in our lives and in our communities.

Desired Outcomes for Collaborating and Coordinating

As we collaborate and coordinate evangelism in the body of Christ, these are our desired outcomes.

1) Increase in the number of people who are reached with the gospel, as resources and efforts are pooled and leveraged for greater impact
2) Increase in the diversity of outreach efforts, as different organizations and churches bring unique strengths and approaches to the table
3) Increase in the level of training and equipping for evangelists, as collaboration allows for a greater exchange of ideas and resources

4) Increase in the level of support and encouragement for evangelists, as collaboration helps to create a sense of community and accountability

5) Decrease in duplication of efforts, as collaboration allows for greater coordination and awareness of what is already being done in each area

6) Increase in the level of innovation and creativity, as collaboration allows for different ideas and approaches to be tested and refined

7) Increase in the number of opportunities for cross-cultural evangelism, as collaboration allows for greater understanding and partnership across cultural and denominational lines

8) Increase in the number of people who are discipled and integrated into local churches, as collaborative efforts prioritize ongoing discipleship and follow-up

9) Increase in the level of impact on local communities, as collaborative efforts are able to address multiple aspects of need and brokenness

10) Increase in the level of enthusiasm and engagement among local churches and communities, as collaboration helps to build excitement and momentum for the gospel message

Tactics for Collaborating and Coordinating

The first is collaborative events. When evangelists join forces, their collective efforts become greater than the sum of their individual efforts. Collaboration brings diverse gifts, talents, and perspectives to the table, enabling a more comprehensive and effective approach to sharing the gospel. Together, evangelists can support and encourage one another, pool resources and knowledge, and learn from each other's experiences. Collaboration also helps avoid duplication of efforts and allows for strategic planning, targeting specific demographics and regions. By working together, evangelists reach a wider audience, break down barriers, and create a greater impact for the kingdom of God. In a world that desperately needs the message of salvation, the collaboration of evangelists brings unity, synergy, and a shared mission to fulfill the Great Commission. The GEA has decided to collectively focus on reaching two nations on two different continents each year.

The second is the fellowship for evangelists. Evangelists often feel isolated, out on their own, desiring to be used by God, but often, their gifts are not fully realized by the local church. Evangelists need a strong fellowship, a place where they can belong, receive encouragement, and where their gifts are embraced and honored. They need opportunities for the promotion of their evangelistic gift and ministry. There is a need for an organization like the GEA that provides training and mentorship for raising up a new generation of young evangelists.

It is time for evangelists to form a "band of brothers" who are united in hearts and minds and committed to working together to finish the task of world evangelism. Evangelists are called to be on the frontlines, leading the way for the church to complete the mission of bringing in an end-time harvest of souls.

Activation and Mobilization

We activate and mobilize Spirit-empowered evangelists:

- We train evangelists how to share a clear gospel message.
- We empower evangelists to preach the gospel with funding, resources, and training on best practices.
- We mentor a new generation of evangelists and release them into the harvest fields of the world.

Desired Outcomes for Activation and Mobilization

As we mobilize evangelists from around the world, these are the desired outcomes:

1) Increase in the number of Spirit-empowered evangelists who are actively involved in sharing the gospel, as they are equipped, trained, and mobilized for evangelistic efforts
2) Increase in the number of regions and people groups reached with the gospel, as Spirit-empowered evangelists are deployed to share the Good News in unreached or underserved areas
3) Increase in the level of creativity and innovation in evangelistic efforts, as Spirit-empowered evangelists bring unique gifts and approaches to sharing the gospel

4) Increase in the number of conversions and salvations, as Spirit-empowered evangelists rely on the power of the Holy Spirit to convict and transform hearts

5) Increase in the number of people who receive healing, deliverance, or other supernatural encounters, as Spirit-empowered evangelists pray for the sick and minister in the power of the Spirit

6) Increase in the level of unity and collaboration among evangelists, churches, and organizations, as they work together towards common goals and vision

7) Decrease in the influence of cultural and societal barriers to the gospel, as Spirit-empowered evangelists rely on the Holy Spirit to break down walls and overcome obstacles

8) Increase in the level of disciple-making and mentoring, as Spirit-empowered evangelists prioritize equipping new believers and helping them to grow in their faith

9) Increase in the level of passion and enthusiasm for evangelism among believers and local churches, as Spirit-empowered evangelists model and encourage a lifestyle of sharing the gospel

10) Increase in the impact of the Church globally, as Spirit-empowered evangelists lead the charge in sharing the Good News of Jesus Christ with the world

Tactics for Activation and Mobilization

The GEA uses both personal and mass methods to reach people with the message of Jesus Christ. Firstly, we train believers in personal evangelism. One-on-one evangelism allows for meaningful conversations and individual connections, where believers can share their faith and answer questions in a personal and tailored manner. Door-to-door evangelism involves going directly to people's homes, sharing the gospel, and praying for their needs. Marketplace evangelism takes place in public spaces, such as malls or street corners, engaging with individuals and initiating conversations about faith. It is essential to focus on developing and training local evangelism teams, equipping believers to share the good news of Jesus confidently and effectively in their communities. By nurturing these personal evangelism methods, individuals can engage with others on a personal level, meeting them where they are and making a lasting impact.

Secondly, we use mass evangelism. School evangelism provides opportunities to share the gospel in educational institutions. Village evangelism targets specific communities, seeking to bring the transformative message of Christ to rural areas or marginalized populations. Stadium events gather large crowds of people into a single location, where passionate preaching, worship, and testimonies can effectively communicate the gospel to many people at the same time. Media evangelism allows evangelists to use modern technology to increase their reach.

Conclusion

Every believer has a vital part to play in fulfilling the Great Commission. We all must continue to work together across denominational lines, ministry networks, and Great Commission movements to reach the lost and bring people into the kingdom of God. Evangelism is a vital part of the church's mission, and it is essential to continue spreading the gospel message to all people, especially to those who have not yet heard it. We must remember that the Great Commission is a command that Jesus gave to all believers, and each of us has a responsibility to share the love of Christ with those around us—whether it be through personal witness, evangelistic events, or support for those who are called to be evangelists. May we be faithful in sharing the gospel message and working towards the completion of the Great Commission until the day when every tribe, tongue, and nation knows the love of Christ.

Notes

1   This chapter is a recompositing of selected parts of the white paper. The full text is found in https://globalevangelistalliance.com/wp-content/uploads/2024/04/GEA-English-White-Paper.pdf.

2   "E21 Launches Historic Global Evangelist Alliance," Global Evangelist Alliance, https://globalevangelistalliance.com/e21-launches-historic-global-evangelist-alliance-2/.

3   Our organization's name comes from the scripture references that follow, with our emphases highlighted. Scriptures paraphrased by author.

4   Barna Group, *Reviving Evangelism: Current Realities That Demand a New Vision for Sharing Faith* (np: Barna Group, 2019), 10.

5   Barna Group, *Reviving Evangelism,* 36.

6   Barna Research Group, *Reviving Mission in the Next Generation* (Colorado Springs: Every Home for Christ, 2021), 48.

7   For information on the Everyone Fund, see https://everyone.earth/.

8   Peter Youngren, "World Evangelism Facts," https://peteryoungren.org/world-evangelism-facts/, accessed May 30, 2023.

7 Prophetic Evangelism: A Round-Table Talk

Cindy Jacobs

If we are to reach everyone for Christ, per the mandate of Empowered21, then it is critical to understand the role of the Holy Spirit's working in the lives of God's people. We need a theology of spiritual gifts that articulates a biblical understanding of the gifts of the Spirit, as well as how they should be applied—especially to evangelism.

There have, of course, been many books written on spiritual gifts. One of the best and most comprehensive, in my opinion, was written by my mentor, C. Peter Wagner.[1] In his study, supplemented by the research of Richard Houts, Wagner expanded the list of spiritual gifts to twenty-eight, beyond the nine that most Pentecostal and Charismatics recognize. While each of the gifts are important and life-giving, I believe that for the sake of evangelism, the gift of prophecy linked with evangelism is one of the most important for us to utilize.

The power of prophetic evangelism is often self-evident in practice, but it is also scriptural. Jesus uses it, for example, in his witnessing to the Samaritan woman at the well (John 4:4–26). Paul later invites all disciples of Christ into this Spirit-empowered ministry in passages such as 1 Corinthians 14. The text begins with the powerful admonition in verse 1: "Pursue love, and desire spiritual gifts, but especially that you may prophesy."[2] The Amplified Version emphasizes the pursuit of this goal even more strongly: "Pursue [this] love [with eagerness, make it your goal], yet earnestly desire and cultivate the spiritual gifts [to be used by believers for the benefit of the church], but especially that you may prophesy [to foretell the future, to speak a new message from God to the people]."

In verse 39, 1 Corinthians 14 bookends the strength of this truth: "Therefore, brethren, desire earnestly to prophesy..." The significance of this ministry gift is explicated throughout the chapter, especially in verses 24–25, where it is linked to the laity and described as prophetic evangelism:

But if *all prophesy* ["the whole church" in v. 23], and an unbeliever or an uninformed person comes in, *he is convinced by all, he is convicted by all*

> (emphases mine). And thus the secrets of his heart are revealed; and so, falling down on his face, he will worship God and report that God is truly among you.

What a fantastic result! Prophetic ministry can open eyes and convert the lost. As one who prophesies myself, I have a conviction about pursuing this gift linked to evangelism. For decades, I have sought to speak supernatural details of a person's life in order to reveal to them that God is real. Many times this leads them to pray to receive Christ as their Savior.

Let me give you an example. One day, I was ministering in Sicily, Italy. As I was ministering, I suddenly felt that there was someone in the meeting who was in the mafia. After I received this information by the Holy Spirit, in what the Bible calls a "word of knowledge" (1 Cor 12:8), I stopped and rather brashly stated, "There is someone here and you are in the mafia. Come down here right now!" Upon reflection, my brashness was probably courageousness, as I suspect the gift of faith (1 Cor 12:9) was being coupled with the word of knowledge (cf., Rom 12:6).

To everyone's surprise, a man came forward. Now, what do you think that God would say to such a person? Perhaps something to this effect: "You are a very bad man and you have to get out of the mafia right now!" However, when one flows in prophetic evangelism, this is not an option. Prophetic expression is redemptive in nature. Scripture exhorts that "he who prophesies edifies the church" (1 Cor 14:4) and that "though I have the gift of prophecy, and understand all mysteries and all knowledge . . . but have not love, I am nothing" (1 Cor 13:2). So, rather than rebuke the man, the Holy Spirit started painting a picture for me of the man's future if he would serve God. To everyone's shock, including mine, he threw his hands up in the air and proclaimed, "But I am a bad man!" To which I replied, "I know! Pray this prayer!" This *mafioso* then proceeded to humbly pray and ask Jesus to come into his life and be his Savior.

So 1 Corinthians 14 is right! Prophetic evangelism is a tremendous way to use the gifts of God to reveal Christ to the lost. When done in love, the prophetic softens unbelievers' emotions towards God. In every person's heart, whether they know it or not, is a longing to know God. Built into our very formation is a hole in the soul that can only be filled by our Creator. In using the gift of prophecy to supernaturally speak to someone's deepest needs—what I call the wilderness in a person's soul—they come face-to face with the living God who loves them and is intimately acquainted with them.

Many in the Spirit-empowered movement would assent to this—and to the gift of prophecy in general. But I contend that the church today has largely used the gift of prophecy to bless each other. Edification, exhortation, and comfort are indeed important (1 Cor 14:3), but I believe that in this time when Spirit-empowered people are uniting around the mission for the greatest harvest of souls that the world has ever known, we must develop training material for ministers to learn how to reach the lost through prophecy. This, of course, does not mean that all will be prophets, but rather that all those who are filled with the Holy Spirit have the power to manifest prophetically as a witness.

This was the promise of Pentecost. Acts 1:8 says, "But you will receive *power* when the Holy Spirit has come upon you; and you shall be *witnesses* to me in Jerusalem, and in all Judea and Samaria, and to the ends of the earth" (emphases mine). The word "power" here means *dunamis*, as in dynamite-like power.[3] Likewise, the word "witnesses" is *martus*, from which we derive the word "martyr." A martyr at that time, according to *Strong's Concordance*, was someone who could provide judicial testimony in a court of law.[4] In the early church, and in many places around the world today, the Christian understanding of this word means to remain steadfast unto death, which testifies to the truth and manner of Jesus' crucifixion and resurrection. Every believer is invited into this call of power to be his witness.

Thus, to reach everyone with the gospel, we need everyone to manifest God's power! Recently, at the EveryONE Asia 2024 conference, I spoke about power in evangelism and this Acts 1:8 text. I encouraged everyone present to receive the power of the Holy Spirit to manifest supernaturally every day and everywhere. I also declared that this generation is dynamite. We can make his name famous so that everyone will see it, and God will use his people prophetically in prayer, worship, and evangelism to bring that forth.[5] Bishop Bill Hamon calls this "the Saints Movement."[6] In the past, the church has largely relied on pulpit ministry to supernaturally release God's power. However, the present pursuit of global awakening will require a broader and more biblical understanding of empowered laity.

Regarding prophetic evangelism specifically, there are various leaders who have pioneered the practice and brought it to the attention of the body of Christ. The first whom I know used it on a broad scale was my good friend, Ed Silvoso, of Transform Our World. In fact, he wrote a whole book on the subject entitled *Prayer Evangelism.*[7] Sean Smith, also a dear friend, has written about it in his book, aptly titled *Prophetic Evangelism.*[8] Both tell numerous testimonies that confirm the power of a simple prophetic word to transform the life of someone who has never known God. They also invite the church to choose a Book of Acts reality, with the pursuit of spiritual gifts tied to bringing the world to Jesus.

Significant predecessors exist in this stream. Many people have heard about the great Argentine revival of 1992, which had roots in the 1980s and earlier. Wagner and Pablo Deiros compiled a history of this revival in their book, *The Rising Revival,* with chapters authored by famous evangelists, including Carlos Annacondia, Omar Cabrera Sr., and Claudio Freidzon.[9] I had the honor of ministering with these leaders during this great move of God, and I learned much about prophetic evangelism from them. Some of this I chronicle in *The Voice of God,* including prophetic intercession over the strongholds of cities and nations, and prophetic acts that pave the way for evangelistic success.[10] Additionally, Silvoso was a major mover and shaker due to his city outreach projects during that time. One of the things that he and his teams did was set up prayer stations at various sites in the city that they were targeting for transformation—and advertise free prayer. Many people, either out of curiosity or earnestly wanting a connection with God, would go for prayer.[11] The results were outstanding! Hundreds of thousands came to the Lord during those times.[12]

Other movements have used prophetic exercises to reach the lost. One that has been used in notable ways is "treasure hunting," at the Bethel School of the Supernatural in Redding, California. The treasure is souls. The students at the school gather and pray for God to speak to them about people they will meet who need the Lord. One story told to me was about a day when a group of students felt instructed by the Lord to go to Home Depot. Once in the store, they walked around looking for treasure. God had specifically shown them that the person they were to pray for would be wearing a baseball cap that said, "Let's go fishing!" So, they patiently walked around the store until they came upon a man wearing just such a hat. The students then approached him and asked if they could pray for him. They said that God had shown them that he had a bad back. The man blustered, caustically replying that he was fine—to which his wife poked him with her elbow and exclaimed, "You know that is a lie! You are scheduled for surgery! Let the kids pray for you!" The man relented to receive prayer. After he was prayed for, he shouted, "What did you do to me?!" He felt the power of God touch his body and was instantly healed! In response, the young people added, "Well, since that is the case, God also told us that you are having problems with your marriage." The tough old man grouchily shot back, "There is nothing wrong with my marriage," to which his wife sharply remarked, "You know that's not true; we are separated!" Right there, the sweet presence of the Lord came into the middle of Home Depot, and the couple got gloriously saved. Prophetic evangelism is so wonderful!

Another friend, Cindy McGill, has the most unusual ministry to the lost using prophetic evangelism that I know of: she attends New Age and pagan festivals. In these spiritually dark places, she sets up prayer tents and advertises free spiritual readings. She specifically uses their terminology out of the conviction that the lost are much more open to receiving Christ when we use their language rather than "Christianese." Her approach is very similar to the concept of "contextualization" that I learned as a student at Fuller Theological Seminary. Whereas the latter term is commonly invoked in global, missional spheres, Cindy is practicing it locally. She simply considers the context of the hearer and works with what they understand due to their culture, belief system, age, and other factors.[13]

One story that Cindy tells is how she and her team set up a prayer tent at an annual festival called Burning Man, which meets at Black Rock City in the Nevada desert. The event is totally Christ-less and anything goes—even clothing is optional! A man came into the tent wearing a pink tutu without anything underneath it. Undaunted, Cindy's prophetic team started giving him his "spiritual reading" (using language without Christianese) when, all of a sudden, he said with tears in his eyes, "I know what this is! This is the power of the Holy Spirit!" He went on to share that he had once been a pastor but had gotten deeply hurt and had walked away from God completely. He then deeply repented and gave his life back to the Lord. He even ended up ministering to others with Cindy's team after that.

Prophetic evangelism is therefore an accelerator and multiplier to see the lost saved. One time when I was ministering in Manaus, Brazil, which is on the Amazon River, I was preaching to a great church of around eighty-five thousand members, pastored by Rene Terra Nova. As I preached, I stopped and began to release a specific word of knowledge that there was a young person involved in gang activity whose life was in imminent danger if he or she did not get out of the gang. I waited and said, "Where are you? Come down here right now!" A young man made his way out of the crowd, and to my surprise fell into my arms weeping! He knew that God was speaking to him about his lifestyle, so right then and there, he gave his life to the Lord. I love prophetic evangelism!

A final story is one the most remarkable testimonies that I have heard, as it regards Spirit-empowered evangelism. It is from the book *Before We Kill and Eat You*, by H. B. and Ruthanne Garlock, subtitled *Tales of Faith in the Face of Certain Death*. Ruthanne was related by marriage to the missionary H.B. Garlock, and they wrote of their exciting story of breakthrough among the cannibals of Liberia. After a season of work there, one chief told this to the Garlocks:

> White man, you have asked us to give up the religion of our ancestors for a new religion, one that has not been tried by our people... We are preparing to consider serving your God, but before doing so we would like to see a demonstration of this power you are talking about. There are many lepers in our village. Would you mind healing some of them?... There are many blind people among us. Please heal some of these. And our people are dying every day.[14]

These words weighed on the missionaries. However, later a woman in the tribe died after giving birth. As was the custom, her body was laid in a refuse heap. Recalling the chief's admonition, the Garlocks decided that it was now or never! In the face of death and cannibalism, the couple crept up to the woman's body, laid hands on her, and commanded the spirit of death to leave her. What transpired next was simply remarkable! The woman's body began to shake and she came back to life! The members of the tribe scattered into the jungle, no doubt thinking that she was a ghost or inhabited by evil spirits. But, soon after, H. B. visited the hut of the husband, who inquired how his wife was. To his delight, she suddenly entered the hut with a stalk of bananas on her head. Needless to say, the chief and the village experienced a collective move of the Holy Spirit and all came to Christ.

These types of evangelistic experiences, of which the gift of prophecy plays a part, are sometimes spoken of as "power evangelism." John Wimber, the founder of the Vineyard movement, wrote a foundational book on this.[15] Power evangelism is particularly powerful in reaching the lost and even whole people groups because, as 1 Corinthians 14:24–25 describes, people are confronted with the reality of the biblical God as he reveals his power, knowledge, and goodness. Prophetic evangelism uses words of knowledge to do this, as well as to speak and invite miracles that God wants to do in a person's life. I believe that God has given Spirit-empowered believers the means to reach the lost, and revive many who need it, through prophetic evangelism.

As of this writing, the fields of the nations of the world are white with harvest (John 4:35). In 2020, the world population was approximately 7.8 billion, of which 2.5 billion were Christians (32.3 percent). Of that 2.5 billion Christians, 644 million (26 percent) were Spirit-empowered.[16] Additionally, according to Johnson and Zurlo, there are more than four thousand unevangelized cultures—they do not have a Bible in their language nor the ability to evangelize themselves.[17] The job of seeing everyone reached for Christ is staggering to say the least! However, it is not too big for God. Nor is it for us, his people, if we avail ourselves of the full power of the Holy Spirit poured out at Pentecost.

Evangelism is, at its core, a Holy Spirit process from beginning to end. His Spirit is more than able to provide the supernatural wisdom and power needed to open blind eyes and reach the remaining population. Let us equip God's people to fulfill the Great Commission, fully empowered, through any and all means.

Notes

1   C. Peter Wagner, *Discovering Your Spiritual Gifts*, exp. ed. (Ada, MI: Chosen Books, 2012). Note that the companion mini-book, entitled *Finding Your Spiritual Gifts*, is a self-assessment of twenty-eight giftings that has been used by thousands of individuals and churches since its publication in 1978.

2   Unless otherwise noted, all scripture references are taken from the New King James Version (NKJV).

3   Bible Hub 2025, s.v. *Strong's Lexicon* 1411: *dunamin*, https://biblehub.com/greek/1411.htm.

4   Bible Hub, 2025, s.v. *Strong's Lexicon* 3144: *martus*, https://biblehub.com/greek/3144.htm.

5   Cindy Jacobs, "EveryONE ASIA2024, General Session 1," Empowered21, YouTube video, July 3, 2024, https://www.youtube.com/watch?v=q9wrcdaMrgs&t=8751s.

6   Bill Hamon, *The Day of the Saints: Equipping Believers for their Revolutionary Role in Ministry* (Shippensburg, PA: Destiny Image, 2012).

7   Ed Silvoso, *Power Evangelism: How to Change the Spiritual Climate Over Your Home, Neighborhood, and City*, rev. ed. (Ada, MI: Chosen Books, 2018). I also highly recommend Ed Silvoso, *That None Should Perish: How to Reach Entire Cities for Christ Through Prayer Evangelism* (Ada, MI: Chosen Books, 1995).

8   Sean Smith, *Prophetic Evangelism: Tactics that Release Signs, Wonders, and Miracles in Your Everyday Life*, rev. and exp. ed. (Shippensburg, PA: Destiny Image, 2021)

9   On a personal note, I am so glad that Wagner and Deiros compiled the history of the Argentine revival for those of us today to use. Wagner used to say, "Any movement that is not written about is not remembered." He would later add, "What if Frank Bartleman hadn't written Azusa Street?" To be sure, it only takes a decade or so for things to be forgotten between generations. Many great moves of God are not remembered simply because they were not chronicled.

10 See Cindy Jacobs, *The Voice of God* (Ventura, CA: Regal Books, 1995), especially 231–256 for testimonies and a reflection on the role of prophetic people in God's plans for cities and nations.

11 Jacobs, *The Voice of God*, 246–250.

12 For a short article with details including numerical data, see Geoff Waugh, "Final Decade of the 20th Century," The Revival Library, https://revival-library.org/histories/1992-argentina-claudio-freidzon/. For a longer anecdotal account, see Richard Riss, "History of the Awakening, 1992–1995," The Revival Library, 1995, https://revival-library.org/histories/1992-1995-history-of-the-awakening/.

13 For more on local contextualized ministry, I highly recommend McGill's self-published manuscript: *Methods to End the Madness Field Guide:*

Proven Strategies & Creative Ideas for Outreach in Today's Culture (Amazon KDP, 2023).

14 H. B. Garlock and Ruthanne Garlock, *Before We Kill and Eat You: Tales of Faith in the Face of Certain Death* (Ventura, CA: Regal Books, 2006), 74.

15 John Wimber, *Power Evangelism* (New York: Harper & Row, 1986).

16 Todd M. Johnson and Gina A. Zurlo, *Introducing Spirit-Empowered Christianity* (Tulsa, OK: ORU Press), 143.

17 Todd M. Johnson and Gina A. Zurlo, *World Christian Encyclopedia*, 3rd ed. (Edinburgh: Edinburgh Press, 2020), 34. See their remarks that most of these are Hindu, Buddhist, or Muslim in the Global South.

Part II

Case Studies in Context

8   The Role of Reinhard Bonnke in Raising National Evangelists in Africa: A Case Study of Teresia Wairimu Kinyanjui-Faith Evangelistic Ministries, Kenya

Charles Obara

Abstract

Africa has witnessed an amazing transformation of its religious landscape in recent decades, making it home to the most Christians globally. Raising missional leaders to shepherd the Spirit-empowered movement at the axis of this stupendous growth should now be one of the most significant undertakings of the church in the majority world. This chapter explores the role of Reinhard Bonnke's Pan-African mission of raising national evangelists. Using a case study of Teresia Wairimu of Faith Evangelistic Ministries in Kenya, it argues that Bonnke's most significant contribution to Christianity in Africa is raising national evangelists through his "Fire Conference" empowerment seminars. These evangelists are now proclaiming the gospel message in the power of the Spirit, adding to the tidal wave of transformation of the religious landscape in Africa.

Introduction

Christianity has grown exponentially in Africa in recent decades with no signs of slowing down. With a Christian population of over 667 million, Africa is home to the largest number of Christians worldwide.[1] Although all denominations have experienced numerical growth in Africa, the Pentecostal-Charismatic stream of Christianity has experienced the most. Pentecostalism has penetrated mainstream Christianity in what has been referred to as the "African Reformation" of the twentieth century.[2] This growth has shaped the contours of Christianity in Africa and challenged the traditional Western categorization of religion in terms of liberals, Evangelicals, Pentecostals, and Charismatics.[3]

Reinhard Bonnke began Christ for All Nations (CfaN) in 1974 in South Africa with a vision of evangelizing the continent of Africa from Cape Town to Cairo. Over the five decades of its operations, CfaN has claimed that eighty million people were converted to Christianity with claims of manifestation of the Spirit's power. This chapter examines Bonnke's missional strategy for evangelizing Africa, with the focus on raising national evangelists as its central theme. It begins with a brief overview of the historical development of Pentecostalism in Kenya before the arrival of Bonnke. It then explores how Bonnke's Pan-African mission spurred the growth of Pentecostal Christianity in Africa through his partnership with the local churches, mass Spirit-baptism, and equipping of local evangelists through the Fire Conferences. Through a case study of Faith Evangelistic Ministries, which was founded by a protégé of Bonnke's Teresia Wairimu, the study argues that Bonnke's most significant contribution to Christianity in Africa was the thousands of local evangelists he equipped through the Fire Conferences. These evangelists are now proclaiming the gospel message in the Spirit's power, drawing many more souls to the kingdom of God. The study concludes with lessons for the Spirit-empowered global movement.

This study is motivated by the transformation taking place in the African religious landscape that has changed the face of Christianity in Africa. It's also inspired by the need for Spirit-empowered transformational leadership to shepherd this movement. Bonnke's success in addressing this critical need offers valuable lessons for missional praxis.

Overview of Pentecostalism in Kenya

Christianity was introduced in Kenya in 1498 when Vasco da Gama, the Portuguese explorer, arrived in Kenya in 1498 at Malindi Bay.[4] From here, the local communities were evangelized in Mombasa with six hundred African converts by the end of the sixteenth century. Other missionary agencies, such as the Church Mission Society, British Methodists, and Scottish Presbyterians, followed later. The first mainline church to experience revival was the Anglican Church in 1912. A charismatic movement known as *Roho* ("Spirit") emerged in this church among the Luo people of western Kenya. Roho's founders were Alfayo Odongo Mango (1884–1934) and his nephew Lawi Obonyo (c. 1911–34).[5] Mango was an Anglican deacon baptized in the Spirit in 1916, who received a special calling in a vision. There seems to have been no contact between these local luminaries of revival flames and the Pentecostal missionaries.

These Anglican "Pentecostals" were not readily accepted in the Anglican church led by Western missionaries as they were considered too emotional.

Revival also broke out among the Quakers in western Kenya. The Abaluya community experienced a revival in the Friends (Quakers) mission in 1927. The local church leaders and American mission authorities discouraged the revival and outlawed public confession of sins and the manifestations of spiritual gifts like prophecy and speaking in tongues. When this did not deter the local revivalists' quest for a Pentecostal experience, they were finally expelled from the mission in 1929. The revivalists established their own local churches, the largest of which was the African Church of the Holy Spirit.[6]

Daudi Zakayo Kivuli (1896–1974), an evangelist among the Luyha, founded the African Israel Church Nineveh (AICN) in 1942, later becoming one of the renowned AICs in Kenya. After experiencing an ecstatic Spirit-baptism in 1932, he embarked on an evangelistic and healing ministry among local communities. Kivuli, worked for Otto and Marion Keller, the pioneer Pentecostal Assemblies of Canada (PAOC) missionaries in Western Kenya from 1925 to 1940 as a supervisor of their mission schools. In 1940, he left the PAOC to establish his church and assumed the title "high priest," with his home becoming the headquarters of Nineveh.[7]

Western Kenya also experienced another wave of revival in 1929, coming from across the border in Uganda. The East African revival, popularly known as the *Tukutendeleza* movement (Praise Jesus) or *Baloloke* (the "saved ones") in Luganda, originated from the Church Mission Society (CMS) church in Rwanda in the 1920s and spread to Uganda, Kenya, and Tanzania. This movement was characterized by public confession of sins and emphasis on personal conversion, leading to being "born again."[8] This movement also encountered opposition from the mainline churches. Anderson observes that the "official" East African Revival movement in the Anglican churches "prevented using spiritual gifts such as speaking in tongues, prophecy, and healing. This often brought it into conflict with those Africans who desired the more tangible evidence of God's presence and power provided by the Pentecostals."[9]

When Charismatic Christianity emerged in Kenya, it found the ground had already been prepared by classical Pentecostal missionaries from the

United States of America and Canada and by the East African Revival movement.[10] The local Pentecostal church leaders collaborated with their Western counterparts, unlike the missionary church leaders who pushed for autonomy. This collaboration birthed what might be referred to as the second wave of Pentecostal revival in Kenya after the earlier one among the local believers. International evangelists like Tommy Lee Osborn and Oral Roberts led this awakening. Osborn held crusades in Kenyan cities—namely Mombasa, Nairobi, Nakuru, and Kisumu—in the 1960s and 1970s. These crusades added new Pentecostal fire in this East African country. Osborn is mainly credited for raising local church ministers and evangelists such as Joe Kayo, Arthur Kitonga, and Wilson Mamboleo, among others, through his school of evangelism.[11] These leaders later founded local ministries and churches such as Deliverance Church, Redeemed Church, and others. These indigenous denominations now have hundreds of churches scattered nationwide and beyond.

The arrival of Reinhard Bonnke in Kenya in 1988 can be considered the third wave of Pentecostal missionary activities in Kenya. Bonnke added a new impetus to the Pentecostal flames from the second wave of revival. An autobiographical sketch of Bonnke is critical to give us a framework for understanding Bonnke's motivation for his Pan-African mission.

Bonnke's Missionary Call to Africa

No Western missionary has had a consistent and lasting impact in Africa like Reinhard Bonnke. Described as the man who changed the face of Christianity in Africa,[12] Reinhard Bonnke is a household name in Africa. His "Africa Shall be Saved" campaign attracted some of the largest crowds ever witnessed in Africa. He preached with great passion, determination, and a sense of urgency. Africans, including their political leaders, responded well to his ministry and came in big numbers to hear him preach.

Reinhard Bonnke was born on April 19, 1940, in Königsberg, East Prussia, to a family influenced by Pentecostalism during the war. His grandfather is said to have been healed of rheumatism by a Pentecostal preacher and was consequently won into Pentecostalism. His father, Herman Bonnke, served in the army during the war before entirely devoting himself to pastoral ministry after the war. His mother, Meta

Scheffler, played a vital role in the young Bonnke's spiritual formation. At age ten, he received a call to join a mission in Africa. Bonnke attended the Evangelical Bible College of Wales in Swansea, which Rees Howells, a disciple of the Wesleyan revival movement, started. Attending this interdenominational college prepared Bonnke for his ministry in Africa. After graduating, on his way home from Wales, he had a brief stopover in London, where he was to make a train connection to Germany. In what might be described as divine providence, Bonnke met Evangelist George Jeffreys, the Welsh revivalist who had founded Elim Church. The ailing evangelist laid hands on him and the power of the Holy Spirit came upon Bonnke so powerfully that he left Jeffreys' house dazed.[13] Bonnke considered this experience as the passing of the baton of revival to the next generation, as Jeffreys passed on a few months later.

The dream of engaging in missionary work in Africa materialized when Bonnke was commissioned by the Velberter Mission in 1967 and sent to South Africa. There, Bonnke was appointed as a preacher to the Apostolic Faith Mission. In South Africa, Bonnke came face to face with the reality of apartheid. Apartheid laws influenced some of his missionary colleagues to the extent that they could not shake hands with non-white. This led Bonnke to move to a small and struggling church in Maseru, which many Western missionaries did not want to be posted to.

In the streets of Maseru, Bonnke could play his accordion and people gathered to hear him sing. After a brief session of singing, he would preach a short evangelistic sermon and make a call for salvation. These efforts paid off as he began to win some converts, who he then directed to his local church. His church started experiencing growth in attendance. Bonnke also established a printing press that printed newsletters and gospel tracts. He hired cyclists to distribute these to the interior parts of this mountainous country. Many people in remote areas were reached through this initiative.

One night, Bonnke had an experience that changed the trajectory of his ministry in Lesotho. In a vision, Bonnke saw a blood-washed Africa, and he claimed that he heard the Spirit whisper, "Africa shall be saved."[14] This experience led him to leave his traditional missionary approach to evangelism and begin mass evangelistic efforts. With a congregation of one hundred members, he held his first mass evangelistic meeting in a stadium in Botswana. The rally started with one hundred people in attendance. Claims of divine healing in this crusade saw the attendance increase exponentially every day to stand at about 10,000 people by the end of the week. This event propelled Bonnke to global fame.

In 1974, Bonnke launched Christ for the Nations (CfN), later renamed Christ for All Nations (CfaN), and moved his headquarters to Johannesburg. He purchased a 34,000-seat dome in which he conducted revival meetings. This dome also filled up quickly. Bonnke shifted to outdoor meetings to accommodate the swelling crowds.

Bonnke's Influence in Africa

Bonnke was very popular in Africa. His mass evangelistic campaigns attracted some of the biggest public gatherings ever witnessed in the history of mass evangelism. In Lagos, it is claimed that 1.6 million people attended his 1999 rally in a single day.[15] Bonnke's meetings also attracted African presidents. President Daniel Arap Moi attended Bonnke's 1988 Uhuru Park crusade in Kenya with several cabinet ministers. Some of his ministers reportedly responded to the altar call. In Sierra Leon, President Ahamed Tajan Kabbah invited Bonnke to address Parliament.[16]

Bonnke significantly influenced Pentecostalism in Africa over the nearly five decades of his missionary engagement. Paul Gifford observes that "there is no denying that CfaN has played a significant role in the growth of Christianity in Africa, going by the number of conversions to Christianity."[17] Bonnke contributed to this growth by promoting mass evangelism, practicing mass Spirit-baptism in his rallies, encouraging ecumenical cooperation among churches, and raising local evangelists through Fire Conferences. We shall now briefly discuss these contributions.

Mass Spirit-Baptism

Bonnke, as a Pentecostal preacher, believed in the spiritual empowerment of believers for effective Christian witness. In his rallies, he emphasized the baptism of the Holy Spirit and prayed for people to be filled with the Holy Spirit. It is claimed that many received the baptism of the Spirit and spoke in new tongues. Daniel King observes that Bonnke emphasized the power of the Holy Spirit in every crusade for three days, and on the third day, he prayed for the crowd to be filled with the Holy Spirit. The Spirit fell on the crowd and they began to speak in new tongues.[18]

This practice promoted Pentecostal spiritualities among converts and the participating churches.

Ecumenical Cooperation

Evangelism was a top priority of Bonnke's "Africa Shall be Saved" campaign. This passion saw him forge partnerships with local churches across the African cities, where he held major evangelistic campaigns, regardless of their denominational affiliations. Bonnke contends, "When it comes to the great and prior interest of evangelism, I work with people of many different spiritual affirmations. CfaN is an evangelist-servant to the churches wherever they labor and whatever their witness or emphasis."[19] This approach has had the positive effect of breaking the silo mentality and uniting the local churches in the cities where he held his rallies. Church leaders realized they could work together to win more people to the kingdom of God. Such cooperation brought in greater witness in a city where he held his rallies than in individual efforts of local churches. It also demonstrates the unity of the body of Christ.

Mass Evangelism Approach

Bonnke would have been an ordinary Western missionary were it not for the vision of the salvation of Africa he claimed to have seen. This vision inspired him to embrace a mass evangelism approach to reach as many people as possible. He relates, "I was a hard-working missionary in Lesotho, but the dream of a Blood-washed Africa haunted me. The vision became more persistent and vivid. An all-consuming desire drove me to make my first ventures towards mass evangelism."[20]

His crusade would draw hundreds of thousands of people. His public rallies would typically take place in the evenings. They were usually divided into three sessions. The first one is what one can call the "warm-up session." Famous local gospel artists would perform in this session. This session served to attract and entertain the crowds. The second session involved Bonnke's preaching. Bonnke would preach pointed sermons that appealed to the hearts of his listeners. The third session involved prayer for salvation and the sick. Gifford observes,

> Bonnke usually tells those desiring healing to·place a hand over the affected organ or area; after rebuking spirits responsible for countless ills and invoking God's powers in all these areas, he calls for the Healing of everyone together.

> Those who claim to be healed are asked to testify on the platform. There, they demonstrate their Healing by performing actions previously impossible for them: for example, by running around the platform if they had been lame, by talking if they had been dumb."[21]

These testimonies were generally not medically certified by a doctor, but they served to pull more crowds to his meetings.

Though Bonnke did not introduce mass evangelism to Africa, his style of doing these rallies has been adopted widely by many local evangelists. Crusade banners and decision cards are used for follow-up; mass media advertisements are increasingly used locally by Pentecostal churches to reach many. These evangelistic rallies take the format of the Bonnke Crusades. The warm-up session of praise and worship is followed by preaching, an altar call for salvation, and prayer for personal needs.

Discipleship Approach

Reinhard Bonnke was keen on turning the converts in his rallies into disciples. He employed a well-designed mechanism for following up on his young converts. Using trained counselors, he would get the contact information of those who responded to the altar call in his meetings and pass this on to local churches that could use the information to follow up on the converts to ensure they were connected to the local churches for discipleship. Bonnke's booklet *Now That You Are Saved* addresses the basics of salvation and has been used widely as a discipleship tool for new converts. CfaN reveals that more than 105 million copies of this booklet have been distributed in and outside Africa.[22] Another booklet, From Minus to Plus, has printed 95 million copies for distribution in homes worldwide.

Raising Local Evangelists

Leadership plays a critical role in the survival of any movement. But leaders only lead for a season and, therefore, must multiply themselves by raising other leaders for the long-term survival of their organization. As it takes a giant killer to produce other giant killers, it takes leaders to raise leaders.[23] Bonnke was keen on nurturing other evangelists to run with his Pan-African vision. He has been described as a socialized charismatic leader who empowered others to run with his vision for the evangelization of Africa.[24] In Lesotho, Bonnke began a correspondence bible school to equip local evangelists for effective ministry. This school attracted a record enrollment of fifty thousand church leaders within five years of operation.[25] These evangelists reached the remotest part of this South African country with the gospel.

Bonnke attended the Billy Graham Conference for Itinerant Evangelists in Amsterdam in 1983 and was very impressed by its organization and impact. This conference inspired him to begin Fire Conferences alongside his evangelistic rallies to equip local evangelists for soul-winning. The first Fire Conference was held in Harare, Zimbabwe, in 1986 from April 21–26 in the new Harare Conference Centre. This conference brought together four thousand African evangelists from sixty countries. The conference aimed to draw together Africa's leading evangelists to devise what Bonnke described as a common strategy to evangelize Africa. Bonnke hoped this conference would ignite a new passion for evangelism among the delegates. The delegates would return to their countries and "set entire nations alight with the name of Jesus."[26]

The Harare Fire Conference drew speakers from the U.S. and Africa and covered topics on evangelism and divine healing, Christian education, intercession, church planting, marriage counseling, etc. The Fire Conferences became Bonnke's modus operandi everywhere he held mass evangelistic rallies in Africa and beyond.

The impact of these Fire Conferences on raising local evangelists is visible in Africa. A case study of Teresia Wairimu of Faith Evangelistic Ministries in Kenya, a protégé of Bonnke, illustrates this well.

Teresia Wairimu, Faith Evangelistic Ministry

One of Kenya's most recognizable figures in mass evangelistic rallies is Teresia Wairimu Kinyanjui. Wairimu was an influential religious leader who often attracted both the top echelon of the political class and people with low incomes.[27] Her megachurch in Karen has hosted retired president Uhuru Kenyatta and current president William Ruto. At the same time, her open-air evangelistic rallies in the 1990s and 2000s in the historic Uhuru Park attracted huge crowds.

Wairimu was born on November 15, 1957, a couple of years before Kenya attained independence from colonial domination in 1963. Her father, a businessman, was detained by the colonialists years before she was born, while her mother worked hard on the farm to fend for her older siblings. The colonial administration declared a state of emergency in Kenya in 1952, which saw many men arrested and others killed for their rebellion (*Mau Mau*) against the harsh British colonial administration. Wairimu grew up in a Christian home, and compared to many children in the village, she enjoyed a reasonably comfortable life and the privilege of attending school.

Wairimu attended Reinhard Bonnke's first crusade in Kenya in 1988. This evangelistic rally was a weeklong campaign in Uhuru Park. Wairimu came into this meeting, smarting from the emotional trauma of a failed marriage to Neilson, a Swedish missionary in Kenya. In a society where divorced women were despised and seen as failures because they could not keep their marriages, Wairimu struggled with guilt and rejection.

This crusade, attended by the Kenyan head of state, spiritually impacted Wairimu's life. Bonnke preached a powerful message under the anointing of the Spirit, with manifestations of miracles that mesmerized her. Wairimu claims that she received emotional healing in this meeting. She was, however, hungry for more of God in her life and hoped that she would serve God the way Bonnke did. Her prayer was, "Dear God, if you can give Bonnke one hundred thousand souls in a day, give me one hundred. I will be a happy woman serving you."[28] Wairimu sought an opportunity for Bonnke to lay hands on her, believing that such an experience would change her life and empower her for ministry. However, her chances were slim due to the massive crowds usually attending his rallies.

After this evangelistic meeting in Uhuru Park, Wairimu began a fellowship of women, who met at her house to pray. She continued to keep tabs on Bonnke's itinerary, hoping to find an ideal meeting where she stood a chance of being prayed for by Bonnke. She reckoned that she might stand a realistic chance of such an encounter if the crusade were held outside Africa, where crowds for his meetings were not as massive.

The opportunity presented itself when Pastor Arne Oystein Rambeck invited Bonnke to minister in his church, *Evangeliehuest*, in Porsgrunn, Oslo. Wairimu traveled to Oslo and stayed with some family friends. On the Sunday Bonnke was going to minister in this church, Wairimu arrived many hours before the service began to secure a seat closest to the pulpit. However, the sanctuary quickly filled up with other people standing in the parking bay. Wairimu recalls that Bonnke preached about the message of the cross and how the cross turns our minuses into pluses in life. During the altar call, Wairimu shot up and ran forward to be prayed for. When Bonnke laid his hands on her, God's power came upon her so powerfully that it threw her meters away from the preacher.[29] She fell back from where she was seated earlier and remained unconscious for hours. Her friends carried her back to her residence and deposited her on her bed to recover from this experience.[30]

The impact of this encounter in Oslo was instantaneous in her ministry. The little fellowship meetings she used to have began to swell as people heard about the move of God in her meetings.[31] She also began to travel across the country, preaching the gospel in prisons, schools, churches, and parks. As her meetings grew in attendance, she moved from home fellowship to bigger halls in Nairobi. Eventually, she moved her meetings to Kenyatta International Conference Center (KICC), the biggest indoor arena. This hall, which seats about five thousand people, also began to fill up quickly.[32] She was forced to hold her meetings outdoors at the famous Uhuru Park, where Bonnke had his first crusade in Nairobi. Her monthly meetings in this venue attracted huge crowds, filling the 300,000-seat venue.

In 1998, Reinhard Bonnke attended one of her monthly meetings incognito. Bonnke was very impressed by what he saw. He recalls,

> I stood at the far edge of the crowd, beyond her field of vision. Two hundred thousand gathered in Uhuru Park that day. Teresia preached with power and authority and saw thousands come to the Lord. Healings manifested. It was like another page was written in the Book of Acts.[33]

Bonnke started engaging Wairimu in his preaching itinerary across Africa and beyond. With her mentor, Wairimu went to many African countries to preach the gospel. She also preached in Bonnke's revival meetings in a Euro Fire Conference and in nations like India, Canada, and Jamaica.[34]

Teresia Wairimu held a monthly evangelistic crusade in Uhuru Park for fourteen years. Her ministry claimed the many conversions and manifestations of the Spirit's power in healing and deliverance. One of the fruits of her ministry was the spiritual transformation of Steve Mbugua, a gang leader involved in a robbery with violent incidents. Mbugua was planning to rob a nearby hotel when he encountered the power of God at Uhuru Park. While waiting for the appointed time to meet up with his fellow gangsters, he fell asleep in the park. He was awakened by loud music and a mammoth crowd singing worship songs. Through word of knowledge, Teresia Wairimu called out his name and asked him to surrender his life to Christ. Mbugua became a Christian amid applause and celebration from the charged crowd.

Mbugua is now a pastor of a church in a slum area of Nairobi called Korogocho. His congregation comprises "reformed people who were once gangsters, prostitutes, drug addicts, and street relics."[35] To meet the needs of these former criminals and poverty-stricken people, he began a program known as the Faith Rescue Network. They equip and support slum dwellers with a form of vocational training. The program aims to "provide knowledge and skills that will help people to earn a decent living as they follow Christ."[36] Courses include tailoring, catering, hairdressing, carpentry, and mechanics.

Wairimu's ministry is holistic, as she notes in her autobiography, *A Cactus in the Desert*. She narrates that the Spirit revealed to her that she could not just preach the word and ignore the pressing needs of the people. The good news includes spiritual well-being, physical provisions, and mental and emotional well-being. Wairimu now runs a megachurch in Nairobi called FEM church, a children's home, and FEM chapters in London and Dallas.

Wairimu is one of the thousands of local evangelists Bonnke raised in Africa during his Fire Conferences that are now transforming the face of Christianity in Africa. With many of his converts reported to have also become pastors, the numbers of those influenced by the late Bonnke could be even higher, making his impact challenging to quantify. CfaN still runs mass open-air rallies across African states led by Daniel Kolenda, a protégé of Bonnke's whom he appointed nine years before his death in 2019.

Lessons for the Spirit-Empowered Movement

Prioritizing Evangelism

Bonnke was focused on the primary task of evangelism with intensity and unparalleled passion. From start to finish, Bonnke concentrated on evangelism and pursued it with admirable vigor and courage. His goal was to "plunder hell to populate heaven." In his tribute, Billy Wilson described him as "the most effective evangelist of the Christian church."[37]

According to CfaN, Bonnke led nearly 80 million people to Christ in his five decades of African ministry.

Divine healing has been viewed as the primary appeal of Pentecostalism in the majority world. Vinson Synan observes that a significant attraction in Bonnke's meetings was the signs and wonders accompanying his preaching, with thousands testifying to miracles of physical healing and exorcisms in his crusades. Bonnke, however, did not make healing the focus of his campaigns. He asserts, "We conduct evangelistic campaigns, not healing campaigns. The healings are signs that follow the preaching of the Gospel. They open the door for salvation on a large scale."[38] The Spirit-empowered movement must focus on sharing the gospel message to win people to Christ. An obsession with miracles has sometimes led to some Pentecostal ministers manipulating people and faking healing to become popular preachers. Miracles accompany the preaching of the gospel and authenticate it while meeting existential needs but should not be sought as an end in themselves.

Spirit-Empowerment

One of the significant features of Reinhard Bonnke's campaigns was his emphasis on spiritual empowerment. His effectiveness in Africa as an evangelist can be attributed to his reliance on the Holy Spirit. Through the Spirit's power, Bonnke performed miracles of healing and deliverance that drew many people, including Muslims, to the kingdom of God. His passion for spiritual empowerment saw him introduce mass Spirit-baptism in his public rallies. Bonnke asserts, "Until the fire falls, evangelism and church activities can be very routine and unexciting."[39] While evangelists must employ all the resources and technology available today, spiritual empowerment is indispensable for effectiveness.

Power Evangelism

The African cosmology is alive to the reality of the spirit world. Africans have been described as notoriously religious people. The spirit world permeates every facet of life, making it impossible to separate the sacred from the secular.[40] Presentation of the gospel in this culture often elicits a reaction from territorial spirits that seek to maintain their hold on the communities. Julie Ma and Wonsuk Ma observe that when a Christian communicator faces a non-Christian community, this often creates immediate spiritual tension. The existing spiritual strongholds feel challenged and will react to this invasion. These strongholds will seek to hinder the communicator or make the people not respond to the gospel message.[41] Bonnke understood this reality very well in Africa. He writes, "In Africa, when you preach the gospel, often you are flying in the face of centuries of superstition, fear and witchcraft."[42] To conquer these territorial spirits, he mobilized teams of intercessors to pray for his rallies. Prayer brings spiritual victory and releases the power of God to perform miracles in the mission field. When God performs miracles of healing and deliverance from the powers of witchcraft and sorcery, many people are drawn to Christ.

The Western missionary movement primarily missed out on this dimension of missions in the Spirit. Their expression of Christianity did not address these spiritual realities. Consequently, many of their converts were superficial Christians who embraced a dualistic worldview. In crisis time, some of them will look for solutions elsewhere. Power evangelism is indispensable in the majority of the world, where an awareness of the spirit world is acute. The outpouring of the Spirit gives the evangelist power to proclaim the gospel with the demonstration of the Spirit's power and hence portrays the superiority of Christ over principalities. This would partly explain why the Pentecostal movement is rapidly growing in the majority of the world. Spirit empowerment is critical to ensuring the gospel witness continues in Africa.

Leadership Succession

Leadership succession has been the waterloo of many Pentecostal and Charismatic ministries in Kenya. This has often had the undesired effect of watering down their Christian witness. Reinhard Bonnke navigated these murky waters of succession by appointing a successor nine years before he passed on. In 2010, he appointed Daniel Kolenda, a young evangelist whom he had mentored for some years, to take over the leadership of CfaN.[43]

During his last crusade in Africa, held in Nigeria to install his successor, the local media was awash with the news of this transition. This event's significance did not escape the attention of church leaders. Deji Okegbile, a Nigerian pastor in the diaspora, commented, "The emerging pastoral and succession paradigm in the Nigerian Church today is tragic and sad; hence, Bonnke's farewell crusade is saying to our leadership that no one is indispensable."[44] He adds, "Bonnke provides a model of intentionally orchestrating missional leadership succession as opportunities to re-energize vision, adapt mission, disciple the people for God's next season of ministry and service."[45] Riding on the wings of his predecessor, Kolenda has been carrying out evangelistic campaigns with equally large crowds in attendance.

Ecumenical Approach

One of the reasons Bonnke attracted large crowds is that he partnered with the local Pentecostal and missionary churches to reach the African cities. In the Nairobi crusade, at least fourteen participating churches were Anglican."[46] As a result of these interactions, some churches became more open to the experience of the baptism of the Holy Spirit. If the vision of Pentecost 2033 is to be achieved, the Spirit-empowered movement may need to open its doors wider to churches that are not traditionally Pentecostal. The unity in proclaiming the gospel message to the world is a powerful witness for Christ in a world that's deeply divided along tribal, racial, and religious affiliations.

Vision for Ministry

Vision for ministry has been defined as "having a clear mental image of a preferred future imparted by God to His chosen servants and based on an accurate understanding of God, self, and circumstances."[47] Bonnke had a divinely imparted vision for the salvation of Africa, and he seems to have rightly understood his role in fulfilling this vision. This vision led him to embrace mass evangelistic strategy and other innovative ways of evangelism. Without this vision, Bonnke would have lived an ordinary life, like many other Western missionaries who came to Africa. Spirit-empowered evangelists need to have a vision for ministry that is bigger than themselves, that will cause them to depend on the Spirit for fulfillment.

Conclusion

This chapter has examined the ministry of Reinhard Bonnke in Africa, specifically his contribution to the growth of Pentecostalism through the raising up of local evangelists. It has argued that Bonnke's missional engagement in Africa added new impetus to Pentecostalism through the pneuma-centric missional approach and mentoring of local evangelists.

The study has also identified some lessons for missional leadership from Bonnke's Pan-African mission.

In conclusion, developing national evangelists is a significant responsibility for guaranteeing the continuity of a movement. Many ministries and churches have sprung up in Africa during revival times, only for such a move of the Spirit to be undermined or quenched by leadership wrangles and succession intricacies. Investing in Spirit-empowered local evangelists is a sure way of raising a pool of leaders who are going to keep the growth trajectory of the Spirit-empowered movement in decades to come. The prophets Elijah and Elisha both had a company of prophets whom they raised to carry on the prophetic mantle over the nation of Israel (2 Kings 2:15-16 and 2 Kings 4:38-41). Reinhard Bonnke contributed to meeting this mentoring gap by raising many local evangelists in Africa and passing on the baton to the next generation. Corollary to his intentional missional leadership development strategy, his missiological impact will be felt in Africa for a long time.

Notes

1   Todd. M. Johnson and G. Zurlo, eds., "Africa," in *World Christian Encyclopedia Online* (Brill, 2020), https://doi.org/10.1163/2666-6855_WCEO_COM_01AFR.

2   Clifton Clarke, *Pentecostalism: Insights from Africa and the African Diaspora* (Eugene: Wipf & Stock, 2018), 11.

3   J. Kwabena Asamoah-Gyadu, "Christianity in Sub-Saharan Africa," in Christianity in *Sub-Saharan Africa*, Kenneth Ross, Kwabena Asamoah-Gyadu, and Todd M. Johnson, eds. (Edinburgh: Edinburgh University Press, 2018), 31.

4   Todd M. Johnson and Gina Zurlo, eds., "Kenya," in *World Christian Encyclopedia Online* (Brill: 2020), https://doi.org/10.1163/2666-6855_WCEO_COM_02KEN.

5   Allan Anderson, *An Introduction to Pentecostalism* (Cambridge: Cambridge University Press, 2004), 112.

6   Anderson, *An Introduction to Pentecostalism*, 113.

7   Anderson, *An Introduction to Pentecostalism*, 113.

8   Kevin Ward, "Historical Overview-Introduction," in *The East African Revival, Histories and Legacies*, eds. Kevin Ward and Emma Wild-Wood (Farnham: Taylor and Francis, 2017), 5.

9   Anderson, *An Introduction to Pentecostalism*, 111.

10 Anderson, *An Introduction to Pentecostalism*, 183.

11 John Brown Masinde, personal interview with author, June 1, 2023.

12 "Reinhard Bonnke: The Man Who Changed the Face of Christianity in Africa," BBC, December 18, 2019.

13 Reinhard Bonnke, *Evangelism by Fire* (Lake Mary: Charisma House, 2011), 59.

14 Bonnke, *Evangelism by Fire*, 6.

15 Bonnke, *Evangelism by Fire*, 224.

16 Bonnke, *Evangelism by Fire*, 482.

17 Paul Gifford, "Africa Shall be Saved, An Appraisal of Reinhard Bonnke's Pan-African Crusade," *Journal of Religion in Africa* 17, no. 1 (1987): 64.

18 Daniel King, "Seven Things I Have Learned from Bonnke," Daniel King Ministries International (blog), https://kingministries.com/king-ministries-blog/seven-things-i-learned-from-reinhard-bonnke/.

19 Reinhard Bonnke, *Mighty Manifestation* (Eastbourne: Kingsway Publications, 1994), 8.

20 Bonnke, *Mighty Manifestation*, 33.

21 Bonnke, *Mighty Manifestation*, 33.

22 Christ for All Nations, "Evangelist Reinhard Bonnke Biography: A Life on Fire, The Legacy of a World Changer," https://cfan.org/reinhard-bonnke#reviews.

23 John Maxwell, *The 21 Irrefutable Laws of Leadership* (Equip: 1991), 138.

24 Charles Obara, "Reinhard Bonnke Charismatic Leadership Paradigm," Spiritus 7, no. 2 (2022): 243–255, 249.

25 Bonnke, *Evangelism by Fire*, 6.

26 Reinhard Bonnke, *Living a Life of Fire: An Autobiography* (Orlando: E-R Productions, 2009), 354.

27 Anthony Njagi, "Teresia Wairimu: Power in Humility," Daily Nation (Nairobi), updated July 5, 2020, https://nation.africa/kenya/life-and-style/lifestyle/teresia-wairimu-power-in-humility-918476.

28 Teresia Wairimu and Anne Jackson, *A Cactus in the Desert: An Autobiography* (Nairobi: Revival Springs Media, 2011), 49.

29 Reinhard Bonnke, *Even Greater: Real Life Stories that Inspire You to Do Greater Things for God* (Orlando: E-R Productions LLC, 2005), 16.

30 Bonnke, *Even Greater*, 17.

31 Wairimu and Jackson, *A Cactus in the Desert*, 63.

32 Bonnke, *Living a Life of Fire*, 448.

33 Bonnke, *Even Greater*, 18.

34 Darmaris Seleina Parsitau and Philomena Njeri Mwaura, "Gospel with Borders; Gender Dynamics of Transnational Religious Movements in Kenya and the Kenyan Diaspora," in *Religion Crossing Boundaries: Transnational Religious and Social Dynamics in Africa and the New African Diaspora*, eds. Afe Adogame, Jim Spickard (Leiden: Brill, 2010), 199.

35 Wairimu and Jackson, *A Cactus in the Desert*, 354.

36 Wairimu and Jackson, *A Cactus in the Desert*, 356.

37 "The Legacy of Harvest: Passing the Torch to this Generation," Christian News Wire, January 9, 2020, https://reinhardbonnke.com/legacy-of-harvest-passing-the-torch-to-this-generation/.

38 "The Legacy of Harvest," https://reinhardbonnke.com/legacy-of-harvest-passing-the-torch-to-this-generation/.

39 Bonnke, *Evangelism by Fire*, 5.

40 John S. Mbiti, *African Religions and Philosophy*, 2nd ed., rev. and expanded (Nairobi: Heinemann, 1989), 1.

41 Julie C. Ma and Wonsuk Ma, *Mission in the Spirit: Towards a Pentecostal/Charismatic Missiology* (Oxford: Regnum, 2010), 66.

42 Bonnke, *Living a Life of Fire*, 268.

43 Matt Sedensky, "Reinhard Bonnke, Preacher who Drew Millions with Promises of Faith Healing Dies," *Los Angeles Times*, December 17, 2019, https://www.latimes.com/obituaries/story/2019-12-17/reinhard-bonnke-preacher-faith-healing-dead.

44 Deji Okegbile, "From Bonnke to Kolenda: a Proverb to Nigerian Christian Leaders on Succession," The Deji Okegbile Blog, November 15, 2017, http://dejiokegbile.com/bonnkes-proverb-to-nigerian-christian-leaders-on-succession/.

45 Okegbile, "From Bonnke to Kolenda."

46 Okegbile, "From Bonnke to Kolenda."

47 George Barna, *The Power of Vision* (Ventura: Regal, 2003), 25.

Digital Evangelism in Africa: OneHope's Spirit-Empowered Mission

Lydia Wonget

Abstract

This chapter explores how OneHope leverages digital technology as a Spirit-empowered channel for evangelism and discipleship across Africa. Grounded in the conviction that the Holy Spirit uses anything and any means to capture people unto himself, the study offers a theological rationale for digital ministry, presents OneHope's strategy for training and deploying online missionaries, analyzes empirical outcomes, and identifies opportunities and challenges in Africa's rapidly evolving digital landscape. Drawing on current data and field reports, it argues that intentional, research-driven innovation coupled with prayerful dependence on the Spirit can form resilient faith communities online and on the ground. It concludes by highlighting some challenges and opportunities, as well as important lessons learned during this strategic shift toward digital outreach. Pertinent questions will be asked: Have there been meaningful and sustainable efforts that are transferable? What challenges have been encountered during this digital exercise?

Introduction

Creativity has been identified as the number one competency of the future.[1] At the helm of OneHope are innovative leaders who harness creativity as a missional imperative. They pursue every appropriate medium by which the Spirit may draw children and youth to Christ. They are constantly working on new processes, projects, products, or services in partnership with other kingdom-minded organizations. The central theme of this chapter is simple: The Holy Spirit uses anything and any means to capture people unto himself, including smartphones, social platforms, artificial intelligence, and immersive digital spaces. OneHope is continually looking for innovation-minded people and training them to generate more creative ideas.[2] This ideal is founded in scripture. Paul said:

> Though I am free and belong to no one, I have made myself a slave to everyone, to win as many as possible. To the Jews, I became like a Jew, to win the Jews. To those under the law, I became like one under the law . . . so as to win those under the law...so as to win those not having the law. To the weak I became

> weak, to win the weak. I have become all things to all people so that by all possible means I might save some. I do all this for the sake of the gospel, that I may share in its blessings (1 Cor. 9:19-23).[3]

This text implies that being open-minded is necessary in order to bring more people into the kingdom of God. Seeing the way more and more people are constantly engaging with digital resources, OneHope recognizes this as an opportunity to reach, disciple, and empower future generations.

OneHope believes that one does not need to be a preacher to be a missionary. They see accountants, secretaries, administrators, mechanics, gardeners, artists, linguists, web designers, scientists, and students as missionaries if they do their work as ministry to the glory of God. OneHope carries a Christian worldview guided by the scriptures where everything anyone does can be sacred and sanctified.[4] OneHope doesn't buy into the thinking that Christian life is divided into "sacred and secular." The belief that everything one does is sacred unto the Lord implies that people from all walks of life are missionaries at OneHope. That is why youths with digital giftings are being trained and recruited to become online missionaries. We are in an age where technology is in the hands of the Spirit.

OneHope is a Spirit-led organization that is called to serve the church in very contextual ways. The coming of COVID-19 influenced OneHope's ministry to innovate and expand its reach digitally. The COVID-19 pandemic, caused by a virus that first appeared in Wuhan province in China and then quickly spread throughout the globe, caused many to be suddenly initiated into online ministry.[5] The challenge of a global pandemic became an opportunity for the world to engage in digital evangelism as a Spirit-empowered instrument for reaching people of all ages for Christ.

Before COVID-19, OneHope had already been working on online initiatives, but during and after COVID-19, OneHope established strategic partnerships in Africa to impact lives through digital evangelism, applying the behavioral skills of questioning, observing, networking, and experimenting. This has yielded fruit. Its African partners have reciprocally developed new ideas and programs that engage upcoming generations on different platforms.[6]

Paulus and Langford assert that the human creation of technology applies ideas to solve problems while the creation of relationships establishes community and civilization. In all human creativity, there remains the distinction between creator and creation. Man creates because he is endowed with the *imago Dei* and given everything that is needed for abundant life.[7] With the rapid multiplication of mobile technology and internet access in Africa, OneHope upheld its commitment to reach and engage children and youth with God's Word by adapting digital efforts to address the needs of African communities. Although Africa is a diverse continent, these innovative digital strategies were meant to address specific needs and challenges. To God's glory, this ministry's digital evangelism initiatives have significantly expanded its reach across nations, especially within Africa. By pulling weight from social media platforms and online content, OneHope has connected with thousands of young people in Africa, presenting the gospel and placing young people in faith communities.

OneHope has been in Africa for many years, partnering with nonprofit organizations, churches, and ministries to engage children and youth with God's Word. OneHope believes God's Word can reach every child and his or her destiny will be changed. To achieve this mission, two great leaders, Taka Ohki and Walada Poulande Aklaesso, have championed the partnership of OneHope with different stakeholders on the continent. OneHope honors and gives trust to its partners. Trust empowers them to feel a sense of partnership, which inspires them to perform better. They also give the same trust in return.[8] With these excellent leaders championing the NextGen ministry, it has been easy to navigate Africa with digital evangelism.

OneHope is intentional and operates with reality in mind. When they want to create a program, their research team finds out information about the product they want to create. After creating and using the material, they research more to find out if it is satisfactory to the people they produced it for. This fulfills the idea of OneHope being an outcome-based ministry.

Methodologically, OneHope focuses on the positive contribution and performance of the whole rather than on individual success. The organization pays attention to different regions for results rather than activities, asking what they can contribute. Asking this question helps in searching for unused potential. This leads to the building of values and the development of people for the future.[9] For example, an understanding of the times and the intrusion of the new normal motivated OneHope to move children and youth ministry online. A crucial aspect of OneHope's work is how they have traversed the continent's different linguistic, cultural, and socioeconomic backgrounds to provide content that aligns with their African partners digitally.

This chapter ascertains that OneHope's Spirit-empowered approach to digital evangelism in Africa yields sustainable discipleship models that complement and sometimes replace traditional in-person methods.

Why Digital Evangelism in Africa

Many people are online, and a good number can be mobilized without movement. Rob Hoskin, the CEO of OneHope, asserts that "the job of OneHope is to serve as a guide to the next generation by endowing them with identity, affirmation, and love for the Word of God."[10] He crafts this assignment from scripture.[11] Rob expresses that parents, leaders, pastors, and teachers are to help the young find divine identity in Christ. These individuals make it possible for students to be surrounded by a community that builds authentic relationships and shows the upcoming generations how to internalize the Word of God. He further states that "the reason for this standpoint is to ensure that whatever life throws at these children and youths they will know where to turn for truth, answers, support, and encouragement."[12] It is in the fulfillment of this assignment that OneHope continues to seek ways and efforts to reach the next generation. The readiness and commitment to reach and disciple for Christ presents new ideas and opens more doors for ministry. The leaders in this organization do not only desire youth to start well, but they desire to see them finish strong.

Paul Stanley and Robert Clinton assert that "few leaders finish well"[13] but that those who finish well do so by being engaged in a mentoring experience through which one person empowers another by sharing God-given resources. This positive dynamic enables people to develop and live up to their potential.[14] Digital ministry in Africa is therefore carried out with the help of mentors and coaches who are currently being trained by OneHope. African students benefit from mentors and coaches both in person and online. The OneHope digital ministry is

Spirit-empowered as destinies are being affected daily. Digital skills are vital for preparing students to work, live, and contribute to the social and civic fabric of their communities.

Digital Landscape in Africa

Digital evangelism became a Spirit-empowered instrument for OneHope during a challenging season. When the challenge of people meeting in person surfaced, the OneHope Training Team asked a very pertinent question: "How do we continue children's ministry in the local church when we cannot meet together?" This underlying question, along with the need for children to be taught, to hear about Jesus, to be mentored, and to be given support to grow, necessitated innovative changes.[15]

Consequently, OneHope initiated monthly online training sessions and invited its African partners to these sessions. In April 2020, the OneHope Training Team introduced the course "Effective Online Ministry" and started by helping users adjust from doing live training to conducting training sessions over Zoom.[16] The OneHope Training Team, under Tena Stone and Andrea Lisboa's leadership, started training individuals from Africa leading to outcome-based ministry. Their trainees developed increased confidence and skills in online engagement. They adapted best online practices and could replicate these in the continent. The team was able to script online content and carry out activities digitally. Futhermore, they introduced developing ministry for the digital world. Pertinent questions were asked, such as who their audience is, what goal they desire to achieve, how people will get to know about the digital programs, and how they will serve users long term. These questions led the team to Liam Savage's wisdom: "Technology scales access, but influence requires relationships."[17] The insight in this phrase led to the five levels of the durable network where beginners become aware in level 1, move on to encounter in level 2, become engaged with the content, subsequently believe in it in level 4, and finally become champions of what they have believed in level 5.[18]

Amazon founder and innovator Jeff Bezos gave an explanation for the inscription that hangs over his fireplace: "Human creativity needs both dreamers and builders."[19] He explains that the "builders get inspired by the dreamers to build, providing a platform for the dreamers to stand on and dream some more."[20] Consequently, learning from Bezos, hypothetical symbolic dreamers and builders from OneHope went ahead after dreaming and built a digital system that keeps growing every day. Cultural values are being operationalized today through digital initiatives, which are here to stay for God's glory in Africa.[21]

OneHope's Approach to Digital Evangelism

With technology in the hands of the Spirit, OneHope harnesses it as a missional imperative. OneHope did not enter the mission of digital evangelism casually, but like the apostles, they desired to "become all things to all people" so that some might be saved (1 Cor 9:19–23). OneHope intentionally engaged in digital evangelism. Their research-driven strategy, with contextualized content, provides seekers with a relational pathway inviting them to deeper discipleship. These online connections lead to mentoring relationships, resulting in capacity building. The OneHope Training Team, started by organizing enrichment training materials in 2020, emphasizing digital engagement. Gifted children's teachers from OneHope and 1for50, like Tena Stone, Andrea Lisboa, Karen Helmuth, Sheryl Grunwald, and the 1for50 leadership team coordinated and involved participants from Africa.[22]

In the digital space, OneHope provides a service, not just products or programs. They craft a digital experience where they will accompany their audience on their journey. They intentionally enable digital missionaries to access and influence seekers. Influence requires relationships. These relationships have significantly impacted young people in Africa.

Increased Access to Content

Digital evangelism has made content sharing more flexible and accessible to people across Africa. With the proliferation of smartphones and internet access, seekers can access sermons, devotionals, and inspirational content through OneHope's digital platforms, social media channels, and mobile apps. Digital access has allowed people in remote and rural areas to connect with the hub. Communities that were previously out of reach are now being reached by God's Word.

In 2020, when COVID-19 hit, education across Africa was hindered as national authorities instituted widespread school closures, leaving children at home with parents, and disrupting their learning.[23] OneHope Cameroon partnered with Full Gospel Mission Cameroon Children's Ministry to use existing content to create interactive videos for children and teens online. The project's technical creator was Daniel Fokam and the project coordinator was Lydia Wonget. Dzouli Sorel, Ruth Neba, Immaculate Awah, and Praise Anufor also participated in the project. Short videos were created from One Hope's children's books, *17 Stories* and *Stories of Hope*, and its teen leadership book *Lead Today*. The team dramatized and acted out the stories live to create content for kids to watch on YouTube. All in all, 214 short videos were created in French and English and were uploaded to the Full Gospel Broadcasting Network YouTube channel. Although these videos are no longer available on YouTube, they served their purpose at the time they were created. Thousands of young people had accessed the videos, and individuals were called to testify. They liked and distributed the videos to friends and relatives. The impact was great. The OneHope national director for Nigeria kept calling to testify of the impact of the videos in his community while children were staying at home and of how parents appreciated the engaging way the work was done.

In Kenya, OneHope along with its Kenyan partners created a series of animated videos that address social issues such as corruption, tribalism, and unemployment, linking them to biblical teachings. These videos have been shared widely on social media, sparking discussions among young people about ways in which they could influence positive societal change.

In OneHope's Facebook community "What If It's True Africa?" seekers engage with different topics digitally. The topics are wisely selected as upcoming generations struggle with questions about depression, low self-esteem, insignificance, sexual purity, and a host of other topics treated in "What If It's True Africa?" For example, one post asks, "If God is in control of everything, why does he cause pain and suffering?" It concludes, "God is not the source of pain but the source of joy." This post got numerous likes and positive reactions from visitors.[24] Topics such as this are contemporary challenges to many online youths. The anonymous way things are presented, with captivating questions, motivates youths to engage in communication with online missionaries.

Enhanced Community Building

Social media platforms and messaging apps have become vital tools for building and maintaining young people's communities. OneHope's digital hub uses different platforms to enhance engagement and discipleship. The digital hub in Africa has a OneHope Facebook community with a community manager, who helps run and encourage the group to maximize growth and who filters comments online. They have also built WhatsApp, Instagram, and TikTok communities. These communities reached 2,228,000 viewers in 2023. OneHope is engaged in training and deploying online missionaries. The Anglophone community manager, Loveday Leonard, had the opportunity to speak to students at the University of Lagos and campus fellowship leaders and he was able to recruit willing students to be online missionaries. He posted photos on Facebook of the Campus Fellowship Leaders Annual Conference (CAFLAC) 2024 gathering where the recruitment and volunteering took place. After recruitment, they train these students in two levels. They also finish level 3 training where online missionaries will then be chosen and recruited.[25]

Growth of Online Missionaries

The "Affect Destiny" (OneHope Africa) online ministry has seen tremendous growth due to digital penetration. Digital ministry has created new avenues for spreading God's Word in new places, with new media. OneHope uses the Echoglobal platform to reach and establish seekers as lovers of Christ. Seekers land on the Echoglobal platform where they are then intercepted by online missionaries who engage them in a conversation until they become established in a physical or online church. Many young people go from seekers (seeker is the name given to people who come initially unaware of what is going to happen) to curious, and finally, to followers. When they become followers and start growing, they often answer the call to be volunteers in online missions, helping to take the gospel to all digital platforms. Online ministries include digital evangelism, online Bible groups, discipleship, and counseling. This enables OneHope to reach a broader audience and cater to the spiritual needs of young people who may not attend traditional church services.[26]

OneHope Africa has gone from interacting with seekers to connecting individuals in a faith community. What If It's True Africa, launched on November 5, 2021, shows statistics for three months, where 12,796 clients sent messages and 10,507 got responses. Of those who responded, 1,370 continued interacting with the state where they received biblical resources. Out of this number, 59 people accepted Jesus into their lives, with 9 connected to the faith community. These results were obtained from only 16 African countries. Assuming more funds and intentionality are implemented to reach all 54 African countries, the growth rate will be extraordinary.[27]

Youth Engagement

Digital evangelism has been particularly effective in engaging teenagers and youth, who are more likely to be active on social media and other digital platforms. By using best-in-class programs and multimedia content, OneHope Africa makes its content and programs contextualized and more appealing to the younger generations. This has also led to the emergence of youth-led movements and initiatives, like OneHope Kenya's program Teen Kulture Show. According Leonard's Instagram account, @Loveday, in the OneHope Africa digital office, as of May 2024, Teen Kulture had five posts, 243 followers, and eight persons with a deeper degree of engagement. What this leader has observed is that those with a deeper degree of engagement end up asking to be trained to be online missionaries.[28]

Empowerment Through Digital Training and Educational Initiatives

OneHope in its digital reach focuses on training church leaders, partners, and volunteers on how to carry out digital evangelism. The empowerment strategies implemented impact the work by building capacity locally. OneHope and its partners organized workshops in South Africa, Kenya, Ghana, Cameroon, Nigeria, Cote d'Ivoire, and Congo DRC to help the youth effectively use Instagram, Facebook, Telegram, YouTube, and WhatsApp to engage with their peers in conversations about faith. These training workshops have equipped both leaders and volunteers with skills to create compelling and engaging content to promote online communities focused on the Gospel. Digital advancements have enabled the establishment of online Christian education programs. These programs offer courses in theology, Bible study, and leadership training, making Christian education more accessible. This has helped in nurturing a new generation of Christian scholars and leaders.

Partnering with 4/14 Academy

OneHope has used digital education as a Spirit-empowered instrument to reach and disciple Africa. In partnership with 4/14, OneHope created the 4/14 Academy where Africans have been trained to be effective children and youth ministers. Children's Global Forum, 1for50, and OneHope have contributed resources or content that appears on the 4/14 Academy website. In the period between September 2020 and June 2024, 32,495 hours of learning have been invested online. A total of 3,660 unique users counted only once have started a course, and 1,936 learners have completed at least one course. Outside the cohorts from Africa, 21,663 learners have completed at least one course. Some of the learners come from the public learner's cohort, increasing the number of learners.[29]

These courses were originally designed to fit an individual, self-paced model, but a cohortative structure was suggested and adopted after doing a demo with African students. OneHope thus created cohorts under the leadership of moderators, which help students finish a group of courses, like 4/14 Academy level 1. When the level is completed, students receive certificates and celebrate with a graduation event before the entire group moves on to level 2. Those who progress more slowly can follow at their own pace, but moderators encourage the group to move up as a whole. At the time of this writing, ten learners have graduated level 4, and two have applied to continue studying for a master's degree at SEU Lakeland. Eight others are serving as online coaches for the Africa Assemblies of God Alliance Children's Ministry Commission (AAGACMC) online certification program for children's ministers. "There is also a six-course collection of 4/14 Academy which brings OneHope's practical, Scripture-rich CM101 training to the digital space. After taking this collection, leaders are equipped with basic skills for ministering to children."[30] The goal of empowering young adults and international students through Spirit-empowered digital education and mentorship is thriving.

Partnering with University Launchpad

In Cameroon and Uganda, OneHope is piloting another digital evangelism and online training program called University Launchpad (UL) for first-year university students. The program focuses on students' personal, academic, and professional development and students grow holistically, in spiritual formation and biblical worldview. UL's flexible courses allow students to learn according to their schedule within a guided program. Students can complete their coursework whether they are working full-time, traveling, or pursuing other interests.

UL is a ten-month program, where students complete two courses in each of five eight-week terms. There are ten courses to complete the program: Divine Design, College Composition, Metanarrative of Scripture, Project Management, Missional Leadership, Quantitative Reasoning, Missional Theology, Practicum 1, Professional Communication, and Practicum II. These ten courses were carefully selected to impact different areas of a student's life.

These courses are designed to help students gain relevant and practical missional work and leadership experience while focusing on their personal and professional development. Upon successful completion of all ten University Launchpad courses, students will receive a UL certificate of completion. OneHope has also officially signed an articulation agreement with Southeast University (SEU). Upon successful completion of University Launchpad, SEU will accept all thirty UL credits towards completing a degree program at the university.

The Digital Landscape in Africa

Internet Penetration and Growth

The penetration and growth of the internet in Africa has enabled more young people to develop new capabilities and competencies. Stephen Covey states that being trusted is the most inspiring form of human motivation as it brings out the best in everyone.[31] Young people who face challenges are often looking for someone to help them. When they get answers online and know the missionary who helped them truly has their best interests at heart, their trust naturally grows. These young people also experience being entrusted when they are given new responsibilities and educated to develop competencies through digital initiatives, which motivates them to perform even better. Digital platforms have accelerated interfaith dialogue with persons who were not aware of the love of Christ, causing them to become curious and open. Some have even gone on to train to become online missionaries and help others who are in their former situation. By using the internet to connect people from different religious backgrounds, OneHope and its partners have seen conversations that started as casually religious—or even non-religious—grow into faith conversations that lead young people to Jesus.

Mobile Connectivity, Social Media Usage, and Measurable Outcomes

Social media is widely used, with cell phones being the primary gateway. On average, users spend three to six hours daily on social platforms. Imagine the impact of these hours being spent interacting with God's Word with online, godly influencers. Facebook is the most popular platform, used by 82 percent of social media users.[32] In Ghana, an online evangelistic campaign led to over five thousand young people downloading the Bible App, with many reporting that they read the Bible more frequently as a result. Follow-up surveys indicated a significant number of individuals expressing a new or renewed commitment to their faith. Other countries in Sub-Saharan Africa have also downloaded the Bible App for Kids, although we currently do not have the exact numerical data.

The impact of OneHope's digital evangelism is evident in measurable outcomes such as increased Bible engagement and conversions. By tracking digital interactions and feedback, OneHope can assess the effectiveness of its programs and make data-driven decisions. Chioma from Nigeria testified, "I asked on WhatsApp if God cared that I was depressed. An online missionary listened for three nights straight. Today I lead a youth prayer room in Lagos." Secondly, Kofi from Ghana said, "Our campus fellowship thought TikTok was frivolous until training showed us how to pair 60-second parables with comment replies. Three students are now attending baptism class."[33]

Digital Economy and Services

Digital payments have seen substantial growth, with 191 million additional individuals in Sub-Saharan Africa making or receiving digital payments between 2014 and 2021. Many countries in Africa are also expanding their digital infrastructure. For example, Mauritania deployed 1,700 kilometers of fiber optic cable between 2021 and 2022, and millions in Uganda and Malawi have benefited from programs aimed at reducing internet costs and expanding broadband access.[34] Digital transformation in Africa is being supported by significant investments and initiatives aimed at improving digital infrastructure and making digital services more accessible and affordable. However, challenges such as high data costs, limited digital skills, and regulatory issues still need to be addressed further to enhance digital inclusion and economic growth in the region.[35]

Challenges and Opportunities

Challenges

Despite its positive impact, digital evangelism comes with some challenges. Issues include digital hostility and cyberbullying of online missionaries and the spreading of misinformation by some seekers. Some online missionaries face harassment and pornography spam. Online missionaries in closed countries face the risk of being exposed to danger. Access to the media is open so anyone can go online to insult and threaten online missionaries. In cases where these missionaries lack prayer support from the team, discouragement might set in.

There are also a limited number of committed online missionaries. There are approximately 150 to 200 messages from seekers on the French platform daily and almost the same number on the English platform. Online missionaries who are unpaid volunteers also complain that they don't have enough data with which to follow-up with seekers.

The high cost of mobile data remains a barrier, with the average cost of one gigabyte of mobile internet being 10.5 percent of monthly per capita Gross National Income (GNI) in 2019. This is significantly higher than the global affordability target of two percent.[36]

Rural bandwidth limitations make large content delivery a significant challenge. The digital content used in Africa had been created in more developed and digitally connected regions, so many areas in Africa struggle to upload and access the provided content due to the very slow network. The parameters used by these platforms require quality technology for quality content.

Lastly, many leaders today are of older generations and are "digital immigrants."[37] Many in this category do not support the ideas of newer generations who are "digital natives," those who grew up in a world where the digital lifestyle was already widely adopted and simply a part of life. Leaders who have the money for equipment are digital immigrants and those who know the proper equipment needed are digital natives. The landscape of technology changes extremely quickly and requires a constant change of equipment, but the leaders who buy the equipment often do not understand or see the need for the constant change in such expensive equipment.

Opportunities

ndeed, the digital landscape in Africa is rapidly evolving, marked by significant growth in internet access and social media usage. Here are some key statistics and trends highlighting the current state of digital development in the region:

No	Social Media Platform	Users
1	Facebook	2.9 billion
2	YouTube:	2.5 billion
3	WhatsApp	2 billion
4	Instagram	1.5 billion
5	TikTok	1.2 billion
6	Snapchat	500 million
7	Twitter (X)	400 million[38]

Table 1. Social Media Active Users from January to May 2024

A glance at 2024 social media statistics (Table 1) indicates opportunities that such platforms, when leveraged, could help in evangelizing and discipling millions of young people digitally. Innovative ideation is what is needed at this juncture. Users spend an average of two and a half hours per day on social media. Young adults (18–29 years old) are the largest users of social networks, followed by the 30–49-year-old age group. Additionally, the metaverse may offer expanded opportunities in the future. In the metaverse, social interactions become more dynamic and immersive, allowing users to meet, work, and play in virtual environments.[39] In a Zoom meeting with online missionary Daniel Fokam, insights were gleaned on how these types of digital spaces could be leveraged and access multiplied.[40]

These are just some of the possibilities: Church organizations that gather many people can partner and get into shared leadership to enhance and maximize technology and media by getting proper equipment and skilled individuals to handle equipment and train others to do the same.

Young people can be equipped to produce creative scripts, and films, and edit contextually authentic narratives for African consumption. The church can partner with internet network providers to lower bandwidth costs for educational and religious content. According to Desmond Phiri, "The smartphone, not the desktop is the primary gateway to Scripture, worship, and mentoring, thus making WhatsApp, Facebook, and TikTok strategic discipleship arenas."[41]

Conclusion

Digital evangelism in Africa has come to stay as it is a Spirit-initiated missionary possibility. Africa is persistently being evangelized, and because it has a young population who are digital natives, intentionally engaging African youth in digital evangelism has the potential to be contextually wise and fruitful. OneHope and its partners have transformed in-person training into online training, which is a leading way of evangelizing and discipling children's ministers, youth ministers, and teenagers. The implementation of online education and the recruitment of online missionaries further helps build authentic relationships cross-culturally and inter-generationally.

The implication of this is that OneHope and its partners share thoughts, ideas, and solutions through proper communication while brainstorming as they work together to expand digital education, discipleship, and evangelism. The latter is not an option but will become the new normal as upcoming generations will be increasingly digital and informed digitally. We conclude by agreeing with Alvin Toffler that "the illiterate of the twenty-first century will not be the ones who cannot read and write, but those who cannot learn, unlearn, and relearn."[42] In context, considering what OneHope has done in Africa through digital evangelism, it is time to unlearn the fact that missionaries can only be found or sent to a physical place. Instead, we must learn to train more online missionaries and help them intentionally disciple people online. It is time to pray, finance, train, and send more online missionaries.

In this, OneHope and its partners in Africa have discovered that training individuals before sending them out as online missionaries prepares them effectively for the field. This entails missionaries being instructed in technology as fully as they are gifted. Technology holds a powerful place in developing young postmodern minds. Information and social media today deeply influence the way people think. Therefore, OneHope and its partners take seriously the mission to engage young minds with scriptures online and think constructively in a godly way. We invite online users to respond to the truth—who is not just an idea but Jesus, a person—presented to them online.34

Notes

1 Richard Florida, The Rise of the Creative Class (New York: Basic Books, 2014), 6.

2 Jeff Dyer, Hal Gregersen, and Clayton M. Christensen, *The Innovator's DNA: Mastering the Five Skills of Disruptive Innovators* (Boston: Harvard Business Review Press, 2011), 1–13.

3 Unless otherwise noted, all scripture references are taken from the New International Version (NIV).

4 Darlene Cunningham, *Values Matter: Stories of the Beliefs & Values that Shaped Youth With A Mission* (Seattle: YWAM Publishing, 2020), 71.

5 Michael J. Paulus, Jr. and Michael D. Langford, eds., *AI, Faith, and the Future: An Interdisciplinary Approach* (Eugene, OR: Pickwick Publications, 2022), 45.

6 Dyer et al, *The Innovator's DNA*, 23–25.

7 Paulus and Langford, *AI, Faith, and the Future*, 107.

8 Stephen M. R. Covey, et al., *Trust and Inspire: How Truly Great Leaders Unleash Greatness in Others* (New York: Simon & Schuster, 2022), 145.

9 Peter F. Drucker, *The Effective Executive* (USA: Harper & Row, Publishers, 1967), 52–55.

10 Barna Report, Produced in Partnership with OneHope, *Guiding Children to Discover the Bible, Navigate Technology, and Follow Jesus* (Barna Group, 2020), 5.

11 See Matthew 3:16–17.

12 Barna Report, *Guiding Children to Discover the Bible, Navigate Technology, and Follow Jesus*, 6.

13 Paul D. Stanley and J. Robert Clinton, *Connecting: The Mentoring Relationships You Need to Succeed in Life* (Colorado Springs: NavPress, 1992), 11.

14 Stanley and Clinton, *Connecting*, 11.

15 Andrea Lisboa, Moving Children's Ministry Online (Part 1), unpublished Paper, Foundations, Enrichment training. PPTX August 18, 2020.

16 "OneHope Training Team, Effective Online Ministry," Unpublished paper, Internal course document, April 2020," https://www.dropbox.com/sh/1nic7ilwayi6g06/AAANv2vsfyYo9sDxglfx_1fDa?dl=0.

17 Liam Savage, For the OneHope Training Team, PFD-DG-ZM-Training Recording (Developing Ministry for the Digital World Enrichment), eng_2020.mp4.

18 Savage, For the OneHope Training Team.

19 Paulus and Langford, eds., *AI, Faith, and the Future*, 6.

20 Paulus and Langford, eds., *AI, Faith, and the Future*, 6.

21 Paulus and Langford, eds., *AI, Faith, and the Future*, 6.

22 Andrea Lisboa, "Moving Children's Ministry Online (Part 2) Foundations,"(unpublished paper, Enrichment training, PPTX, September 1, 2020).

23 Save the Children and UNICEF, "Africa: COVID-19: Millions Out of School, Jeopardizing the Future of Millions of Children," AllAfrica, April 3, 2020. UNESCO Institute for Statistics, "COVID-19 in Sub-Saharan Africa: Monitoring impacts on learning Outcomes," MILO Report (2020): 55.

24 What If It's True Africa, "If God is in control of everything, why does he cause pain and suffering," Facebook, October 16, 2023, https://web.facebook.com/wiitafrica/?_rdc=1&_rdr#. A post on October 16, 2023 showed 9,1000 likes and 300 comments, and a post on May 22, 2024, showed 161 likes, and one comment.

25 Loveday Leonard, Facebook post capturing campus students volunteering to be trained as online missionaries, February 9, 2024.

26 Innocent Ekoue Zoom Training for Africa Assemblies of God Alliance Children's ministry Commission, online missionaries, March 25, 2025, https://www.ohafrica.echoglobal.org. Testimony from Innocent who has about three hundred members attending his online church he planted through the Echoglobal platform. It functions like a normal physical church except that it holds its services online.

27 What If It's True Africa, https://web.facebook.com/wiitafrica/?_rdc=1&_rdr#.

28 Loveday Leonard, Zoom meeting, personal information and testimonies with Lydia Wonget, June 6, 2024.

29 Some of the learners from Africa joined not in groups but in the 4/14 Academy public sector, and since we could not extract only Africans from

the public sector learners, we did not include the data in this report. The implication of this is that more leaders have been trained through the 4/14 Academy in Africa than mentioned in this report. Information provided by Chrissy Schaeffer.

30 4/14 Academy, "Children's Ministry Foundations," https://414academy. pathwright.com/library/children-s-ministry-foundations-164186/349074/about/.

31 Stephen M. R. Covey, et all, *Trust & Inspire: How Truly Great Leaders Unleash Greatness in Others* (New York: Simon & Schuster Paperbacks, 2022), 143.

32 "Social Media Usage Trends in Africa: GeoPoll Report," GeoPoll, https://www.geopoll.com/blog/social-media-usage-trends-in-africa-geopoll-report,

33 OneHope International, *Digital Evangelism in Africa: Case Studies from Nigeria and Ghana* (internal report, OneHope International Global Ministry Resources, March 2025), 12, 15.

34 "Digital Transformation Drives Development in Africa," World Bank, https://www.worldbank.org/en/results/2024/01/18/digital-transformation-drives-development-in-afe-afw-africa.

35 Insights from OneHope Digital Hub team, Loveday Leonard (Manager - Anglophone) and Innocent Ekoue (Manager - Francophone), personal interviews, June 6, 2024.

36 "Digital Transformation Drives Development," World Bank, accessed June 6, 2024.

37 A digital immigrant is one who is entering the digital landscape with the mindset of one who comes from another culture or upbringing.

38 Numbers are rounded approximations from Smart Insights, https://www.smartinsights.com, accessed on June 4, 2024.

39 Smart Insights, accessed June 4, 2024.

40 Zoom meeting with Daniel Fokam on June 4, 2024. The metaverse is a shared, collective virtual space created by the convergence of physical and virtual reality, including augmented virtual environments and virtual reality. Metaverse platforms enable real-world economic transactions, with the use of cryptocurrencies and non-fungible tokens.

41 Desmond Phiri, ed., *Digital Discipleship in Africa: The Church's New Frontier* (Nairobi: HippoBooks, 2024), 15–16.

42 Alvin Toffler, *Future Shock* (New York: Random House, 1970), 414.

10 A Sister Duo for World Evangelization: An Instance of Flowering of Missionary Renewal in the Catholic Church

Hyeon Ju (Sabina) Cappello Lee

Abstract

The activation of Catholic laity into evangelization and missionary discipleship cannot be understood in separation from the Second Vatican Council through which the Church undertook rethinking itself and reworking its engagement with the world. As this top-down shift was transforming the theology and praxis of the Church, concurrently at the grassroots level, Catholics experienced a new Pentecost, which has grown to be the Catholic Charismatic Renewal today. This article explores how missionary renewal has precipitated the emergence of lay Catholic evangelists in recent decades. With that in mind, the lives and ministry of Lavinia and Alicia Antoine are presented as a concrete instance of lay Spirit-empowered female evangelists continuing the mission of the Church, i.e., the mission of Christ.

Introduction

The traditional model of missions in the Catholic Church was historically linked to the geographical expansion of the Church. Missions were about bringing one model of church life to newly discovered continents, replicating that model, and then maintaining it in mission territories. Furthermore, missionary activities were exclusively assigned to ordained priests or the religious while the laity would participate in the missionary activities of the Church through financial support or prayer. Under these circumstances, the ordinary way—perhaps the only way—for a lay woman to participate in the mission of the Church was in and through motherhood, i.e., educating her children in the faith.[1] Consequently, a lay person engaged in evangelization is a relatively new phenomenon for the Church, developing only in the latter part of the twentieth century. This study will examine two streams of renewal contributing to this missiological shift: the Second Vatican Council and the arrival of Pentecostalism into Catholic congregations. It will explore how these two streams have set in motion the mobilization of the laity into evangelization and missionary discipleship and reflect on that in a final case study.

The Second Vatican Council as the Event of Ecclesial Conversion

In the aftermath of WWII, the Catholic Church called on bishops worldwide to address the trend of secularization forcefully impacting the world. John XXIII prayed that the Second Vatican Council would bring to the Church a time of renewal as if for a new Pentecost: "Renew your wonders in our time, as though in a new Pentecost..."[2] In seeking the renewal of the Church, the overriding thrust of the Council was twofold: pastoral and missionary. O'Malley observes that the Council, in dealing with the crisis of the modern world, called for abandoning confrontation, condemnation, and hostility in relation to the world, in order to take up a new approach of engagement, persuasion, and reconciliation.[3] Komonchak adds that John XXIII "did not want a series of condemnations, but a positive presentation of the faith; he wanted this conciliar exercise of the magisterium to be pastoral in character. In these respects, Trent would not be an adequate model for Vatican II."[4]

The insistence of the Council on pastorality meant more than taking up a friendlier mode of engagement with the world. It eventually transformed the way the Church was conceived. Prior to Vatican II, the Church was understood to be "*a societas perfecta*, an institution in possession of changeless, divine truth in its doctrinal and moral proclamations" that had "stood solidly for centuries in a defensive mode against the modern world."[5] However, Bevans and Schroeder point to a radical change made during Vatican II. The Council retreated from the institutional view of the Church as "an unequal society" consisting of "the pastors and the flock," based on the striated model of "civil society." Instead, the Church was redefined as a "mystery," and understood to be "a people, a communion, and mission, conceived as the participation in the dynamic communion of God's triune life; that is, the Church was a sacrament of salvation, a sign and instrument of God's saving presence toward and within all creation."[6] The traditional juridical vision of the Church was overcome and replaced by renewed ecclesiology that retrieved the biblical category of mystery and gave birth to the sacramentality of the Church:

> Since the Church is in Christ like a sacrament or as a sign and instrument both
> of a very closely knit union with God and of the unity of the whole human
> race, it desires now to unfold more fully to the faithful of the Church and to
> the whole world its own inner nature and universal mission.[7]

The Redefined Identity and the Role of Laity in the Mission of the Church

Turning to the biblical conception of the Church, *Lumen Gentium* defined
the Church as "the People of God," developing more dynamic concepts
such as "the Body of Christ" and "Sacrament of Unity."[8] This fruit of
ecclesial conversion of the Council is attributed to Congar's contribution.
His "total ecclesiology," which envisions the Church as fully inclusive of
the laity, equally called to participate in the salvific mission of Christ, was
reflected in the documents of the Council; in particular, *Lumen Gentium*.[9]
The concept of the Church as the Body of Christ gave rise to the general
priesthood of the faithful: "Christ the Lord, High Priest taken from among
men" made the new people "a kingdom and priests to God the Father."[10]

> The term laity is here understood to mean all the faithful except those in
> holy orders and those in the state of religious life specially approved by the
> Church. These faithful are by baptism made one body with Christ and are
> constituted among the People of God; they are in their own way made sharers
> in the priestly, prophetical, and kingly functions of Christ; and they carry out
> for their own part the mission of the whole Christian people in the Church
> and in the world.[11]

The rethinking of ecclesiology by the Council Fathers thus produced
a renewed understanding of the identity and role of the laity. There
are numerous teachings in the conciliar documents that reflect such a
development: *Ad Gentes* 35, 36, and 41 teach that everyone in the Church
is called to participate in the mission of the Church;[12] *LG* 7 defines the
Church as the Body of Christ; and *LG* 10 sheds light on the general
priesthood of the laity. *Lumen Gentium* affirms that, by virtue of baptism,
the baptized participate in the priesthood of Christ. Hence the whole
faithful are called to actively participate in the mission of the Church.[13]

Drawing from the idea of the common priesthood of all the baptized,
which flows from the priesthood of Christ, Vatican II updated the
identity and mission of the laity. *Apostolicam Actuositatem* stressed the

responsibility of the laity to fulfill the mission of the Church[14] while Paul VI added a teaching that invoked unity through the Holy Spirit:

> Our own times require of the laity no less zeal: in fact, modern conditions demand that their apostolate be broadened and intensified... An indication of this manifold and pressing need is the unmistakable work being done today by the Holy Spirit in making the laity ever more conscious of their own responsibility and encouraging them to serve Christ and the Church in all circumstances.[15]

The teachings of the post-Vatican II development has sealed this shift. John Paul II, in *Christifideles Laici*, affirms that the Lord himself entrusts the laity with a great responsibility to fulfill his mission, particularly proclaiming the gospel.[16] Benedict XVI introduces the concept of "co-responsibility of all the members of the People of God in their entirety," emphasizing the role of the laity sharing in the mission of the Church.[17] In the same vein, Francis, affirming that evangelization as the "first task of the Church,"[18] declares that "in virtue of their baptism, all the members of the People of God have become missionary disciples" who are "agents of evangelization" along with professional clergy.[19]

The Redefined Understanding of the Mission of the Church

The Conciliar effort for ecclesial renewal also resulted in a shift in missiology, thanks to which the understanding of mission became unfettered from the narrow concept of the past.[20] Bevans affirms that Vatican II was essentially "a missionary council" that reasserted the Church's sacramental and missionary presence in the world as "a sacramental sign...of grace and wholeness."[21] *Lumen Gentium* further articulated that the sacramentality of the Church signifies how the mystical and the social dimensions are fused in an inseparable reciprocity, which guarantees not only unity but also distinction at the same time. The unity between the two dimensions—mystical and social—found in the sacramentality of the Church reflects and flows from the asymmetrical dual unity of the mystery of the Incarnate Word, who is fully man and fully God, thus illuminating the mystery of the indissoluble union between the invisible and the visible dimensions, at the same time, preserving their distinction. Mission itself becomes sacramental because the Church on one hand signifies God's offer of salvation and on the other hand is the instrument thereof."[22]

Ad Gentes highlights the renewed vision of the mission of the Church as essentially rooted in Trinitarianism, connecting the Church's mission with the mission of Christ and the mission of the Holy Spirit: "The pilgrim Church is missionary by her very nature, since it is from the mission of the Son and the mission of the Holy Spirit that she draws her origin, in accordance with the decree of God the Father."[23] This affirms that: 1) Mission is primarily linked to God himself and his character of love and the mission of the Church flows from *Missio Dei*; 2) The pilgrim Church is missionary by her very nature; 3) All Christians are called to mission; 4) Mission no longer signifies a territorial concept but a fundamental attitude of the Church wherever it is; 5) Mission is not about going to places but serving people in other cultures or one's own; and 6) The Church is a sacramental sign of Christ in the world.

Evangelii Nuntiandi, promulgated in 1975 by Paul VI, further developed the conception of mission of the Church by introducing the concept of evangelization as containing a rich, complex, and dynamic reality.[24] Based on *Ad Gentes* 2, Paul VI affirms that evangelization is the "grace and vocation proper to the Church" and the very identity of the Church: the Church "exists in order to evangelize, that is to say, in order to preach and teach, to be the channel of the gift of grace, to reconcile sinner with God, and to perpetuate Christ's sacrifice in the Mass, which is the memorial of His death and glorious resurrection."[25] The Holy Spirit was acknowledged as the principal agent of evangelization, and the understanding of mission expanded to incorporate more than the explicit proclamation of the gospel. It also included promotion of the rights and duties of every human being and family life, international relations, peace, justice, development and liberation. Instead of using the term "inculturation," renewed mission began to speak about participating in the cultural and political life and becoming people of dialogue.

Building on the achievements of *EN*, John Paul II presents a rich and multilayered concept of mission and evangelization in *Redemptoris Missio* in 1990.[26] John Paul II, while emphasizing one fundamental mission of the Church, teaches that due to the diversity of situations in which the Church finds itself, there are three dimensions of the missionary activity of the Church: 1) the first evangelization, missionary activity *ad extra*; 2) missionary activity *ad intra*, which is pastoral care for the faithful; and 3) the new evangelization, which centers on reaching out to the baptized who, in part or totally, lost the living sense of the faith.

The Renewed Understanding of Ecumenism and Charisms

The work of the Conciliar Fathers, engaged in rigorous self-examination and thoroughgoing communal discernment over four years, is celebrated as an event of *aggiornamento*, an Italian word to denote bringing the Church up to date. Updating also brought new elements to the Catholic consciousness. After defining the essence of the Church as missionary, and declaring missionary involvement to be a call and responsibility of all the baptized, the Conciliar innovation enabled all the baptized to fully participate in the mission of the Church. Then two other fruits of the Second Vatican Council were equally crucial to the unleashing of the current of God's grace[27] into the Church, as they are closely linked to the insertion of a renewal in the Spirit into the lives of everyday Catholics. To begin with, the composition of the Council, by virtue of allowing non-Catholic observers in it, indicated the changed posture and mindset of the Church toward non-Catholic Christianity, which was more open and less judgmental. Furthermore, the Catholic Church moved away from the position of seeing itself as the exclusive representation of the Church of Christ on earth and acknowledged the need for and importance of Christian unity:

> This Church constituted and organized in the world as a society, subsists in the Catholic Church, which is governed by the successor of Peter and by the Bishops in communion with him, although many elements of sanctification and of truth are found outside of its visible structure. These elements, as gifts belonging to the Church of Christ, are forces impelling toward catholic unity.[28]

Unitatis Redintegratio ("Decree on Ecumenism")[29] signals a shift in the official teaching of the Catholic Church regarding unity. It recognizes ecumenism as a priority for the Catholic Church and articulates Christian unity in a new way. The document begins with a statement that "the restoration of unity among all Christians is one of the principal concerns of the Second Vatican Council," and affirms that "Christ the Lord founded one Church and one Church only."[30] The Conciliar Fathers also underscored the importance of unity as a task of all the baptized. In the past, unity meant only one thing—the return of "separated brethren" to the fold. In contrast, *Unitatis Redintegratio* frames Christian unity in terms of the restoration of the One Body:

> The attainment of union is the concern of the whole Church, faithful and shepherds alike. This concern extends to everyone, according to his talent, whether it be exercised in his daily Christian life or in his theological and historical research. This concern itself reveals already to some extent the bond of brotherhood between all Christians and it helps toward that full and perfect unity which God in his kindness wills.[31]

It was affirmed that "Catholics must gladly acknowledge and esteem the truly Christian endowments from our common heritage which are to be found among our separated brethren," even learning from them because of the unity brought by the common indwelling Holy Spirit:

> It is right and salutary to recognize the riches of Christ and virtuous works in the lives of others who are bearing witness to Christ, sometimes even to the shedding of their blood. For God is always wonderful in his works and worthy of all praise. Nor should we forget that anything wrought by the grace of the Holy Spirit in the hearts of our separated brethren can be a help to our own edification. Whatever is truly Christian is never contrary to what genuinely belongs to the faith; indeed, it can always bring a deeper realization of the mystery of Christ and the Church.[32]

Another intervention that eased Catholics into the move of the Holy Spirit was the renewed understanding of charisms and the charismatic dimension of the Church the Second Vatican Council documents delineated:

> It is not only through the sacraments and the ministries of the Church that the Holy Spirit sanctifies and leads the people of God and enriches it with virtues, but, "allotting his gifts to everyone according as He wills, He distributes special graces among the faithful of every rank. By these gifts He makes them fit and ready to undertake the various tasks and offices which contribute toward the renewal and building up of the Church, according to the words of the Apostle: "The manifestation of the Spirit is given to everyone for profit." These charisms, whether they be the more outstanding or the more simple and widely diffused, are to be received with thanksgiving and consolation for they are perfectly suited to and useful for the needs of the Church.[33]

The Church defined charisms as the gifts the Holy Spirit gives to the whole Church, including both the laity and the clergy, for the sake of the edification of the Body. But what is noteworthy was the fact that the Second Vatican Council provided a way to overcome a dichotomy between the hierarchical dimension and the charismatic dimension of the Church. By holding together both the institutional—visible—dimension and the mystical Body of Christ, i.e., the spiritual and invisible dimension of the Church, as one seamless reality, the Second Vatican Council secured a vast playing field for the laity to operate in as agents of evangelization and missionary discipleship with the power that comes from the Holy Spirit. Christ, the one Mediator, established and continually sustains here on earth his holy Church—the community of faith—hope and charity, as an entity with visible delineation through which he communicated truth and grace to all. But, the society structured with hierarchical organs and the Mystical Body of Christ, are not to be considered as two realities, nor are the visible assembly and the spiritual community, nor the earthly Church and the Church enriched with heavenly things; rather they form one complex reality which coalesces from a divine and a human element.[34]

The Catholic Charismatic Renewal

On the 1st of January 1901, Pope Leo XIII offered a Mass and prayed for the fresh coming of the Holy Spirit on the Church and the world.[35] While Catholics had to wait to see the answer to this prayer for decades, in the Protestant world, the move of the Holy Spirit broke out almost immediately in Topeka, Kansas,[36] which eventually gave rise to Pentecostalism, a worldwide renewal movement in the Spirit, which was characterized by the baptism in the Holy Spirit, speaking in tongues, and charisms. Catholics were kept out of this Protestant movement for decades. But when all the necessary components—the renewed understanding of missiology, the renewed understanding of Church as the mystical Body of Christ, the renewed understanding of the role of the laity in the mission of the Church, the embrace of ecumenism and the inclusion of charisms—were put in place, the doors of the Catholic Church flung open to the move of the Holy Spirit.

The Catholic Charismatic Renewal began in contact with a renewal in the Spirit, in Seattle, U.S., where Fr. Dennis Bennett, an Anglican Priest, after having received the baptism in the Holy Spirit, offered Friday meetings from 1960 for seven years.[37] Following, awakening and revival occurred at the Duquesne Weekend in 1967, where a group of Catholic young adults experienced the baptism in the Spirit.[38] From then on, the fire that finally reached Catholics spread all over the world and grew into a formidable movement, precipitating small and large prayer groups, covenant communities, conferences, seminars, schools of evangelization, and missionary, evangelistic initiatives and ministries—by and large, initiated and led by laity.

Spirit-Filled Female Evangelists in the Catholic Church

Through the Catholic Charismatic Renewal, countless men and women have been transformed by virtue of an encounter with Jesus in the power of the Holy Spirit. The most common way the renewal movement in the Spirit spread in the Catholic context was through a "Life in the Spirit Seminar" (LSS). An LSS was designed to help participants to deepen a relationship with God the Father, in and through the Son, Jesus, and receiving the baptism in the Holy Spirit. Commonly, it is in the setting of an LSS and prayer groups that Catholic women have learned to take active roles in the work of evangelization and discipleship. In other words, the renewal movement in the Spirit has made the charismatic dimension of the Church come alive while giving opportunities to women which otherwise might not have been made available for them. Thanks to the move of the Spirit, many women in the Catholic Church have found creative and innovative ways to be involved in leadership by taking care of people in need, starting prayer groups, establishing covenant communities, or initiating ministries and apostolates.

The most prominent female Catholic evangelist of our time is Mother Teresa, who preached a simple message of God's unconditional love, available for even the most wretched. Other well-known and highly respected lay female evangelists are:

- Ursula Bleasdell, endearingly called "Auntie Babsie," an international speaker and evangelist from Trinidad and Tobago
- Barbara Shlemon Ryan from the U.S., known for her inner healing ministry
- Patti Mansfield, one of the first Catholic youths who received the baptism in the Holy Spirit at Duquesne University and who subsequently became an iconic figure of the Catholic Charismatic Renewal Movement
- Michelle Moran, a former president of ICCRS (International Catholic Charismatic Renewal Services) and founding member of Sion Community

- Dorothy Ranaghan, a cofounder of People of Praise Catholic Ecumenical Covenant Community
- Sr. Techie Rodriguez, a founder of the Lord's Flock, a Catholic Covenant Community in the Philippines.

There are a multitude of women who have been touched by the love of God and begun preaching, teaching, and serving others in the power of the Spirit.

A Sister Duo from Malaysia

Just before the world became mired in the COVID-19 crisis, Lavinia and Alicia Antoine burst upon the scene resolved to live as disciples of Jesus and encourage others to do the same. This sister duo is from Malaysia, a predominantly Muslim country. They were born to Jude and Veronica Antoine, whose lives were deeply touched by the move of the Holy Spirit in the Catholic Church, and who dedicated themselves to the work of evangelization and missionary discipleship.[39] Lavinia and Alicia grew up in a household characterized by docility to the Holy Spirit, absorbing the missionary dynamism of their parents. In 2016, the two Antoine teens visited Poland to participate in World Youth Day. Returning home, they launched a youth ministry called Kasih, in the Archdiocese of Kuala Lumpur, Malaysia, inspired by being part of millions of Catholic youths gathered in Poland to celebrate Jesus. The objective of Kasih was to reach out to other teens with the gospel and lead them to a personal encounter with Christ.

Having discerned the leading of the Holy Spirit, Lavinia and Alicia Antoine stepped out in full-time ministry in the year of 2019. They relate that their parents were initially hesitant to bless their desire to serve as full-time missionaries, as they understood the challenge and difficulty attached to the lifestyle of a full-time missionary in the Catholic setting. However, the sisters moved to Slovakia and established the Kasih House of Mission (KHOM) with the aim of equipping young Catholics and mobilizing them into evangelization and mission in the power of the Holy Spirit.

Today, Lavinia and Alicia preach the gospel, pray for baptism in the Holy Spirit, and teach on new life in the Spirit—how to receive prayer languages, how to pray for and receive healing and deliverance, how to move in the gifts of the Holy Spirit, and more—in the context of retreats, conferences, rallies, parish missions, and evangelistic programs. They have been to Indonesia, the Philippines, India, Japan, Sweden, Poland, Germany, United Kingdom, Romania, Azerbaijan, Mauritius, Tanzania, Kenya, Uganda, and Australia. Currently there are four other full-time missionaries working alongside Lavinia and Alicia whose faith journeys have also been marked by the power and Person of the Holy Spirit. Each of these young professionals came to have an experiential knowledge of Jesus and a fresh outpouring of the Holy Spirit through the ministry of Lavinia and Alicia. They therefore decided to leave their promising careers and join the ministry of KHOM. The agenda of KHOM set for the year 2024 reflected their focus on discipleship, and offered three types of discipleship and formation programs in Slovakia and Poland.

The timing of Lavinia and Alicia's work of building up a ministry of evangelization and missionary discipleship is worth mentioning; it is taking place precisely as declining church attendance and membership is accelerating, especially in the Global North. In 2019, Pew Research Center reported that both Protestant and Catholic populations were declining, with many joining the ranks of "nones" or religiously unaffiliated groups. In the U.S., for example, 17 percent described their religion as "nothing in particular," an increase from 12 percent a decade prior. Across the globe, agnosticism and atheism are on the rise, as are non-Christian religions.[40]

What makes things worse is the fact that the retreat from the faith is more pronounced among younger demographics. In 2019, Barna reported that "the percentage of young-adult dropouts has increased from 59 to 64 percent. Nearly two-thirds of U.S. 18–29-year-olds who grew up in church tell [us] they have withdrawn from church involvement as an adult after having been active as a child or teen." But despite the alarming rate at which young people are retreating from Christianity, Barna also identifies an emerging category of young people who are still highly engaged in church life and value scriptural engagement, church attendance, and discipleship; these are categorized as "resilient disciples."[41] Additionally, the example of Lavinia and Alicia Antoine suggests that there is yet another category of young people, though a far smaller sample in the Church, who not only value discipleship personally—exemplified by a resilient disciple—but also make disciple-making their primary goal.

Conclusion

Thanks to the shifts precipitated by the Second Vatican Council and the Catholic Charismatic Renewal, Catholic laity has been integrated into the mission of the Church. This missionary renewal of recent decades has given women unique opportunities to become active agents. The story of Lavinia and Alicia Antoine indeed constitutes a distinct example of Spirit-empowered female evangelists who are continuing the mission of the Church today. But the real significance of their story does not lie in continuation as much as how they are breaking new ground. They are effectively reaching out to Millennials, Gen Z, and Gen Alpha in the context of the Global North. They are reversing the trend of disconnection from church life. They have invested in creating a culture of mission and discipleship, and in doing so, are presenting an innovative model of co-responsibility exercised by the laity in the context of the Catholic Church.

This article has been adapted to fit the scope and focus of the project highlighting Spirit-empowered female evangelists, and is based on the original article by Dr. Hyeon Ju (Sabina) Cappello Lee under the same title.

Notes

1   This statement is not meant in any way to undermine the dignity of motherhood, which is a gift from God for the benefit of the whole human race, or the importance of religious education at home but to underline the extent of mission engagement of Catholic lay women in the past.

2   John XXIII, *Humanae Salutis*, December 25, 1961, in *the Documents of Vatican II*, ed. Walter Abbott (New York: American Press, 1966), 709.

3   See J. W. O'Malley, "Trent and Vatican II: Two Styles of Church," in *From Trent to Vatican II: Historical Investigations*, eds. R. F. Bulman, F. J. Parrella (Oxford University Press, 2006), 311–315. O'Malley presents a clear analysis of how the style of the VCII was different from all the other councils for forsaking the usual, i.e., negative approach in dealing with "enemies" of the Church, which expressed hostility and condemnation. The agenda of VCII was to establish an effective way of communicating with the world, signaling to offer "medicine of mercy rather than that of severity," and reconciliation with "modernity, which was a code word for the decline of civilization into irreligion and immorality that had been under way for centuries." According to O'Malley, the vocabulary employed at the VCII reveals the new approach: the operative words were

"persuasion, reconciliation," while "threat, intimidation, surveillance and punishment" were rejected; and words such as "reciprocity, cooperation, partnership and collaboration," and horizontal words such as "brothers and sisters" and "people of God" were preferred, with the vocabulary of "dialogue and collegiality."

4 J. A. Komonchak, "The Council of Trent at the Second Vatican Council," in *From Trent to Vatican II: Historical Investigations*, eds. R. F. Bulman, F. J. Parrella (Oxford University Press, 2006), 62–63.

5 O. Rush, "Towards a Comprehensive Interpretation of the Council and Its Documents," *Theological Studies* 73, no. 3 (September 2012), 554. For more about *societas perfecta* see A. Codd, "The Pastoral Context as a Living System: Implications for Theology and Practice," in *Pastoral Ministry for Today: "Who Do You Say That I Am?" Conference Papers 2008*, ed. T. G. Grenham (Dublin: Veritas Publications, 2009), 66. Codd explains that "After the Council of Trent (1545–1563) the self-understanding of the Catholic Church was predominantly (if not exclusively) juridical and its vision of itself was largely that of a 'perfect society'—*societas perfecta*. The motif of the perfect society was preserved in official ecclesiology right up to the publication of the encyclical of Pius XII, *Mystici corporis*."

6 See S. B. Bevans, R. P. Schroeder, *Constants in Context: A Theology of Mission for Today* (Maryknoll, NY: Orbis Books, 2004), 286.

7 The Second Vatican Council, "Dogmatic Constitution on the Church," *Lumen Gentium*, November 21, 1964, 1, http://www.vatican.va/archive/hist_councils/ii_vatican_council/documents/vat-ii_const_19641121_lumen-gentium_en.html, accessed February 8, 2020.

8 *LG*, sections 9, 7, and 1 and 9, respectively.

9 See R. Beal, *Mystery of the Church, People of God* (Washington D.C: The Catholic University of America Press, 2014), 14–16, 205–210. Beal identifies Congar's "total ecclesiology," which Congar proposed as an alternative to the dominant Catholic ecclesiology at that time, as "an ecclesiological synthesis of the mystery of the church in all its dimensions," which includes both the clerical church and "the people of God in the fullness if its truth." In her description of how Congar's "total ecclesiology" influenced the Vatican II Council, Beal explains that the council abandoned the dominant juridical view of the Church and replaced it with the concept of Congar's "total ecclesiology while supporting the idea of giving a primacy "to the sacramental over the juridical and to Christian ontology of the spiritual reality of the Christian man over the structures of service and command."

10 *LG* 10. For more on the priesthood of all the baptized, see P. De Mey, "The Sacramental Nature and Mission of the Church in *Lumen Gentium*," *International Journal for the Study of the Christian Church* 14, no. 4 (October 2014), 352–353. De May explains that "the priesthood of all believers is rooted in baptism and confirmation, the ministerial priesthood also in the sacrament of ordination. The *relatio* justifies their essential difference by pointing out that only the ordained priesthood is 'representative' and therefore able to act liturgically 'in the name of the whole people.'" (*LG* 10).

11 *LG* 31.

12 The Second Vatican Council, "The Decree on Mission Activity of the Church," *Ad Gentes*, December 7, 1965, http://www.vatican.va/archive/hist_councils/ii_vatican_council/documents/vat-ii_decree_19651207_ad-gentes_en.html, accessed February 16, 2020.

13 *LG* 10.

14 See The Second Vatican Council, "Decree on the Apostolate of the Laity," *Apostolicam Actuositatem*, November 18, 1965, 1, http://www.vatican.va/archive/hist_councils/ii_vatican_council/documents/vat-ii_decree_19651118_apostolicam-actuositatem_en.html, accessed March 17, 2020.

15 Paul VI, "Apostolic Exhortation, Evangelization in the Modern World," *Evangelii Nuntiandi*, December 8, 1975, http://www.vatican.va/content/paul-vi/en/apost_exhortations/documents/hf_p-vi_exh_19751208_.evangelii-nuntiandi.html, accessed March 7, 2020.

16 John Paul II, "Apostolic Exhortation, On the Vocation and the Mission of the Lay Faithful in the Church and in the World, *"Christifideles Laici,"* December 30, 1988, 32, http://www.vatican.va/content/john-paul-ii/en/apost_exhortations/documents/hf_jp-ii_exh_30121988_christifideles-laici.html, accessed April 3, 2020.

17 Benedict XVI, "Address of His Holiness Benedict XVI, Opening of the Pastoral Convention of the Diocese of Rome on the Theme," *Church Membership and Pastoral Co-Responsibility*, August 10, 2012, http://www.vatican.va/content/benedict-xvi/en/speeches/2009/may/documents/hf_ben-xvi_spe_20090526_convegno-diocesi-rm.html, accessed February 10, 2020. Benedict XVI teaches, "They must no longer be viewed as 'collaborators' of the clergy but truly recognized as 'co-responsible', for the Church's being and action, thereby fostering the consolidation of a mature and committed laity." While stressing the co-responsibility between the laity and the clergy, Benedict affirms the important role the clergy has to play: "This common awareness of being Church of all the baptized in no

way diminishes the responsibility of parish priests." See also J. Cavadini, "Co-Responsibility: An Antidote to Clericalizing the Laity?," *Church Life Journal: A Journal of the McGrath Institute for Church Life* (March 2020), https://churchlifejournal.nd.edu/articles/co-responsibility-is-the-remedy-for-lay-clericalism/, accessed March 14, 2020. Cavadini explains that "the theology of co-responsibility begins by invoking Vatican II's rediscovery of the priesthood of the baptized, the mystery of the People of God as a royal priesthood, with each member ordered towards the prophetic, royal, and priestly vocation to 'declare the wonderful deeds of him who called [us] out of darkness into his marvelous light,' that is, to mission, to evangelization."

18 *EG* 15, 110, 111.

19 *EG* 120. For the absolute importance of co-responsibility, see Francis, "Apostolic Exhortation, On the Proclamation of the Gospel in Today's World," *Evangelii Gaudium,* November 24, 2013, 27, http://www.vatican.va/contet/francesco/en/apost_exhortations/documents/papa-francesco_esortazione-ap_20131124_evangelii-gaudium.html, accessed March 11, 2020. Francis articulates his objection against clericalism: "Lay people are, put simply, the vast majority of the people of God. The minority—ordained ministers—are at their service" (*EG* 102).

20 For more detail on ecclesial conversion, see S. O. Sheridan, *"Gaudium Et Spes*: The Development and Implementation of the Church's Role in Evangelization in the Pastoral Constitution on the Church in the Modern World," *The Jurist: Studies in Church Order & Ministry* 71, no. 1 (November 2011): 95. Sheridan sheds light that apart from theologians who were demanding changes, there had been various movements attempting to bring changes to the Church: "the liturgical movement that called for reform of the liturgy, the biblical movement that called for a renewed understanding of Scripture, and the ecumenical movement that called for dialogue with other Christians. . ."

21 S. B. Bevans, "Mission at the Second Vatican Council: 1962–1965," in *A Century of Catholic Mission: Roman Catholic Missiology 1910 to the Present,* ed. S. B. Bevans (Oxford: Regnum Books International, 2013), 101.

22 De Mey, "The Sacramental Nature and Mission of the Church in *Lumen Gentium,*" 349–350. De Mey explains that "The Church also needs to be aware of its living relationship with Christ. 'The church, as the kingdom of Christ already present in mystery, grows, visibly in the world through the power of God' (*LG* 3). Understandably, a sacramental ecclesiology at this place also contains a reflection on the Eucharist. 'Through the sacrament of the eucharistic bread, there is represented and produced the unity of the faithful, who make up one body in Christ' (*LG* 3)."

23 See the Second Vatican Council, "Decree on the Mission Activity of the Church," *Ad Gentes* (December 7, 1965), 2, http://www.vatican.va/archive/hist_councils/ii_vatican_council/documents/vat-ii_decree_19651207_ad-gentes_en.html, accessed February 16, 2020. See also Bevans and Schroeder, *Constants in Context*, 287–288, especially "*AG* has provided a strong, consistent reason of considerable theological depth; that is, the church is in mission because it has been graciously caught up in the *missio Dei*, the very mission of God in creation, redemption and continual sanctification."

24 See Paul VI, "Apostolic Exhortation, Evangelization in the Modern World."

25 *EN* 14. See also Bevans and Schroeder, *Constants in Context*, 305–307, 311–321.

26 See D. Dorr, "'*Redemptoris Missio*': Reflections on the Encyclical," *The Furrow* 42, no. 6 (June 1991): 341–347. *Redemptoris Missio* is characterized by 1) its Christocentric focus; 2) an expanded understanding of mission which includes interreligious dialogue, which is acknowledged a constitutive dimension of the mission of the Church; 3) the concept of mission that overcomes boundaries and turns its attention to the neglected, whether territorially, socially or culturally; 4) the concept of mission as a multifaceted reality which includes inculturation, interreligious dialogue, development, work of charity, forming new communities, etc. Dorr evaluates that "the distinction between the mission of re-evangelization and mission 'to the nations' is one of the most important elements in the encyclical."

27 See Matteo Calisi, *The Current of Grace of the Catholic Charismatic Renewal: Origins and Current Events*, speech in Rome, February 11, 2023, https://www.academia.edu/100334565/_THE_CURRENT_OF_GRACE_OF_THE_CATHOLIC_CHARISMATIC_RENEWAL_Origins_and_current_events_by_Matteo_Calisi?email_work_card=title, accessed October 3, 2023. Calisi explains that Francis articulated the importance of the Charismatic Renewal Movement in the Catholic Church by elevating it from one of the renewal movements that come and go in the Church to the current of grace which is necessary for and available to every Christian.

28 *LG* 8.

29 The Second Vatican Council, "Decree on Ecumenism," *Unitas Redintegratio*, November 21, 1964, https://www.vatican.va/archive/hist_councils/ii_vatican_council/documents/vat-ii_decree_19641121_unitatis-redintegratio_en.html, accessed October 17, 2023),

30 *UR* 1.

31 *UR* 5.

32 *UR* 4.

33 *LG* 12. See also *AA* 3, which decrees that, "For the exercise of this apostolate, the Holy Spirit who sanctifies the people of God through ministry and sacraments gives the faithful special gifts also (cf. 1 Cor 12:7), "allotting them to everyone according as He wills" (1 Cor 12:11) in order that individuals, administering grace to others just as they have received it, may also be "good stewards of the manifold grace of God" (1 Pet 4:10), to build up the whole body in charity (cf. Eph 4:16). From the acceptance of these charisms, including those which are more elementary, there arise for each believer the right and duty to use them in the Church and in the world for the good of men and the building up of the Church, in the freedom of the Holy Spirit who "breathes where He wills" (John 3:8)."

34 *LG* 8.

35 See A. Schrek, *A Mighty Current of Grace: The Story of the Catholic Charismatic Renewal* (Frederick, MD: The Word Among Us Press, 2017), 20.

36 For the Topeka outpouring on the new year holiday, see Schrek, *A Mighty Current of Grace*. Also Calisi, *The Current of Grace of the Catholic Charismatic Renewal*.

37 Calisi identifies Fr. Bennet's Friday meeting as the first contact point where Catholics met with a renewal in the Spirit in *The Current of Grace of the Catholic Charismatic Renewal*.

38 For more about the Duquesne phenomenon, see Schrek, *A Mighty Current of Grace*, 23, 27–28, 30–39.

39 Jude and Veronica encountered Jesus through the Catholic Charismatic Renewal in Malaysia as young adults. Since they were married, they have served at different capacities of leadership in the Catholic Church in Malaysia. At one point in their lives, they felt led to "put down the net into the deep" and as a result, they left their professional careers and became a full-time lay missionary couple fully dependent on providence, which is quite a rare path among Catholics even today. They founded and led the Catholic Youth Evangelisation School (YES) for the Archdiocese of Kuala Lumpur, Malaysia, and have traveled to thirty-five different countries preaching the uncompromising message of faith in the Person of Jesus Christ. They currently lead Kerygma Ministry, preaching, teaching, and praying for healing and deliverance in the name of Jesus.

40 Pew Research Center, "In U.S., Decline of Christianity Continues at Rapid Pace," *Pew Research Center*, October 17, 2019, https://www.pewresearch.

org/religion/2019/10/17/in-u-s-decline-of-christianity-continues-at-rapid-pace/, accessed December 30, 2023. Pew notes that "43% of U.S. adults identify with Protestantism, down from 51% in 2009. One-in-five adults (20%) are Catholic, down from 23% in 2009 . . . Self-described atheists now account for 4% of U.S. adults, up modestly but significantly from 2% in 2009; agnostics make up 5% of U.S. adults, up from 3% a decade ago."

41 Barna, "Church Dropouts Have Risen to 64%—But What About Those Who Stay?," *Barna*, September 4, 2019, https://www.barna.com/research/resilient-disciples/, accessed December 30, 2023.

11　From Creeks to the Ganges: A "Small Man History" of the Pentecostal Evangelist, Reverend N. E. Singh

David Emmanuel Singh

Abstract

"From Creeks to the River Ganges" is how this paper conceptualizes the "small man history" of the Pentecostal evangelist, Reverend Newton Emmanuel Singh (henceforth, "Singh," 1930–2014). His story reflects a humble highland creek, which when joined up with other creeks and streams becomes the Ganges. His story, as that of a creek, begins on the Highlands and contributes to the "river" of Pentecostal Christianity in the Hindi heartland of northern India. The argument is simple: Singh was a Spirit-empowered evangelist who trained disciples for mission permeated with worship and service. This story may inspire on its own, but when articulated with other micro stories, its significance as a contributor to vernacular Christianity may become more visible and better appreciated.

Why Tell His Story?

This study focuses on two settings of Reverend N. E. Singh's ministry. First is his little-studied frontline of mission, in caste-ridden rural and semi-urban settings, where one still finds his protégés from the Assemblies of God's (AG) Bible school. Second is the mission he served in Manihari over four separate periods. Singh's work in Manihari began around 1947 at a "mission initiated through the" Norwegian independent Pentecostal church at Narvik, called Smyrna. Renamed Bethel Pentecostal Church (BPC) in the 1980s, it joined an association of churches in Manihari, Katihar, Dankhora, and Banda. These churches do not fit any of the existing Indian Pentecostal denominations, as their inception owes to the

Figure 1: N. E. and Suhasini Singh, partners in mission

173

1906 Pentecostal revival in Norway and India. The question therefore becomes: why is a story such as Singh's worth telling?

While biography as methodology can be viewed skeptically—for promoting a narrative where a "great man" or "isolated genius" is singlehandedly responsible for intellectual or cultural accomplishments[1] —yet biography as an approach to research is highlighted by Thomas and Znaniecki for informing scholars' understandings of individual interactions that create and shape context.[2] "Small man history" can be insightful and transformative, especially when historians bring such stories to light in their own horizons to "explain the past and to connect it to our present, and ourselves."[3] Focus shifts from systems and structures to individuals, as windows into their worlds, and allows generalizations to arise through simple conclusions from narratives or observations.[4] Jansen and Whittle thus argue for a shift in approach from a single, linear narrative concerned with "established cannons and hegemonic discourses," to a multiplicity of discourses even if they appear insignificant, marginal, or non-linear. [5]

Who is qualified to tell such stories of individuals deemed small and marginal? I admit that in telling the story of Singh, as his son, there are methodological and ethical dilemmas from being an insider.[6] I do not claim detachment or objectivity, but I commit to transparency in acknowledging challenges and seeking ways to minimize them.

Who was Singh?

Singh studied at a Church Missionary Society (CMS) mission school near the erstwhile Mughal center of power, Sikandra (Agra). He hailed from a devout family of high caste converts at the Himalayan village of Bungidhar. His great-grandfather identified himself as a *thakur*, which, among others things, means "the master of the estate." The region's connection with the empire (conscription for the army) facilitated the movements of Christian missions, particularly of those related to the Methodist Episcopal Church (MEC) and the CMS.[7]

Singh's choice of Pentecostalism deserves attention. The Methodist church of Singh's grandfather was intensely missionary. MEC's focus was on a region considered the hardest for Christianity to penetrate: "There is no other land so difficult to win for Christ as India, and no other land which in the intellectual and religious endowments of its inhabitants, promises such an abundant harvest."[8] They rejoiced despite the scarcity of fruit among lower and higher castes.[9] Unlike the Missionary Society, which was criticized for its one-sided emphasis on missions at the expense of pastoral ministry, MEC was a missionary church equally committed to pastoring converts through discipleship and education.[10] Singh's early role models were family members who had converted to Christianity before him and were products of this balanced approach. From MEC reports, both Tibet and Garhwal hills were noted as mission opportunities, with the church missionally active through preaching, teaching, and healing outreaches. Notably, while healing prayer was an essential part of their practice, the church understood healing to encompass hospitals, dispensaries, and asylums.

Singh's decision to work as a peripatetic Pentecostal evangelist could appear atypical given that both his grandfather and father were with mainstream church-led missions. However, he was the only one among his eight siblings to follow his grandfather and father's path in Christian ministry. Additionally, his preparation for evangelism and discipleship enveloped by Spirit-led worship and service indeed came partly through his father, George (alias, Iman; 1914–1963).[11] The reason behind George's decision to move from MEC to CMS is difficult to gauge. We know MEC began work in North India in 1856 and grew from one conference to thirteen by 1960. In the seventies, MEC voted against union with the Church of North India and was constituted as the Methodist Church of India.[12] This process of institutional inwardness (restricting freedom for evangelism) had likely begun well before the change and could be why George shifted to CMS. It appears Singh was following his father's example of choosing a tradition that afforded greater freedom to balance pastoral and evangelistic ministries.

Singh's attraction to the wandering ideal came from Sadhu Sundar Singh (henceforth, "the Sadhu"). He often spoke of him and told me stories of the Sadhu's travels to the higher Himalayas, especially to Tibet. He acquired these anecdotes not from readings but directly through George, who reportedly had heard them from the Sadhu himself. In one of these anecdotes, Singh mentioned George encountering the Sadhu on one of his trips from Tibet. Footsore, unkempt, and emaciated from the long and arduous journey through the passes, the Sadhu sought renewal with George, who cut his hair and helped with his recovery. Being aware of the Sadhu's critique of formal theological education in the Anglican tradition, Singh chose to be trained at a Pentecostal Bible school known for its experiential and practical preparation for evangelism in the language of the masses.

His choice of a Bible school, and later, the North India Bible Institute (NIBI), was critical for other reasons: this is where he met Suhasini, a fellow Pentecostal and a Bengali orphan raised at the Manihari mission in the Santhal tribal region and at an AG orphanage at Bettiah. He also met the American Pentecostal evangelist Marguerite Flint (1892–1963). She was a woman demonstrably empowered by the Spirit to serve in India for forty years (1815–1958). Her three reasons for being a missionary remained Singh's guides: "First, for my sake (because when we fail to hear the cry of the needy, we die); second, for their sakes (because millions of people in India are without Christ); third, for His sake (because Jesus died for India)."[13] Singh had another reason for seeing her as a mentor: like him, she had a close family connection with the Spirit-led missionary tradition of Methodism. She had begun her ministry at Bettiah, where she set up a school and an orphanage for two hundred girls (where Suhasini studied). She also helped set up a school for girls in Hardoi, which later morphed into a Bible school, and, subsequently, a graduate-level Bible institute, NIBI.

In one of her reports, Flint spoke of a spiritual revival on April 7, 1934, when classes had to be terminated. She reports, "Oh, the transforming power of the Holy Ghost! How glad I am for Pentecost. We have a Pentecostal Bible school in very truth now and He is in our midst."[14] In the picture published in Oberg's piece, about twenty years after the revival, Flint is seated garlanded with a colleague and thirty young girls behind them, one of whom is Suhasini. The school grew into an institute where Singh completed his undergraduate program with Suhasini, graduating in 1956. Here began a partnership that lasted a lifetime.

Singh's first recorded ministry as an evangelist followed his graduation and marriage at Manihari in the 1950s, well before it became BPC. The couple chose for a time to live in a mud hut in the remote Santhali village of Hurlajudi, the site of the first converts among the Santhalis in this part of Bihar. Singh's areas of operation gradually expanded to other Santhali regions across the states.[15] The couple relocated to the highlands adjoining Tibet and Nepal, with Singh continuing his peripatetic evangelism in this hardest of places, mostly walking and living by faith. After five years, in 1961, the AG recognized Singh's work by awarding him a license to preach. He subsequently felt called to pursue graduate-level training at NIBI, completing it in 1966. His affiliation with NIBI continued until his retirement, firstly, through three further periods of full-time work in Manihari as an evangelist-pastor. Secondly, after the Manihari mission became part of an organized body called the BPC Association, he chose the AG as his base. Singh continued, however, to be a revival and evangelistic speaker, not just among the Santhals in Manihari but throughout the Hindi belt. NIBI gave him the opportunity to prepare young evangelist-pastors; it also gave him the freedom to exercise his own evangelistic calling, mainly through the training of his students but also on his own as a travelling preacher.

Empowered by the Spirit

Singh's objective was not just to be a pastor-teacher; he saw his ministry as channeling the Spirit for evangelism and discipleship soaked in worship and service. Singh never emphasized speaking in tongues, not when he was with the AG, and not at Manihari. This choice can most likely be attributed to Singh's childhood and family background in the Methodist and Anglican traditions. This was never an issue for anyone during his time at NIBI. His emphasis was on the exercise of power through Spirit-inspired evangelism and discipleship, and in the easily overlooked miracles mediated through worship and service. Singh expressed his experience of the Spirit's fullness in terms of Christology. He was, again, atypical among most Indian Christians, especially the Sadhu. Some Indian Christian conceptions appear close to being "Christo-monist"— but not Singh's. His experience was Trinitarian, as Kärkkäinen describes it: "Trinity is not an appendix to the notion of the one God; rather, the 'name' of the biblical God is Father, Son, and Spirit,"[16] and again, "The Spirit, at work in the world after the cross, is the spirit of the crucified and risen Christ."[17] Singh was, like the Sadhu, Christocentric in this sense; this was an experiential assertion rather than a reasoned intellectual position.

Evangelism

Method

A pastor in Manihari, Franci Murmu, notes that "Cornelius and Simone were Singh sir's early associates. Jona Hemrom joined [Manihari] when

I was a student at [NIBI]." I spent considerable time with Cornelius Hemrom in his village at Neema. He was one of the five early converts here when I visited often as a child. Hemrom spoke about his own role as the head *ojha* (shaman). His younger brother died from *bonga* (spirit) possession. *Bongas* tormented him with "evil eyes and fangs." Hemrom had been unable to save him. He was terrified, as the village seemed to be under "dark clouds." This crisis[18] led him to earnestly seek freedom from evil and a "clean place." He found these among the missionaries from Manihari where he went for worship and fellowship along with other converts on foot. It was Jesus and the Holy Spirit who took his fear away, "cleaned him" from evil, and led him to the clean place he had been searching. He gave up being an *ojha* and began serving Christ despite opposition from his family. He had no formal education or training in theology and yet grew as a leader with help from his wife and Singh, who discipled him.

Hemrom described to me some of the things I knew as a child when I accompanied Singh on his bicycle:

> Singh and I used to travel around in villages to preach the gospel of Jesus. We had only two modes of transport: bicycles and bullock carts. He used to speak in Hindi and I translated for him. We would have our breakfast, leaving home at around 8 a.m. every day, and return late in evening. We would go to a village and go right up to the *pradhan* (head) to seek his permission. We always managed to get their permission because the heads knew nothing or little about Jesus and they were curious. They would urge us to talk. I translated for Singh. We were always together...I do not remember the years we were not together.[19]

Another report reveals that the Santhals were hungry for the word of life. Singh would preach for an hour or longer with anecdotes and songs, and then, on demand, he would continue speaking until it was impossible to continue. They never carried anything to eat for the day. The believers or seekers invited them into their open-air verandas. The lead woman of the family would seat the guests, wash their feet in clean bowls, and wipe them. She would then reappear and offer traditional greetings before others would appear. Gradually the crowd would build up. Santhali culture is rich in a variety of songs, often with accompanying dance. As an *ojha*, Hemrom had used *jhal* (a homemade instrument). Songs with Santhali tunes preceded the preaching of the Word; they ended with prayers for the sick, followed by refreshments. Hemrom related several stories of their travels to distant places with clusters of villages where they would need to get the permission not just from the village heads but from local non-Santhali politicians as well. Despite the difficult terrain, Singh and Hemrom covered a large territory.

Another respondent confirmed much of the above but added interesting details about Singh often sleeping on straw beds in the open, often with no food for days on his extended travels. He was also moved with compassion for the naked or ill-clad tribal community that often suffered from natural calamities like floods or famine. This is what began his emphasis on evangelism accompanied by service. He led teams distributing clothes and food. Sacrificial service was an essential part of the gospel, independent of the Western debates on evangelism and social responsibility or holistic-integral mission.[20]

Francis is one of many who connect the two locations of Singh's ministry, Manihari and NIBI. His grandfather and father were converts from the Santhali village of Harlajudi. Francis described the establishment of the Manihari church on December 27, 1951, with the first baptism of nine from the village. He confirmed another source's report that Singh and Suhasini lived in a small mud hut in this village right after their wedding in Manihari in 1956. They ministered in the village and the surrounding areas and helped with a modest school in the village.[21]

During Singh's tenure, there were several spikes in baptisms:

I always thank God for—twice around this time, there were mass baptisms: 1971 and 1972. These were results of hard labour of all those who went ahead. At one time seventy-nine people were baptized [another report suggests 100 at one time]. It all happened directly through Pastor Singh's ministry and it was a big number for that time. Each time of these baptisms, Singh *sir* remained standing the entire day for the baptisms. Pastor Cornelius assisted. Following these, the number remained roughly around twenty to forty annually.[22]

I remember these baptisms because I was part of one of them, as a little boy of ten.

One of Singh's students from a state holy for Hindus reported Singh wished nothing more than to prepare students for evangelistic and church-planting ministries. Ganesh reported that Singh remained an evangelist even when very old and frail, often using all his breaks and holidays for evangelistic and revival conventions throughout the north, especially the Santhal region.[23] This is what Rudra, one of innumerable witnesses, says:

> Singh's ministries in Uttarakhand and Uttar Pradesh have blessed countless lives. A great Gospel preacher and bible teacher, Singh was immersed in the scriptures. His preaching was accompanied with the songs of praise, which he sang with his ever-present accordion. He sang new songs and taught them. His preaching was always in a language people understood because it was embellished with real-life stories as illustrations people never forgot. He came to my region three times to preach the word in Pauri, Duggadda, and Bijnor. His personal simplicity enhanced the reality of proximity with God whose servant he was and remained until the end.[24]

Some of Singh's conventions lasted a week and included independent Pentecostals, AG, Baptist and mainline Charismatic churches. Many of the places he ministered in have been noted in existing research as centers for conversions. Singh's was one of many contributions that arguably prepared the ground for conversions.

Reasons for Conversions

Singh followed in the footsteps of others including a local minister, Nathaniel Tudu, instead of charting a new course. He recognized some of the continuities between the Santhali religion and Christianity. He saw them as signs of the Spirit's work of preparing them for faith in Jesus. Hemrom reports how simple their message was. It centered on Jesus and his power to bring them to a "clean place" and to save them from the spirits and from hell. The Spirit of Jesus also saved them from becoming spirits that suffered, or caused others to suffer, and from the eternal suffering of hell:

> [Our] message was all about Jesus. We often preached from John 3:16. It was simple. Believe in Jesus, as he is able to save you from hell (*narak*). We reminded them of their rite of passage involving the branding of boys with a tika on their arms [or tattoos on girls].[25] We reminded them that this was, like circumcision, meant as a physical reminder of Jesus' suffering for us. The sign itself does not have the power to save you from hell. Jesus saves.[26]

This was a sign of Santhali readiness for life in heaven or death in hell. The ceremony is called *jivan-maran* (life and death):

> They already had some idea of *swarg* and *narak* (heaven and hell). When they encountered the Christian message, they responded positively. They saw in Jesus someone who bore the pain of branding on their behalf through death

so they could have *jivan* free from the eternal suffering of *narak*. The mark on their arm was merely a sign of their desire for life; Jesus made it certain. He also made expiatory sacrifices redundant.[27]

The Santhali also saw a reflection of Christianity in their practice of hospitality and oral traditions. For example, they saw in the story of the original couple (*pilchuvada-pilchugudi*) parallels with the biblical story of Adam and Eve. The tradition of *marangu* (hill) had similarities with the biblical story of Moses ascending the mountain and the teaching on human proclivity for sin and its consequences. Such traditions made it easier to speak of sin as not just moral failings but as defiance against God, which leads to death in *narak*; God does not cause this death, sin does. Like the Sadhu, in Singh's evangelistic outreaches and preaching, he embraced an experiential sense of God's suffering love in the incarnation, death, and resurrection of his son, God for us. Forgiveness was not merely about removing punishment brought about by sin; forgiveness was the consequence of the ultimate act of love of Jesus for all. Humanity only needed to turn to him and receive his forgiveness to be cleansed of their sins and installed in a "clean place."[28] Within the normative framework, conversions are seen as the work of the Spirit. In the Santhali case, "Food for work...opened doors for the gospel even in places where people were resistant to [Christianity]."[29]

In the last years of his life, Singh lost his eyesight to glaucoma and was afflicted with Parkinson's disease, severely restricting the movements of the wandering evangelist. He would remember the Santhalis and others he served who saw sickness, suffering, and death as being evil or consequences of sin. He thought about his sufferings but remained resolute that suffering was neither purposeless nor a penalty for sin. Rather, it served to keep believers conscious of the price paid by Jesus to give us life, to remind them to be Christ-like, and to be an opportunity to demonstrate the power of God.

Francis illustrated the point about Singh's position on suffering and sickness as an opportunity for the demonstration of God's power and love for individuals. His father, Petrus Murmu, had been converted and baptized through Singh's ministry. He became seriously ill and came close to dying from tuberculosis. Despite being Christians, the family tried *ojhas*, to no avail. Petrus was brought to Manihari where he was nursed while receiving ceaseless prayers led by Singh in a tent on the campus. Despite the prognosis, he experienced a miraculous healing to the glory of the living Christ for all to see. This led to Francis's conversion and commitment to ministry. He went on to study under Singh at NIBI.[30]

Discipleship

We will now shift focus to Singh's training young Christians for a lifetime of Spirit-led evangelism and service. He did this both when he was in Manihari and at NIBI. The common refrain was that the Spirit manifested his power in Singh, not through extraordinary feats but through ordinary gifts, expressed through preaching and teaching enriched with worship and sacrificial service.

One of the gifts often emphasized was humility. Moses, a pastor from a Highland town of Pauri, reported that Singh manifested this gift of the Spirit in mentoring youth. Moses made a distinction between two Hindi words when applying them to Singh: *namrata* and *vinamrata*. The former refers to humble behaviors while the latter is about the deeper disposition from where the behaviors arise. Singh, he asserted, "couldn't not be humble." It was a work of the Spirit, from Moses' perspective: "I am never tired of speaking about his example. He was the embodiment of Christ-likeness for me."[31]

Neeraj, another student of Singh, related this story of the day he graduated, conveying his experience of the power of God:

> I was an arrogant person. If today, I am a humble minister of God, it happened because of Singh *sir*. The preacher spoke about the anointing of Elisha on my graduation. My only prayer was, "Lord, I want someone to lay their hands on me. I do not know who this person will be. I would like a double portion of your anointing on them." As the teachers were laying their hands upon the graduating students on their knees, I felt a hand upon my head. I open my eyes and saw Singh sir. I prayed in my heart and asked God to give me the double portion of the Spirit through him. If today people say Neeraj is a humble man, I remember those days. God transformed me that day for life. I have never seen anyone as humble as him.[32]

Music was another "ordinary" gift Singh exercised. There is a picture taken after singing songs of praise to God that shows him with a team comprising women, men, and children, seated in front of the Prime Minister of India, Indira Gandhi (1917–1984);[33] his beloved accordion still hanging from his shoulder even though he is seated. One of the kids seated in the front was Ashish Maxton, now a vicar of a large city church; he credits Singh for his use of music in his own ministry.

Figure 2: Singh (far right) with the India Every Home Crusade team; at the Indian Prime Minister's residence, Indira Gandhi standing (center) in the background.

His role model, the Sadhu, loved the sitar, an Indian string instrument. The Sadhu had given up playing partly because the sitar, being bulky, was unsuitable for itinerant evangelism. But he loved music as a means of worship, which he saw as an essential element of effective evangelism and training. He sang, but was not very good at it.[34] Singh not only sang, but he played the sitar, violin, and guitar as well. The instrument he used in worship was the accordion. He carried it with him everywhere.

Singh understood the Genesis 1:28 notion of subduing the earth as a command to be creative and caring. He obeyed this command with delight, through his music and through creative Bible teaching that included performances with handmade visual aids. The AG youth—now lawyers, doctors, and engineers—recall Singh's instruction: "These [stories] sowed the seeds of godly conscience in our hearts; he modelled this. The many stories he told us have been a guiding force in our lives."[35] Another witness said, "He was truly creative in making the stories of the Bible come alive."[36] An allusion to two of the performative choruses should suffice: one inspired by Matthew 6:26 was about a little bird on a tree branch. The singers (children) urge the bird to interpret the meaning of her songs. In response, the bird says that she sings the praises of her Lord, who is love. Loving people, even enemies, becomes possible for those who invite Jesus into their hearts. Another was inspired by 1 Kings 17: here, a raven sings a noisy tune as it picks up a piece of bread from an unspecified place and flies off purposefully to deliver it to someone hungry. As the delivery is accomplished, it continues its unmusical singing. The singers (children) then tell the story of this raven's mission, which was to feed

Elijah as directed by God. The cycle of singing continues, embedding the message and the song deeper into the kids' memories. One Hindu student, now a lawyer in the high court said, "I do not know another preacher who reflected his own teachings as did Singh sir. He will always be in my thoughts… A teacher affects eternity; he can never tell where his influence stops."[37]

As in the Psalms, Singh's performative songs, music, and object lessons welled up from joy, sorrow, praise, and lament. This flavored his exchanges with people and drew their attention towards Jesus. Singh never copyrighted anything. His stories and songs were free for use. One Pentecostal pastor sent me one of the last songs Singh taught his congregation. It speaks of life as if it were a rented apartment: one cannot inhabit it forever. Just as the rising sun eventually sets and morning turns into night, our early life ends but another begins. The faithful walk on petals of flowers, but not before they have experienced the thorns. Dreams last mere moments, and men are mere mounds of earth destined for their tombs (those buried) or the piers (those cremated). The song then invites singers or listeners to allow the spirit of Jesus into their lives and warns them about distractions such as the fleeting enchantment of wealth or youth.

Moses and Ganesh, both missionary pastors in Garhwali hills, still remember Singh's sermons laced with songs and music. One, from Proverbs 30:25, emphasized wisdom and preparation for personal and spiritual battles ahead. Unlike the ants, Singh emphasized, humanity has a special position in the created order as bearers of the image of God. How much more wisdom and power would be in store for us, if only we allowed the Spirit to bathe us with his gifts for ministry?

On weekends, Singh took his students to diverse evangelistic settings, including the annual interfaith gatherings. He wanted his students to develop their passion for evangelism and break new grounds without being polemical. In one such outing, near the town's main government college, Christian youth engaged college students in intense conversations. This led to angry outbursts from the college youth. Tracts that the Christian youth were handing out were confiscated and strewn on the roadside. As the scene became rowdier, someone kicked the cardboard box that contained the tracts. It landed on a young Bible student's head, covering him up to his shoulders. In panic, the perpetrator rushed out of the gathering in haste, grabbed hold of a rickshaw, and demanded to be taken promptly to

"God." What he meant was the Assemblies of God, which everyone in town knew because of the AG high school!

A Hindu pupil from the AG high school recalls attending the chapel where Singh addressed them:

> We have temples all around but few churches. I had never been into a church before. It looked bare, like a classroom with pews and a wooden "plus sign" on the wall. I had no idea what it was. Sir explained to us what this sign was. The story he told us moved me to tears. I felt angry—why should someone like Jesus suffer? Then I learned, this was the whole point. He suffered to forgive. This speaks to me—forgiveness is infinitely more powerful than vengeance...I still have a NT in my office. When I need guidance, I read it....I do not know another teacher who reflected his own teachings as did Singh *sir*.[38]

Significance

Today, there is perceptible mission drift at both of the locations where Singh served. It is not hard to speculate on the reasons. New socio-political realities, combined with the changing Christian mission leadership (family-run enterprises, as opposed to Spirit-led movements), severely lack the courage and the call needed to remain faithful. A Muslim caretaker at Manihari, now in his nineties, bemoans the current mission drift, but is a witness of the sacrificial outreaches to villages in the past, as well as the fruits of these in the expanding membership in centers across the region. Despite the emerging evidence of such drifts in the centers, such as NIBI or Manihari, Singh's sphere of ministry was much larger, with intersecting spheres across north India. These have evolved into newer movements despite the failing mother institutions. Just a few pieces of evidence should suffice here.

Singh's protégés emphasize the practical and vernacular aspects of their preparation, in addition to leadership by example. They feel called to evangelistic work in rural India because they hail from where most Indians live. One of them notes:

> Those with a true heart for ministry lose nothing even if they miss the intellectual aspects of training—this can be covered through independent readings and experience on the field. What one learns from role models stays; it leaves a permanent impression on you. One learns from their spiritual *gurus*—now 20 years since graduation—what they showed us about evangelism and service helps us even today.[39]

Anil Abraham was barely seventeen when he came to NIBI as a convert from Punjab. He comes from a devotional sect called Kabirpanth, which believes in one personal God and emphasizes devotion. Like many converts from this sect, he saw visions, one of which was about setting up a base in a small town in Punjab: "I saw big crowds and I was told that these were my people and that I should preach to them."[40] He started to work with just two or three families, gradually expanding to villages around the town. Now this AG-affiliated rural church has five additional rural locations and is set to reach fifty villages in the years ahead. Abraham is from the NIBI cohort of 2003–2006. There were sixteen students in his class, all of whom are now working as evangelists like him. He is one of many "Pastors of Punjab" who are finding "a fertile ground among Punjab's most oppressed castes to spread their faith and expand their flock."[41] A recent *India Today* article features the impact of these charismatic Christian preachers, who are drawing people to Christianity in large numbers. So significant is this movement that it is making both Hindus and Sikhs "apprehensive."[42] Many of Singh's students are working in the *devbhumi* (the land of the gods). One of them, Ganesh, has, besides his mother church in the highland town of Pauri, several house churches purely populated with converts. This promises to be another Punjab.

Deva Maran is one of twenty from the class of 1996 who are all active missionary pastors, predominantly in the Chhattisgarh state. He spoke of a number of Nepali students who are all ministering in Nepal. He has a base church in the ancient Hindu city of Varanasi from where they are expanding work in five rural districts. In his interview with me, he spoke of people responding to the Spirit following healing, exorcism, and the preaching of the word. He spoke of the persecution of pastors working with him, some of whom are still in prison. In the outskirts of Varanasi, recent research by Kerry Chirico highlights a massive Charismatic revival among the "backward classes" and "scheduled castes." While they worship Jesus, they remain unbaptized, which characterizes conversion in this BJP state and others, and raises questions about the nature of church and Christian identity.[43]

Another graduate from the 2002–2005 cohort, Peter Yesu, has been a missionary pastor at a small town called Korba in Chhattisgarh. He has about three hundred converts as members in his church, who are helping plant churches at four other locations. Yesu's NIBI cohort of twelve are still in touch with each other through WhatsApp; he knows they are similarly growing in other northern states.

Chad M. Bauman's work explores Christianity and Dalit religion in Chhattisgarh between 1868 and 1947. It shows how missionary interactions with a group called the Satnamis[44] has led to a Satnami-Christian identity. These conversions, like most, were not purely religious as there were other socio-political processes involved. However, these conversions were not coerced (as is often the charge); there is evidence of material self-interest but also a search for an ideal, which has led to an indigenous or hybrid Christian identity.[45] This context explains not just the high number of NIBI students from the region during Singh's time, but also the continuing impact of their ministries in the state.

Because Singh's ministry at Manihari was not narrowly provincial, the mission drift observable in Manihari does not characterize the wider and independent networks of mission initiated by Manahari's Pentecostal church. Hemron and Singh's travels took them to adjoining states of West Bengal and the region now in the state of Jharkhand. Churches planted in these regions and others distant from Manihari have grown and expanded their own networks independent of the Manihari mission. Hemrom noted: "We went to Bengal for missions. Our sphere of ministry was much larger than Manihari. It is the converts who expanded the mission."

Even within the sphere of Manihari missions, villages like Harlajudi retain a Christian presence, with more than half of the village being Christian. There is even a church in the village constructed by Christians here. The movement of God continues because of new leadership, such as Francis', who is following in Singh's footsteps in expanding the sphere of mission beyond Manihari. The former spoke of his work and his visions:

> We had a scattering of the congregation and we had to work hard to make a new start...We saw a vision of people giving their children to us to be educated as Christian. We have now started work in Amdabad as it was an unreached area [untouched by Manihari]. There are also some believers from Yadav, Kumhar, and Paswan, besides Santhali.[46]

Flint's schools and hostels for girls in Bettiah, Hardoi, and Orai have similarly been extended independently of Manihari. Her approach to evangelism, which prioritized Christian engagement in society, reflects nineteenth- and twentieth-century missions as discussed in Okkenhaug and Summerer's edited works on Christian missions in the Middle East.[47] Ganesh has continued in this tradition, studying first under Singh and then proceeding to his master's degree in social work as a way of integrating evangelism and service. In the *devbhumi,* one of the holiest places for Hinduism, this approach of serving people first is opening doors across the state. As in the Punjab, house churches are springing up, and "believing without belonging," a phrase from Davie,[48] has now become common. Although it particularly characterizes Western Europe, it captures a bit of what some missiologists call "the insider movement"—a movement of people who come to Christ without belonging to a church.[49] This notion is not above critique,[50] but arguably, many of Singh's pupils from the AG school fell in this category of converts. This too is worth exploring in the future.

Conclusion

One hopes that this study offers enough evidence of how God empowers seemingly unimportant individuals for his work and why such stories are worth telling. I used the image of creeks turning into a river to highlight this story in the Hindi heartland. Singh's evangelistic, pastoral, and teaching ministries were informed by his own practice of Spirit-empowered evangelism. His emphasis on evangelism and training of evangelists was enriched by an all-encompassing lifestyle of worship and service. He remained focused on the frontlines and on training protégés for the expanding spheres of the Sprit's work in the Hindi belt.

Singh's story may inspire those who serve God despite fear of shifting socio-political landscape or drifts in mission. It also provides a modest warning against rigid institutionalization, appropriation of Spirit-empowered offices as hereditary possessions, and increasing inwardness of churches that choke up the Spirit's movements. Samson, Singh's youngest son, who along with his wife, Suman, were Singh's prime caregivers, reported: "On his deathbed, just a few hours before he passed, Papa called us all and urged us to read the following verse from 2 Timothy 4:7: 'I have fought a good fight. I have finished my course. I have kept the faith.' His last wish was to have this verse inscribed on his tombstone where it now rests with his remains."[51]

Notes

1 Robert J. Richards, "The Role of Biography in Intellectual History," *KNOW: A Journal on the Formation of Knowledge* 1, no. 2 (2017): 295–318.

2 William I. Thomas and Florian Znaniecki, *The Polish Peasant in Europe and America*, 2 vols. (Boston: Richard G. Badger, 1920).

3 Julia Laite, "The Emmet's Inch: Small History in a Digital Age," *Journal of Social History* 53, no. 4 (Summer 2020): 963–989.

4 Douglas Walton, "Abductive, Presumptive and Plausible Arguments," *Informal Logic* 21 (2) (2001): 141–169.

5 Dennis Jansen and Mark Laurence Whittle, "Introduction: Storytelling in the Margins," *Junctions: Graduate Journal of the Humanities* 5, no. 1 (2020): 1–13.

6 Jenny Fleming, "Recognizing and resolving the challenges of being an insider researcher in work-related learning," in *International Journal of Work-Integrated Learning* 19, no. 3 (2018): 311–320.

7 This involves conflating the role of the soldiers with both the saints (martyred soldiers) and saint-evangelists.

8 Frederick B. Price, *India Mission Jubilee of the Methodist Episcopal Church in Southern Asia: Story of the Celebration Held at Bareilly, India, from December 28th, 1906* (Calcutta: Methodist Publishing House, 1907), 162.

9 Price, *India Mission Jubilee*, 163.

10 Price, *India Mission Jubilee* 164–67.

11 *"Iman,"* in Urdu, means faith or faithful, but it could also have been a shortened form of "Immanuel."

12 J. N. Hollister, *The Centenary of the Methodist Church in Southern Asia* (Lucknow Publishing House, 1956), 169 ff.

13 Ruthie Edgerly Oberg, "This week in AG History–April 7, 1934," Assemblies of God, April 8, 2021, https://news.ag.org/en/article-repository/news/2021/04/this-week-in-ag-history-april-7-1934.

14 Oberg, "This week in AG History."

15 Santhals belong to the Austroasiatic group possibly in antiquity from Southeast Asia.

16 Veli-Matti Kärkkäinen, "How to Speak of the Spirit among Religions: Trinitarian 'Rules' for a Pneumatological Theology of Religions," *International Bulletin of Missionary Research* 30, no. 3 (July 2006): 122.

17 Kärkkäinen, "How to Speak," 123.

18 See Lewis R. Rambo, "Theories of Conversion: Understanding and Interpreting Religious Change," *Social Compass* 46, no. 3 (2016): 259–271.

19 Interview, Cornelius Hemron, January 5, 2022.

20 C. René Padilla, Mission Between the Times (W.B. Eerdmans Publishing Co., 1985) and Samuel Escobar. *A Time of Mission: The Challenge for Global Christianity* (Langham Global Library, 2013).

21 Now there is a government school and a church in this village.

22 Interview, Francis, January 6, 2022.

23 Interview, Ganesh, August 10, 2022.

24 Interview, Rudra, September 3, 2022.

25 The branding was done with a piece of cloth tied in a knot and set on fire. It was then pressed against the arm until it turned into ash.

26 Interview, Cornelius Hemron, January 5, 2022.

27 Interview, Cornelius Hemron, January 5, 2022.

28 Burnett Hillman Streeter and A. J. Appaswamy, *The Sadhu: a study in mysticism and practical religion* (Delhi: Mittal Publications, 1987), 158.

29 Interview, Jona, January 6, 2022.

30 Singh also raised a different type of young "converts" as a "moral teacher" at the campus-based AG School for 8–11-year-olds. Space constraints would not allow me to include those details here.

31 Interview, Moses, January 3, 2022.

32 Interview, Neeraj, July 3, 2022.

33 V. V. Giri (1894–1980), the fourth President of India, was also present at this occasion, though he is not in the picture.

34 Streeter and Appaswamy, *The Sadhu*, 18–19.

35 Interview, Manik, February 3, 2022.

36 Interview, Manik, February 3, 2022.

37 Interview, Manik, February 3, 2022.

38 Interview, Manik, February 3, 2022.

39 Interview, Yesu, September 5, 2022.

40 Interview, Neeraj, July 3, 2022.

41 A. S. Mahajan and S. Menon, "Pastors of Punjab," *The India Today,* November 8–14, 2022, 33–47.

42 Mahajan and Menon, "The Pastors of Punjab," 33–47.

43 Kerry San Chirico, *Between Hindu and Christian* (Oxford University Press, 2022).

44 A nineteenth-century sect among the "untouchables" in Middle India.

45 Chad M. Bauman, *Christian Identity and Dalit Religion in Hindu India, 1868–1947* (Grand Rapids: William B. Eerdmans Publishing, 2008).

46 Interview, Francis, January 6, 2022.

47 Inger Marie Okkenhang and Karène Sanchez Summerer, eds., *Christian Mission and Humanitarianism in the Middle East, 1850–1950*, Leiden Studies in Islam & Society 11 (Leiden: Brill, 2020).

48 Grace Davie, "Believing without Belonging: Just How Secular is Europe," Pew Research interview, December 2005, https://www.pewresearch.org/religion/2005/12/05/believing-without-belonging-just-how-secular-is-europe.

49 Herbert E. Hoefer, *Churchless Christianity* (Pasadena: William Carey Library, 2001).

50 Ayman S. Ibrahim and Ant Greenham, eds., *Muslim Conversions to Christ: A Critique of Insider Movements in Islamic Contexts* (New York: Peter Lang, 2018).

51 Interview, Sam and Suman, January 2, 2022.

12 Female Cell Leaders as Spirit-Empowered Ground-Level Evangelists: A Case Study of Yoido Full Gospel Church

Younghoon Lee

Abstract

According to John Christopher Thomas, "One of the most prominent issues in church ministry in the twenty-first century is the role of women."[1] Recently, leadership that reflects feminine values, such as relationship orientation and democratic participation, is considered an alternative mode of leadership for the future. Unlike traditional male-centered leadership, female leadership that is characterized by inclusiveness, grace, sacrifice, loving service towards others, and affection is required in today's world. These characteristics, when put together, become a dwelling place for God's love through his Spirit. This study proposes that the use of cell groups and female leadership could be the future direction for the church. First, this study will explore a biblical perspective concerning cell groups and female cell leaders. Second, this study will disclose a relationship between cell groups and church growth by describing the origin and operation of cell groups in Yoido Full Gospel Church (YFGC). Third, this study will explore the activities of YFGC female cell leaders and how establishing them in the 1960s was innovative in light of social norms and perceptions. Finally, this chapter will demonstrate that YFGC female cell leaders have helped redefine Korean women's identity by leading cell systems, and by serving and contributing to the movement of the Holy Spirit and church growth in Korea.

Introduction

We contend that the most efficient way to deliver the gospel to people in the twenty-first century is through small groups. According to the "Korea Church Small Group Activity Survey," which was released by the Pastoral Data Research Institute on June 6, 2023, nearly four out of five people (77 percent) responded that they were participating regularly in small groups.[2] The survey also shows that the more Christians participate in a small group regularly, the more a church grows. A cell group composed of small groups grows, divides, expands, and directly affects the growth of the main church, acting as a type of small church within the larger church.

However, church growth also depends on the ability of cell leaders who lead the small groups. The cell leader essentially has an apostolic mission to preach the gospel by being filled with the Holy Spirit. The ability of the lay leader can affect whether small groups become active and churches experience revival. Yoido Full Gospel Church (YFGC) has experienced explosive growth with apostolic missions through the work of cell leaders empowered by the Holy Spirit. Jang-hwan Kim identifies that the way YFGC was able to grow—from a tent church that started with five people in Daejo-dong, Seoul, to the world's largest church with 780,000 people—is the result of a "mustard seed" of cell group ministry.[3] Furthermore, Catholic theologian Jeong-myung Son endorses that cell groups caused YFGC's "explosive growth," emphasizing female cell leadership as the key growth factor.[4]

In this regard, this chapter will now explore the future direction of the church by introducing how the ministry of female cell leaders led to the growth of the church and affected the Korean church and society.

A Biblical Perspective Concerning Cell Group and Female Cell Leaders

In both the Old Testament and the New Testament, we find examples of effective small groups and of the role of female leadership in strengthening God's people. Throughout scripture, forms of cell ministry were established to reduce the workload concentrated on one leader by sharing it with others.

The Prototype of Cell Ministry in the Bible

In the Old Testament, the prototype of biblical cell or small group ministry can be found in the narratives of Moses. In Exodus, Moses had to deal with everything that happened to the people of Israel in the process of fleeing Egypt. However, it was not easy for Moses to handle everything by himself. Jethro, Moses' father-in-law, encouraged him to share his workload with others. In Exodus 18:21–22, Moses accepted his advice and established a thousand leaders, a hundred leaders, fifty leaders, and ten leaders to whom he delegated his work and authority. The passage shows one huge congregation gathered in one place, centered on Moses, subdivided into small groups. Carl F. George notes that these events in Exodus 18 show a change in leadership system, from one man leading alone to a shared responsibility amongst small group leaders. The establishment of this prototype cell system meant pluralistic leadership.[5]

In the New Testament, the emergence of small group ministry can be seen in the formation of cells at the household level.[6] For instance, the church at Philippi was established by Paul in Macedonia, starting in the home of Lydia, a seller of purple goods in Thyatira[7] (Acts 16:14–15). Likewise, multiple churches began in homes including: Ephesus, in the home of Priscilla and Aquila; Corinth, in the home of Gaius; Colossae, in the home of Philemon; and the Laodicean church, in the home of Nympha (1 Cor 16:19; Rom 16:23; Col 1:1–2, 4:15).[8] Acts 2 notes that the members of the first church continued to joined as a prototype of a cell group, united by teaching, fellowship, the breaking of bread, and prayer. As a result, the believers within these churches praised God, enjoying the fellowship with sincere hearts, and growing as the Lord added to them more who were being saved (Acts 2:42, 47). In this narrative, David Yonggi Cho perceives cell ministry and the role of cell leaders in church growth. In *The Story of My Church Growth*, he highlights the presence of two assemblies in the early church, inspired by the accounts in the first two chapters of Acts. The first is the assemblies that were meeting at the temple; and the second is a family meeting where people fellowshipped by breaking bread.[9] Cho states that three thousand people were baptized and became believers on Pentecost, when the church began, and that it was impossible for only twelve apostles to care for this number of believers, so the leaders of family gatherings filled in the gaps.[10]

In the church as Christ's body, which Paul emphasizes in Ephesians, it is important that all the saints work together because each body is made up of its constituent parts and grows together. Paul describes God making some people apostles, some prophets, some evangelists, some pastors and teachers, and doing so to make the saints whole, to do the work of service, and to build the body of Christ (Eph 4:11–12). In the same respect, Paul implies that the laity in the first church should handle a part of the ministry in the form of spiritual gifts. For instance, Barnabas was a representative lay leader in the first church. As a member of the Jerusalem church, Barnabas worked with the apostle Paul, whom he'd met at Daso. He played the role of spokesperson for Paul in the Jerusalem community, co-teaching the saints with Paul while continuing to establish local leaders. Lay leaders like Barnabas played a major role in the revival of the first church.

Female Co-Workers of Paul

It is notable that some of the lay leaders that Paul worked with were female volunteers, who were co-workers in his ministry.[11] Women's social status in the ancient Roman Empire was minimal; Helmut Koester describes them as excluded completely from public society.[12] In this male-centered context, Paul made the revolutionary argument that "there is neither Jew nor Gentile, neither slave nor free, nor is there male and female, for you are all one in Christ Jesus (Gal 3:28).[13] Paul respected women and trusted them. For example, Paul trusted Phoebe by delegating to her the task of sending a letter to Rome. Additionally, Paul complimented Priscilla's faith and deemed her a person who would sacrifice her own life for others (Rom 16:4). Junia is also described as having great influence in the Christian community. She was an apostle who had begun following Christ before Paul (Rom 16:7).

Furthermore, Paul not only had women join in central ministry within the church community, but he also gave them reasonable authority. John Walton et al. notes that Paul introduced Phoebe as a *diakonos* (διάκονος) of the church in Cenchrea, not a volunteer.[14] When Paul mentions his own co-workers (c.f. 1 Cor 3:5; Eph 3:7; Col 1:23), he uses the term *diakonos* (διάκονος) several times (Eph 6:21; Col 1:7, 4:7; 1 Tim 4:6).[15] Paul uses *diakonos* as a term referring to a servant of God rather than limiting the term to mean a specific position within the church.[16] In particular, Paul uses *diakonos* in its typical masculine form when referring to Phoebe. Although her role was not performed by women in general, the term denotes her as a leader or pastor of the church.[17] By implication, female leadership must have been recognized and accepted in the family of the first church, given that Phoebe was introduced to the Roman church as serving as the *diakonos* of the church in the Cenchrea.

Priscilla, who was also introduced as a co-worker of Paul's, was described as a leader independently in charge of missions, not as merely an assistant in mission endeavors, according to Frank Thielman.[18] In

Acts 18, Priscilla stayed with Paul in Corinth for a year and a half, and later preached the gospel with him, travelling with him until reaching Ephesus. What is noteworthy here is that Priscilla and Aquila even taught scripture to Apollos, a native of Alexandria (Acts 18:24–26). Priscilla was therefore in a teaching position of some authority.

Junia was also an outstanding leader. Thielman, again, argues that Junia was called "the apostle," although there is debate about this (Rom 16:7).[19] Among the ministers serving in the first church, there were many prophets and teachers. However, few people could be called apostles. It was impossible for a woman to be delegated as an apostle. Nevertheless, the reason why Junia might be called "the apostle" by Paul was because she was an influential leader.

Cell Groups in Yoido Full Gospel Church

Convinced by scriptural warrant, YFGC adopted the position that cell ministry needed to change from pastor-centered leadership to cell-leader-centered leadership. This section will explain how cell groups were created and now operate in YFGC, and how they relate to the growth of YFGC.

Origin of the Cell Group

YFGC cell groups originate from a season of hardship turned into opportunity. In 1964, when the number of YFGC members had reached about three thousand, it became difficult for Cho to lead the church alone. Due to the influx of saints, Cho could not take a day off, and physical and mental fatigue accumulated. One day, Cho collapsed at the pulpit. From 1964 to 1965, he had to spend most of his time in bed due to health problems.[20] During this time, Cho's pride was revealed to him through God's word: "Blessings will come only through himself, whom God specifically uses."[21] Just as Peter still tried to live by his own zeal and power even after he received Jesus as his savior, Cho found that he had been acting like Peter before God. He realized that "ministry is the work of God, not an individual's work."[22]

In particular, Exodus 18:18 made Cho realize the need for cell ministry.[23] Cho discussed this pericope, of Moses and Jethro, with another pastor, his mother-in-law, Ja-shil Choi. The next week, Cho conveyed to all the deacons his intention to create a cell ministry.

However, the cell ministry faced difficulties from the beginning, especially because Cho tried to establish a woman as the head of the cell system.[24] The male saints refused to accept women as leaders, as a matter of tradition. In Korean society at that time, when Confucian culture was prevalent, most social institutions and communities relied on male leadership. The church was no different. It was not easy for Cho to decide how to proceed because establishing female cell leaders and delegating the authority of ministry to them might cause division within the church.[25] However, there was no other alternative because male saints had no time for cell leader responsibilities, like home visitation, due to their jobs.

Cho prayed for God's will in solving this issue. While meditating on the words of Romans 16, he discovered that the hidden workers in the Roman church were women: Phoebe, to whom Paul delegated authority to care for the church, and women such as Priscilla and Mary, Tryphena, and Tryphosa, who were mentioned as Paul's co-workers in Christ.[26] In the end, the voice of God was the decisive factor in Cho's establishing a female layperson as the leader of a cell group:

> God asked Pastor Cho who he was born from. God then asked, "Who remained and watched until the end when I was crucified, who came to pour oil on my body when I was in the grave, and who witnessed the resurrection for the first time?" Pastor Cho realized that Jesus was served by loyal women while he was fulfilling his ministry in the world.[27]

Obeying God's words, despite people's concerns and opposition, Cho selected, trained, and appointed twenty female cell leaders to teach the Bible to the saints, to pray with them, and to go out and preach the gospel with them to reach their neighbors. This is how the cell group began to be the growth engine of YFGC.

Operation of Cell Groups

In the early days, the operation of the YFGC cell group was not smooth. Systematic education and role allocation for lay leaders were not properly carried out.[28] Female cell leaders had not yet had the opportunity to systematically study the Bible and theological doctrine. They had to study Bible passages alone, which they would then teach in their cell group, resulting in frequent mistakes. Some cell leaders did not understand the doctrine of the Trinity, for example, so they taught that

Jesus and the Holy Spirit were gods below God. Some even taught that people could not be saved without speaking in tongues.[29] As a result, there was confusion in the church.

Cho realized the need for comprehensive education for all cell leaders. He convened a meeting for the entire group of cell leaders and handed out a script that contained what cell leaders would teach the saints at their meeting. Cho also taught in detail how to guide cell worship.[30] Furthermore, he had other cell members share roles and responsibilities in cell meetings. For example, if one person served as presider in cell worship, the other served as preacher.[31] Cell meetings became more systematic over time.

YFGC's typical cell meeting consists largely of four things: worship, Bible study, fellowship, and evangelism. Cell meetings progress in a sequence of preaching or teaching by the cell leader after meditation, the Apostles' Creed, praise, and joint prayer. After finishing with the Lord's Prayer, they have fellowship. Bible study consists of a seven-step curriculum that focuses on the fivefold gospel, four-dimensional spirituality, triple blessing, and absolute positivity. After studying the Bible, cell members share their prayer requests and testimonies. Then, they pray for unbelievers. The cell leader is required to follow a certain timeframe. If the cell meeting is meant to last for an hour, cell leaders can spend twenty minutes on prayer and Bible study and then spend the rest of the time praying for individual problems and for unbelievers. This allocation shows how much they value prayer for individual problems and for unbelievers.

Evangelism practices vary within the cell system. Being in a large district motivates groups to evangelize through an evangelism seminar. Large districts encourage attending a prayer meeting for the fullness of the Holy Spirit and for evangelism every month. In addition, cell groups invite unbelievers by regularly holding street missions and joint family worship.[32] Small districts also practice street missions. For example, every week small district groups conduct street missions near parking areas or subway stations, and hold a customized evangelism event to reach pregnant women and children. Various events such as a special prayer meeting, missionary prayer meeting, lost souls outreach, rice cake or fish-shaped-bun-sharing ministry, and Bible-reading outreach ministry are increasing the participation rate of cell members.[33]

Currently, YFGC has a research institute, the International Theological Institute, that independently produces and edits educational textbooks for cell groups. The International Theological Institute publishes textbooks for cell worship, including study guides and materials for Bible school, Bible college, and Bible graduate school. Study guides for cell worship in particular, also called one-to-two discipleship training, consist not only of scripture, but also Christian doctrine and ethics, and the full gospel faith (fivefold gospel, threefold blessing, sevenfold faith of full gospel, four-dimensional spirituality, absolute positivity, and so on). The cell leader uses these textbooks to teach cell members. Through this systematic and diverse operation method, a cell group is activated, and the church experiences revival and growth.

Cell Groups and Church Growth

In his book on successful home groups, Cho compares cell groups to cell tissues:

> Everything exists through cell tissue and grows through cell division. The church is not a dead organization. The church is the body of Jesus Christ, and the Holy Spirit is alive and moving in it. . . what are the cells as Christ's body. It cannot be said too often that it is [the] cell group.[34]

Indeed, YFGC cell groups continue to divide and expand like biological cells. When there are more than twelve members in a cell, it is separated to form a new cell, and when the cell is revived, a new cell is created again from that cell. In that way, the cell system, which started with twenty groups, had expanded to 126 cells two years later in 1967. After the construction of the Yoido Full Gospel Church building in 1973, YFGC's cell groups became more active, expanding to 394 cells in 1973; 542 cells in 1975; 1,604 cells in 1976; 4,818 cells in 1978; and 6,351 cells in 1979.[35] The cell groups led the growth of the church, and in 1979, YFGC finally achieved a hundred thousand saints.

YFGC, which continued its remarkable growth[36] into the 1980s and 1990s, tried to change the cell system according to the times. In December 1999, YFGC carried out the central district system to improve the church. The main purpose of the central district system is to manage and operate by combining two or three existing small districts into a single district to increase the efficiency of the ministry.[37] On January 3, 2001,

Cho emphasized that the cell system should be reorganized to cultivate evangelical workers at the Wednesday service, and from April to June of that year, all leaders underwent ten weeks of training for the new cell system. The leaders were educated in ecclesiology, discipleship, small group leadership development, leader qualifications, and vision casting for cell group growth. Currently, YFGC holds monthly seminars for cell leaders to train them in cell member management and cell meeting facilitation. On April 18, 2001, there was a ceremony of appointment for cell leaders. At that time, a total of 14,118 cell leaders were established from various generations for men, women, youth, and children.[38] As a result of these efforts, in 2008, YFGC grew into the world's largest church with 780,000 saints. YFGC's growth surprised the world beyond Korea and became a credible example to support Cho's argument that "the secret of church growth is the family cell group."[39]

In 2008, under the leadership of Reverend Younghoon Lee, who was appointed as the second pastor, YFGC named satellite churches that were to become independent churches. Twenty independent churches separated from the main church the following year, along with 330,000 saints. As a result, the number of YFGC saints decreased from 780,000 to 450,000.[40] Due to these changes, the district composition of YFGC was reorganized resulting in changes to the cell system itself.[41] For instance, a district for thirty- and forty-year-olds was newly established, and a revived small district was elevated to a large district.[42] In addition, in 2009, YFGC began to produce and broadcast "video cell worship." This practice expanded to other districts. The video cell worship was available through the YFGC website and app. Through these changes and innovations, YFGC grew to 560,000 in 2018.[43]

In 2020, YFGC's "one-to-two training system" was introduced as a method of revitalizing the cell system for expansion. The system consists of one cell leader and two cell members, but up to five people can attend depending on the number of people being evangelized. If the number increases to six, a new leader will be established to lead another two cell members. Cell groups continue to be divided in this way.[44]

YFGC's system for building a successful cell ministry was not only reproduced in other churches in Korea, but also spread to many churches abroad. YFGC is also preparing for the revival of the next generation by establishing more cell leaders through the program.

YFGC Female Cell Leaders

One of the great advantages of the cell ministry is that trained lay workers can use their God-given gifts effectively to lead efficiently. The YFGC cell system was a place of ministry for lay workers—particularly female cell leaders.

Background of YFGC Female Cell Leadership

Missionaries entered Chosun, now Korea, to preach the gospel at a time when most of the country followed Confucian culture and values and there was much discrimination against women, which limited women's role in society. These missionaries tried to use education and Christian evangelical propagation activities to eliminate false customs and ideas that led to gender discrimination. Mary Scranton, for example, was a female teacher from North Methodist Church in the United States, who began teaching women at her home in Jeongdong, Seoul, in 1886. This marked the founding of *Ewha Hakdang* (school), Korea's first modern women's educational institution.[45] Since then, many Christian schools, Bible academies, and women's missionary societies have been established for women. New educational efforts to guarantee women's rights, break patriarchism, and advocate for Chosun women's human rights also helped produce many female ministers. Even after they received professional education, early female ministers in the Korean church faced discrimination and were prohibited from preaching or teaching male saints due to the patriarchal culture that was prevalent in Korean society at that time. However, they continued to undauntedly preach the gospel.

The reason why the Pentecostal church in particular was able to be revived was because of the influence, hard work, and dedication of Korean female ministers, such as Mary Rumsey, who first introduced the Pentecostal faith to South Korea after she experienced the Holy Spirit at a revival rally on Azusa Street; Meon Jeong, who was called the mother of Pentecostal faith in North Chungcheong Province in South Korea and who helped plant Imok Full Gospel Church, Cheongju Full Gospel Church, and Joongang Full Gospel Church;[46] Gui-im Park, who helped spread the Pentecostal faith and planted churches such as the Christian Sooncheon Pentecostal Church during the early history of the Assemblies of God in South Korea. These female ministers directly or indirectly influenced YFGC's female leadership.

One woman in particular, Ja-shil Choi, led the Korean Holy Spirit movement through fasting, prayer, speaking in tongues, and divine healing and played a significant role in the origin and development of YFGC. Her childhood had been dark. She had tried to commit suicide after experiencing her mother's illness and father's death. However, God opened her eyes to the gospel after she heard a sermon by Sungbong Lee. Although, at first, her faith was not solid and she even struggled with doubt due to personal circumstances and difficulties, after thirty years, she experienced the baptism of the Holy Spirit and was given the gifts of divine healing, speaking in tongues, and prophecy. There were numerous testimonies of her healing gift, including of her healing a seven-year-old paralytic patient, an elderly woman who was called a small shaman, and a woman who had evil spirits.[47] Moreover, Choi showed that the role of women can be extended to having a significant influence on society, beyond family, by leading large domestic and international conferences.

YFGC's female cell leadership was greatly influenced by Choi. Her charismatic ministry was so powerful that she could have chosen to be in independent ministry. However, just as Barnabas put Paul at the forefront of his ministry, she handed over the leadership of the ministry to Cho at YFGC. She then devoted herself to establishing female cell leaders at YFGC, supporting Cho's vision. Since the days of tent churches, Choi had conducted street missions with other female saints to preach the gospel after Sunday worship. The women's evangelism ministry was established in 1959. With Choi, this organization actively participated in home visitations and funerals as well as street evangelism. After 1965, the women's evangelism ministry joined the prison ministry. Since 1975, they have been preparing bread and wine for the Lord's Supper.[48] Choi's influence was evident in the training of female cell leaders. She knew better than anyone else the importance of prayer in ministry. Since 1962, YFGC has held regular weekly prayer meetings, praying for Cho's ministry every Saturday afternoon and praying for female evangelical executives and for lost sheep every Tuesday. In 1970, when there were problems with the construction of the Yoido sanctuary, the women's evangelism ministry started a daily all-night prayer meeting. After the construction was completed, the daily all-night prayer meeting developed into a prayer meeting for the country and the people, for churches and pastors, for the filling of the Holy Spirit, and for individuals and families. Once, an article reported in a newspaper that Japanese men had come over and corrupted Korean female college students.[49] Choi, angered, held a prayer meeting with exhorters and female evangelical executives, weeping and crying bitterly.[50] She was a mother of prayer and a model of female leadership in YFGC for how to serve in the church, including in evangelism, service, and relief. In honor of Choi's fasting prayers and divine healing ministry, the Osanri Choi Ja-shil Memorial Fasting Prayer Mountain, established in 1973, is still visited by countless Christians from all over the world who want to experience God's grace and miracles.

Activities of YFGC Female Cell Leaders

YFGC's female cell leaders are armed with Pentecostal spirituality and work more passionately than anyone else in ministry, including in worship, prayer, evangelism, and service. Currently, the activities of YFGC female cell leaders are very diverse, and their roles can be largely organized into five categories.

First, female cell leaders excel in giving nurturing words for the spiritual growth of cell members. Words are spiritual bread, and the faith of the saints grows through words. However, it is not enough to listen to the Word of God declared by the pastor at the pulpit. The saints share the Word of God in cell meetings and talk about how to apply it in their lives. Female cell leaders encourage cell members to share the Word of God and talk about the application of the Word, explaining to them what they don't yet understand.

Second, female cell leaders lovingly take care of cell members. From the beginning, YFGC considered care ministry to be very important within the cell system. One group shared a testimony about how cell members, under the leadership of the cell leader, actively helped a member whose house had been flooded and who had nowhere to go. One opened their home to the saint, who had suffered much loss in the deluge. Another brought food and clothing. Others brought medicine and money. In addition, all the cell members fixed the damage caused by the flood.[51] Through such caring ministry, cell members formed a family relationship, and it became a solid community of love.

Third, female cell leaders consult and pray for cell members. Cell leaders maintain intimate relationships with cell members through meeting frequently and they know their members' situations better than anyone else. Therefore, cell members are able to open their hearts more comfortably to cell leaders. Cell leaders can be joyful and yet still cry together with their members, considering their cell members to be their family. Female cell leaders can perform better as counselors because they can easily understand the problems and pains that only women face. As a result, YFGC has a very high proportion of female saints.

Fourth, female cell leaders lead their cell members to evangelize. God wants to send his people out to fish for lost people. The cell system is like the net that fishermen use, as it is relatively more accessible to unbelievers than churches.[52] When the net is thrown into the world, new believers come to church. Just as a dense net can catch many fish, when the cell system is systematic and the relationships of cell members are strong, it leads to more souls coming to the Lord and settling into a church. Female cell leaders are like missionaries who use all their effort in the service of the gospel. They set an example for others and evangelize with passion. They also try to revive the cell system while encouraging cell members to participate in evangelism.[53]

Lastly, female cell leaders serve as a channel for communication.[54] As the church grows, it is not easy for pastors alone to understand or attend to the personal situations of numerous saints, or to convey their pastoral policies to all the people in the church. Female cell leaders serve as a pathway between pastors and saints, almost like nerve tissue. Just as the brain receives messages from nerve tissue throughout the body, cell leaders inform the district pastor of their cell members' personal life problems and prayer requests as well as their spiritual status. Cell leaders also convey pastoral guidelines or church information down to cell members. These activities by female cell leaders greatly help the pastor to understand and lead the saints in their district.

Characteristics of YFGC Female Cell Leadership

There are four main characteristics of female cell leadership at YFGC. First, female cell leadership at YFGC is transmitted through apprenticeship. As mentioned earlier, one difficulty that appeared in the early years of cell ministry was the need for cell leadership training. Accordingly, YFGC holds a special seminar for cell leaders twice a year, in spring and autumn, and all cell leaders must attend and be educated. Although it is important to be educated in these seminars, practical teaching is also disseminated through a one-to-one process, or apprenticeship training. In Mark 3:14, the reason why Jesus called his disciples was for them to be with him. The disciples who were with Jesus watched and learned everything Jesus did. They were able to naturally learn Jesus' ministry. The same goes for female cell leaders. Newer cell leaders spend a lot of time with experienced cell leaders, who teach them how to raise cell members in the Word of God, how to serve them with love, and how to pray for them. This method, which is in line with the Pentecostal tradition of emphasizing experiential faith, greatly contributed to the growth of YFGC female cell leaders as faithful workers of the full gospel.

Second, YFGC female cell leadership is a leadership based on vision. A clear goal articulates a ministry's direction. Therefore, leaders must set specific goals for the community and then have that goal at heart and dream of it being achieved. Cho had emphasized that cell leaders have to dream when they become established in the cell system.

> Let's embrace a dream that each of leaders grows your cell and produces another one before the end of the year. Nurture this dream in your heart in the morning and evening prayers, and it will be before my eyes tomorrow. The Holy Spirit comes only to those who have dreams and works with them.[55]

At YFGC, female cell leaders practice the four-dimensional spirituality of Cho and the faith of absolute positivity of Younghoon Lee. That is why they experience the grace of God by faith.

Third, female cell leaders at YFGC function as spiritual mothers. In her book on women's leadership, Hye-sung Jeon describes women's character as being considerate of others placing importance on the process rather than the result, and making sure everyone develops and grows together.[56] In this respect, female cell leaders possess excellent empathy and inclusivity based on the motherly nature of most women. This is a big advantage over male leadership. Female cell leaders embrace and care for cell members with maternal affection. For example, one of our women's leaders went up the prayer mountain with[57] cell member even though the leader was pregnant. Another distributed snacks to children wandering on the street and preached the gospel to them. Female cell leaders often devote themselves to ministry day and night for the poor. Finally, YFGC female cell leaders are armed with the fullness of the Holy Spirit and a passion for evangelism. The female cell leaders attend almost all public services (dawn service, Wednesday service, Friday service, Sunday services) and cry out day and night. They believe that they cannot fulfill the mission as cell leaders unless they were full of the Holy Spirit manifests as a passion for evangelism. Whenever women cell leaders pass by their neighbors' houses, they pray for them, even giving up time meant for sleep for the sake of evangelism. One female leader did laundry to evangelize a neighbor and went to church carrying another woman's child on her own back because the child's mother was sick. Another's leaders' passion for evangelism was so great that a humorous saying was coined: "First of all, if you are appointed out as a target of evangelism by a female cell leader, there are only two ways [out]: One is that you must leave [this] world. The other is that you must attend YFGC."[58] At YFGC, cell leaders are given red bags as gifts when they are appointed. These bags have become a symbol representing YFGC female cell leaders, so much so that their hard work and dedication to the ministry is called "the Miracle of the Red Bag." Their enthusiasm for ministry is so great that it has been said to be even stronger than most pastors.

It is no exaggeration to say that the passion of female cell leaders for the fullness of the Holy Spirit and evangelism made YFGC what it is today. This is a confession of faith from one of them:

> I am constantly working hard to spread the gospel and share with others the 'God of healing and grace' that I have encountered. Last year, I received the first prize for evangelism from the Yangcheon Archdiocese. However, I have never thought of evangelism as a special mission. I just worked hard because I thought that, as a Christian, I should naturally obey the Lord. My wish is to establish a family of faith and devote myself to the Lord for generations. I also want to establish one hundred churches for the Lord. That is why I am preaching the living God without rest even today.[59]

Influence of YFGC Female Cell Leadership

At the time that the first female cell leaders were established in YFGC, it seemed impossible for a woman, who was generally in charge of housework, to become a leader in church and Korean society. There was prejudice against, and negative views of, female leaders both from inside and outside the church. However, female cell leaders devoted themselves to their mission with confidence. When they first began serving as cell leaders, no one expected them to survive for decades. However, up until the present, YFGC female cell leaders have been actively serving and contributing to the movement of the Holy Spirit and church growth throughout Korea.

Reproduction of the History of the Pentecostal Holy Spirit Movement

H. Vinson Synan, a world-renowned Pentecostal theologian, mentions that the reason why the Pentecostal movement has expanded worldwide from the twentieth century to the present is because of the baptism of the Holy Spirit, speaking in tongues, and divine healing. In the Pentecostal Holy Spirit movement, believers want to experience the power of the Holy Spirit as those in the first church did—speaking in tongues, miracles, and divine healing. Within the YFGC cell system, the power of the Holy Spirit is experienced frequently. For example, one testimony tells of a saint who came to the church through the evangelism of a female district leader, and there experienced the baptism of the Holy Spirit and speaking in tongues:

> In November 2016, I wanted to receive the gift of speaking in tongues. I prayed, "Lord, give me the gift of speaking in tongues. I would like to have a close relationship with you through speaking in tongues." I sought it. When I shared in cell group that I desired the gift of speaking in tongues, my cell leader prayed for me, sharing how she received it. I prayed for an hour every morning and evening. After two days, I prayed again and suddenly received the gift of tongues. Since then, prayer time has been fun.[60]

In another testimony, a leader at YFGC was diagnosed with end-stage ovarian cancer. It was hard for her to maintain her quality of life because cancer had spread to her organs. However, cell members prayed for her with all their heart. As a result, she was healed completely. She testified to the following:

> The reason why I, who had no chance of living, was able to come to church is because of the constant prayer of district and cell members. . . . I have a new life. Thanks be to the Lord our God who gave [me] a new life. I will cheer up again and work hard to evangelize. Give glory to our God.[61]

There are many testimonies of those who have been healed, have experienced the Holy Spirit, and have been blessed under the leadership of female cell leaders. Consider one more testimony:

> As I was working hard as a female cell leader, God gave me a blessing. When I first believed in Jesus, I was so poor that I had no food, and no money for transportation. I lived in tears. But God gave me blessings in health and

finances. Many people say, "After you believed in Jesus, you succeeded." Now I preach all the time the gospel that our God is good. I declare that our Father is [in] control [over] our life and death.[62]

Female leaders who have directly experienced the power of the Holy Spirit have devoted themselves more to cell ministry and preached the gospel more diligently. These practical testimonies show that the Spirit-empowered movement is being reproduced in this world through YFGC cell systems and female cell leadership.

Improvement of Female's Social Status in Korea

Looking back on Korean history, women's rights were very poor just a century ago. A patriarchal social structure based on Confucianism limited the roles and activities of women. Women were educated differently from men, and it was commonly argued that women did not need to be educated. The role of women was limited to helping their husbands and doing housework well. Expressions such as "Sam-Jong-Ji-Do," "Yeo-Pil-Jong-Bu," "Chil-Geo-Ji-Ak," and "Nae-Wei-Bub" represent the situation of women well.[63] Women who were subordinated to the male authority of the household had no freedom of choice. They lived a passive life. Women's ideas and talents were ignored completely. Even by the time Korean society began to develop on the wave of modernization after liberation, women were still far behind men in having educational access. For example, although by 1966, 90 percent of men and women were enrolled in elementary school, the middle school enrollment rate for women was only 33 percent, and the high school enrollment rate was only 19.6 percent. This indicates that women's access to educational and social activities in society were very limited at the time.[64] Under these circumstances, activities for women in church changed the lives of Korean women and had a profound impact on the improvement of women's status at home and in society.

YFGC female cell leaders specifically contributed to the improvement of the status of women in Korea. YFGC women cell leaders re-established their identities by leading cell systems. They realized that they could play a primary role in the family and society as independent beings. The experience of devotion to, and love for, cell members became a driving force in the lives of female leaders and gave them confidence. The following is one testimony to that fact:

> I married into a thoroughly Confucian family. I was the eldest daughter-in-law of the twelfth generation. . . . There was always pressure in my mind as the eldest daughter-in-law of the twelfth generation. I had to live by caring [for my] brothers-in-law, including my cousin's brother-in-law. It was not easy for me to live and care for the family as the eldest daughter-in-law of the twelfth generation, including my whole family. One day, I went to my acquaintance's house in Yoido due [to an errand for my husband]. She led me to YFGC accidentally. I listened to the preaching and began to go to church. Since then, my life has changed 180 degrees. I have devoted myself to evangelism and delivering Christ's love to others. I have confidence as a woman through my various experiences in church.[65]

One of the slogans that YFGC members often shout is: "We can make it! All things are possible! Let's do it!" Confidence based on the belief in absolute positivity has influenced the life of female cell leaders.

The Bible discourages discrimination between men and women. When God created men and women, God did not create men to be over women, but rather created each to complement and cooperate with each other. Women created in God's image also have value and dignity equal to men. It has been said that YFGC spearheaded the true biblical value of womanhood in Korean society before other conservative churches. The bold acceptance and full support of female cell leaders at YFGC has helped change people's perspective on women in Korean society.[66]

Conclusion

Future-thinking scholars mention that an unprecedented period of change—an era of a new normal—is approaching. They predict that existing methods will no longer work in the twenty-first century and that new methods will be formed to change the world. Looking back at the history of the church, the organization of church, and its method of ministry, we can see that they have changed according to the demands and needs of the times—and must continue to change. Otherwise, the church risks being eliminated.

In this era of change, the church should pay attention to female leadership.[67] Currently, a leadership style that reflects feminine values such as being relationship-oriented and valuing democratic participation is an alternative that society should consider for the future. Kim explains that the reason why female leadership draws attention today is that "there is a growing demand for more participatory and democratic leadership, along with pointing out that traditional and vertical leadership does not efficiently cope with changes in social consciousness, organizational changes, and industrial changes."[68] Today, female leadership is needed, and with it, women's characteristic inclusiveness, grace, and nurturing that is unlike traditional male leadership. Female leaders characteristically show sacrifice and loving service for others, which can be a dwelling place for God's love through his Spirit. In this era of extreme individualization, this will be a suitable alternative and a way for churches to build healthy communities.

The good news is that Christianity is a religion of renewal and reform. In the 1960s, to establish a lay woman as a leader of cell group was innovative in light of the social norms and perceptions, but it then became a driving force in building the YFGC of today. More than sixty years have passed since then, and many women's rights have been restored in our lives today. However, unfortunately, it is still difficult to find female leadership in certain places. Senior leadership of the church, for example, is often still occupied by men. The church should remember "the fact that women are the majority members of Christianity in the world," as Helen Kim argues, and take innovative steps again.

In 2023, YFGC realized the need for female leadership and established forty-seven female pastors. As a result, YFGC drew worldwide attention. It will continue to be innovative in the future, giving female pastors and saints the same authority without discriminating against men, and hiring more female leaders for key positions in the church. Furthermore, YFGC will conduct more in-depth research on the role of women in the church in order to create an environment where women can maximize their capabilities. We hope that the history of the Holy Spirit, poured into people without any discrimination, will be full of testimonies from all nations as predicted by the prophet Joel:

> And afterward, I will pour out my Spirit on all people. Your sons and daughters will prophesy, your old men will dream dreams, your young men will see visions. Even on my servants, both men and women, I will pour out my Spirit in those days (Joel 2:28–29).

Notes

1 Jin-seon Kim, 오순절의 불꽃이 된 여인들 [*Women Who Became a Flame of Pentecost*] (Seoul: Qumran, 2022), 107.

2 "개인화 시대 소그룹 문화가 건강하게 교회 성장 이끈다" [In the age of individualism, small group culture leads to healthy church growth], *Koshin News*, June 9, 2023, https://www.kosinnews.com/news/articleView.html?idxno=28424.

3 Yonggi Cho, *Desiring Ministry 45 Years* (Seoul: ICG, 2004), cited in a letter of recommendation.

4 Jeong-myung Son, *Pastor Yonggi Cho's Theology and Ministry that Catholic Theologian Has Seen* (Seoul: Dong-Yeon, 2022), 287, 222–225.

5 Carl George, *Prepare Your Church for the Future* (Grand Rapids: Revell, 1992), 23.

6 Hyun-cheul Oh, "Small Group as Community Moving Forward with Christ's Life," *Bible and Theology* 65 (2013): 10; Yonggi Cho, 성공적 구역 [*Successful Cell Groups*] (Seoul: Seoul Logos, 1978), 34–35.

7 Darrell L. Bock, *Acts*, Baker Exegetical Commentary on the New Testament (Grand Rapids: Baker, 2007), 34; Cho, *Successful Cell Groups*, 34.

8 Han-ok Kim, "Reality and Alternative of Small Group in Korean Church," *Theology and Practice* 12 (2007): 10; Cho, *Desiring Ministry 45 Years*, 76.

9 Yonggi Cho, *The Story of My Church Growth* (Seoul: Seoul Logos, 2006), 123.

10 International Theology Institute, *A Minister of Yoido* (Seoul: Seoul Logos, 2008), 402–405; Cho, *Successful Cell Groups*, 34; Cho, *Desiring Ministry 45 Years*, 74–76.

11 Ji-cheul Kim, "Paul and Female Mission Co-workers," *Korea Presbyterian Journal of Theology* 13 (1997): 29.

12 Helmut Koester, *Introduction to the New Testament: History, Culture, and Religion of the Hellenistic Age* 1 (New York/Berlin: Walter De Gruyter, 1995), 62–64.

13 Unless otherwise noted, all scripture references are from the New International Version (NIV).

14 John H. Walton, Victor H. Matthews, Mark W. Chavalas, and Craig S. Keener, *The IVP Bible Background Commentary*, trans. Korea IVP (Downers Grove: IVP, 2010), 1722–3; Frank S. Thielman, *Romans*, Exegetical Commentary on the New Testament, trans. Hwa-Ryoung Han (Grand Rapids: Zondervan, 2008), 744–5. Συνίστημι δὲ ὑμῖν Φοίβην τὴν

ἀδελφὴν ἡμῶν οὖσαν ‹καὶ› διάκονον τῆς ἐκκλησίας τῆς ἐν Κεγχρεαῖς (Romans 16:1).

15 Thielman, *Romans*, 744–745.

16 Thielman, *Romans*, 745.

17 Thielman, *Romans*, 745.

18 Thielman, *Romans*, 745.

19 Thielman, *Romans*, 753–754.

20 Young-hoon Lee, 희망의 목회자(영산 조용기 목사 평전) [*A Pastor of Hope: A Critical Biography of Youngsan Yong-gi Cho*] (Seoul: Seoul Logos, 2022), 121.

21 Lee, *A Pastor of Hope*, 118.

22 Lee, *A Pastor of Hope*, 121.

23 Lee, *A Pastor of Hope*, 121; International Theological Institute, *A Minister of Yoido*, 402–409; Yoido Full Gospel Church 50 Years History Compilation Committee, *Yoido Full Gospel Church 50 Years History* (Seoul: Seoul Logos, 2008), 95–98.

24 As described in International Theological Institute, *A Minister of Yoido*, 406–409.

25 Lee, *A Pastor of Hope*, 126.

26 Lee, *A Pastor of Hope*, 126; International Theological Institute, *A Minister of Yoido*, 407.

27 Lee, *A Pastor of Hope*, 126.

28 In the early days, Pastor Cho realized that there were two problems in cell group operation: (1) care without education, (2) evangelism without education.

29 Lee, *A Pastor of Hope*, 128.

30 Lee, *A Pastor of Hope*, 129.

31 Yoido Full Gospel Church 50 Years History Compilation Committee, *Yoido Full Gospel Church 50 Years History*, 97; See Sung-guk Kim, Gi-bok Peak, and Youn Choi, *CEO조용기* [*CEO Yonggi Cho*] (Seoul: CGI, 2006), 174–177.

32 "대교구별 전도 및 정착을 위한 노력" [Striving for Large District Evangelism], *The Full Gospel Family Newspaper*, April 14, 2013, http://www2.fgnews. co.kr/html/2013/0414/13041411312317110000.htm.

33 Yoido Full Gospel Church 60 Years History Compilation Committee, *Yoido Full Gospel Church 60 Years History* (Seoul: Seoul Logos, 2018), 294–295.

34 Cho, *Successful Cell Groups*, 16.

35 Yoido Full Gospel Church, *Yoido Full Gospel Church 50 Years History*, 431

36 Yoido Full Gospel Church, *Yoido Full Gospel Church 50 Years History*, 431

37 Yoido Full Gospel Church, Yoido *Full Gospel Church 50 Years History*, 231.

38 Yoido Full Gospel Church, *Yoido Full Gospel Church 50 Years History*, 281.

39 Cho, *Desiring Ministry 45 Years*, preface.

40 Yoido Full Gospel Church 60 Years History Compilation Committee, *Yoido Full Gospel Church 60 Years History*, 177.

41 Yoido Full Gospel Church, *Yoido Full Gospel Church 60 Years History*, 180–184.

42 Yoido Full Gospel Church, *Yoido Full Gospel Church 60 Years History*, 184.

43 Yoido Full Gospel Church, *Yoido Full Gospel Church 60 Years History*, 206.

44 "구역활성화 위해 '일대이 양육 리더 교육' 실시" [One-to-Two Leader Training Education to Revitalize Cell], *The Full Gospel Family Newspaper.* February 9, 2020, http://www.fgnews.co.kr/front/view.do?first_category_id=4&second_category_id=23&id=107024.

45 Young-Kyu Park, 한국기독교회사 1 [*History of the Korean Church* 1] (Seoul: Lifebook, 2008), 369.

46 Kim, *Women Who Became a Flame*, 214.

47 Choi and Cho laid the foundation for the current Yoido Full Gospel Church. Choi was called "Hallelujah Lady." It is a nickname she got from people because she would always greet them, saying, "Hallelujah," with a bright smile.

48 Lee, *A Pastor of Hope*, 135–136.

49 Kim, *Women who Became a Flame of Pentecost*, 260.

50 Ja-shil Choi, 나는 할렐루야 아줌마였다 [*I was Hallelujah Lady*] (Seoul: Seoul Logos, 1988), 424.

51 Cho, *The Story of My Church Growth*, 131–134.

52 Younghoon Lee, *Faithful Worker* (Seoul: CGI, 2012), 19.

53 "지구역의 역사와 중요성" [History and Importance of District and Cell], *The Full Gospel Family Newspaper*, April 13, 2007, http://www2.fgnews.co.kr/html/2007/0413/07041320410817110000.htm.

54 Lee, *Faithful Worker*, 20.

55 Cho, *Successful Cell Groups*, 59.

56 Hye-sung Jeon, 여자 야망 사전 [Women's Authentic Leadership] (Seoul: JoongAng Books, 2007), 48.

57 "세상의 중심에 여성이 있다" [There are Women in the Center of World], *The Full Gospel Family Newspaper*, March 7, 2008,http://www.fgnews.co.kr/front/view.do?first_category_id=3&second_category_id=252&id=122777.

58 Church Growth Institute, *The Power of Growth of YFGC* (Seoul: CGI, 2008), 146–147.

59 "조현순 집사(양천대교구) – '때를 얻든 못 얻든 쉼 없이 전도해요'" [Deacon Hyunsoon Cho (Yangcheon district): I Keep Going to Preach to Gospel Regardless of Circumstance], *The Full Gospel Family Newspaper*, May 27, 2012, http://www.fgnews.co.kr/front/view.do?first_category_id=7&second_category_id=42&id=91965.

60 "도인순 집사(종로중구대교구) – 고난의 길을 지나 축복의 땅으로 (Deacon In-sun Do (Jongno district): Through the Path of Hardship, into the Land of Blessing)," *The Full Gospel Family Newspaper*, September 16, 2018, http://www2.fgnews.co.kr/html/2018/0916/18091609202519110000.htm.

61 "김옥란 권사(강서대교구)—난소암 말기와 전이....절망 속에 새생명 얻어" [Exhorter Ok-ran Kim (Gangseo district): The End of Ovarian Cancer but New Life], *The Full Gospel Family Newspaper*, November 24, 2019, http://fgnews.co.kr/front/view.do?first_category_id=7&second_category_id=42&id=106523.

62 Cho, *Successful Cell Groups*, 125.

63 Sam-Jong-Ji-Do (三從之道) is that there are three ways for women to follow: (1) obey your father at a young age, (2) obey your husband, and (3) follow your son after your husband dies. Yeo-Pil-Jong-Bu (女必從夫) means that a wife must follow her husband. Chil-Geo-Ji-Ak (七去之惡) means seven reasons for expelling a wife: (1) disobeying her parents-in-law, (2) failing to give birth to a child, (3) committing obscene acts, (4) being jealous, (5) having a bad illness, (6) being talkative, and (7) stealing. Nae-Wei-Bub (內外法) is a precautionary method for men and women to avoid facing each other.

64 Encyclopedia of Korean Culture, "Women's Education," https://encykorea.aks.ac.kr/Article/E0036367.

65 "어윤희 권사: 내 인생을 바꾼 예수님 사랑" [Exhorter Youn-hee Uh: Christ's Love that Changed My Life], *The Full Gospel Family Newspaper*. November 4, 2018, http://old.fgnews.co.kr/U_pdf/2018110404.pdf.

66 International Theological Institute, *Sanctification of Christian in the Ministry of the Holy Spirit* (Seoul: ITI, 1997), 161.

67 Kim, *Women Who Became a Flame of Pentecost*, 107.

68 Kim, *Women Who Became a Flame of Pentecost*, 103.

13 Spirit-Empowered Evangelists and Divine Healing: A Korean Pentecostal Perspective

Jun Kim

Abstract

This chapter examines the inherent link between healing evangelism and church growth, specifically through the lens of three illustrious Korean healing evangelists: Ikdu Kim, Seongbong Lee, and Yonggi Cho. The research provides a detailed examination of the theological evolution experienced by these three Spirit-empowered evangelists. Importantly, this investigation aims to comprehend the distinct contextual factors that have collectively shaped their respective healing theologies. The interaction of these elements not only shifts our focus to the prevailing contextual challenges but also paves the way for potential future trajectories in the healing movement. All these insights serve the grand aim of magnifying the efficacy of evangelistic efforts.

Introduction

Global evangelism faces significant challenges today, with the growth rate of Christianity slowing in recent decades despite broader outreach efforts. While more people than ever before have access to the gospel, conversion rates—particularly in Asia—remain low. This trend calls for a reexamination of evangelistic strategies that can effectively address the evolving cultural, spiritual, and socio-economic landscape.

This study explores how Spirit-empowered healing evangelism can serve as a response to emerging missiological, worldview, religious, and theological challenges. By examining the ministries of Ikdu Kim, Seongbong Lee, and Yonggi Cho, it investigates how healing evangelism has contributed to substantial church growth in Korea and what insights can be drawn for contemporary evangelistic efforts. The aim is to highlight how healing, when theologically grounded and contextually sensitive, can remain a vital and transformative force for church growth in Asia and beyond.

A Korean Healing Movement and Church Growth

The contributions of several Korean healing evangelists call for comprehensive study, with particular emphasis on the works of Ikdu Kim (1874–1950), Seongbong Lee (1900–1965), and Yonggi Cho (1936–2021) since their theological development has formed a representative Korean healing movement. Within the sphere of the Korean church, Kim rose to prominence as an instrumental figure, devoting his life to healing ministries and spearheading an indigenous Korean healing movement. Lee, standing as a bridge between Kim and Cho, developed a healing theology through interaction with Western theology and maintained the vitality of the healing movement during two critical junctures in Korean history: the Japanese colonization and the Korean War. Later, under Cho's leadership, the healing movement evolved further as he refined the healing theology, systematized its principles, and championed its global acceptance.

The healing ministries of these three individuals spanned over a century, from 1900 to 2008, in the following chronological order: Kim (1900–1940), Lee (1940–1960), Cho (1960–2008). Their theological progress has become emblematic of the Korean healing movement, as clear theological continuity can be traced amongst them. Lee was a disciple of Kim,[1] and Cho's mother-in-law, Ja-shil Choi, received spiritual guidance from Lee. As Cho and Choi embarked on their joint ministries, their theological viewpoints evolved reciprocally. While Cho primarily focused on preaching, Choi initially devoted more effort to healing ministries.

Understanding the contextual factors that influenced the development of the healing movement led by Kim, Lee, and Cho necessitates the examination of three key aspects: shamanism, Japanese colonization, and the Korean War. Korean Christians were originally drawn to the healing narratives in scripture, which resonated with their deeply ingrained "belief systems," as Julie C. Ma describes them.[2] The practice of healing and exorcism within Korean churches was not a product of Western missionary influence[3] but instead stemmed from deeply rooted religious traditions. It is often observed that shamanism was a major religious context that partially influenced the spiritual worldview of the three healing practitioners.

Moreover, the political and economic conditions accompanying the healing movement brought forth the concept of holistic healing. This approach addressed not only physical afflictions but also emotional turmoil, as Korean society wrestled with *han*—a concept defined as "an accumulation of suppressed" and "condensed experiences of oppression."[4]

The healing evangelism carried out by Kim, Lee, and Cho was a natural response to the unique socio-political-economic-religious contexts faced by the Korean church. Their healing ministries demonstrated effectiveness not in only spreading the gospel but also in motivating converts to become Spirit-empowered evangelists. Missionary Harry A. Rhodes recounted the revival sparked by Kim, stating:

> Nevertheless, the whole New Era Movement which began in our Korean Presbyterian Church more than a year before had not produced any appreciable results in and around Seoul until Reverend Mr. Kim launched his meetings. From that time on the whole aspect of our evangelistic work has changed.... As a result of these meetings, the number of church members has continued to increase.... Many families with only one church-going member now joined the church all together, and there were many backsliders who received new strength. Church members were inspired to evangelize, and each Sunday they would go out in large groups to evangelize.[5]

Intriguingly, when Kim's healing ministry catalyzed considerable church growth through individual and familial conversions, it posed a challenge to the traditional modus operandi of Protestant evangelism. As Kim's evangelistic success was credited to his Spirit-empowered evangelism, Cho similarly asserted, "It was divine healing that turned many toward God"[6] and precipitated group conversions, as illustrated in his account:

> In the morning I got word that the young man had run out of the house and began to tell all of the neighbours what had happened. All of the Buddhists and other non-Christians in the town knew the situation, and they were amazed at the power of God. Since then most of the people in that part of town have been saved because of the healing power of God.[7]

It is significant to acknowledge that the role of healing as a catalyst for substantial church growth is corroborated by the experiences of these three Spirit-empowered evangelists. This is particularly noticeable when considering that Cho's healing ministry was instrumental in building his church into the largest congregation globally.

Emerging Challenges and the Breakthrough of Healing

Missiological Challenges in Asia

The critical need for strengthening evangelistic activities in Asia is glaringly apparent when reflecting on Asia's status as the continent least influenced by Christianity. As of 2020, a slim 8.2 percent of its population identified as Christian. This figure is dwarfed by the representation of 49.3 percent in Africa, 92.1 percent in Latin America, and 65.1 percent in Oceania.

Paradoxically, despite the urgent demand for evangelistic endeavors in Asia, only a minor fraction of worldwide missionaries are currently committed to Asian missions: a mere 14.3 percent. This allocation is rather surprising, particularly when compared to the 22.8 percent and 24 percent of missionaries assigned to Africa and Latin America respectively.[8] The fact that the least evangelized yet most densely populated region is receiving minimal support from global churches is deeply concerning.

However, the focus of evangelism in Asia should hinge on the quality of the efforts rather than the volume. Historical data indicate that the success of Asian missions is not primarily dependent on the sheer number of missionaries deployed. For instance, between 1900 and 1970, while 43.1 percent of global missionaries were situated in Asia compared to 14.1 percent in Africa, Asian churches only gained 73,792,000 new followers by 1970. In contrast, African churches increased by 130,383,000 new members.[9] Intriguingly, the growth in African churches was nearly twice that of Asian churches, despite having only a third of the number of missionaries.

Year	KAG[10]	YFGC[11]	Percentage[12]
1958	3,684	5	0.13%
1964	4,261	2,000	46.93%
1970	17,172	8,252	48.05%
1980	199,916	132,940[13]	66.49%
2001	1,225,512	752,401	61.39%
2003	1,192,514	788,441	66.11%

Table 1. Population Comparison between KAG and the YFGC

Further statistical analysis reinforces this point. Despite evangelism reaching 60.1 percent of the Asian population by 2020, Christians in Asia only made up 8.2 percent of the population. This implies that, for every one hundred individuals who had the opportunity to hear the gospel, only roughly fourteen would choose to remain Christian or to convert to Christianity due to evangelistic efforts in Asia. This conversion rate substantially lags behind the sixty-four out of one hundred individuals in Africa who would likely respond positively to evangelism.

These figures imply that success in evangelistic work isn't secured merely by increasing its scale in Asia. While the data could suggest that Asia presents a significant challenge as a mission field, it could also support the argument for revising in the methodologies of evangelism in Asia and adopting a more effective approach.

Despite the comparatively slow growth of the Christian population in Asia, the region's Spirit-empowered churches have displayed exceptional evangelistic effectiveness. From 1970 to 2015, in East and Southeast Asia, Pentecostal-Charismatics emerged as the fastest-growing group with a 6.1 percent growth rate. This group expanded twentyfold, while Evangelicals grew elevenfold.[14]

This trend is validated by the rapid growth observed among Korean classical Pentecostals, with Yonggi Cho being the most notable example. His first church, typically referred to as Daejodong Cheonmak Gyohoe, or the tent church in the Daejo area of Seoul, started with only five members (Cho, Choi,[15] and Choi's three children) in an old American service tent on May 18, 1958. As mentioned above, the tent church experienced swift growth due to several significant healing events.[16]

Table 1 reveals steady growth in the Korean Assemblies of God (KAG) membership, which aligns with the expansion of Cho's church. Since 1964, when Yoido Full Gospel Church (YFGC) accounted for nearly half of the denomination's population, its growth has significantly influenced the KAG's demographics. Remarkably, despite entering the arena of Korean Christianity relatively late, the KAG has ascended to become one of the three major denominations in Korea alongside the Presbyterian and Methodist churches within just four decades.[17] Consequently, it's understandable that KAG attributes much of its progress over its fifty-year history to Cho, placing his contribution on par with that of the early Korean Pentecostal missionaries.[18]

The particular religious and economic contexts of Asia are generally understood to have catalyzed church growth. This is especially noticeable when Pentecostal-Charismatic groups employed potent evangelistic strategies, emphasizing elements such as "supernatural healing, miracles, deliverance and the promise of divine assistance."[19]

Worldview Challenges

The Spirit-empowered movement's rapid growth in Asia is often linked to its spiritual practices, which resonate deeply with the religious sensitivities of the region.[20] The movement has been especially appealing to those who are socially marginalized or economically disadvantaged.[21] However, a critical question arises in the present rapidly changing context: can Asian Pentecostals and Charismatics still carry out effective evangelism through healing, especially while the economy grows, the political persecution subdues, and the deeply rooted religious belief system gets overshadowed by agnosticism or atheism?

Mary Ho has raised a relevant precaution for Asian Christians, as she observes the escalating trends of secularism, materialism, and the pursuit of wealth. She warns that these phenomena may become potential barriers to the growth of the church, as follows:

> While persecution fuels spiritual fervour, materialism breeds a new faith that wealth can solve all problems. In the context of Asia's economic growth, prosperity theology which claims to guarantee divine provision, health and well-being has gained popularity, validating the accumulation of wealth in capitalist economies. In many cities wealthy churches encourage Christian business networking. Nevertheless, the focus on wealth breeds secularism.[22]

Ho suggests that this thriving economy might eventually nurture a generation of atheists and agnostics.[23]

However, around 1970, the religious landscape experienced a significant shift with the advent of postmodernism.[24] It brought forth a worldview that sees humans and the world as integrated and recognizes spiritual needs as vital.[25] The dilemma, therefore, lies in the coexistence of two contrasting worldviews: religious postmodernism and non-religious secularism.[26] Crafting an effective evangelistic strategy that bridges these disparate perspectives poses a formidable challenge.

The challenge becomes even more complex when we consider the diversity of Asia, as noted:

> Asia is a region of clashing extremes, where polar forces hang in fragile tension. It houses some of the fastest-growing economies but is home to two-thirds of the world's poor. It hosts the world's most populous atheistic state but also vast numbers of Buddhists, Muslims and Christians.[27]

The ever-evolving socio-political, religious, and economic landscape may contribute to the slower progress of evangelism in Asia compared to other continents. This might stem from the ongoing struggle of Evangelicals to present an unchanging gospel in a continuously "fluctuating cultural setting."[28] In this context, some may question the efficacy of Pentecostal-Charismatic evangelism in Asia's booming economy. The critical query is whether the message of health and wealth blessings will still resonate with individuals who have risen above poverty and are less prone to illness due to economic and medical advancements.

John Wimber's healing ministry offers a thought-provoking perspective on this issue. Wimber identified the Western worldview of secularism, materialism, rationalism, and nominalism as the primary impediments to his healing ministry when he started his Spirit-empowered evangelism.[29] However, his ministry saw extraordinary growth when he pivoted his evangelistic approach to power evangelism, leveraging signs and wonders as demonstrations of the kingdom of God. It's worth noting that Wimber's evangelistic ministry had already achieved significant success before incorporating power evangelism. As an Evangelical pastor, he had guided many individuals toward Jesus. "By 1970, he was presiding over 11 Bible studies, attended by over 500 individuals! His efficacy as an evangelical pastor resulted in him being requested to helm the Charles E. Fuller Institute of Evangelism and Church Growth."[30] Yet, it took him about fifteen years to undergo a paradigm shift in 1977, recognizing the importance of spiritual gifts in promoting effective evangelism on another level. Upon launching his healing ministry, the church experienced extraordinary growth: "About 120,000 people call about 500 Vineyard churches home throughout the United States."[31]

In this light, the rising threat of secularism and rationalism to Christianity could be counteracted by the supernatural manifestation of divine healing. It's vital to understand that spiritual empowerment as a witnessing tool isn't merely a characteristic of Pentecostal-Charismatic churches but a universal principle and divine intervention that transcends contextual barriers. In this respect, Wimber's claim rings true: "Power evangelism is not excluded from any culture. We have seen that it can flourish in Western societies with the same results that occurred in the first century or that are reported from Africa, South and Central America, and Asia today."[32] It could be suggested that the spiritual gift of healing is universally effective, applicable to all individuals across different contexts. Thus, Spirit-empowered evangelism is still believed to remain relevant and effective in Asian regions.

Religious Challenges

There has been some skepticism towards healing evangelism, with critics drawing parallels to shamanistic rituals such as exorcism and *anchal*,[33] a prayer for the sick. However, despite these apparent similarities, Christian healing incorporates its own unique cultural and religious contexts. For instance, Ikdu Kim's healing movement within the nascent Korean church was perceived as closely intertwined with spiritual warfare,[34] where illnesses and adversities were often regarded as punishments from malevolent spirits.[35] Within this context, Myeong-seob Heo contends that healing and exorcism are defining traits of the early Korean church.[36] It is believed that there was a discernible necessity for healing the sick through exorcism in the mission fields of Korea, particularly during its nascent period.[37] In this regard, healing tended to focus on individual sins that might cause the sickness.

With shamanism serving as a prevalent religious backdrop, Seongbong Lee emphasized healing as a form of spiritual warfare. He attributed most illnesses to evil spirits acting through sin. This perspective was formalized when Lee founded a healing ministry named "Immanuel Commando" following the Korean Army's reclaiming of Seoul on September 28, 1950.[38] This ministry was particularly notable for its adoption of military terminology, a strategy Lee had not employed prior to the Korean War. In the inaugural report of Immanuel Commando, Lee extended the use of military metaphors: "array" for gatherings, "veteran" for the lead pastor, "soldiers" for church members, and "rearmament" for spiritual renewal. He viewed his revival ministry as a "hand-to-hand fight" against the "large force of Satan."[39] In this framework, Lee's interpretation of healing extends beyond individual experiences; it is a pivotal element in the salvific battle between Christians and Satan, with illness cast as a weapon utilized by the spiritual adversary. Lee's conception of spiritual warfare therefore ties in with a broader process of soul winning.

Lee's perspective on spiritual warfare is also echoed by Yonggi Cho, who argues:

> Our struggle, by its very nature, is spiritual. We are obliged to curb the authority of the devil and propagate spiritual peace under the banner of Jesus Christ. Thus, our world is a crucible for the ongoing combat between the Holy Spirit and the devil.[40]

Cho's standpoint is unequivocal; our combat is spiritual, even amidst physical ailments.

The evolution of Korean healing theology is evident, transitioning from a belief system where sin leads to sickness, to a notion where sickness is employed by Satan as a tactic to impede the expansion of God's kingdom. However, even though this perspective facilitates understanding of the supernatural realm, it may precipitously lead individuals to infer that most sicknesses have a spiritual root cause. Hence, the Korean healing movement requires a more balanced perspective on the natural causes of illness and the suffering experienced by righteous individuals.

Additionally, the concept of healing as spiritual warfare should ground its theological foundation more firmly in Trinitarian theology, focusing on Jesus's grace, God's loving nature, and communion with the Holy Spirit. This approach is necessary to prevent healing evangelism from devolving into a fear-driven religious ritual that relies on human merit and potentially misuses power. Furthermore, while shamanism holds that healing is a blessing granted to devout worshippers, this belief should not be allowed to mutate into a theology of blessings that effectively nullifies the theology of the cross. In this context, the desire for the gift of spiritual discernment should be as fervent as the pursuit of the spiritual gifts of healing.

Theological Challenges

Healing, when viewed as a spiritual gift, typically leads to discussions that are predominantly pneumatological and ecclesiological. This is due to the prevailing belief that healing gifts are primarily intended for the edification of the church, as in 1 Corinthians 14:12. Yet, the field of healing theology still necessitates a soteriological evolution to fully appreciate its complexity.

From the very beginning, Kim embraced the idea, stating, "If such miracles [healing] were to happen today, would it not be a great testimony that would overthrow the foul thoughts of those who oppose the truth of the Bible?"[41] To Kim, divine healing was the most compelling evidence of God's existence, a surefire way to win over nonbelievers.

In contrast, Lee's healing theology is distinct from Kim's perspective. His understanding of healing originates from a theological tradition that identifies the redemptive works of Jesus as the primary source of healing.[42] Thus, healing is seen not just as an event within the church or a potent method for displaying God's power and love, but also as a central message of the gospel to disseminate.

Echoing these sentiments, Cho presents a theological progression from Lee's approach. He emphasizes the concept of holistic salvation, encompassing spiritual, physical, and material restoration. In Cho's understanding, healing becomes a critical aspect of soteriology. However, his concept of healing theology has expanded considerably to cater to diverse societal needs molded by ever-changing socio-political-economic contexts. Cho's approach encapsulates not only individual healing but also societal well-being, promoting the idea that personal salvation is inherently tied to the community. This outlook propelled him towards various social initiatives beginning in the early 1980s.[43]

But Cho's theological journey did not stop there. By 2005, it had evolved towards a concept of cosmic healing. For Cho, this was a pivotal moment, leading him to recognize a blind spot in his pastoral work just three years prior to his retirement:

> I recently began to realize some shortcomings of my forty-seven-year ministries. The Bible clearly says that for God so loved *the world* that he gave his one and only Son. It does not say that God gave his Son for God so loved *the man*.... My evangelistic ministries have been man-centered without including the world.[44]

This signified a substantial shift in theological paradigms, as the restoration of wholeness through the redemptive works of Jesus should envelop all areas impacted by sin and the Edenic Fall. Consequently, the beneficiaries of divine healing should extend beyond humanity to all creatures, as "the creation was subjected to futility" and "the whole creation has been groaning in travail together until now" (Rom 8:20–22).[45]

Despite the progression in theological understanding from Kim to Cho, there still exists a notable lack of eschatological perspective. It is both shocking and disheartening that numerous Spirit-empowered leaders have been implicated in various ethical scandals. These issues highlight an overemphasis on earthly life to the point of valuing it more than devotion to God and the promise of heavenly rewards. Healing theology, fundamentally rooted in the kingdom principle of *already but not yet*, should continuously remind us of this. As healing embodies God's kingdom power by liberating the sick, today's Christians should ardently aspire to and live for the eschatological healing that will ultimately usher us into perfect restoration.

A dispensationalist viewpoint presents an additional theological obstacle to church growth through healing. Despite the comprehensive debates between cessationists and continuists from the 1960s to the 1990s, disagreements persist.[46] Many Evangelical churches today generally accept sign gifts, refuting teachings on tongues yet remaining open to continuous revelation from God.[47]

The 1974 Lausanne Congress on World Evangelism, one of the most influential international Evangelical conventions, underscored the link between effective evangelism and the Holy Spirit. The conference, organized by renowned Evangelical leaders Billy Graham and John Stott, and attended by over 2,300 evangelical leaders from 150 countries, yielded a significant document known as the *Lausanne Covenant*. This document outlines "the necessity, responsibilities, and goals of spreading the gospel."[48] Notably, the essential role of Spirit-empowered evangelism is articulated within the document: "We believe in the power of the Holy Spirit. The Father sent his Spirit to bear witness to his Son; without his witness ours is futile."[49] It is further stated that "the whole Church becomes a fit instrument in His hands, that the whole Earth may hear His voice," only possible through spiritual *fruits* and *gifts*.[50]

Despite a consensus within Evangelical circles regarding the intrinsic connection between evangelism and spiritual gifts, a substantial faction of conservative Protestants maintains an anti-Pentecostal-Charismatic position. This stance has hindered the full potential of church growth and evangelism, despite the significant contributions from the Spirit-empowered movement towards global evangelism. The case of Ikdu Kim, the pioneering Korean healing practitioner, is illustrative. Kim's launch of his healing evangelism ignited theological debates due to differing interpretations between Korean Christians and Western missionaries.[51] Despite Kim's influential role as moderator of the Korean Presbyterian Church and the impact of his healing ministries post-1920, cessationist perspectives prevailed over indigenous beliefs in divine healing.[52]

Sadly, it has been more prevalent to impose imperialistic decisions on mission fields, rather than fostering indigenous theological development, by allowing local theologians and practitioners to develop their biblical interpretations on healing. Another example is the case of Yonggi Cho, who faced accusations by a dominant Korean Protestant Church starting from 1983 that he was propagating pseudo-Christianity. After thorough investigation, the church retracted their objection in 1994, acknowledging that "most of Cho's theology is based on the characteristics of World Pentecostal beliefs."[53]

It's worth noting that today's evangelical subculture remains predominantly rooted in the modernist worldview.[54] Materialism, challenging the existence of a supernatural realm, has still led many conservative Protestants to believe that miraculous healing isn't applicable in today's context,[55] a belief reinforced by their lack of personal experience with such healings. While this study does not aim to endorse Pentecostal-Charismatic beliefs, it strives to raise awareness of how Western perspectives have often been imposed on mission fields without adequate sensitivity to varying contextual factors. This tendency can impede growth, especially in the Global South. While this study is not designed to justify the theological foundation of healing evangelism either, it attempts to reemphasize the conclusive message of the Evangelical agreement of the *Lausanne Covenant*:

> Therefore, in the light of this our faith and our resolve, we enter into a solemn covenant with God and with each other, to pray, to plan and to work together for the evangelization of the whole world. We call upon others to join us. May

> God help us by his grace, and for his glory, to be faithful to this our covenant! Amen, Alleluia![56]

It is important to note that this preeminent Evangelical document, acting as a covenant with God and one another, establishes a deep ecclesiological foundation. Its fundamental message is that we need each other's diversity to spread the gospel in unity.

Conclusion

This research explores the efficacy of healing evangelism in Korea through the ministries of Ikdu Kim, Seongbong Lee, and Yonggi Cho. As a theological continuum emerged among these three figures, unique Korean contexts such as shamanism, Japanese colonization, and the Korean War significantly shaped the Korean healing movement. The adaptability of healing evangelism to these contexts spurred remarkable church growth. Under shamanism's influence, healing was viewed as a form of spiritual warfare, where individual sins were seen as leading to sickness, and where Satan used illness as a weapon to hinder God's kingdom expansion. This supernatural worldview aided the three healing evangelists in merging Western theology with local beliefs, crafting an indigenous healing movement as a potent tool for evangelism.

The concept of holistic healing, addressing both physical ailments and emotional distress, emerged from the hardship endured under Japanese rule and during the Korean War. The promise of hope through comprehensive healing became essential for the marginalized and impoverished. As people witnessed the Spirit-empowered ministries of healing, they became influential evangelists, contributing significantly to church growth.

Despite emerging challenges, healing evangelism remains a potent tool for evangelization, especially as the growth rate of the Christian population in Asia has slowed compared to other continents. As Asia needs a more impactful, high quality evangelistic approach, healing continues to play a pivotal role in gospel dissemination. Although the Asian Church may appear to be losing its momentum for growth—facing challenges from rising secularism, materialism, and rationalism leading to agnosticism and atheism, postmodern religious relativism, remnants of human-centric shamanistic beliefs, and dispensationalism—healing evangelism is believed to continue to resonate with diverse Asian groups. This is because it persistently adapts to societal changes through Spirit-empowered evangelism. However, it is crucial to employ healing evangelism judiciously to ensure it doesn't devolve into merely meeting people's needs or increasing the Christian population. Healing should be viewed as a holistic restoration of individual, communal, and cosmic wholeness, always reminding us of eschatological healing—the promise of perfect and everlasting restoration in *parousia*.

Notes

1 Seongho Lee, *Kim Ikdu Mogsa Seolgyo Mit Yakjeonjib* [The Sermons and Biography of Ikdu Kim] (Seoul: Hyemunsa, 1977), 175.

2 Julie C. Ma, "Miraculous Divine Activity and Religious Worldviews," Carl F. H. Henry Center at Trinity Evangelical Divinity School, January 3, 2020, https://henrycenter.tiu.edu/2020/01/miraculous-divine-activity-and-religious-worldviews/.

3 The group of Western missionaries here refers to those who were under the influence of fundamentalist Protestantism, especially conservative Calvinism. It should be noted that those from the Catholic, Anglican, or Orthodox traditions were not ardent supporters of the cessationists' view. However, it is an inevitable result that the Korean church in the beginning was greatly affected by the Presbyterian group in terms of dogmatic issues. This is because they were taking the lead as the largest Christian group in terms of Korean missions.

4 Dane J. Adams, *Christ and Culture in Asia* (Quezon City, Philippines: New Day, 2002), 97.

5 Harry A. Rhodes, "Some Results of the Kim Ik Tu Revival Meeting in Seoul," *Korea Mission Field* (May 1921), 113–114.

6 Yonggi Cho, *Spiritual Leadership for the New Millennium* (Seoul: International Theological Institute, 2002), 84.

7 Yonggi Cho, *More Than Numbers* (Waco: Word Books, 1984), 87–89.

8 Gina A. Zurlo and Todd M. Johnson, *World Christian Encyclopedia*, 3rd ed. (Edinburgh: Edinburgh University Press, 2019), 32.

9 Zurlo and Johnson, *World Christian Encyclopedia*, 8.

10 The numbers include the membership of the Yoido Full Gospel
   Church (YFGC). Jongdal Im, *Gidokgyo Daehan Hananimui Seonghoe
   Osibnyeonsa: Yeoksapyeon* [The 50-Year History of the Korea Assemblies
   of God:1953– 2004] (Seoul: Creation Publisher, 2005), 434.

11 Cho, *Widaehan Somyeong: Huimang Mokhoe 50 Nyeon*, 431.

12 This indicates the YFGC's percentage of the Assemblies of God population.

13 Kwang-il Kim, "Gidokgyo Chibyeong Hyeonsange Gwanhan
   Jeongsinuihakjeok Josa Yeongu," [A Psychiatric Study of the Phenomenon
   of Healing Practice in Christianity] in Korea Christian Academy,
   Hangukgyohoe Seonglyeongunddongui Hyeonsanggwa Gujo [Phenomenon
   and Structure of the Holy Spirit Movement in the Korean Church] (Seoul:
   Christian Academy, 1981), 299.

14 Francis D. Alvarez SJ and Todd M. Johnson, *Christianity in East and
   Southeast Asia* (Edinburgh: Edinburgh University Press, 2020), 500.

15 Cho first met Ja-shil Choi in Bible college. He helped Choi with her ministry
   after graduation, and they started their church together. Choi became Cho's
   mother-in-law in 1965.

16 The healings of Choi's oldest son suffering from acute pneumonia, a woman
   who had been paralyzed for seven years, a crippled beggar, and two deaf
   women were sensational enough to bring many non-believers to the church.
   See N. L. Kennedy, *Dream Your Way to Success* (Plainfield, NJ: Logos
   International, 1980), 166; Yonggi Cho, *Widaehan Somyeong: Huimang
   Mokhoe 50 Nyeon* [Great Call: 50 Years of Hope Ministry] (Seoul: Yoido
   Full Gospel Church, 2008), 74; 82–83; Yonggi Cho, *To God Be the Glory*
   (Seoul: n.s. 1973), 42.

17 Im, *Gidokgyo Daehan Hananimui Seonghoe Osibnyeonsa*, 376.

18 Cho, *Widaehan Somyeong: Huimang Mokhoe 50 Nyeon*, 270.

19 Mary Ho, "The Future of Christianity in East and Southeast Asia," in
   Christianity in East and Southeast Asia, eds. Kenneth R. Ross, Francis D.
   Alvarez SJ, and Todd M. Johnson (Edinburgh: Edinburgh University Press,
   2020), 481.

20 Septemmy E. Lakwa, "Mission and Evangelism," in *Christianity in East and
   Southeast Asia*, eds. Kenneth R. Ross, Francis D. Alvarez SJ, and Todd M.
   Johnson (Edinburgh: Edinburgh University Press, 2020), 405.

21 Julie Ma, "Pentecostals and Charismatics," in *Christianity in East and
   Southeast Asia*, eds. Kenneth R. Ross, Francis D. Alvarez SJ, and Todd M.
   Johnson (Edinburgh: Edinburgh University Press, 2020), 336.

22 Ho, "The Future of Christianity in East and Southeast Asia," 489–490.

23 Ho, "The Future of Christianity in East and Southeast Asia," 490.

24 Ed Stetzer, *Planting New Churches in a Postmodern Age* (Nashville: Broadman and Holman, 2004), 120.

25 Paul G. Hiebert, "Healing and the Kingdom," in *Wonders and the Word*, eds. James R. Coggins and Paul G. Hiebert (Winnipeg: Canada, Kindred, 1989), 117.

26 Robert E. Webber, *Ancient-Future Evangelism* (Grand Rapids: Baker Books, 2003), 56.

27 Webber, *Ancient-Future Evangelism*, 126

28 Stetzer, *Planting New Churches in a Postmodern Age*, 24

29 John Wimber, *Power Evangelism* (New York: Harper and Row, 1986), 70–72.

30 "History and Legacy," Vineyard USA, https://vineyardusa.org/about/history/.

31 Vineyard USA, https://vineyardusa.org.

32 Wimber, *Power Evangelism*, 45

33 *Anchal* refers to the practice of percussive therapy, involving the application of pressure using the palms of the hands-on areas of discomfort or illness within the body.

34 D. K. McKim, "Spiritual Warfare," in *Westminster Dictionary of Theological Terms* (Grand Rapids: Zondervan, 1996), 268. Spiritual warfare refers to a "New Testament theme expressed in images of combat and athletics to indicate the cosmic struggles of those in the Christian life against the powers of evil." Additionally, "Spiritual warfare is a multilevel conflict between good and evil initiated on the supernatural plane with the prehistoric rebellion of Lucifer and transferred onto the natural plane with the fall of man. Satan, man's adversary, continues to work to deceive and divert people from salvation in Jesus Christ, and to harass and hinder Christians through enticement to sin and exploitation of weaknesses." See Thomas. B. White, *The Believer's Guide to Spiritual Warfare* (Grand Rapids: Servant Publications, 1990), 23.

35 J. R. Moose, "What Do the Korean Worship?" *The Korea Mission Field* (May 1905): 88–90.

36 Myeong-seob Heo, "Chogi Haguk Gyohoeui Sinyu Ihae" [Understanding Healing in the Early Korean Church], *Seonggyeol Gyohoewa Sinhak* 11 [*The Holiness Church and Theology* 11] (Spring 2004), 163; see also Myeongsu Park, *Hanguk Gyohoe Buheungundong Yeongu* [A Study on the

Revival Movement in Korean Church] (Seoul: Institute of the History of Christianity in Korea, 2003), 67.

37 Heo, "Chogi Haguk Gyohoeui Sinyu Ihae," 147.

38 Seongbong Lee, *Malo Mothamyeon Jukeumeuro* [If You Cannot Preach in Words, Preach by Death] (Seoul: Word of Life Books, 1993), 112.

39 Lee, *Malo Mothamyeon Jukeumeuro*, 125.

40 Cho, *Spiritual Leadership*, 51.

41 Taek-kwon Im, *Joseon Yesugyohoe Ijeogmyeongjeung* [A Testament of Miracles in the Joseon Jesus Church] (Seoul: Christian Literature Society of Korea, 1921), 34.

42 This idea is well extracted from the theological frameworks of Lee and Cho. Divine healing is one of the core doctrines of the fourfold gospel for Lee and the fivefold gospel for Cho. See Lee, *Malo Mothamyeon Jukeumeuro*, 100; and Yonggi Cho, *Ojung Bokeum Iyagi* [The Story of the Fivefold Gospel] (Seoul: Seoul Logos, 1998).

43 Cho's practical efforts are manifest in his support for a range of causes, including heart surgeries, orphans, international refugees (including North Koreans), flood victims, impoverished local churches, foreign workers, the elderly living alone, the handicapped, Holt International Children's Services, blood donation drives, medical services for the impoverished, nature conservation, and the establishment of Elim Rehabilitation Centre and a heart hospital in North Korea. Post-retirement, in 2008, Cho devoted his life to assisting marginalized communities through the Sharing Love and Happiness Movement. See *Cho, Widaehan Somyeong: Huimang Mokhoe 50 Nyeon*, 181–191 and 284–291; Gwuisam Cho, *Youngsan Choyounggi Moksaui Gyohoe Seongjanghak* [The Church Growth of Rev. Yonggi Cho] (Gunpo, Korea: Hansei University Press, 2009), 34; Tai-Il Wang, "Dr. Yonggi Cho's Understanding of the Social Salvation," *Journal of Younsan Theology Supplement Series 1: The Spirituality of Fourth Dimension & Social Salvation*, ed. Mun-hong Choe (Seoul: Hansei University Press, 2012), 205.

44 Hyeong-geun Lim, *Cho Yonggi Moksa Ildaegi: Yeouidoui Moghoeja* [Biography of Rev. Yonggi Cho: The Minister of Yoido] (Seoul: Seoul Book, 2008), 563.

45 Unless otherwise noted, all scripture references are taken from the Revised Standard Version (RSV).

46 Timothy Lim, "Protestants," in *Christianity in East and Southeast Asia*, eds. Kenneth R. Ross, Francis D. Alvarez SJ, and Todd M. Johnson (Edinburgh: Edinburgh University Press, 2020), 296.

47 Lim, "Protestants," 296.

48 "Lausanne I: The International Congress on World Evangelization," Lausanne Movement, https://lausanne.org/gatherings/congress/lausanne-1974/, accessed September 12, 2024.

49 John Stott, "The Lausanne Covenant," Lausanne Movement, https://lausanne.org/content/covenant/lausanne-covenant#cov/, accessed September 12, 2024.

50 Stott, "The Lausanne Covenant," Lausanne Movement.

51 Gyeongbae Min, *Taehan Yesugyo Changnohoe Baeknyonnsa* [A Centennial History of the Presbyterian Church in Korea] (Seoul: General Assembly of the Presbyterian Church in Korea, 1984), 354.

52 Yonggyu Park, *Anak Sangol: Hanguk Gyohoe Buheung Mogsa Kim Ikdu Jeongi* [The Backwoods of Anag: The Biography of Korean Revivalist Rev. Ikdu Kim] (Seoul: Christian Sinmunsa, 1968), 90.

53 Cho, *Widaehan Somyeong: Huimang Mokhoe 50 Nyeon*, 158.

54 Stetzer, *Planting New Churches in a Postmodern Age*, 115.

55 See recent criticism on the Pentecostal-Charismatic movement in John F. MacArthur, *Strange Fire* (Nashville: Nelson Books, 2013).

56 Stott, "The Lausanne Covenant," The Lausanne Movement.

14 Spirit-Empowered Women in a Japanese Context: Lessons from Kyoko Funatsu's Life and Ministry

Yoriko Yabuki

Abstract

Reverend Kyoko Funatsu was one of the Pentecostal women of the Holy Spirit who impacted many lives through her ministry and leadership in Japan. She prioritized her personal prayer time and Bible study no matter how busy she was. She was humble but courageous for God's mission. Many lives were led to Christ to be saved, healed, and encouraged through Kyoko's preaching and pastoral care. Japan has its own cultural context impacted by Shintoism, Buddhism, and Confucian teachings, yet the Holy Spirit worked through Kyoko's life to glorify God in Japan. Pastors who got saved through Kyoko's ministry shared about her life-changing impact with honor and respect. John 15:7–8 says, "If you remain in me and my words remain in you, ask whatever you wish, and it will be done for you. This is to my Father's glory that you bear much fruit, showing yourselves to be my disciples." As this chapter introduces Kyoko's Spirit-empowered life, may each reader be challenged to seek the Holy Spirit, who can do a mighty work through their lives wherever they are. May our heavenly Father receive all the glory through each reader for the twenty-first century.

Introduction

The Japanese national flower is the *sakura*, or the cherry blossom. Japanese people love to have a picnic under the *sakura* tree to enjoy being in nature with their family and friends. Many foreigners visit Japan and spend money to see *sakura*. However, *sakura* bloom for only two weeks and then they are gone. The *sakura* tree itself does not die; it lives and stays dormant to prepare for the following year.

We can liken this to our lives and our calling. God has been preparing his vessels by allowing us to take time before public ministry and by using many trials and much pain to strengthen us until we can fully stand by faith and trust in God alone. Jesus, too, prepared for thirty years before he began his public ministry. Moses was prepared for eighty years. Joseph was prepared through others' jealousy, abuse, and maltreatment, years before becoming a national leader who influenced other countries through the pharaoh of Egypt.

Reverend Dr. Kyoko Funatsu gave her life to God to bring God's words to many in Japan. She listened to God's heart through her fervent prayers and served as a Pentecostal preacher and pastor for those who lived in Japan. God prepared her through great loss and trials before God would use her for his great work in Japan. Through her corroboration with the Holy Spirit, new churches were birthed. In this chapter, we will see how the Holy Spirit empowered this female Japanese pastor, who said yes to God even within the male-dominated culture of Japan. The story of Kyoko Funatsu shows several key spiritual principles from which we can learn.

This chapter first describes Kyoko's childhood and her family background. Then, it will introduce how Kyoko became a Christian, received God's call, and used her time at Central Bible College for future ministry. This chapter also introduces how Kyoko started a Spirit-empowered church and what were the outcomes of her evangelism in Japan. Finally, this chapter will point out the lessons we can learn from her attitude and actions in ministry and leadership.

Kyoko's Childhood and Her Family Background

Japan had a patriarchal culture throughout the Meiji era. The Japanese government gave voting rights only to the fathers in each family. His wives and children had to obey this human-given authority for major decisions. Both boys and girls could go to school, however, they had and were given different educational goals under Confucian culture. Only boys could go to college to work and lead society—girls went to the school to learn *Ryosai Kenbo* ("good wife, wise mother") to serve their future families. Once they were born in Japan, gender determined their future and role in their lives. In patriarchal culture, honor and respect is crucial for keeping the society in harmony.

Kyoko Funatsu (born "Yamaguchi") was born in Kagoshima prefecture on September 3, 1933. Her father served as a professor of advanced agriculture and forestry. He later served as a social education expert for the Ministry of Education of the Japanese government. Even in the midst of his busy schedule, he would take his first daughter, first son, and second son to different places to learn new things. Kyoko's father had a dream for his firstborn son not only to carry the Yamaguchi family into the future but also to become a good educator in Japan. His firstborn son, Kyoko's eldest brother, was admitted to Tokyo University to get a master's degree to become a professor.

Kyoko was the fourth child. She usually stayed at home with her younger brother and her mother. She didn't know much about her father, but her mother told her that Kyoko's personality was the most similar to her father's. Kyoko's family moved to Tokyo after Kagoshima. Their house was located in Nakameguro in Tokyo. Two ladies were hired to take care of the house. She grew up playing with her younger brother in a wealthy educated home in Tokyo, Japan. In such an environment, Kyoko was able to devote herself to reading and studying.

One day, however, she saw someone bringing a box to her family with deep sadness. At the age of eight, she could not understand what was happening in her family. She was told that her father had been killed in a train accident while he was in a taxi, although the taxi driver had never had an accident in his entire life and had been hired by the government. At the age of 48, Kyoko's father was returned to his home as only bones in a box!

The Yamaguchi family experienced great sadness. The government showed its respect and honor to Kyoko's late father and his family. Yet, according to Japanese patriarchal culture, the family's hope rested on the firstborn son. Kyoko's family anticipated that he would be successful like his father. But a few months before his graduation from Tokyo University, before he could earn his master's degree and begin work, he was struck with serious tuberculosis and passed away at a very young age.

After this, the family experienced a series of moves and life changes. Kyoko's older sister left home to get married to a man who lived in Hiroshima. Kyoko's second eldest brother was deployed to fight in World War II. Only her mother, Haru (meaning "spring" in Japanese), Kyoko, and her younger brother remained. Kyoko's mother was mentally ill and she could not make decisions about things. She even sold their house for some sweet potatoes to live on. She began to depend on Kyoko to live.

When Kyoko was a young teenager, in the midst of all those tragedies in the Yamaguchi family, she dreamt of becoming an English teacher or businesswoman. While she was a high school student, she took a YMCA night class to learn English. She devoted herself to learning English for her future career. After graduating, she applied to work at a military base as an English typist. They noted Kyoko's good English skills and her willingness to work, so they hired her. Soon, she was transferred to the medical department to work as a typist, handling all the official documents. She loved working there and using her English skills as a business professional.

One day, one of the American ladies who worked at the American base invited Kyoko to a church in Yokohama. Kyoko had never heard about church or Christianity, but she was interested in going with her American coworker.

At the Shinohara Church, Pastor Tomino Ito welcomed Kyoko warmly. Ito had lost her husband, who had been the lead pastor for the Shinohara Church, while he was deployed by the government. According to her daughter, Mikami, her father's last words to his wife were, "Please take care of the church." He knew he would not be coming back to his church, nor to his family. Ito became a widow and a single mother of four children. She trusted God financially and served his church as she had promised her husband.

Kyoko began to hear the gospel from Ito, as well as from her son, Reverend Akiei Ito, who later became a long-serving general superintendent of the Japan Assemblies of God (AG). Kyoko confessed her sins before God, accepted Jesus Christ as her Lord and Savior, and experienced clear conversion. She shared her faith with her mother as well as her younger brother, her only family members.

Kyoko wanted to receive the baptism of the Holy Spirit with speaking in tongues. But whenever the church had a time of prayer, others received the Spirit-baptism—but not Kyoko. She kept seeking the power of God for over a year. After months of waiting, she began to think that she would no longer believe in the baptism of the Holy Spirit if she did not receive it the next time she prayed. Then, as she was yelling to God in prayer, she suddenly began to speak in tongues and to experience the power of the Holy Spirit. Her Christian life was changed. From then on, she read her Bible more and understood it better. She kept praying in the Spirit.

One day, when she was on a train, she saw all black around her and heard the voice of the Holy Spirit say, *"Kenshin shiro. Kenshin shiro,"* which means,

"Surrender all for God. Surrender all for God." She could not carry the burden from God by herself, so she shared her experience with her pastor, Tomino Ito. She told her that God was calling her to go to Central Bible College to be equipped to preach the gospel as a pastor, saying, "I would rather train you only than have a big church."[1] These words meant that Ito knew that even by disciplining only Kyoko, through Kyoko dedicating herself to serving God, God would bring many lives into his kingdom.

Kyoko had a good salary from her job at the military base and a fulfilled life, but she gave these all to God and decided in faith to go to the Central Bible College in Tokyo. When Kyoko shared her decision with her mother, her mother blessed Kyoko's decision to go to the Bible school so Kyoko would influence many lives someday, as her husband had.[2]

Kyoko's Preparation for God's Call at the Bible School

The Japan AG was established in 1949 with the help of missionaries of the U.S. Assemblies of God. They appointed Reverend Kiyoma Yumiyama as the first general superintendent. Central Bible College (CBC) was established in the following year, 1950, as a Japan AG training school for pastors. Rev. Yumiyama was appointed as the first general superintendent of Japan AG and later became a principal of the CBC.

Kyoko enrolled in Central Bible College in Tokyo in 1953 with fifteen other students. According to Koichi Kitano (a future principal of Central Bible School), who was one year senior to Kyoko, nine of the sixteen new students were female, and as a result, the ratio of male to female students at Central Bible Seminary had changed. Kitano realized that not only their numbers, but also their unique personalities and rich gifts began to dominate the school. Kitano called Kyoko *"joketsu,"* which means a woman who has a firm temperament, excellent wisdom, and who is rich in executive ability.

Kitano said Kyoko was usually the first person to go into the prayer room and pray in the Spirit with a loud, clear voice, from five in the morning. He didn't want to be behind this CBC freshman, so he took a Bible and *zabuton* (a Japanese cushion) and began to wake up earlier to go to the prayer room to pray. Gradually, the prayer room became filled with Bible college students, who were all filled with the Holy Spirit, praying loudly in the morning, which even received complaints from the neighbors.

One day, when the principal, Yumiyama, asked the students to share their future mission and vision, Kyoko immediately raised her hand and said, "I want to preach at the Hansen Isolation Sanatorium." The CBC students were silent for a moment. Although Yumiyama himself had already been doing door-to-door evangelism at tuberculosis sanatoriums, he was shocked to have to preach to patients with this disease, which was the most feared disease at the time because of its high infection rate and its aftereffects.

When Kitano returned to CBC in 1992 after being overseas, students were regularly visiting the Hansen's disease sanatorium. Kitano said that Kyoko must have been the one who initiated this.[3]

While at CBC, Kyoko decided to give one-tenth of her day to God. She prayed for two hours and forty minutes a day and had deep communion with the Holy Spirit. Her voice of prayer and passion for mission work later led to the founding of Kanazawa Christ Church in Kanazawa, Yokohama, which became one of the leading churches in the Japan AG, according to Kitano. He believed Kyoko's Spirit-empowered life was the reason why many pastors had a heart for church planting in different parts of Japan.[4]

One day, in Kyoko's sophomore year, Yumiyama told Kyoko to go to Kanazawa Ward, Yokohama City, and preach the gospel for the birth of a new church. Kyoko went with other students and, using a drum, got the attention of the people in the street, preaching the gospel in a loud voice. Though she was a Japanese woman in her early twenties, the Holy Spirit opened people's hearts one by one. When Kyoko graduated from the CBC, she was appointed as a licensed Japan AG pastor for this new church, Kanazawa Christ Church.

Kyoko's Church Planting in Yokohama

Church-Planting with Her Mother

Kyoko had devoted her life to praying, preaching, evangelizing, and serving as a pastor at Kanazawa Christ Church in Yokohama as a single female pastor appointed by the Japan AG. Her mother, Haru Yamaguchi, served the Lord actively as the first dedicated staff for this church. She was the first principal of the church Sunday school. Yamaguchi taught Bible stories to kindergarteners weekly. She really loved children. She prayed for Kyoko and joined her in her evangelism. When Kyoko was sick and weak after serving in the ministry, Yamaguchi decided to live at the church with her and cooked her meals, cleaned the church, and cut the grass. She wrote letters to people asking them to come to church, recorded church meetings, decorated the sanctuary with flowers, made posters, helped church finance, and supported Kyoko's ministry wholeheartedly. People who came to church called Yamaguchi "mother" because Yamaguchi loved the church people as she loved her own daughter, Kyoko. Yamaguchi always encouraged Kyoko with words of affirmation, saying, "Your preaching today was wonderful. My faith is strengthened by your message more than any other preachers!" Kyoko understood how much she was encouraged by Yamaguchi's encouraging spirit. Yamaguchi's father was the president of a well-known company, and he once came to visit his daughter and granddaughter. Yamaguchi told Kyoko that she could not believe that Kyoko, such a wonderful woman of God, was "born from my womb."[5]

Kyoko and Yamaguchi served God together, serving the people who came to the Kanazawa Christ Church during its first ten years. After Kyoko got married and had three children, Yamaguchi was able to see her three grandchildren before she went to heaven in 1977.

Kyoko's Spiritual Grandmother Influence

Beginning on July 2, 1958, tent meetings were held for a week at Kanazawa Christ Church. Kyoko was twenty-five or twenty-six years old at the time and was an eloquent and passionate preacher who spoke the word of God. Kiyoshi Kubota, a student of Kanto Gakuin University, came to a meeting for the first time and, after, was invited to come back to the church. "There will be a Yakiniku party next week, so please come again," he was told, so Kubota attended the Sunday service the following week. That day, Kubota decided to become a believer; he was baptized on November 17. Kubota described the church service at that time:

> About thirty people attended the service, and the small, one-story wooden church was filled to capacity. However, it is said that there was a meeting filled with the Holy Spirit. Young people came to the church one after another and had faith, and both the pastor and the members were praying fervently. Their prayers could be heard from the road dozens of meters away, and they were always full of energy. The church conducted roadside evangelism every week, and its members were passionate about evangelism.[6]

Under Kyoko's guidance, Kubota decided to dedicate his life to God and entered CBC as the first student from Kanazawa Christ Church. After his studies and training at the CBC, upon graduating, he started pioneering evangelism in Sugita Ward in Yokohama. He established a new church and became the pastor.

It was through Kubota's evangelism that Kiyoshi Tsuchiya was saved. Tsuchiya would later go to the CBC in Tokyo to become a Spirit-empowered pastor in the Nigata prefecture as well as serve as general superintendent for the Japan AG for several years. Kyoko didn't know that someday she would become a spiritual grandmother of her Assemblies of God Fellowship through her Spirit-empowered local evangelistic meeting. God's plan and vision was greater than anyone's plan. Spirit-empowered ministry leads to a greater future for greater influence.

Kubota said, even after his time at Kanazawa Christ Church, young people were saved and went to the CBC, but they carried Kyoko's evangelistic spirit with them wherever they were sent for church planting in Japan. At the time, Kubota shared, the Japan AG had a long history of gender discrimination. Female pastors were not allowed to become ordained ministers, so when someone would be baptized in water, female pastors had to invite male ordained pastors to perform the water baptism. However, in later years, female pastors were produced one after another and were then recognized as ordained ministers. Says Kubota, it can be said that Kyoko also played a role in raising the status of female pastors.[7]

Through Kubota's pastoring and evangelism, Etsuko Nogawa got saved and received God's call. Nogawa went to the CBC and became a female minister. She not only became a female pastor for Kohnan Zion Church as a church planter, but was also elected CBC teacher to teach about pastoring as a woman in leadership. She also showed excellent leadership leading the female pastors' network of the Japan AG. Kyoko didn't know that she would also become a grandmother who influenced many through Kubota's obedience to God.

In 1958, the same year Kubota came to Kanazawa Christ Church, Masae Kakizaki visited the Kanazawa Christ Church for the first time. She was only sixteen years old, a sophomore in high school. She had attended the Misaka Catholic Church as well as the Baptist Kanto University Chapel before, but she saw a difference when she went to this Pentecostal church where Kyoko was leading. Kakizaki shares that Kyoko was only twenty-six years old, but her preaching was like a fire that captured Kakizaki's mind and heart.[8] She began to join the Sunday service weekly, and the Saturday youth group. She began to realize Jesus Christ and God's greatness as her personal savior. At the time, she didn't realize what made Kyoko's preaching so passionate and powerful that it touched her heart; she later learned that it was the power of the Holy Spirit.

Kakizaki saw eight other young men and women give their lives for God because they realized God's calling in their individual lives. They were sent by Kanazawa Christ Church to the CBC in Tokyo and became Japan AG-credentialed ministers, sent to plant churches, impact more people's lives, and birth more leaders in God's kingdom.

Kakizaki was one of the eight of God's called in this youth group. When God called her, she shared with her parents her decision to go to Bible school. Her parents were not Christians. They went to Kyoko's place with anger and criticism, yet Kyoko listened to them patiently. Kakizaki told her parents she would not go to Bible college just to stop their arguments, so her parents calmed down. However, she could not change her decision to follow Jesus. She eventually left home for Jesus, went to the Bible college, and became an evangelist.

Kakizaki is now eighty-three years old, but she does not regret her decision. She is so honored to have been used by God as an evangelist throughout her entire life. She wants to give all the glory and praise to God's wonderful name.

Kakizaki not only gave her life for God, but also raised her children for Jesus. Her son, Koichi, which means "light first," is currently leading a Yokosuka Church as a lead pastor. He began after Kakizaki's husband passed away. Koichi and his wife have been raising four children who all love the Lord; they are serving the Lord as one family. He was even elected to serve as the South-West Kanto district superintendent from 2018 to 2020 to lead churches, saying, "Let us go back to the Pentecostal!"

Kyoko's Influence on the Next Generation of Spirit-Empowered Ministers

In 1961, an outdoor service was held at Kanazawa Christ Church at the Yokohama Sankeien Garden. Ms. A,[9] who participated in the event, was a high school student at the time. Through Kyoko's sermon, Ms. A learned about how Jesus Christ became the savior of humankind. Ms. A learned about worship and the significance of obeying the Bible, living a life of prayer, and evangelizing others. One day, when Ms. A went to church, Kyoko told her that, even though Ms. A had lost her parents when she was in third grade and had been raised by her grandmother and uncle, Jesus had never abandoned her. Kyoko sang a hymn for Ms. A and made her feel God's love. Through the prayer, Ms. A was led to experience salvation. Ms. A later experienced the baptism of the Holy Spirit with speaking in tongues. She became a Sunday school assistant under Kyoko's guidance. Ms. A gave her life for God and went to the CBC. Occasionally, Kyoko would give Ms. A advice and guide her on the path she should take. Although the advice was not easy for her—and could even be strict—Ms. A said she was glad to follow the advice because it was always a God-centered, not human-centered idea.[10] At that time, Ms. A said there was a tendency within the church to give priority to men, but Kyoko's presence brought hope and self-reliance to other women in the teaching profession.

Here is another story of a female high school student who was ministered to by the Holy Spirit through Kyoko's ministry. Her name is Kiyoko Osaka. She moved from Tokyo to Yokohama due to her father's work and had a difficult time at her new high school. When she received her first grade, she felt her value as a person being measured based on that. She felt life was hopeless. Noticing the heaviness Osaka was carrying, Ms. A, who was sitting in front of Osaka's desk in the classroom, told Osaka that she had recently become a Christian and asked if Osaka wanted to go to church with her. Osaka remembered her experience at Sunday school when she was little at the church in Tokyo. She had wonderful memories of listening to Bible stories and receiving fun games and sweets, so she decided to go to church with Ms. A.

While Osaka was listening to Kyoko's Spirit-empowered sermon, she encountered Jesus Christ and couldn't stop crying, falling off her chair and crying out loud with conviction of sins and joy of finding the place to be. Freed from the burden of sin she had been carrying, she skipped and returned home. That night, she confessed her sins to her parents and told them of her decision to become a Christian.

While Osaka was in high school, she accepted God's calling and decided to go to the CBC instead of finding a job. Her family strongly opposed it, but she went to the CBC in Tokyo, despite her family's opposition. At that time, Kyoko was twenty-nine years old. Osaka said Kyoko supported Osaka's life during her Bible college days. Osaka was appointed to serve at her mother church, Kanazawa Christ Church, in 1964, where she worked as an evangelist.

Osaka's daily role was to open the church door at 5 a.m. for early morning prayer and to pray with people before they went to work or school. During these times, a young man would be waiting for the lock to open, swinging a bat every morning. Osaka remembered how this young man was on fire for the Lord. He was always the first to come to the morning prayer meeting. His name was Yukio Funatsu (he would later become Kyoko's husband). All Osaka remembers was Yukio Funatsu's *"sawayaka,"* which means refreshing spirit.

After her two years of training as an evangelist at Kanazawa Christ Church, she married and became the pastor of a church in Hokkaido. Osaka's first-born son, Taro, is currently serving as a lead pastor of the Yamate-cho Church in Hokkaido, where Kiyoko and her husband preached the message of Jesus' salvation to many people. Taro serves as a professor at the Full Gospel Theological Seminary in Japan where Yonggi Cho established a Bible school for many to become ministers. Through Kiyoko Osaka's dedication to God, Spirit-empowered evangelism has spread to her family and reached many from the next generation, now through her son.

There have been cases of people going out on roadside evangelism in teams, stopping to hear the gospel, attending church meetings, and being saved. One day, during Osaka's roadside evangelism, Shintoku Ikehara stopped to listen to the gospel message. He decided not to go to the public bath, but instead to go with this group to the church. There, he heard the message from Kyoko and became a Christian. Later, he dedicated his life to serve in ministry and went to the CBC in Tokyo. After his graduation, he was sent to the city of Yokosuka to plant a new church as its pastor.

When Ms. A became a CBC student, she had to go a church for her internship. Kyoko sent Ms. A to Yokosuka church to assist Pastor Ikehara. Later, after Ms. A graduated from the CBC, she received a marriage proposal from Ikehara. They got married and spent two years together at Yokosuka before they were appointed to go to Okinawa for church planting as missionaries to America, a year before Okinawa was returned to the Japanese government.

Shintoku Ikehara focused on church planting and built a big church in Okinawa. He served as executive presbytery for many years for the Japan AG and his leadership influenced many pastors. On the other hand, Ms. A focused on Christian childhood education. She established two kindergartens and spoke to the children about knowing Jesus Christ as their Savior while they were young. Ms. A retired from pastoring in 2020, but she still oversees more than a hundred staff as the principal of the two schools, with many graduates serving the Lord all over Japan.

Just like with Ikehara, God also used street evangelism to open Sachio Hiratsuka's heart to the gospel. He kept coming to the Kanazawa Christ Church and joined the others in kneeling to pray. Whenever he listened to people speaking in tongues, he felt like he was at the day of Pentecost that was written about in Acts 2. He felt God's presence and, in 1962, decided to be baptized in water. He had been hired by the Kamakura city hall to work on the city's architecture, but when Kyoko spoke to Hiratsuka and asked him to go to the church in Yokosuka and serve God and Ikehara, the new pastor for the new church, Hiratsuka said yes to Kyoko.

Hiratsuka lived with Ikehara and paid the rent. He served at the church plant and united his heart with the new pastor. The first convert was a daughter of a Buddhist priest, Etsuko. She later became Hiratsuka's wife and together they had two daughters. He went to the Yokosuka church because he felt, through Kyoko's guidance, that God had sent him there to serve in the mission field.

Later, his first daughter, Mariko Hiratsuka, visited Kanazawa Christ Church at the age of nineteen.[11] She had always heard about why her father had become a Christian. When she came to the church herself, she felt the Holy Spirit. She received the baptism of the Holy Spirit. She then started serving as a Sunday School teacher. Through her, Kyoko's second daughter, Yoriko Yabuki received love and care when she was a teenager.

Kyoko's Influence on Her Daughters

Kyoko eventually married Yukio Funatsu and had three children. Her new role as a wife and a mother has enriched her experience and allowed her to reach more people. She never stopped her regular prayer life, her study of

God's words, and her ministry by the Holy Spirit. Her influence on her two daughters is obvious through their lives. They both serve the Lord locally and globally as Spirit-empowered women of God.

Her first daughter, Masako, was born in 1968. Masako said she learned the most from her mother, Kyoko, about the significance of praying in tongues and trusting God alone.[12] When she studied in a Bible college in Malaysia and ministered to many Japanese families during and after Bible school, she could see how greatly the Holy Spirit moved among people's lives to lead them to becoming saved. Masako had seen Kyoko's solid Bible message, initiative to lay hands on people receiving the baptism of the Holy Spirit, and clear and strong discipleship. Masako connected to God through her mother's strong influence.

Masako said those are the reasons why the church foundation is strong. Japan went through poverty and strong discrimination against women, especially right after World War II. In the midst of such cultural pressure, God had chosen Kyoko to bring about many wonderful things to glorify God before men and women. God used Kyoko and Yukio Funatsu as a couple to build the church together and go to different parts of the world to preach together.

Later, when Masako returned to Japan, she and her husband would minister to people from over twenty-six nations as pastors for the Kanazawa Christ Church international church group. Since 2023, Masako has been appointed as a lead pastor along with her husband. God has given Masako a pastoral gift and is using her at the church, even after her mother Kyoko had stepped down and retired from ministry. Kyoko's Spirit-empowered example is still in Masako's pastoral ministry as a female pastor.

Kyoko's second daughter, Yoriko, was born four years after Masako. Kyoko didn't understand why Yoriko was so quiet and why it was difficult to read her thoughts. God saved Yoriko at the age of eight, and poured out the Holy Spirit on her at the age of ten with speaking in tongues. Later, she graduated from the Assemblies of God Theological Seminary (AGTS) in Springfield, Missouri, with a degree in Intercultural Studies, then returned to Japan and served in the youth ministry where Kyoko had been leading as a pastor for a long time. Yoriko served in the women's group alongside Kyoko for five years at Kanazawa Christ Church (2000–2005) as a Japan AG licensed minister.

Yoriko's husband was led to Christ through Kyoko's preaching. He went to the CBC to become a minister. After his graduation, Yoriko's husband and his family moved to Springfied to learn at AGTS. Yoriko heard the voice of the Holy Spirit tell her to evangelize Japanese people. When she said yes to God, she met Japanese people. One by one, God led them to Christ through Yoriko's personal evangelism. Yoriko listened to the Holy Spirit to create a National Japanese Fellowship while she was writing a missiology course at AGTS. Later, Yoriko and her husband were appointed to become missionaries from the Japan AG to the U.S. AG for that vision. Kyoko included Yoriko in prayer every morning. God has helped Yoriko and her husband to accomplish these tasks with the power of the Holy Spirit in 2015. After serving four terms, they moved back to Japan and continue to serve as local AG ministers for the growth of the National Japanese Fellowship.

When an AGTS professor invited Yoriko to take a doctoral course, Kyoko was the one who strongly encouraged Yoriko to do so. Later, Yoriko pursued her Doctor of Ministry degree. God has given Yoriko the gift of teaching and has opened doors for Yoriko to teach on Biblical Theology of Women in Ministry and Leadership at the Asia Pacific Theological Seminary (APTS). In her fourth year of teaching, in 2025, she had twenty students from eleven nations. One of the students was from the Samoan Assemblies of God who strongly believed the role of women is not leading, but supporting their husbands. However, he received the call during the class to establish women in ministry and leadership in his Samoan AG national group. Another student from Papua New Guinea confirmed that she would start women in ministry in her national denomination. Yoriko was also invited to teach missiology at the CBC in Tokyo in 2022 and 2024, where Kyoko had gotten her degree to become a pastor. Yoriko was elected as one of the executive committee members of the Asia Pentecostal Society, serving from 2021-2024. In 2024, she became one of the members for the Joint Consultative Group of World Pentecostal Fellowship to speak about Pentecostalism at the World Council of Churches in Switzerland. She currently preaches Sunday services for people from different nations at Revive International Church in Tokyo, Japan, as a church planter, leading people to Christ and baptizing them in water with her husband, Rev. Daisuke Yabuki. Japanese and international students have been discipled through their ministry and filled with the baptism of the Holy Spirit. She and her husband both continue to commit to nurturing God's missional church to the world. Her mother Kyoko's gift of teaching and church planting influenced Yoriko deeply. Kyoko's influence was also spreading to many male and female Bible college students through Yoriko, inspiring them to follow in her steps.

Kyoko's two daughters are faithful to God's call, using their pastoral and teaching gifts to honor God for others and influence others locally and globally with the power of the Holy Spirit.

Lessons from Kyoko Funatsu's Life

There are many countries with patriarchal and male-dominant cultures in the world. Yet, when you read the Old Testament and New Testament, God has been working with both men and women through the power of the Holy Spirit. God could even use a Japanese female single minister, as well as a wife and mother, for his glory.

Here are several lessons we can learn from Kyoko Funatsu: First, Kyoko drew near to God every morning. "Draw near to God and he will draw near to you" (Jas 4:8).[13] Her alarm always rang before 5 a.m. She went to church in the dark, prayed to God with other people in the church, shared the Bible message, led several people to lead prayer, and concluded the prayer meeting with the Lord's Prayer. She often said we are not able to live without prayer.

Second, her ears and heart were always open to God. She often woke up early at 3 a.m. since she heard the message from the Holy Spirit. She took a pen to write down notes so she would not forget what God was saying to her. She also spoke in tongues and interpreted the meaning for edifying the church. Her advice was clear and led people to God, as she herself listened to God.

Third, Kyoko did not compromise in speaking truth from the Bible. She had no fear about confronting anything in her preaching and discipleship. In Japan, communication is not clear. People do not express their opinions in order to preserve harmony in groups. However, Kyoko didn't follow these rules or compromise. She spoke the truth clearly to others. She used God's words to preach, and the Holy Spirit brought conviction of sins, leading many people to repent and be filled with joy in God.

Fourth, Kyoko demonstrated love with words and gifts. Kyoko listened to people's stories with compassion. Her active listening led people to God. She always covered others with love and prayed for others by laying her hands on the person. She smiled and showed love to people so people could connect to her pastoral ministry.

Fifth, Kyoko discerned the Holy Spirit. The Holy Spirit gave Kyoko wisdom to solve her problems. She could discern if something was from the enemy or the person's spirit or from God. She had often fasted and prayed to cast out the devils from people's lives in Jesus's authority.

Sixth, Kyoko was diligent about her quiet time with God. She guarded her quiet time daily. When her second daughter came back from school and opened her mother's room, she would find Kyoko studying the words of God quietly. Kyoko took off to have solitude with only God for a few days and would return refreshed for ministry again.

Seventh, Kyoko used her strength in speaking English. Many English-speaking guest speakers came to Kanazawa Christ Church. Kyoko used her skills to interpret the speaker's English into Japanese. She was anointed and ministered to other people with the guest speakers. When Yukio Funatsu became a board member of Church Growth International upon the invitation of Yonggi Cho, Kyoko along to interpret for her husband. Kyoko's international work increased the church's influence.

Eighth, Kyoko extended her hands generously to those in need. Kyoko responded to people's needs. She understood that people suffer a lot. She was generous and honored God's heart.

Ninth, Kyoko was humble before God and corrected her words and actions through sincere apologies. She knew God's call and the excellent gifts God had given to her for his church. But even with her strong leadership, she had the humility to check what was in her heart. If she felt she'd offended her husband or children, she would come to them and apologize humbly with words. She knew what the Holy Spirit had convicted her of and wanted her to do, for healthy relationships. She did not blame others but took responsibility when she made mistakes.

Tenth, she expressed her love and joy with her smile. Her laughter made people around her happy. She was authentic in conversation. She smiled at people, even shaking her hands or waving her hands from a distance. Her smiles made people feel God's love and acceptance, and their significance.

Conclusion

Spirit-empowered people move people's hearts. The Spirit is able to do amazing things that people cannot imagine. God knows what he is doing. God called this Japanese woman who had lost her own father and brother, whom she had depended on, and used her to be a mother and grandmother to many. God revealed himself to Kyoko and answered her prayers. Kyoko guarded the vision. She knew God called her to take care of his sheep. Don't stop believing in the one who called you because he is able to do "more abundantly than all that we ask or think, according to the power at work within us" (Eph 3:20).

Notes

1   Kyoko Funatsu, as told to the author in a personal interview on July 18, 2016.

2   Yukio and Kyoko Funatsu, *The Church Birthed by the Vision* (Tokyo, Japan: Inochino Kotobasya, 1985), 123.

3   Koichi Kitano, as told to the author in a personal email on January 21, 2024.

4   Kitano, personal email, January 21, 2024.

5   Kyoko Funatsu, as told to the author in a personal interview, July 18, 2016.

6   Kiyoshi Kubota, as told to the author in a personal interview, February 2, 2024.

7   Kubota, personal interview, February 2, 2024.

8   Masae Kakizaki, as told to the author in a personal interview on March 18, 2024.

9   Not her real name, but the name given to preserve anonymity.

10 Atsuko Ikehara, as told to the author in a personal interview on February 25, 2024.

11 Mariko Hiratsuka, email interview with the author, February 17, 2024.

12 Masako Selvaratnam, as told to the author in a personal interview, January 20, 2024.

13 Unless otherwise mentioned, all scripture references are from the English Standardized Version (ESV).

15   How to Prepare to Reach Out to Refugees

Stavros Ignatiou

Abstract

As the country of Greece is situated at the southernmost part of Europe, it becomes an obvious initial destination for people who can be identified as "displaced" or "refugees." The majority of these people are Muslim since the countries which they flee from are predominantly Islamic. As a Christian community based in Athens, Greece, we felt the need to reach out to these people, with the intention of helping with their basic needs. This chapter describes the process we went through personally and professionally, including the method and strategy we established, in order to be more effective in our outreach.

Introduction

I remember when the first refugees arrived outside our door; we were completely unprepared. We knew that we needed to reach out to them, but we did not know how.

We did not know them; they did not know us. They were from a different cultural background and spoke a language that none of us understood—none of us spoke Arabic, Farsi or Dari, or any other language spoken by the refugees.

We were scared. We were scared about whether we were doing the right thing, scared about whether we were going to be taken advantage of, scared about what other people would say, scared about how our neighbors would react. The list went on and on. We kept telling the refugees that we were Christians—as if they did not know—but at the same time, I believe we were a little bit scared of each other.

The whole process of reaching out was complex. We needed to prepare ourselves but there was no time, which made things even more complex. In the beginning, the whole process seemed very simplistic. Just feeding people did not seem enough. We somehow knew that something else needed to be done. We were present, and in proximity, but at the same time we felt that the message we wanted to give was somehow not being delivered clearly.

This was an emergency on all levels, as far as I was concerned. As a leader at Athens Christian Center (ACC) and a local church pastor, I felt I had to assess the situation, to find solutions, and to convey to our members that what we were doing was right—and theologically correct. So, I started thinking and praying for guidance.

Prayer

Prayer was the first thing I did. I knew God's will: the refugees needed to somehow hear the gospel. I felt it was my responsibility to make that happen—I just had no clue how to do it. I felt that the Holy Spirit impressed on me one sentence: "Don't be afraid of change." That was spot-on since my whole world had gone through an unexpected change that I felt ill-equipped to respond to adequately.

The first thing I had to do was accept the advice from leadership professor J. Robert Clinton: "Change happens. It can be deliberate. Most of the time it is not."[1] I have heard many people talking about change and how much it is needed, but when the opportunity arises to get practical, many back away. Change, after all, is not an easy thing. Change, according to John Kotter, "takes you into a territory that is new and less well known, or even completely unknown."[2]

The Process of Leading Change

While in prayer, I felt that the Holy Spirit was clearly asking me to lead the change. I decided to follow Kotter's advice in *Leading Change*, where he unfolds an eight-stage process where change is managed and led. Even though Kotter's ideas are business- and management-oriented, I found his principles quite practical and applicable in our ministry setting. His eight stages are as follows:

1) Establish a sense of emergency.
2) Create a guiding coalition.
3) Develop a vision and strategy.
4) Communicate the vision behind the change.
5) Empower employees for broad-based action.
6) Generate short-term wins.
7) Consolidate gains and produce more change.
8) Anchor new approaches in the culture.

In my opinion, a church is an organization that goes through these eight stages when change is managed or needed. I tried to put these into practice even though I took the risk to distance myself from cliché phrases and church language.

Establishing a Sense of Emergency

Step number one from Kotter's book needed to be established in the church context. The local church had to sense the emergency. Kotter believes that "failing to establish a high enough sense of emergency" is the biggest error an organization can make.[3] Our problem as a local church was that the church was not prepared for that emergency when refugees were suddenly standing outside our door. In that moment, the Holy Spirit reminded us that the church of Jesus must visibly show the compassion of Christ to the world. As Jesus, our perfect example, was in the world, so the church should be also.

In our next service, 1 John 2:6 was preached, which declares that "He who says he abides in Him ought himself also to walk just as He walked."[4] John is speaking to the church, the body of Christ, which is a complex organism. As such, Snyder and Runyon remind us that "an incarnational model of church life and witness is very complex and sometimes chaotic."[5]

That was our picture at the time—complex and chaotic—and we needed help. Understanding the church's complexity, I had to take some brave steps and ask for help. My theological issues and differences from other believers needed to wait; we were in emergency mode and needed help from the rest of the body of Christ, both locally and internationally. That realization and understanding led me to take the next step: we needed to create, as Kotter puts it, a "guiding coalition."

Creating a Guiding Coalition

According to Kotter, "Individuals alone, no matter how competent or charismatic, never have all the assets needed to overcome tradition and inertia except in very small organizations."[6] So even though we were not a big organization, we needed help because our challenge was much bigger than what we could manage. Kotter goes on to say, "Failure here is usually associated with underestimating the difficulties in producing change and thus the importance of a strong guiding coalition."[7]

It was at this moment that I experienced a miraculous intervention. Many friends of mine, mainly from abroad, started getting in touch with me and asking how they could help. It was through this that our guiding coalition started to be formed. Everyone on board came with different ideas for financing the effort, sending teams, and even writing a newsletter. Then, when all the ideas and resources were on the table, a vision needed to be developed or redefined and a strategy agreed on.

Developing a Vision and Strategy

Step three was to re-emphasize our vision and, even more importantly, to develop a strategy. In doing this, many clarifications and reminders were needed to get everyone on board. As Kotter puts it, "Vision plays a key role in producing useful change."[8] Our big challenge was that we needed to adopt that vision and apply it to our new reality. Even though we were a church engaged in missions, we still needed some readjustments. We needed to change from "Let's go to them" to "They came to us." Believe me, that was not as easy as some thought it would be.

This is the first time we realized what an *incarnational approach* really meant. We understood that an incarnational approach was costly. We understood how costly incarnation was to Jesus and that this was now our task. I cannot find better words to describe "incarnation" than those Alan Hirsch uses. Speaking of incarnation as a lifestyle, he argues that "if God's central way of reaching his world was to incarnate himself in Jesus, then our way of reaching the world should likewise be incarnational."[9] Hirsch identifies four dimensions of the incarnation of Jesus that we are called to imitate: presence, proximity, powerlessness, and proclamation.

Presence: Hirsch says, "One of the profound implications of our presence, as representatives of Jesus, is that Jesus actually likes to hang out with the people we can hang out with. They get the implied message that God actually likes them."[10] Even from the beginning of our outreach to refugees, we noticed that they liked to be with us. Especially for our Muslim refugees, it was significant that they perceived us as friends rather than enemies. It was, in fact, because of our faith that we liked them. They came to the conclusion that if we liked them, then our God must also like them.

Proximity: Hirsch exhorts, "If we are to follow Jesus' footsteps we really need to be directly and actively involved in the lives of the people we are seeking to reach."[11] With this perspective, we came up with the idea to start a program called Integration. In our Integration program, which involves learning in a very relaxed environment, our purpose was not to forcefully integrate the refugees into our culture, but for us to integrate into theirs. We were the ones who needed to connect, to understand, to learn together, and to really help them. Jesus came to help us and so we are called to go to them to help them.

Powerlessness: Hirsch states, "We cannot rely on normal forms of power to communicate the Gospel."[12] Did we know that? Yes, we did. We had all kinds of limitations in this endeavor, with the language barrier being the biggest. We could not communicate. The only thing we could do at that initial stage was to humbly and quietly serve. That really put us in a very awkward and challenging position. These were the moments that Philippians 2:6—where Jesus, in his humility, did not consider equality with God to be grasped —became real to us. We intentionally became their servants and "put our theology aside" in order to concentrate our efforts on love and service.

Proclamation: Proclaiming the message of Christ was our biggest challenge because we did not think we could do it, at least in the beginning. But what kind of incarnation would we have without being able to share the gospel? The only thing we had at that moment were our actions. Actions speak louder than words. The story of the gospel in those moments came out not in words but in action. In fact, in the long run, more results emerged from our silence than from our speaking.

The Vision Behind the Change

As previously mentioned, communicating the vision for change was quite a challenge. Change is not always comfortable, and communicating it was even more uncomfortable at times. Furthermore, the change that I needed to communicate required many clarifications since our people were presented with new facts. In any case, the change was first communicated because of my actions. As Kotter states, "Communication comes both in words and actions."[13] As the main leader, I really put myself on display and led by example. I was out there serving, cooking, cleaning, smiling, trying to engage, and so forth. People saw how I was helping the refugees and how passionate I was in what I was doing. One reason for that was that I had once been a refugee. My personal experience not only allowed me to understand their situation but also to be passionate about what I was saying and doing.

In communicating the vision for the change, I wanted to introduce some new terms and new approaches, and in doing that I had to redefine "church." My first attempt required that I see the church from inside out. What is church? First and foremost, the church is people. Edmund P. Clowney states, "According to the Bible, the church is the people of God, the assembly of the body of Christ, and the fellowship of the Holy Spirit."[14] Even though that seems very basic, I felt that my people needed to hear it and digest it well. Sometimes, as a leader, I get the feeling that people confuse church with its leadership and somehow cut themselves off from the rest of the body. With this reminder, I wanted to shift attention back to all the people of the church, no matter what their role was in the local assembly.

In this case, when we talk about the people of God, inevitably, we are discussing the church. According to Alan Roxburgh, "The church is an ecclesia, which means an assembly that has been called out in the public way as a sign, witness, and a foretaste of where God is inviting all creation in Jesus Christ."[15] This aspect of church needed to be clarified and emphasized, since the church, in the Greek mentality and context, has been confused with the building and the clergy. Understanding the church as people of God really brought a new perception, understanding, and even revelation to members. It was evident that the level of responsibility had been raised and could be observed in their serving. Furthermore, people became proactive instead of reactive. It was wonderful to see.

Empowering Employees for Broad-Based Action

As previously mentioned, the situation looked like an emergency to me, in which I had no other option but to respond. The need at that moment was to employ as many hands as possible in this. As Kotter puts it, "The implementation of any kind of major change requires action from a large number of people."[16]

The first thing to be done was to remove impediments from people's minds. This had been done through the previous steps to a certain degree. The obstacle now was not so much the people, but the structure of our church. We needed to think a little bit outside the box. The mentality had started to change in that our members understood that we were not here to preserve ourselves, but to expand, grow, and develop, even if that meant taking significant risks. It was time for us to think of our church as a living organism or a living system. In the words of Hirsch:

> A living system approach seeks to structure the common life of an organization around the rhythms and structure that mirror life itself. In this approach we seek to probe the nature of life. We seek to observe how living things tend to organize themselves and then try to emulate as closely as possible this innate capacity systems to develop higher levels of organization to adapt to different conditions and to activate latent intelligence when needed (emergence)."[17]

Unfortunately, I came to the conclusion that our local church in Athens had been so influenced by the world around it that it had allowed a shift from a biblical perspective to a more secular one. Our local church was perceived to be an organization or institution where its members and staff were constantly engaged to maintain or preserve itself. My purpose was not to have a church—or a living organism, in this case—with no structure. On the contrary, we needed structure to support us but not to govern us. Our local church had an urgent need: to see itself as a movement. Hirsch defines "movement," using sociological language as:

> a group of people organized for, ideologically motivated by, and committed to a purpose which implements some form of personal or social change, who are actively engaged in the recruitment of others, and whose influence is spreading recruitment of others, and whose influence is spreading in opposition to the established order within which it originated.[18]

From this definition, one word stands out clearly: engagement. Being in the ministry for more than forty years, I know that engagement does not just happen. People cannot be engaged if they are not motivated. Equally, they cannot be engaged if they are not committed to a purpose. Commitment and motivation are crucial factors in engagement.

To see the whole matter in a more spherical way, we also need to recognize that engagement is not done in the atmosphere of an institution but in the environment of a movement. If we are part of a "frozen" church, we certainly do not have the right soil to cultivate engagement. Hirsch, in quoting Bill Easum, states: "The key to unfreezing the church to be with Jesus in a mission field is to view our congregations and denominations as the roots and the shoots of an organic movement that goes far beyond organizational survival."[19] Certainly, with the coming of refugees, our local church in Athens was forced to think outside the box. Our organizational structure was under pressure—the kind of pressure that someone feels when pushed outside their comfort zone.

Generating Short-Term Wins

After all the previous steps were taken, we started seeing some results. On one hand, some of the refugees kept coming back, not only asking for help but also seeking relationships. They had questions, and some of them started asking for prayer. On the other hand, only a slight increase in church members' engagement was observed overall.

I tried not to get disappointed, as I had bigger expectations, but as Kotter maintains, "real transformation takes time." He continues, "Most people won't go on the long march unless they see compelling evidence within six to eighteen months that the journey is producing expected results. Without short-term wins, too many employees give up."[20]

I then started sharing with our congregants what was happening: testimonies, miracles, stories, pictures, and videos, along with acknowledging and recognizing our staff and volunteers for our sacrificial outreach to the refugees. Short-term wins are essential—even though I had failed to see their value up to that point—because they show that sacrifices are worthwhile, help refine vision and strategies, decrease resistance, and build momentum.

Consolidating Gains and Producing More Gains

While short-term wins are necessary, declaring victory too soon would be a mistake. Victories here and there, even after years of hard work, do not indicate that we have finally arrived. Kotter warns, "Declaring victory too soon is like stumbling into a sinkhole on the road to meaningful change."[21] I have seen this happen in our organization. After getting too enthusiastic about an isolated win, we "went home" thinking that all was okay, and the war was over—without realizing that when weary soldiers get home, it becomes very difficult for them to return to the battlefield.

The question is, how did we consolidate our short-term gains to produce more gains? The answer is simple. First, we stuck to the process. At this stage, we needed to get more people to promote and to develop. Helpers, employees, and volunteers had to be those who truly believed in the vision for change, as they would be the ones implementing it.

One problem that always occurs under serious and continued consideration is resistance. Even when we were successful, some people insisted that we should not give too much attention to it because the refugee problem would soon cease to exist. Yet, five years later, refugees continue to flow in, and the situation has become even more complex, with many different dimensions.

The question again was, why does this resistance keep returning? Sometimes it is because of insecurity. People don't want to leave their comfort zone. "None of us have been down that road before," or "How can we trust those people?" or "We should be careful with them," or "We are here for the Greeks," were some of the concerns that formed the resistance party. This resistance led me to critically analyze our church, Athens Christian Center. I began to analyze the profile of people involved in our ministry, starting with the staff of ACC, since I considered this absolutely necessary in the process of change. According to Clinton, "Change participants can be favorable or unfavorable to change."[22] In this case, I needed to concentrate on those who were unfavorable—the resistant.

I found that other reasons people had for not being in favor of, or being resistant to, the changes we needed to make were rooted mainly in practical circumstances. Some people just didn't like change. Others already felt overloaded in the ministry. The truth is that some of our leaders were already doing too much and there was no spare time left in their weekly schedule for any extra ministry work. Another reason for resistance, in my opinion, was that many drastic changes needed to happen over a short period of time.

Yet, I wanted to keep these people on board. Leaders at any level are key people in whatever they do. I knew that everyone needed to put in a lot of effort to bring about the desired change. Unity or togetherness was, and is, crucial.

Anchoring New Approaches in the Culture

I personally did not give the whole process any rest until I knew that change had started to sink into our system. Kotter states, "In the final analysis, change sticks only when it becomes *the way we do things around here.*"[23]

Many people fail to understand how important culture is to any organization when it comes to success. As Mike Smith asserts, "It is your culture that will determine whether your strategy works and is sustainable. It is the culture you create that is going to determine whether your players perform and execute." He continues, "Every week you will face difficult circumstances that are completely out of control."[24] Thus, the real challenge was to anchor our new approach within our existing church culture. Kotter adds, "Anchoring a new set of practices in a culture is difficult enough when those approaches are consistent with the core of the culture."[25] The greatest challenge becomes how to use change to bring more change. Change is constant, fast—so fast that most of the time we find ourselves unable to keep up with it.

Conclusion

Looking at the big picture of this great work amongst the refugees, particularly those from a Muslim background, one thought comes to mind: the people of God, the body of Christ, the church, must live incarnationally and in proximity with the people they desire to reach. That is not an easy task. Many things must be taken into consideration before the existing local body of Christ becomes incarnational and fully operational.

Additionally, it is extremely challenging in some cases since existing churches must go through major changes. Existing organizations and structures must undergo internal changes even as the outward change is knocking at the door. Nevertheless, our engagement with refugees for the last few years has brought us many steps forward. The urgency created by the unprecedented change challenged us to see the problem as an opportunity for bringing transformation.

Notes

1   J. Robert Clinton, preface to *The Making of a Leader: Recognizing the Lessons and Stages or Leadership Development* (Colorado Springs: NavPress, 1988), 1-1.

2   John Kotter, New preface to *Leading Change* (Boston: Harvard Business Review Press, 2012), vii.

3   Kotter, *Leading Change*, 4.

4 Unless otherwise noted, all scripture references in this chapter are taken from the NKJV.

5 Howard A. Snyder and Daniel V. Runyon, *Decoding the Church: Mapping the DNA of Christ's Body* (Eugene, OR: Wipf and Stock, 2002), 43.

6 Kotter, *Leading Change*, 6.

7 Kotter, *Leading Change*, 7.

8 Kotter, *Leading Change*, 8.

9 Alan Hirsch, *The Forgotten Ways: Reactivating the Missional Church* (Grand Rapids: Brazos Press, 2006), 133.

10 Hirsch, *The Forgotten Ways*, 134.

11 Hirsch, *The Forgotten Ways*, 134.

12 Hirsch, *The Forgotten Ways*, 134.

13 Kotter, *Leading Change*, 10.

14 Edmund P. Clowney, *The Church: Contours of Christian Theology* (Leicester, UK: Inter Varsity Press, 1995), 28.

15 Alan J. Roxburgh, *An Introduction to the Missional Church Conversation* (Eagle, ID: Allelon Publishing, 2008), 7.

16 Kotter, *Leading Change*, 10.

17 Hirsch, *The Forgotten Ways*, 182.

18 Hirsch, *The Forgotten Ways*, 191.

19 Hirsch, *The Forgotten Ways*, 187.

20 Kotter, *Leading Change*, 12.

21 Kotter, *Leading Change*, 14.

22 Clinton, *Making of a Leader*, 3–19.

23 Kotter, *Leading Change*, 14, emphasis mine.

24 Jon Gordon and Mike Smith, *You Win in the Locker Room First: The C's to Building a Winning Team in Business, Sports, and Life* (Hoboken, NJ: John Willey & Sons, Inc., 2015), 9.

25 Kotter, *Leading Change*, 163.

16 Niilo Yli-Vainio: Evangelist in Finland and Beyond

Arto Hämäläinen

Abstract

This article examines the elements that comprised the impact of the ministry of Finnish evangelist Niilo Yli-Vainio, who was the catalyst of a revival in Finland that changed the lives of thousands of people. His ministry was also pivotal in other European countries, as well as in Africa, Asia, Australia, the former Soviet Union, and North and South America. Analyzing the circumstances, his message, and the response of the audience, this chapter aims to point out key factors in Yli-Vainio's ministry. It uses qualitative assessment in evaluating his message and the results of his ministry. Some quantitative assessments are made as well concerning the number of people touched by his ministry. Because he also served in countries and cultures foreign to him, attention is paid to the element of contextualization. This study considers both theological and missiological aspects of his ministry to learn useful practices for world missions and evangelism from his life.

Introduction

Many countries can name their heroes, those who were instrumental in bringing revival. What Jonathan Edwards meant for the spiritual awakening of the United States is widely known, not to mention the impact of Charles Finney and D. L. Moody. Of course, the fame of Billy Graham and Reinhard Bonnke has spread to all corners of the world. Norway names Hans Nielsen Hauge and Thomas Barratt; Sweden recalls Carl Olof Rosenius and Lewi Pethrus. Finland had several Lutheran revivalist influencers like Lars Levi Laestadius, Paavo Ruotsalainen, and Henrik Renquist.

Finland has not had Pentecostal pioneers like Barratt and Pethrus. There have been several persons with great influence, such as Eino Manninen in Helsinki, but there have not been any clear *primus inter pares*. However, a little more than a half century after the arrival of Pentecostalism in Finland, God raised up the Pentecostal pastor and evangelist Niilo Yli-Vainio to bring revival to Finland. His influence was not limited only to Pentecostalism, nor only to Finland. Thousands of people have been

"

touched in other European countries, as well as in Africa, Asia, Latin America, North America, and Australia.

Background and Context of Yli-Vainio's Ministry

Niilo Yli-Vainio was born on February 23, 1920, in Alahärmä, Finland. He died in Spain on November 16, 1981. Yli-Vainio first worked as an assistant in a pharmacy and then in a cartridge factory in Lapua, where he met his wife, Linnea. Soon he was drawn into the Second World War. He became a combat medic in the Finnish army and was sent to the front lines in the east. At the end of the war, he found himself in an awkward situation, close to a minefield, where Soviet soldiers approached him. The fallback to the Finnish side was very difficult. He was not able to sleep for eight days as he took care of wounded soldiers who needed help. Finally, he tried to hide from the shooting in a mud puddle, praying for God to help his fellow soldiers. While retreating back to Finland, still in the midst of the battle, a grenade hit his arm and he was seriously wounded. Thus, for him, the war ended in that moment.

Figure 1: Niilo Yli-Vainio

After the war, Yli-Vainio began to show interest in religious matters by reading the Bible, causing him to understand his need of salvation. Later, in January 1946, he went to a revival meeting in Lapua, his hometown. However, making a decision to follow Jesus at that meeting was a big challenge. He later remembers that his heart was beating tremendously fast. He asked his brother-in-law, who was sitting beside him, to check his pulse, and even he was surprised at its speed. When the preacher asked those who desired to be saved to raise their hand, Yli-Vainio felt his hand was as heavy as a stone. But, finally, he got the courage to do just that.[1]

Following Pentecostal doctrine, Yli-Vainio was baptized in water and became a member of the local church in Lapua. The baptism took place in the Lapua River in the midsummer of 1946. Then, the next month, in July, he experienced the baptism of the Holy Spirit.

Before receiving the baptism of the Holy Spirit, he had carefully studied the matter in the New Testament, which increased his thirst to experience it himself. He later related how the desire to be filled with the Holy Spirit had continued to increase and finally had become so overwhelming that he prayed for it day and night. He also noticed that his desire to witness about the Lord grew, but he felt that he lacked the power and ability to do so. Then, that July, he participated in the national Pentecostal summer conference in Helsinki. Day and night prayer meetings were part of the program. A special focus in these prayer meetings was praying for those who wanted to be filled with the Holy Spirit. One afternoon, he knelt beside a bench and started thanking Jesus silently. While doing this, a warm heavenly stream came down and overwhelmed him. At the same time, he started to speak in new languages that he did not understand.[2]

In 1947, after having experienced divine healing from heart problems,[3] Yli-Vainio committed himself to full-time ministry in the Pentecostal movement. He served as the pastor in several smaller churches in Midwest Finland as well as in some Finnish churches in Sweden. After moving back to Finland, he became the pastor in Espoo, located around the capital. His next place of ministry was the city of Vaasa on the western coast of Finland. He became the senior pastor of a mid-sized church there.

While serving at that church, however, he experienced burnout and felt it necessary to resign. He moved to a smaller town with his wife. He suffered from depression and thought that his ministry was over.[4] Then, in 1967, Yli-Vainio found out that he had cancer. He underwent surgery for the cancer but had an ostomy for the rest of his life. His wife also got cancer, which was operated upon and partly removed.

Revival and Renewal

In those days of severe hardship, Yli-Vainio was invited to come to Australia by a couple who had become believers during one of his meetings. He went there in December 1976 and stayed for seven weeks. During that visit, he experienced a renewal of his ministry.[5]

After returning to Finland, his messages had a fresh new dimension. Before, he was famously known as a straightforward evangelist, who would describe the horrors of hell in dramatic colors. Later in his ministry, he described these previous sermons by stating that, as a young preacher, he had tried to frighten people into faith. Why? Because he had felt an urgency—people were on their way to hell.[6]

After his Australia trip, Yli-Vainio's preaching took on a new tone; no more frightening of the people. He was full of love toward his audience. The main focus of salvation in Jesus Christ did not change, but the way he presented his message was different. The atmosphere was free and welcoming, accepting everyone just as they were. That approach started to draw people to his ministry.

After his renewal as an evangelist, he stated that he would never return to his earlier way of preaching, at any cost. People can be saved in an easier way. He came to the conclusion that the flames of hell, or the "terrifying thunderbolts on Mount Sinai,"[7] or any of that kind of threatening were not necessary. Even his own efforts were not needed; he only needed to rest in Christ.

I personally remember those days at the beginning of the revival. We were living as a family not far from Lapua, which became the starting place of the revival. People came in droves to the sports hall of Lapua, from all directions of Finland, and soon also from other countries. The hall was packed; people arrived by bus and car from everywhere. The atmosphere was very special. We felt it must have been like that when Jesus met with the crowds. It was holy and full of expectancy for anything that God might do.

Yli-Vainio became known and appreciated as an evangelist in the 1970s and early 1980s. Everywhere he ministered, whether to smaller or larger crowds, people became believers and then became members of Pentecostal churches. Though not always in big crowds, his ministry always bore the fruit of seeing conversions. His desire was to also lead them to experience the baptism in the Holy Spirit. After his renewal in Australia, his audience started to grow, and invitations from outside of Finland increased as well.

Religious and Political Landscape of Pre-revival Finland

In what kind of context did he minister in Finland? The Lutheran church was dominant. Along with it, the Greek Orthodox church had a special status, recognized by the state, that gave it some special benefits. The free churches, like the Pentecostal church, were protected by the law of religious liberty and could be officially registered. Pentecostals, however, were operating as a network of local churches, locally registered under the civil law as associations. It was only later, at the beginning of the twenty-first century, that Pentecostals became registered as a national church body. However, even before that, during the time of the officially loose fellowships, local Pentecostal churches closely collaborated in various ways. They used registered associations for different kinds of ministries like world missions, media (publishing and radio and television ministry), Bible schools, social ministry, and rehabilitation work among those suffering from addiction.

The Pentecostal church was the largest free church in Finland with more than forty thousand baptized members. Doctrinal tensions related to baptism remained between Pentecostals and the Lutheran church due to the Pentecostal practice of the believer's baptism and rejection of the infant baptism. This caused some disagreement in ecclesiology as well. The Charismatic movement had reached the Lutheran church and renewal movements inside it had changed its attitude to become more open to Pentecostals, but some prejudices still prevailed.

The 1970s in Finland was the time of an oil crisis, which was painted in dark colors in the minds of the people. Politically, Finland was in a Cold War context and was wanting to be neutral. It had to adjust, however, to the reality that its neighbor Russia was a superpower with nuclear weapons. Although the living standard had risen slowly after World War II, much insecurity was still in the air. It was in this context that Niilo Yli-Vainio appeared as an evangelist.

Although Yli-Vainio was a central figure in the revival, which started in 1977 after his visit to Australia, there were other practical things that paved the way for the revival. He actively inspired people to spread Christian evangelistic literature, music, and sermon cassettes. Thousands of copies of books and recordings were sold. The Pentecostal publishing house spread tens of thousands of copies of evangelistic magazines and Christian newspapers, sometimes over one million copies. Niilo Yli-Vainio was one of the most eager promoters of these activities. It was a great time for sowing seeds. The revival did not come in a vacuum. Yet, everything exploded in 1977 and onward. Yli-Vainio's evangelistic ministry effloresced.

As the ministry of the evangelist was elevated in the Pentecostal churches, Niilo Yli-Vainio became a model and inspiration. During the peak of Niilo Yli-Vaino's ministry, I was a young pastor in the church in Oulu, the largest city in Northern Finland. He visited the city a few times. Those visits initiated the revival that started there; they were the igniting force, although, in the long run, it was not dependent on them. He created awareness and interest among all people, not only among believers. In that way, he paved the way and inspired believers to evangelize their relatives, friends, and neighbors.

This reflected what is written in Ephesians 4:11 about the role of the different ministry gifts. Some were gifted and called by the Lord to be evangelists. However, it is important to observe the reason for this work of evangelism: to prepare the believers for the work of service (v. 12). This phenomenon could be seen in Yli-Vainio's ministry. New believers were eager to win other people to Jesus.

According to Veli-Matti Kärkkäinen, in 1996 there were 223 Finnish-speaking Pentecostal churches with 46,300 members and 32 Swedish-speaking churches with 2,700 members.[8] The effect of the Yli-Vainio revival was huge. Back in 1970, there were only 29,600 baptized members in the Pentecostal churches. By 1980, the figure had risen to 36,700.[9] The new revival can be seen as the catalyst for this growth. It should be noted that not all people who became believers became members of the Pentecostal Church. The revival also touched other churches. Many new believers joined the Lutheran church or other free churches in Finland, rather than the Pentecostal churches.

Characteristics of the Yli-Vainio Revival

Revival meetings had been one of the essential activities of Pentecostalism in Finland beginning in 1911, and a little bit earlier in the Swedish-speaking area. Usually, the morning services on Sunday were more for teaching and worship. Sunday evening services were evangelistic in nature. Also, now and then, revival meetings were organized as a series of gatherings on weekday evenings. Those meetings included music by a choir or soloists and congregational singing. Personal testimonies from those who had become believers were quite common in those meetings. Then an evangelist or pastor preached a message that culminated in an altar call.

This format was quite the same as that which originated during the great revivals in the US, as used by Finney and other revival preachers. Finney had started the practice called the "anxious bench." People who wanted to become believers or wanted help for their various needs could come forward to a special area in the front where they were then prayed for. The invitation to come forward was known as the "altar call."[10] This was also the practice in the Finnish Pentecostal churches.

In Yli-Vainio's meetings, besides those desiring to accept Jesus as their personal Savior, the altar call also gathered those who wanted to be healed physically. He also prayed for those who wanted to be filled with the Holy Spirit. Of course, there were people with various other problems as well who wanted prayer.

Yli-Vainio observed that the more he preached about the Holy Spirit and about the features, authority, and power of the Holy Spirit, the more he was filled with compassion for people. This would burst out through him as loving words. The more he emphasized forgiveness and atonement and the unlimited love of Jesus' sacrifice, the more powerful the divine presence became in his ministry.[11]

A unique thing that happened in Yli-Vainio's meetings was that many would fall down when he prayed for them. Sometimes this happened without anyone laying hands upon the person. This power experience was a mystery for Niilo, and he wondered what the secret was behind it. The phenomenon of "being slain in the Spirit" in his meetings did not happen to everyone he prayed for. He never focused on it being an important matter in and of itself, nor saw it as a sign of the measure of spirituality. Paul writes about the *energēmatōn* (1 Cor 12:5), which means the effect of the power. He does not explain it in detail, but states that these phenomena are various. The falling down seems to fit that category. Yli-Vainio was not the only one seeing this happen in the ministry. Many ministers during the revival connected to Yli-Vainio's saw this happen when they prayed for people. In the first months of his renewed ministry, Yli-Vainio recorded over nine thousand people falling down in his ministry.[12]

Yli-Vainio later said that he had not planned to be in a ministry that involved the phenomenon of falling down. This just happened to take place. At first, when this happened, he was afraid. Soon, however, he reconciled with the understanding that God's Spirit was behind it.

The duration of his new ministry was short. He started with this new anointing in 1977. He finished his ministry in 1981, when he died while jogging in the mountain area close to Vitoria in Spain. His total ministering time was about one thousand days. Yet, during those years, he reached millions of people with the gospel, in different countries, including hundreds of thousands of Finns. He sold over six hundred thousand copies of his books of his printed sermons and writings.[13]

Yli-Vainio's home field was the Pentecostal church. He never left his home movement, although some people encouraged him to start a separate ministry. He did not choose that option, although some Pentecostal ministers were critical of his way of working. He was, however, open to other Christian churches. Some of the Lutheran bishops appreciated him and his ministry. Many priests were charismatically oriented and shared his views about the need of revival and a fresh move of the Spirit.

Niilo Yli-Vainio's Success Factors

What was the key to Yli-Vainio's success? We can answer with this one concept: the anointing of the Holy Spirit. He urgently felt dependent on it. Before ministering, he usually felt himself to be totally empty. His belief was that, whether he leaves the pulpit alive or dead, it did not matter. "I will never get used to it." He felt his only role was to be used as an instrument in God's hand.[14]

He felt that pride was a struggle for preachers. During the hardships of life, he learned that "even if the dead would be raised and sick people would be healed like cars in line, I would not steal your (God's) glory." Only God must be honored.[15] He was a humble man willing to give all glory to God.

The message of Yli-Vainio was cross-centered. He was powerfully able to describe Christ's death and its effects. He followed Paul's pattern of focusing on Jesus and him crucified (1 Cor 32:2). He described his status in this way: "The realized fact is that Jesus has died on the cross for my sins and delivered me from the chains of death and I live. If you want to separate me from faith, you need first to eliminate Jesus and nullify his death on the cross. However, no elite army on earth is able to do that. Jesus is veritably one unique sacrifice."[16]

Joy was an essential feature in the life of Yli-Vainio. The many hardships that he met through the years could not destroy it. In one of his books, he asked the reader: "Do you know what kind of person Niilo Yli-Vainio is? Listen, he is a joyful man. He is full of glee."[17]

He was aware of his fame in Finland, and also of the fact that some saw him as a future politician. He knew that he could possibly win the votes to become a member of parliament. He stated that the wives of alcoholics, "suffering people, these burden carriers," would have voted for him.[18] He recognized the problems caused by the reckless use of alcohol in Finland. Therefore, he promoted a march protesting against loosening the rules for selling alcoholic drinks. The motion was being considered in the parliament at that time.[19] He felt, however, that his ministry as an evangelist was more important and so he never joined any political parties.

Niilo was close to suffering people. Whether they were sick, poor, or struggling with addictions, he had compassion towards them. That concern crossed the border between this world and eternity. In his early years of ministry, this concern appeared as frightening scenarios in his sermons. In the new anointing he had in his later years, the concern was displayed as empathic love toward his listeners.

One key to his success was that he was a folksy man. He skillfully contextualized his speaking and conversations. This facet was clearly seen in a situation that I personally witnessed in Hamburg, Germany, in 1980. I was participating in a short-term Bible class with the Elim Pentecostal congregation. Yli-Vainio was there at that time preaching an evangelistic campaign in the Elim Church. When he arrived, I was asked to serve as interpreter for him, not in the public meetings, but in his everyday needs and interactions. The church offered him coffee when he arrived there. We were sitting together at the coffee table, starting to drink the coffee. He then asked an interesting question of the German waiter: "Did Stalin kill all the cows in Germany?" The waiter was a little bit stunned by the question. The reason for the question, however, soon became clear. Milk was lacking on the table!

The way Yli-Vainio behaved in this situation unveils his sensitivity in cross-cultural situations. He had been a soldier of the Finnish army in World War II. Germany was a main player in it, and Finland and Germany had some collaboration as well, although Finland tried to keep a measure of sovereignty amidst this collaboration. By using this humorous picture in his request for milk, he skillfully touched on the Finnish-German history without referring to painful memories of the war. The same kind of approach could be found in his sermons. I myself saw how well he communicated with a German audience, and I heard other reports of similar interactions with people from other countries as well.

In his early years, Yli-Vainio had performed as an amateur actor in the theater. Those skills served him well later on in his evangelistic ministry. I was present in Hamburg when he used the example of a steam locomotive train as an illustration in his sermon. As he spoke, you really felt like you were hearing all the sounds of the train as it went speeding down the track, followed by smoke and clouds of steam. You felt as though you were one of the passengers.

Without doubt, the major attraction of Yli-Vainio's ministry was healing. Allan Anderson refers to recent studies that indicate healing as the most important category for understanding the expansion of Pentecostalism during the twentieth century.[20] Was that not the same with Jesus' ministry? Miracles of healing drew people to him. Marja Toukola presents nineteen well-documented healing miracles related to Yli-Vainio's ministry.[21] Some of the cases are documented by a medical doctor, while some are testimonies about the miracles that are verified, not only by the former sick person, but by people who know the person and who are able to testify of the change.

The diaries of Yli-Vainio document the healings and the numbers of people who claimed to be healed during his ministry. Between the end of February and the end of May in 1980, Yli-Vainio recorded about four hundred healings in his diary.[22] Of course, one may ask how trustworthy these statistics are, but, surely, these recordings show a general trend. People felt that they were helped. In some cases, the change may have been more emotional without facts of a clear physical change. However, in comparing this to the documents Toukola gathered, there seems to be no doubt that miracles had taken place. Still, the fact that people were convinced of God's touch in their life has value, besides the experiences of those whose healing testimonies are also backed up by medical documents.

One of the secrets of Yli-Vainio's effective ministry was surely his fasting. By reading his diaries in Mauno Saari's book *Saarnaaja* (which means "the preacher"), the reader may wonder how often he fasted. It is also amazing that he, as a sick man with an ostomy, could fast so much. For example, on October 30, 1980, he wrote in his diary, "I was fasting for the trip in Germany. I feel myself so weak in body that I hardly can manage."[23] He was not fasting to gather merits before God, but he understood that there was a divine connection between it and the ministry.

Global Influence of Yli-Vainio's Ministry

Although the expanded ministry of Yli-Vainio lasted only for a few years, he reached an extraordinary number of countries. Outside of Finland and Scandinavia, he visited and had evangelistic events in Argentina, Australia, Austria, Canada, France, Germany, Israel, Japan, Kenya, Netherlands, Singapore, Spain, Switzerland, Taiwan, Thailand, United States, and Uruguay. Most of the countries outside Scandinavia were countries with which the Finnish Pentecostal churches collaborated through their mission organization (today, Fida International).

Yli-Vainio left the seed of revival. For example, during his meetings in Argentina, he wrote in his diary on January 23, 1979: "I believe a revival is starting in Argentina." He also influenced the ministry of Carlos Annacondia, who became one of the most famous evangelists in Argentina and beyond. Annacondia's larger ministry started in 1982.[24]

The influence of Yli-Vainio also spread to countries he never visited as an evangelist. Rauli Lehtonen, the long-time general secretary for missions of the Swedish Slavic Mission and a mission executive in the Pentecostal church in Sweden, is a very knowledgeable source of the spiritual development in Eastern Europe. Lehtonen reports that a revival that had roots in Yli-Vainio's work in Finland reached Estonia. Tallinn, the capital of Estonia, became the center of the revival, which deeply touched areas of the Soviet Union. Russia, Ukraine, and the Caucasus were impacted, and lasting fruit in these places is evident even to the present day. The center of the revival was the Oleviste church in Tallinn. People started to come from different parts of the Soviet Union to participate in the revival. The lives of tens of thousands of people were changed.

Lehtonen reports that, according to Slavik Radchuk, an evangelist who has worked for Reinhard Bonnke's ministries, almost two hundred Slavic churches were established in the United States alone as a result of Yli-Vainio's revival movement.[25]

The pastor of the Oleviste church, Rein Uuemõis, relates that before the coming of this revival, the church had a prayer group that gathered regularly for a long period of time to pray in homes. Some Finnish friends visited that group and prayed with them for Holy Spirit baptism. From that event, the revival fire started to spread. A spiritual bridge was created between Finland and Estonia. The revival in Finland touched Estonia and, from there, large areas in Eastern Europe. Tom Kraeuter writes in *The Great Soviet Awakening* that hundreds of thousands of people experienced a spiritual renewal and hundreds of new churches were established.[26] Divine healings took place. Many of those healed had been suffering from cancer, blindness, and deafness, or were lame or victims of other diseases.[27]

Yli-Vainio's Revival and General Characteristics of Revival

Ian R. Hall has studied revival movements throughout history and found some basic features in them. Is it possible to see these things relating to Evangelist Yli-Vainio and the movement ignited as a result of his ministry? Hall, in his meritorious book *Times of Revival*, reflects on the elements and features in revivals. Several synonyms are used for that phenomenon like "renewal," "awakening," or "refreshing." "Revival," however, seems to be the most commonly used term. It includes the connotation of something that happens to a believer. Revival is used interchangeably with "evangelical awakening" or "spiritual awakening." Also, expressions in the Bible such as "times of refreshing" and "times of visitation" belong in this same category. "Renewal" belongs to this group of terms suggesting revitalization of church structures and individual faith.[28]

Can we call the movement that was started by the ministry of Yli-Vainio a revival? Did it influence and inspire believers? Were they renewed, awakened, and refreshed? Yes, these things really took place. It happened in the prayer meetings in Tallinn. It was evident in the evangelistic rallies in Finland. Believers received a fresh touch of the Holy Spirit. The reason they came to those meetings could have been their need for healing from sickness or their need for help for various other difficulties they were facing. However, the fresh presence of the Holy Spirit encouraged them to be open, to repent, and to experience a renewal in their spiritual life. After that, they became eager to share their faith with others. This then led unbelievers to accept Jesus as their Savior. Because of this, the churches started to grow.

The effects of the revival continued even after Yli-Vainio's death. His ministry renewed the need to evangelize people worldwide, not only in Finland. During his lifetime, the Pentecostal mission organization, together with the local churches, stated that their goal was to increase the number of missionaries by one hundred people in five years. This goal was achieved in four years.

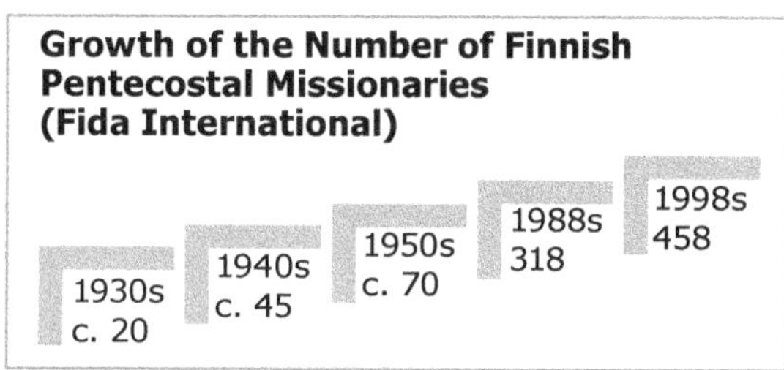

Figure 2: The number of Finnish Pentecostal missionaries has increased since the 1930s.[29]

Conclusion

Niilo Yli-Vainio was, without a doubt, the most influential evangelist in Finland during the last century. Perhaps, having a widespread international ministry like Yli-Vainio, only Provost Kalevi Lehtinen from the Lutheran church could be placed in the same category. Yli-Vainio was a catalyst for a nationwide revival in Finland. Nothing similar had been experienced there since the awakenings through the Lutheran revival movements in the eighteenth and nineteenth centuries.

This revival was characterized by the healings of people, which ignited a great interest in the gospel in Finland and beyond its borders. People travelled to Lapua by private car and by bus and filled the sport arena from week to week. Besides the healing experiences, people falling down under the supernatural touch of God's Spirit created curiosity. People wanted to see for themselves and observe what was going on.

The large missionary work of Finnish Pentecostal churches paved the way for Yli-Vainio's international ministry, but Yli-Vainio was also an eloquent speaker whose folksy manner gripped his listeners. He was capable of crossing cultural bridges, contextualizing his message to be easily accepted. The audience recognized his empathic attitude towards people who were suffering, sick, and depressed. His own life story included many hardships and much suffering. That kept him humble and free from pride and a feeling of superiority.

Jesus was the center of his message. Yli-Vainio's core message was love for Jesus and Jesus' love for the people who were reconciled by his death. In his earlier years, he would preach sermons that frightened people. But in his later ministry, the atmosphere was more focused on Jesus, attracting the hearers to the person of Jesus himself.

Nobody knows how many people have been touched by his ministry. They no doubt number in the millions. Not everyone has met him personally, but they may be served by people who had become believers in his meetings, been healed there, or listened to his preaching on radio, television, cassettes, or videos. His preaching is now available on YouTube and other outlets, so his influence continues even today.

Notes

1   Marja Toukola, ed., *Suomen herättäjä: Niilo Yli-Vainion syntymästä sata vuotta, 1920–2020* (Virrat: KKJMK, 2020), 170–171.

2   Toukola, *Suomen herättäjä*, 173–174

3   Toukola, *Suomen herättäjä*, 17.

4   Mauno Saari, *Saarnaaja: Niilo Yli-Vainion taistelu, testamentti ja päiväkirjat* (Porvoo-Helsinki-Juva: WSOY, 1983), 27.

5   "Niilo Yli-Vainio," Wikimedia Foundation, https://fi.wikipedia.org/wiki/ Niilo_Yli-Vainio#Varhainen_el%C3%A4m%C3%A4, last modified 11 November 2024.

6   Saari, *Saarnaaja*, 268–269.

7   Saari, 269.

8   Veli-Matti Kärkkäinen, "The Pentecostal Movement in Finland," *Journal of the European Pentecostal Theological Association* 23, no. 1 (2003): 102–28, https://doi.org/10.1179/jep.2003.23.1.007.

9 Eero J. Antturi, "Helluntaiherätys tänään," in *Helluntaiherätys tänään*, eds. Kai Antturi, Juhani Kuosmanen and Valtter Luoto (Vantaa: Ristin Voitto, 1996), 65.

10 Ian R. Hall, *Times of Renewal: A History and Theology of Revival and Spiritual Awakenings* (Oradea: Metanoia, 2023), 219.

11 Saari, *Saarnaaja*, 135.

12 Saari, *Saarnaaja*, 137.

13 Saari, *Saarnaaja*, 251.

14 Saari, *Saarnaaja*, 266.

15 Saari, *Saarnaaja*, 265.

16 Toukola, *Suomen herättäjä*, 119.

17 Saari, *Saarnaaja*, 268.

18 Saari, *Saarnaaja*, 262.

19 Saari, *Saarnaaja*, 222–226.

20 Allan Anderson, *To the Ends of the Earth* (Oxford: University Press, 2013), 149.

21 Toukola, *Suomen herättäjä*, 86–125.

22 Saari, *Saarnaaja*, 449–451.

23 Saari, *Saarnaaja*, 370.

24 "1984 Argentina Revival," Beautiful Feet, https://romans1015.com/1984-argentine-revival/.

25 Toukola, *Suomen herättäjä*, 69–70.

26 Toukola, *Suomen herättäjä*, 71.

27 Toukola, *Suomen herättäjä*, 70–72.

28 Hall, *Times of Revival*, 15–16.

29 Arto Hämäläinen, *The Spirit and the Structure* (Helsinki: Fida International, 2005), 269.

17 Spirit-Empowered Mission in Chilean Pentecostality

Alfred Cooper

Abstract

This article seeks to bring together theology, pastoral praxis, and missiological strategy from the Latin American church in Chile. It will narrate and expound lessons from the 1909 Pentecostal revival and the fast-growing renewed Anglican church, La Trinidad de Las Condes. I will first establish theological criteria that open the wider church to "Pentecostality," the concept Bernardo Campos creates that helps eliminate false distinctions between so-called "Spirit-empowered" churches and those of non-Pentecostal traditions. Complementing Pentecostality, my concept of Pneuma plasticity enables a fresh pneumatological understanding of the work of the Holy Spirit that encourages full reception of the Spirit's missional power from a non-Pentecostal theology. Then, I will draw from the varying Pentecostalities and methodological strategies that these two differing Chilean churches have developed, each under the Holy Spirit's guidance, both producing fruitful and "limitless" missional structures as they mobilize the majority of their members in testimony, discipleship, and leadership training.

Introduction

"¡Chile para Cristo!" ("Chile for Christ!") is a cry that still rings out among today's three thousand and more Pentecostal denominations or "Pentecostalities," as Bernardo Campos calls the Pentecostal expressions of denominational local churches.[1] The Iglesia Metodista Pentecostal (IMP) and the Iglesia Evangélica Pentecostal (IEP), over the first half of the past century, became a fast-growing movement that reached into every village and mountain vale in Chile where small churches have continued to worship since the Pentecostal revival broke out in 1909 under the pastorate of Willis Hoover in Valparaiso's Episcopal Methodist Church. Later, division and multiplication under new Chilean legislation that facilitated the acquisition of legal status for church denominations led to the diversity of Pentecostal denominations today, continuing Hoover's missional work in and beyond Chile. Reminiscent of a Paul and Barnabas crisis between missionary

journeys (Acts 15:36–41), the divisions are often scandalous, but the multiplication of fruit has continued.

Despite the growth structures still in place, the Pentecostal movement has slowed down over the last twenty years among the poorer and lower middle classes, where it had previously found fertile ground to sprout and spread. This may be due to the factors mentioned in *"El Obispo Durán y La Jaula de Hierro,"* the disturbing article by Luis Orellana and Miguel Ángel Mansilla on the scandals and corruption within some of the significant Pentecostal churches.[2]

Since the 1970s, however, the cry was taken up, surprisingly, by renewed Anglican churches in Santiago's wealthier, more Chilean European sectors in the capital cities' Barrio Alto (upper neighborhood), one of which figures in this study. The central thesis of this report is that both the burgeoning Pentecostal churches and the upcoming Anglican church of La Trinidad de Las Condes[3] would say that Chile will only be won for Christ by the enabling power of the Holy Spirit. I will suggest in this chapter that the mission-enabling power of the Spirit that Pentecostals have so convincingly demonstrated in their kingdom-spreading efforts over the last century is equally available to mainline and traditional denominations (like Anglicanism) and, similarly, is effective in enabling mission effort from those platforms as well. Both churches can access the new wine and develop the appropriate wineskins. Beyond the well-known Charismatic movements that come and go in waves of Spirit visitations, what is required is a sustained understanding of the *nature* of the Spirit's desire for the church and a constancy in reception modality for that fullness of enabling to become expressed in world outreach through a mobilized church. To the church, it was declared that "you will receive power when the Holy Spirit has come on you; and you will be my witnesses..." (Acts 1:8).[4] The Spirit is given to the church for mission and, I suspect, may be withdrawn in part when the church stops spreading the kingdom.

Reception of the Spirit

Let me first establish what the Pentecostals rightly affirm: that only the Holy Spirit can kindle and rekindle the fire of passion for the gospel and the mission in the believer's heart. As Paul exhorted Timothy, "For this reason I remind you to fan into flame the gift of God, which is in you through the laying on of my hands. For the Spirit God gave us does not make us timid, but gives us power, love and self-discipline" (2 Tim 1:6–8). Interestingly, both churches vary in their understanding of the baptism and reception of the Holy Spirit. Willis Hoover's Pentecostalism sought a baptism of the Spirit from 1907, when he and his wife heard of the Pentecostal revivals in Mukti, India, through a pamphlet sent by Minnie Abrams, a college friend of Mary Hoover's.[5] They held to a subsequential theological understanding in that a further, sometimes second or third, experience of the Holy Spirit after regeneration, called the "baptism of the Holy Spirit," was sought and seen as essential to the movement's characteristic and success in mission.

In contrast, Anglicans who also "received" Spirit-enabling *dunamis* are not subsequential in doctrine, though certainly in the expectation and experiences that receive "more and more" of the Spirit. As I analyze their missiological and theological development in each case, I will deal with this difference and hope to resolve the contradiction from the vantage point of Campos' Pentecostality and my theory of Pneuma plasticity.

Wine and Wineskins, Locomotives and Rails

Churches that multiply evangelism and church planting usually discover access to both the "new wine" and the "new wineskins," the new structures necessary for the kingdom of God to find expression in the context of that mission. We can agree with most commentators that the "new wine" Jesus spoke of refers to the Holy Spirit given under the new covenant. F. F. Bruce, for instance, in his commentary "The Gospel of Matthew" interprets Matthew 9:17 in this way.[6] John Wesley, Matthew Henry, and John MacArthur also share this similar understanding in their writings. In the context of changes concerning Jewish "fasting," "feasting with the Bridegroom," and Sabbath-keeping, Matthew 9:14–17, Mark 2:18–22, and Luke 5:36–39 refer starkly to a coming dispensation of time when God's people will be activated in a way different to life under the Law. Similar to Christ's exclamation to the woman at the well, referring to how the Father will now seek worshippers who worship in Spirit and in truth, we infer that there is a new community life in the Spirit that, as he clarifies in John 7:37–39, the disciples will later experience after his resurrection. Therein lies the importance of the book of Acts that models what this new wineskin will look like as it describes the missional communities and the effective outreach of conversion growth that spreads so dynamically around them (cf. Acts 2:32–47; 6:7; 8:1–8; 13:1–3; 19:1–11).

I will maintain that churches will always need to access the Spirit and develop the mission structures through which the Spirit enables and can multiply the church. The power in the locomotive needs the rails to run effectively. My interest in these two very diverse churches is that both have accessed the new wine of the Spirit from different theological perspectives and have developed new strategic wineskins of growth. I intend to show that Spirit-empowered mission is accessible to all churches, both Pentecostal and non-Pentecostal.

Something Remarkable in Valparaiso

Something remarkable occurred in the Methodist Episcopal Church in Valparaiso in 1909, with lasting missional effects in Chile over the nearly thirty years following (measured by Hoover's death in 1936). It is now accepted and has been amply documented and analyzed.[7] Authorities like Luis Orellana, a socio-historian and probably the foremost authority on Chilean Pentecostalism today, who regularly publishes fresh and updated insights into the history of the movement,[8] proposes that this was "the first autonomous Pentecostal movement in Latin America," and that it became impossible to ignore because the revival grew in numbers and social influence to such a degree[9] that it warrants continued study. Chilean Pentecostalism is part of a broader phenomenon from which the universal church has learned much. David Stoll's book (and question): *Is Latin America Turning Protestant?*[10] explores what had become an observable sociological and historical reality by 1991: "The fastest growing church movement in Latin America over the last 50 years of the twentieth century was Pentecostalism. The International Board of Mission estimates that the Pentecostal population in Latin America, by the year 2025, will have swelled to 680 million."[11]

In 2020 (after which it is difficult to find reliable figures), the third edition of the *World Christian Encyclopedia* counted 644 million Pentecostal-Charismatics worldwide and nineteen denominations and fellowships. Paul Freston confirmed this observation in 2008 in his book *Evangelical Christianity and Democracy in Latin America:*[12]

According to 2006 figures from the World Christian Database, Pentecostals and Charismatics now represent around 30 percent, or around 150 million, of the Latin American population of 360 million people. In contrast, they represented only 4 percent in 1970 . . . the conclusion that evangelicalism has become the dominant form of Christian practice in the Global South is inescapable.[13]

Similarly, Miguel Alvarez, in his book *Integral Mission*, a study of Latin American *missio Dei* of Pentecostal churches, builds the challenge of his book—that they should engage more thoroughly in the political and social aspects hitherto neglected—on their very significant growth rate.[14] Therefore, studying Pentecostalism in Latin America today seeks to understand, indeed, something remarkable: one of the leading forces affecting Latin culture and society.

The Pentecostal revival that broke out in Chile in 1909 was the first to show signs of this unprecedented growth in Latin America. Allan Anderson comments: "Many of the first Pentecostals in Latin America were Chileans, and in the early years, this was the most successful of the different Pentecostal nations in the continent."[15] Various national census readings give percentages for the population of Protestants or *Evangélicos*: in 1920 at 1.45 percent,[16] at 5.6 percent in 1960,[17] then 15.14 percent in 2002, reaching 16.62 percent in 2012.[18] Out of a national population of 17,574,003 Chileans, 2,145,092 called themselves *Evangélicos*.[19] The *Evangélicos* have been the object of much study over the last sixty years, from anthropological,[20] historical,[21] and sociological[22] viewpoints. These studies have majored chiefly on the effects of the movement on Chilean underclasses, the social impact of Pentecostal mission to the poorest and most marginalized, and their gradual rise to cultural and political influence over the last century. Hoover, however, in the first pages of his book, relates all to what he calls the "real secret," a relationship with the person of the Holy Spirit:

I believe the real secret of all this is that now we really and truly believe in the Holy Spirit—we truly trust him—we truly *know*[23] him (italics mine)—we truly obey him—we truly give him liberty. We believe truly that the promise in Acts 1:4 and Joel 2:28, 29 is for us. We have ceased to merely believe and speak of the doctrine while continuing on without hope in our usual routine. Thus, now we believe, wait and pray and he has done these things before our eyes. Blessed be his name.[24]

This chapter explores how both Pentecostals and non-Pentecostals (in this case, Chilean Anglicans) can access the same "secret," the person and power of baptism of the Holy Spirit, for the mission of God.

Theological Controversies Around Spirit-Empowerment

Several attempts have been made to systematize the theology on the third person of the Trinity, the Holy Spirit, to unite broader criteria and increase consensus on his person and work. However, the doctrine of the Holy Spirit has been a source of discord and division in the church. In Latin America, these divisions have generally emerged as reactions to a "Pentecostalism without a theology" or "theology without Pentecost." Faced with extravagant phenomenology, theologies without scriptural foundations, harmful charismatic extremes, and unbalanced messages such as prosperity theology, Christians have reacted with fear and caution. When a theological tower is removed from ecclesial or social reality, the church can fall into an equally harmful cessationism. Relating to the *dunamis* and gifting of the Spirit has marked the church with disbelief and immobility, which separates the fruit, the fire, the gifts, and the entire activity of the Holy Spirit from the mission of Christ. As Francis Chan writes in *The Forgotten God*:

> From my perspective, the Holy Spirit is tragically neglected and, for all practical purposes, forgotten. While no evangelical would deny His existence, I'm willing to bet there are millions of churchgoers across America who cannot confidently say they have experienced His presence or action in their lives over the past year. And many of them do not believe they can.[25]

Pentecostals and renewed Anglicans in this study both learned to rely on the enabling power and guidance of the Holy Spirit in a relationship with him. Interestingly, as I intend to analyze, both access Spirit-empowerment from different theological understandings of baptism of the Spirit.

Let me build my study, first, from Willis Hoover's missional understanding of the Acts of the Apostles. Second, I will refer to Bernardo Campos' theory of Pentecostality to show how his theory enables the entire church to experience the Pentecost event and its origin. All churches have their origin, Campos says, in the Pentecostal phenomenon and can therefore expect power for mission to be readily available today as in the Acts of the Apostles. Further, I will apply my own theory of Pneuma plasticity[26] to strengthen the understanding of how the Holy Spirit's person and power for mission is available to the whole church today from a more precise concept of the Holy Spirit's nature and essential outworking in the believer and the church.

The Book of Acts as Willis Hoover's Mission Manual

In 1902, when Willis and Mary Louise Hoover were asked to leave the English school they were leading in Iquique and take up the pastorate of Valparaiso's Methodist Episcopal Church, Willis was asked a question stemming from the studies the church was diligently exploring on Luke's Acts of the Apostles: What prevents our being a church like the early church? Hoover's answer charted the theological direction for the coming revival: "Nothing prevents it, except whatever impedes it from within, ourselves."[27] He was speaking from a Wesleyan Radical Holiness Movement perspective. When he placed his hand on his heart, he thought that entire sanctification would lead to an Acts of the Apostles mission. Yet, with his words and gesture, he validated Acts of the Apostles as a proper model for New Testament mission and for all time. Describing the revival church that was birthed in 1909, he says:

> It is called "Pentecostal" because it believes the happenings on the day of Pentecost were the inauguration by the Holy Spirit of the church Christ wanted, permanently, until his return in person. It believes that the book of Acts of the Apostles does not represent the end of the workings of the Holy Spirit in the church but rather establishes the norm set up by Christ by which the church ought to be guided in fulfilling its great mission on earth.[28]

The pamphlet from Minnie Abrams[29] described Pentecostal manifestations and giftings, provoking in the Hoovers a hunger for more of the Spirit's power. The fact that they knew the author personally caused the Hoovers to examine the story more closely.

> The marvel for us was that the pamphlet spoke of a clear and definite baptism in the Holy Spirit and fire as *something in addition to justification and sanctification* (italics mine)... Until then, we had believed that these two elements encompass the totality of the Christian experience.[30]

This noting of subsequence, a *third* experience of the Spirit, appears to have confused the Hoovers at first. "I was confused, and my wife and I talked it over. But the facts were there, so plain, so wonderful, so desirable, that we began to think and seek."[31] Their growing interest soon became the conviction: "that there were deeper Christian experiences we had not reached. A new hunger awakened us to have everything God had for us."[32]

Hoover was ahead of his time. Acts is understood to be more than mere historic narrative, but as a valid window to early church mission principles by such eminent theologians as James Dunn,[33] William and Robert Menzies,[34] Walter Hollenweger,[35] Allan Anderson,[36] Harvey Cox,[37] Gordon Fee,[38] and Max Turner.[39] Their useful conversations around the nature of the Holy Spirit and his action in the Acts of the Apostles validate Acts as doctrinally and missionally relevant today. This vision of the baptism of the Spirit, which led to the Acts of the Apostles' mission as the norm set up by Christ, seized the Hoovers, as it did the entire Pentecostal movement emerging at the turn of the twentieth century in the world. Hoover implemented the Wesleyan practices in the *Book of Discipline*: continuous street evangelism, cell group "classes" for discipling, church planting. These he found perfectly adequate rails for the spread of the Pentecostal revival locomotive to run on.

I believe it to be a crucial aspect for church extension that Acts indeed be understood as Luke's historical mission record and manual for all the time that Jesus continues to "do and teach" in the church (Acts 1:1) until his *parousia* (Acts 1:10–11).

Bernardo Campos' Theory of Pentecostality

Out of Latin America, Campos' observations of Pentecostalism led him to formulate his theory of Pentecostality. Campos divides his classic book, *El Principio Pentecostal*, into three sections. The first he devotes to Pentecost itself, a hermeneutic of the common event, and the second part to Pentecostality, where he seeks to build a theology of Pentecostality around the Messianic happening and the Pentecostal event in terms of ecclesiological, social, and consequential ethics. A third part is devoted to "Pentecostalisms," the history of the diverse Pentecostal churches, and expressions of the Pentecostal principle. He claims that the manifestation of the principle of Pentecostality, of common ancestry in the church capable of embracing, theologically, the life of all God's people, is a sign and hope for the uniting of the church and, by extension and example, even becoming a uniting catalyst for humanity. Beginning, therefore, with the Pentecost event and the church's re-interpretation of Joel and the Sinai encounter, Campos expounds the common thread that weaves the history of all churches ("all churches are founded in Pentecost"[40]) and usefully describes their historical development from their earliest Catholic and Orthodox origins through to the massively diverse Protestant, Evangelical, and, of course, Pentecostal families of churches. He shows that the history of the church has always alternated between its latent charisma and its necessary authority, that the Pentecostal principle appears again and again in all church history. It is only focused on in a specialized way with twentieth-century Pentecostalisms. These are significant in bringing the Pentecostal principle to the fore but divisive in separating themselves (as did Hoover) from the body of the wider church.

> We can interpret the history of the church as the history of the conflict between charisma and institution: the history of the predominance of the one over the other (manifestation) or the repression of the other (latency).[41]

By this, he means that "manifestations" of the Spirit are often repressed into "latency," where the potential Pentecostality is kept latent, though always present like magma in a volcano. Campos traces how Pentecostal theology, as in the book of Acts, that is born of a genuine experience with the Holy Spirit and that is not repressed, draws the church dynamically along the path of transformational mission as, indeed, occurred in Chile between the years of 1909 and 1936. He defines his concept of "Pentecostality" in relation to and as distinct from what he calls "Pentecostalisms," the diverse Pentecostal churches that identify with the baptism of the Holy Spirit, as a study of the social, collective identities from which we can construct and rationalize an objective systematization of the global Pentecostal identity.[42]

> We must define Pentecostality as that universal experience that expresses the Pentecost event as an over-arching ordering principle of the life of those who identify with the Pentecostal revival and who build from it a Pentecostal identity. Pentecostality would thus be the principle and type of religious practice, informed by the Pentecost event; a universal experience that brings Pentecostal and post-Pentecostal practices to the category of "principle" (arch-order) those Pentecostal and post-Pentecostal practices that seek to become historical concretions of that primordial experience (of Pentecost).[43]

For him, therefore, baptism of the Spirit falls into a broader concept and dimension of Pentecostality where Holy Spirit empowerment is available to all believers and not exclusively Pentecostals. Pentecostal churches challenge us in pointing to the possibility of rediscovering the Acts of the Apostles' Christian empowerment for mission through immersion and gifting in the Holy Spirit today. This theory of Pentecostality thus opens all churches to understand that they can access Pentecostal power and gifting.

My Theory of Pneuma Plasticity

Prompted by deliberation on Hoover's theological understanding, I derived a personal theory concerning the characteristics and nature of the Holy Spirit's persona that I call "Pneuma plasticity." By this term, I mean one of the attributes of the nature of the Holy Spirit, the capacity to "indwell" a person fully and yet "come upon" that person again through several experiences, anointings, and further infillings. As Jesus was born of the Spirit and no doubt was full of the Spirit, yet was visited powerfully by the Spirit at his baptism,[44] so will the Spirit come upon us in missional power.

Confusion often arises among believers, as I have illustrated with Hoover's own theological quest for understanding on Spirit-baptism, on account of the personhood and the spiritual nature of the Holy Spirit as an agent of the Trinity in bringing Jesus' life, love, and power to the believer and the church. Some of my more Reformed Anglican colleagues object: "Is not the person of the Spirit fully contained within the temple of the believer? Was not the Spirit's person fully received at Pentecost? How can it be possible for the *indwelling* person to *come upon* the indwelt again and again?"

Interestingly, a Catholic theologian, Raniero Cantalamessa,[45] leader in the Catholic Charismatic movement and prelate to the Pope, has observed this problem and confusion among those being renewed in their Christian walk by the recent movements of the Spirit in his church:

> How can the church now invite the Holy Spirit to "Come, visit, fill"? Does not the church believe that she has already received the Holy Spirit at Pentecost, and that we have already received the Holy Spirit in our individual baptism [Catholic, baptismal regeneration]? What sense can it make to say: "Come, visit, fill" to someone who is already present? The problem is there in scripture as well. On the day of Pentecost all were filled with the Holy Spirit, but just a few days later we find a kind of second Pentecost when all over again "all

were filled with the Holy Spirit," and among them were some of the apostles who had been present at the first Pentecost.[46]

Quoting Thomas Aquinas, Cantalamessa attempts to resolve the problem by picturing an indwelling Spirit who "begins to be in a new way in those he makes temples of God." In the context of what he identifies as "the greatest spiritual upsurge of all the history of the Church," he tries to explain baptism of the Holy Spirit as a "special grace that lies at the core of all this vast spiritual revival." However, he does not explain the nature of the "grace" and leaves it, with Aquinas, as a "mystery".[47]

Hoover's experience and teaching on the baptism of the Holy Spirit prompt us to develop such a doctrine from his own theological growth and, in extension, to it. Can the Spirit manifest in a person, regeneration, sanctification, empowerment in separate moments, all the while indwelling that person and revisiting, "coming upon" that person from "outside," so that he/she will grow in the Spirit, day by day? This ability, fully innate and essential to the nature of the Spirit, I call Pneuma plasticity.

Traditional Pentecostals usually understand the separation of regeneration and empowering as distinct actions of the Spirit. However, like Hoover, they are often confused by the expectation of subsequent experiences in the economy of the Spirit's salvation and sanctifying work. This need not be the case if we understand personal growth in a personal Spirit who is endowed with pneumatic properties that cause him to work in many and diverse ways and through many and varied signs (Heb 2:3,4), both indwelling and "re-immersing" or "baptizing," revisiting a believer, time and again, day by day.

Anglicans speak from a Reformed understanding of baptism of the Spirit, referring to initiation and reception of the Spirit at regeneration. Gordon Fee highlights the controversy over subsequentialism[48] and describes how it arose as an experience-based projection of blessings received. It is understandable, he says, as a reaction to a frustratingly dead church and absence of missional expression. However, even though he is a Pentecostal, he holds to the Anglican Reformed understanding as "better theology." I agree with his argument that Pentecostals are scripturally right in their longing after the Acts of the Apostles' dynamic Christianity contrasted with the traditional forms of their times, if scripturally wrong in their proposal of normative subsequence in the baptism of the Holy

Spirit. However, his theological conclusions, mainly from Protestant Reformed teaching, leave an open debate concerning subsequence. The importance of this explorative approach to the subject of Spirit-baptism is that, from the perspective of Pentecostality, both Pentecostal and Anglican theology can access the fullness of missional power from the Spirit.

Pentecostal Pentecostality

Hoover developed his Pentecostality around four main manifestations of the Spirit: presence, power, purity, and proclamation. The "manifestations of the Spirit" (which he preferred to the classical "tongues as initial evidence" theology), which began in 1909, led to a sovereign presence and power that heightened still further the sanctifying process of purity he saw so essential to true revival. However, the recapturing of Wesleyan proclamation of the gospel has characterized, often in great sacrifice, the Pentecostal movement in Chile.

As I write, I am visiting Chillán's IMP Pentecostal churches that are celebrating 101 years since the gospel arrived in Pentecostal power in the city. I shared in the mother church where it happened many years ago and also in one of their twelve daughter churches. There, I looked around at the hundred or so committed believers: a girl of four played timbral in perfect rhythm with the guitars and banjos while the two choirs sang alternately. A man with no legs played the accordion joyfully in a wheelchair. One after the other, members were called out to testify or sing. The place lit up every now and again with the presence of the Spirit—the reason, they continually declared, they were there at all. There were testimonies of glory, victory over pain, loneliness, sickness, and the misfortunes and tragedies of lower-middle-class life in Chillán. At least twenty times, they rose to their feet and shouted the triple *"¡Gloria a Dios!"*

I was housed at the home of Joel and Rosie Olate and their two daughters, Bárbara and Génesis (the four-year-old timbral player mentioned above). Joel is a car restorer, owns a taxi firm, and has two houses and a block of apartments that he rents out. His is the very typical upward mobility that is observable among Pentecostal families. They tell me they have "done very well, by God's grace."

The Olates recount how the "Matrix church," as they call it, the original plant out of Hoover's revivals in 1923, grew so much that in Chillán there are now two mother churches and eight *locales* (mission churches) in various Chillán neighborhoods. They work in a leadership team that helps in their *locale*, Villa Alegre, where they preach in the streets, worship, teach, and facilitate the children's work on Mondays, Wednesdays, Fridays, and weekends. They also informed me of another eight circuits outside the city, among the towns surrounding Chilllán. These are Wesley-style preaching circuits where new churches that have also arisen continue growing fast. Turns of preachers from the Chillán churches serve them. Every Sunday, one of the four sectors of those circuits comes to the mother church and "celebrates God's rich blessings upon them."

On questioning Rosie whether or not she had been baptized in the Spirit, she was unable to reply in theological terms but spoke of a "wonderful prayer meeting when "an instrument" laid her hand on me and I was immersed in such glorious waves of power that my life was changed from that moment on."[49] She reflected what Juan Sepúlveda will show of how Pentecostalism grows its theology out of its experience of the living Christ.[50]

Talking to Bishop Bernardo Cartes, celebrating seventy years since the Lord called him to be a member of the IMP church in Chillán, he corroborated this "Pentecostal system of growth" and its history, which he has observed personally.[51] He also explained to me how a Pentecostal preaches: "I wait on the Lord for a text which may be as simple as 'Jesus stopped....'[52] Then, often just before going to the pulpit, the Holy Spirit gives me the vision of where I am to go with the word, the teaching I am to give around why Jesus stopped before the woman and stops before us, and then he leads me to speak these things out. Some may balk, but who can fault the hermeneutic or homiletic methods when they have seen so much fruit from it? I felt that I was privileged to be on the inside of Hoover's work, the secret again of 'now really knowing him.'"

Anglican Pentecostality

A fuller understanding of Pentecostality became important to Anglicans in the Barrio Alto context of Santiago as they set about working around their mission methodology for a section of the city that Spanish-speaking non-Catholic churches had never reached. Since Allen Gardiner's arrival there in 1838, Anglicans had traditionally worked only with the indigenous peoples of southern Chile. They had refrained from Spanish work among the Catholic population. However, in 1974, a Society of Anglican Missionaries and Senders (SAMS) missionary team started two small home groups in 1974. A synod held in 1975 in the English Anglican church previously known as St. Andrew's was called to prayer to conclude its business. It was decided that the missionary bishops would pray for the national pastors. There was a sudden and unexpected outpouring on the assembly, resembling Pentecost. Pastors received, danced, rejoiced, spoke in tongues, prophesied, and worshipped for at least an hour. That night, the preacher spoke from Hebrews about how God would "shake all things" (Heb 12:25–28). Suddenly, after a time of united intercession, an earthquake shook the entire church, reminding them of Acts 4:31: "After they prayed, the place where they were meeting was shaken. And they were all filled with the Holy Spirit and spoke the word of God boldly." It was almost as though God were asking the assembled synod, "What kind of Anglican church do you want? Your kind or my Spirit-filled kind?" Several of those present chose the latter and began to seek God's leading for what a Chilean, Spirit-filled church should look like!

In 1983, the Anglican church of La Trinidad in Las Condes began in a living room. Initial work had been done through house groups led by mission partners in two focal points that later came together in the Anglican Church of Providencia, where the 1978 synod had been held. After receiving the commission to start churches in the Barrio Alto sector, the young new pastor of Providencia, who began with a few pews in the front row of the old English Anglican church, was forced to spend hours in prayer and fasting to discover how the work should be implemented. He came away with a simple phrase: "Plant churches that grow without limits." This seeking led to unexpected visitations of the Holy Spirit influenced by the Wimber revivals in the UK under David Pytches, who had been a bishop in Chile (1959–1977).

Since the enterprise entailed starting without a congregation, there opened up an Acts of the Apostles way ahead over the following years that involved seeking and learning directly from the Spirit for how to proceed with this Anglican missional work. There began a clear "pneumatic" or Spirit-led guidance of the congregation that led to a method that was taken up and developed in the church plant, La Trinidad de Las Condes, and has since been used to plant more churches: (1) "Much prayer, much blessing!" (2) "New people bring new people"; (3) "Everyone a disciple"; (4) "Mobilize" the entire congregation in their giftings and evangelism; (5) "Train leaders into the Army"; and (6) "Pepper the world with churches." These became principles by which the new wineskins were fashioned. First, through God's leading, it was decided that the church would begin every Saturday at 6 a.m., with everyone spending time in prayer and vigils as Jesus did early every morning. Second, personal evangelism was taught to every new believer, many of whom began to bring their family and friends to such programs as Marriage Encounter and Cursillo, devised with that aim in mind. New believers were immediately put into a beginner's group where they learned the introductory Christian walk in community, led by the pastor they could relate to. It also became natural in that context to mobilize and find jobs for everyone according to their gifting in the church so that everyone was active and had a spirit of service. Then it became apparent that there would never be new Bible school-trained pastors unless they were trained in a "boots on the ground" local church leadership training program, PROGROMIN (PROgramme of GROwth and MINistry). The Seminary by Extension for All Nations (SEAN)[53] program was used to disciple and train believers and new leaders. People were called and sent on missions through this specialist program and through personal leadership discipling by the pastor. Gradually, as local missions began to take shape around neighborhood clusters, new churches were formed with team leadership. So, six new churches were planted in the previously unevangelized sector of the city that are still there today. Several other missions were also planted on summer evangelistic teams along the north and south of Chile.

As I write, I look back at the Sunday when we held a service with prayer for healing. The church filled to capacity (four hundred people), and later, during the ministry time, as people fell to the ground, demons were cast out, and healing was manifest, I could not help but reflect: "I am seeing the New Testament come alive in my church!" As I described these scenes at our Bible college the next day, I asked two questions: "Is this Anglican?" and then, "How much more *biblical* should our Anglicanism be?"

Conclusion

Campos' principle of Pentecostality opens the doors for understanding foundational Spirit-empowerment as open to all believers and churches. All Christians originate from the church at Pentecost. What is needed is an understanding of the Spirit's nature and work in order to comprehend how he can come upon us in power again and again. Spirit-baptism can undoubtedly be regarded as a Christian initial reception of the Spirit (Rom 8:9-11; 1 Cor 12:13). However, the baptism of the Holy Spirit needs to be sought continuously in the Spirit's work in the believer. Regeneration leads to sanctification and empowerment. It is this empowering that Pentecostals have understood so well, calling it the experience of the baptism of the Holy Spirit. Understanding that the Spirit can initiate and later bless a Christian as many times as they ask (Luke 11:9) is explained under the concept of Pneuma plasticity. To many non-Pentecostals, Spirit-baptism can start at initiation but needs to continue with the full work of the Spirit.

When an Anglican bishop lays hands on the candidates at their confirmation, he speaks out the Pentecostal principle:

> Defend, O Lord, this your servant with your heavenly grace, that he/she may continue yours forever; and daily increase in your Holy Spirit, more and more, until he/she comes into your everlasting kingdom. Amen.[54]

Hoover and Cranmer combine to enable the vital Spirit-empowered mission needed in today's complex and dark world. The Spirit came powerfully upon Jesus, who already had the Spirit in fullness. Both traditionally defined Pentecostal and non-Pentecostal churches can rely on the Spirit to repeatedly come upon them as they seek to exemplify the new wine and the missional wineskins of the Acts of the Apostles.

Notes

1 Dr. Bernardo Campos (who sadly passed away October 15, 2024) was a Peruvian Pentecostal pastor and theologian since 1975. He earned his bachelor's degree in theology at the Evangelical Seminary of Lima. He continued his studies at the *Instituto Superior Evangelico de Estudios Teologicos* (ISEDET) in Buenos Aires in 1989 and obtained his master's degree in Science of Religion at San Marcos National University in 1998.

He finalized his doctoral studies in 2008 at Rhema University, USA. He was a professor of contemporary theology, and taught Religious Sciences, History of Dogma, and Missiology and Ministries at the Peruvian Evangelical Seminary (Presbyterian), the Wesleyan Seminary of Peru (Methodist), the Alliance Bible Seminary of Peru (AC & MP), and more recently in the Davar School of the Tabernacle of God Church. He authored over ten books, the most important of which are *El Principio Pentecostal* and *Experiencias del Espíritu*, quoted in this chapter.

2 See Luis Orellana and Miguel Ángel Mansilla, "El Obispo Durán y la Jaula de Hierro," *Le Monde Diplomatique* edition (Instituto de Estudios Internacionales, 2017).

3 Founded in 1983 from a house church initiative that was started by a group of Anglican missionaries from the South American Mission Society, the church grew to its current size of over one thousand members and six daughter churches in Santiago's upper middle class. See Barbara Bazley, *"Somos Anglicanos"* (Santiago: Editorial Interamericana, 1995).

4 Unless otherwise stated, all scripture references are taken from New International Version (NIV).

5 See Mario G. Hoover, *History of the Pentecostal Revival in Chile*, Santiago: Ebenezer Publishing House, 2000, 33. Though North American, Hoover wrote his book in Spanish. Mario Hoover, his grandson, produced his excellent and very useful English translation (especially to English researchers).

6 F. F. Bruce, *Matthew* (Scripture Union Publishing, 1978).

7 Walter Hollenweger, *Pentecostalismo* (Buenos Aires: Editorial Aurora, 1976); Allan Anderson, *Spreading Fires: The Missionary Nature of Early Pentecostalism*, 1st ed. (New York: Orbis, 2007); John Kessler, *A Study of the Older Protestant Missions and Churches in Perú and Chile* (Goes, The Netherlands: Oosterbaan & Le Contre N.V., 1967).

8 Luis Orellana, *El Fuego y la Nieve* 1 (Hualpén, Chile: CEEP Ediciones, 2006); Luis Orellana, "El Futuro del Pentecostalismo en América Latina," Red Latinoamérica de Estudios Pentecostales (RELEP), *Voces del Pentecostalismo Latinoamericano*, IV, eds. Daniel and Luis Orellana Luis (2011): 141–56; Luis Orellana, Claudio Colombo, and Zicri Rojas, "Los Pentecostales en Chile: Sus Principales Representaciones Sociales en el Siglo XX," *Religião & Sociedade* 39, no. 3 (December 2019): 82–99. Luis Orellana and Miguel Ángel Mansilla, "El Obispo Durán y la Jaula de Hierro," *Le Monde Diplomatique* edition (Instituto de Estudios Internacionales, 2017).

9   Anderson, *Spreading Fire*, 201.

10 David Stoll, *Is Latin America Turning Protestant?* (California: UCC Press, 1991)

11 Todd M. Johnson, Gina A. Zurlo, Albert Hickman, and P. F. Crossing, "Christianity 2016: Latin America and Projecting Religions to 2050," *International Bulletin of Mission Research* 40, no. 1 (January 2016): 22–29.

12 Paul Freston, *Evangelical Christianity and Democracy in Latin America* (Oxford: Oxford University Press, 2008).

13 Freston, preface to *Evangelical Christianity*, xi.

14 Miguel Alvarez, *Integral Mission* (Oxford: Regnum, 2016).

15 Anderson, *Spreading Fires*, 201.

16 Dirección de Estadística y Censos, 30 Junio, 1920.

17 Empadronamiento de 1960.

18 Censo Instituto Nacional de Estadística 2012, 2017.

19 Though the term *"Evangélicos"* refers to all non-Catholic Christians in Chile, a majority of these, calculated by national census at over 80 percent, are Pentecostals.

20 Rodrigo Moulian, *El Sello del Espíritu derramado sobre la Carne* (Valdivia, Chile: Kultrún, 2017).

21 Orellana, *El Fuego y la Nieve*.

22 Eugenia Fediakova, "Somos Parte de esta Sociedad," Evangélicos y política en el Chile post autoritario. En los sectores populares y lo político: acción colectiva, políticas públicas y comportamiento electoral de *Revista Política*, vol. 43 (Santiago, Chile: Primavera, 2004).

23 Mario G. Hoover (see footnote 5) translates his grandfather Willis' original Spanish *"reconocemos"* as "recognize." However, I have chosen "know" as the Spanish is thus better represented: the meaning is more like "we now know and recognize him."

24 Hoover, *History of the Pentecostal Revival in Chile*, 33.

25 Francis Chan, *The Forgotten God* (Colorado Springs: David C. Cook, 2009), 15.

26 Alfred Cooper, "A Gem in the Water" (Doctoral Thesis, Chapter 6.10, Oxford Centre for Mission Studies), 236.

27 Hoover, *History of the Pentecostal Revival*, 4.

28 Hoover, *History of the Pentecostal Revival*, 119.

29 See Gary McGee, "Baptism of the Holy Ghost and Fire! The Mission Legacy of Minnie F. Abrams," *Missiology: An International Review* 27, no. 4 (1999), https://doi.org/10.1177/009182969902700410.

30 Hoover, *History of the Pentecostal Revival*, 9.

31 See Willis Hoover, "The Wonderful Works of God in Chili," *The Latter Rain Evangel* 3, no. 7 (April 1911): 19–20.

32 Hoover, *History of the Pentecostal Revival*, 10.

33 James Dunn, *Baptism in the Holy Spirit*, 2nd ed. (London: SCM Press, 2010).

34 Robert P. Menzies, *The Development of Early Christian Pneumatology with Special Reference to Luke-Acts* (Sheffield, England: Sheffield Academic Press, 1991).

35 Walter Hollenweger, *The Pentecostals* (London: SCM Press, 1972).

36 Anderson, *Spreading Fires*; Allan Anderson, *Introduction to Pentecostalism: Global Charismatic Christianity* (Cambridge: Cambridge University Press, 2013).

37 Harvey Cox, *Fire from Heaven: The Rise of Pentecostal Spirituality and the Reshaping of Religion in the Twenty-First Century* (New York: Addison Wesley, 1995).

38 Gordon Fee, *God's Empowering Presence* (Baker Academic, 2009).

39 Max Turner, *Power from on High: The Spirit in Israel's Restoration and Witness in Luke-Acts* (Sheffield: Sheffield Academic Press, 1996).

40 Bernardo Campos, *El Prinicipio Pentecostalidad* (Salem, OR: Kerigma Publications, 2016). See Section Three of the book for this prevaling theme on the unity of churches beginning at Pentecost.

41 Campos, *El Principio Pentecostalidad*, 98.

42 Campos, *El Principio Pentecostalidad*, 132.

43 Campos, *El Principio Pentecostalidad*, 130.

44 See Damon So, Jesus' *Revelation of His Father* (Great Britain: Paternoster, 2006).

45 Raniero Cantalamessa OFM Cap is an Italian Catholic cardinal and priest in the Order of Friars Minor Capuchin and a theologian. He has served as the Preacher to the Papal Household since 1980, under Pope John Paul II,

Pope Benedict XVI, and Pope Francis. Cantalamessa is a proponent of the Catholic Charismatic Renewal.

46 Raniero Cantalamessa, *Come, Creator Spirit,* 1st ed. (Minnesota: Liturgical Press, 2003), 53–54.

47 Cantalamessa, *Come, Creator Spirit,* 53–54.

48 Gordon Fee, "Baptism in the Holy Spirit: The Issue of Separability and Subsequence," *Pneuma* 7, no. 2 (1985): 87–99.

49 Rosie Olate, personal communication with author, April 20, 2024.

50 Juan Sepúlveda, "Características Teológicas de Un Pentecostalismo Autóctono: El Caso Chileno," in *En La Fuerza Del Espíritu,* ed. Benjamín Gutierrez (Guatemala: AIPRAL/CELEP, 1995). Juan Sepúlveda, "The Power of the Holy Spirit and Church Indigenisation: A Latin American Perspective," in *Pentecostals and Charismatics in Latin America and Latino Communities* (New York: Néstor Medina and Sammy Alfaro, 2014).

51 Bernardo Cartes, personal communication with author, January 2023.

52 Referring to the incident with the woman with the issue of blood in Mark 5 and Luke 8.

53 SEAN (https://seaninternational.org) is a program of theological training that aims to put into place the "bottom rungs" of the educational ladder. Devised by Archdeacon Tony Barratt in the sixties, he and a team wrote, edited, and published a program that covers the scriptures and teaches basic pastoral skills for Majority World pastors.

54 Thomas Cranmer, "Confirmation Prayer," in *The Book of Common Prayer* (New York, Seabury Press, 1979).

18   Oral Roberts and Billy Graham: A Friendship that Influenced the Christian World

John Paul Thompson

Abstract

This study explores the relationship between Oral Roberts and Billy Graham. Their personal admiration for each other and their public display of friendship influenced their own ministries, the attitudes of the broader Evangelical community, and even the development of holistic mission and a broader understanding of gospel in the Evangelical world. Two catalytic public moments together are considered in this chapter: Roberts speaking and praying at Graham's World Congress on Evangelization in Berlin, and Graham speaking at the dedication of Oral Roberts University.

Introduction

Two world-renowned evangelists of the twentieth century, Oral Roberts and Billy Graham, stood side-by-side on the new campus of Oral Roberts University (ORU) in Tulsa, Oklahoma, on April 2, 1967. That day, the crowds on the lawn swelled to nearly twenty thousand, all to personally witness these two spiritual giants bless the establishment of a Christian university forged from the fires of healing evangelism. In the post-World War II era, these two evangelists had become the premiere leaders in their particular streams of Evangelicalism. Billy Graham was at the helm of the populous Evangelical movement, and Oral Roberts represented the Pentecostal-Charismatic movement of the mid-twentieth century, considered by many to be the subset of Evangelicalism.

Although these two Christian communities shared the same roots of American fundamentalism and Protestant pietism, suspicion lingered between them. This public display of solidarity between Billy Graham and Oral Roberts surprised many Christians and contributed credibility to the fledgling university. On that day, the Christian world in America witnessed a friendship and shared passion for education between two icons of American Christianity. Billy Graham's declaration over Oral Roberts University became part of the lore passed down to generations of students. The friendship between Oral Roberts and Billy Graham not only impacted the university but also contributed to Roberts' journey into mainstream American Christianity and to the evolution of Evangelical thought regarding the nature of the gospel, evangelism, and mission in subsequent years.

A Friendship as Fellow Evangelists

This friendship had begun seventeen years earlier, in the summer of 1950 in Portland, Oregon. Graham and Roberts had each been leading crusades across the country for three years. Roberts had intentionally traveled to Portland to hear Graham preach and hopefully meet him. They first met by chance in the hotel before the evening crusade. Billy and Ruth Graham spotted Roberts in the cafe and hollered at him to come join them. Graham spontaneously asked Roberts to pray at his crusade that evening. Roberts tried to decline, saying, "That might not be the thing to do because I'm very controversial [due to] my healing ministry." To which Graham responded, "You are not controversial in my services." Though many Evangelicals did not accept Roberts and his ministry at the time, Graham had already secretly visited one of Roberts' crusades in Florida several nights the year before. Some of his family members had also been prayed for by Roberts.[1]

Mutual Respect and Interaction

The two deeply respected each other, valued each other's ministry, and shared a long-standing friendship. Roberts publicly expressed his belief that Graham was "the greatest of our century," saying, "He has the greatest crowds; he has the widest influence on government leaders."[2] He affirmed that Graham had "a great soul-winning call." Meanwhile, Graham recognized Roberts had the gift of healing.[3] He even confided with Roberts that the reason he did not pray for the sick in his crusades was simply that he did not have the healing gift that Roberts had.

Graham affirmed that their objective was the same even though their method and approach were different.[4] In 2009, almost sixty years after their first face-to-face meeting in 1950, each of them reflected on their friendship. Roberts stated, "Billy was the most generous man in the ministry I've ever met. He accepted me as a brother. He said he fell in love with my ministry. I counted him as the number one evangelist in the world. We became very close friends." Similarly, Graham said, "Oral Roberts was a man of God and a great friend in ministry. I loved him as a brother. We had many quiet conversations over the years."[5] Those conversations included periodic personal correspondence and times together.[6]

They occasionally spent time together in each other's world over the decades. At least three times (1950, 1965, and 1974), Roberts traveled to a Billy Graham crusade or meeting, which typically included Roberts addressing the crowd, and Graham and Roberts having personal conversations.[7] At least twice, Graham visited Roberts at ORU. Graham spoke at the dedication of the university in 1967, and again at the dedication of the massive Mabee Center on the campus five years later, in 1972. When Roberts ministered in North Carolina, Graham invited Roberts and his wife to brunch in their home. When Graham was near Tulsa, Roberts drove to Oklahoma City to be with him. They had extended time together as well at the Berlin Congress on World Evangelization in 1966. Their long and personal friendship is even reflected in the gift Roberts sent Graham late in their lives: a walker identical to the one he was using, to which Graham replied, "Oral, you've sent me the Cadillac!"[8]

On the one hand, this friendship made sense as they shared several similarities. They were the same age, born in the same year of 1918. Both launched into crusade ministry in the same year of 1947. Both quickly became renowned evangelists holding crusades throughout the United States and internationally as well. Both grew up and were shaped by the American fundamentalism of the first half of the twentieth century, which bred a deep conviction on the authority of scripture and holiness.

Representatives of a New Evangelicalism

After the Second World War, a new Evangelicalism emerged out of fundamentalism, and both men played significant roles in this emerging stream. New Evangelicals sought to leave behind the strong separatism that had developed in fundamentalism, and they desired to have cultural influence. Graham was at the populist center for the new Evangelicalism. Both he and Roberts called all Americans to a life-transforming faith and preached their versions of that message beyond the walls of the local church to all in the surrounding society. They proclaimed the gospel in the largest tents money could buy, in stadiums, and on television to speak to all Americans. Seeking to influence culture, Graham met with every American president, from Truman to Obama, and was seen as the pastor to presidents. Likewise, Roberts met with presidents from Kennedy to Bush, and he hosted many cultural icons, including actors, singers, and political figures on his prime-time television specials between 1969 and 1975.[9]

Mutual Passion for Christian Education

For Roberts, his initial calling into ministry included building a university. He heard the voice of God in the car while being transported to the revival meeting where he would be prayed for and subsequently healed from tuberculosis. He heard God say, "Son, I am going to heal you and you are to take my healing power to your generation. You are to build me a university and build it on my authority and on the Holy Spirit."[10] During the years of his healing crusades, as he traveled to various cities, he would intentionally visit universities to gain ideas. He had conversations with professors, students, and architects.[11] He told audiences in his crusades that he would one day build a university. In the 1950s, he and his family often prayed over a piece of farmland on the south side of Tulsa, Oklahoma, that he had his eye on for a future campus. In 1960, over a meal in Virginia with Pat Robertson, who founded the Christian Broadcasting Network that year, Roberts wrote down the ideas that had been percolating in his mind over the course of his conversation with Robertson. The words would later be etched on the university chapel wall for generations of students to see: "Raise up your students to hear my voice, to go where my light is dim, where my voice is heard small, and my healing power is not known, even to the uttermost bounds of the earth. Their work will exceed yours, and in this I am well pleased."

Roberts founded Oral Roberts University in 1963, with the first cohort enrolled in 1965. Graham came to dedicate the new university in 1967. Graham shared with Roberts that he, too, had seriously thought about establishing a Christian university for several years, but felt he did not have the bandwidth to do so. He was thrilled that Roberts had built a magnificent university.[12] In his dedication speech, he highlighted that "during the past three hundred years, many of America's great universities were founded by evangelists."[13] He believed it was deeply significant that Oral Roberts University was founded by an evangelist. Graham declared to the crowd of eighteen thousand gathered that day, "The first objective of Christian education is a quest for truth," and that quest is "linked also to evangelism." He articulated how Christian education was critical to the future success of Christianity in the modern world, stating, "Christian education is at the center and must be at the center of an awakened, revived Christianity. The future of the entire missionary program, the future of informed witnessing Christians, the future of an enlarged Christian concern and influence are all at stake in higher Christian education today."[14] Graham had asked Roberts in Berlin the year before, "When are you going to invite me to your university?" Roberts immediately responded, asking him to come to dedicate the university. Their shared belief in the necessity for Christian universities with high academic excellence was an additional similarity that continued to strengthen their friendship.

Hurdles to Friendship

While both men shared a number of similarities, their differences could have easily prevented them from developing a friendship. Roberts attracted negative press, and he knew this could create problems for Graham by association. Roberts suggest to Graham that it might not be a good idea for Roberts to pray at Graham's crusade in 1950. Then, while Roberts was ministering in North Carolina, Graham sent a man to invite Roberts and his wife to his home for brunch, but Roberts turned down the invitation because he "did not want to infect" Graham with the controversial nature of his own ministry. Graham responded, "No, I want you," and sent the man back to bring the Roberts to his home. Roberts remarked after that they had a conversation about the Lord following a delightful brunch.[15]

Graham demonstrated his genuine friendship at the Berlin Congress on World Evangelization in 1966. Even though he had been invited to chair a panel session on healing, Roberts was very hesitant to go. Afterward, he wrote to his *Abundant Life* readership:

Only the warm invitation of Billy Graham and Carl Henry had prevailed upon us to go.... Perhaps any reluctance on our part was that our ministry of evangelism and healing have been considered by some to be on the periphery of the great stream of evangelical Christianity. We felt a deep love and appreciation for these men for their sacrificial labors to win souls. However, since the healing ministry had not been understood to be an integral part of the mainstream of the gospel, we were not sure how our ministry would be accepted or what our contribution could be to the Congress. Billy Graham, his

> team, and these leaders reached out to us in Christian love and we reached out
> to them. It was soon evident there were no real barriers between us.[16]

At the Congress, Graham invited Roberts to eat dinner with him and the other key leaders there. Graham decided to invite him to address all the delegates in a general session. "It was an audacious decision that would bring immediate attacks from fundamentalists and conservative critics."[17] Graham leveraged his own position and influence despite the offense he knew other participants would take. He introduced Roberts at the evening plenary session to all the delegates with these words:

> Our prayer is going to be led by a man that I have come to love and appreciate
> in the ministry of evangelism. He has just built, and is in the process of
> building, a great university. He is known throughout the world through his
> radio and television work, and millions of people listen to him. I am speaking
> of Dr. Oral Roberts, and I'm going to ask him to say a word of greeting to us
> before he leads the prayer.[18]

Warren Hultgren, a Southern Baptist minister, the pastor of the First Baptist Church of Tulsa, and Roberts' friend, had strongly encouraged Roberts to go to Berlin. Being present when he then spoke and prayed at that plenary in Berlin, Hultgren observed the historic nature of the moment. He felt it was "the 'unconscious turning point' in that conference and in Oral's life."[19] Graham's risky and strategic move shifted perspectives for many of the gathered leaders of the Evangelical world, and it did become a catalytic moment in Roberts' life.

Mutual Influence

The friendship of these two world-renowned evangelists created space for and fostered mutual influence on each other and, because of their prominent roles in the body of Christ, had broader ramifications. Biographer David Harrell chronicled Roberts' movement from the tributaries of Pentecostalism into the mainstream river of Evangelicalism and American Christianity. His upbringing and early ministry were immersed in the classical Pentecostal world. Pentecostals of the first half of the twentieth century in America were on the periphery of society in general and in the Christian world as well. Their typical economic poverty and holiness ethics kept them out of mainstream American life. Emotional worship, emphasis on Spirit-baptism as a second work of grace evidenced by speaking in tongues, and the exercise of other spiritual gifts from 1 Corinthians 12:1–3 relegated Pentecostals to the periphery of American Christianity. Though they were fundamentalists in their affirmation of the authority of scripture and their eschatology, many fundamentalists were cessationists. Consequently, Pentecostals were often viewed by other fundamentalists with skepticism at best.

Movement to Mainstream

In the late 1960s and 1970s, Roberts intentionally moved into the circles of mainstream Evangelical Christianity. In the late sixties, Roberts left his Pentecostal denomination and joined the mainline Methodist church. With a membership of eleven million, it dwarfed his Pentecostal denomination of sixty-five thousand.[20] At the same time, he closed the chapter of two decades of crusade ministry and launched primetime television specials and a weekly Sunday morning program to capture the American viewing audience. Ten million people tuned in to his first primetime television special in 1969. In 1973, over thirty-seven million watched the spring primetime show.[21] Many were reading Roberts' magazines and books as well. His magazine *Abundant Life* grew to one million in monthly circulation.[22] He wrote books that were distributed worldwide, and his quarterly devotional, "Daily Blessings," had a quarterly circulation of 250 thousand.[23] He had become a household name in America, and much opposition had fallen by the wayside. People everywhere were reading his books and magazines and watching him regularly on television. By 1970, Roberts had been accepted by the leaders in the Evangelical world (apart from the fundamentalist cessationism contingency). *The New York Times* wrote in 1973 that "in the wake of his plunge into prime-time television, Roberts commands more personal loyalty than any other clergyman of the nineteen-seventies. Graham is obviously the dominant figure of the era, but he is a more impersonal force."[24]

Three forces in the 1960s propelled Roberts out of the Pentecostal shadows of the first half of the twentieth century into the limelight of mainstream American life and American Christianity: the formation of his Christian liberal arts university, the groundswell of the Charismatic Renewal in the 1960s, and the friendship of Graham. At times, these components overlapped. Graham gave the university legitimacy when he came to dedicate it in 1967. The Charismatic Renewal gave the

Pentecostal experience legitimacy in the Evangelical and ecumenical wings of Protestantism, as well as among Roman Catholics. Oral Roberts University became a hub for leaders in the Charismatic Renewal to pass through and to congregate with Roberts, who was positioned to be a connector and facilitator in the movement.

Integral to the story of Roberts' trek from the periphery to the center was Graham's hand of friendship. Despite their different backgrounds and methodologies, they were united in their passion for the gospel, evangelism, and cultural influence. Though Roberts experienced persistent opposition from various quarters of the Christian community, Graham appreciated, accepted, and publicly applauded him. Graham leveraged his position of influence on his behalf. Just nine months after Graham boldly showcased him at the Berlin Congress plenary, Graham again faced opposition from his own constituency by coming to the new campus of Oral Roberts University to help dedicate it. Biographer David Harrell reports, "Graham's supporters feared he would be irreparably damaged by such a close association with Oral; his office in Minneapolis was flooded with letters warning him of the risk."[25] Five years later, Graham again came to the university campus and joined Roberts on one of his primetime specials to dedicate the new basketball arena and auditorium, the Mabee Center. Graham repeatedly invited Roberts to stand beside him publicly: in front of his crusade crowds in Portland and Denver, then in front of the leaders of the Evangelical world gathered in Berlin, and finally in front of the world, dedicating the ORU campus, not just once but twice.

The divide between Pentecostals and Evangelicals was still present, but the seeds of change had been sown through that friendship, and early fruits were appearing that today have grown into maturity. Harrell observed,

> Roberts's friendship with Billy Graham—highlighted by Oral's presence in Berlin and Graham's dedication address at ORU—did much to lessen tensions between charismatics and evangelicals.... While many evangelicals remained reserved about Pentecostals and Roberts—the movements still remain "half-sisters" with considerable "sibling rivalry"—Oral's embrace by Graham was sufficient to open many doors.[26]

Harrell wrote those words in 1985. Today, almost forty years later, the Evangelical and Pentecostal worlds are nearly one and the same: no longer "half-sisters" with "sibling rivalry." The seeds are now full grown.

With the swell of the subsequent third wave of Pentecostalism (or neo-Pentecostals, as classical Pentecostals like to refer to them) and the global growth of all three Pentecostal streams—classical Pentecostalism, Charismatics, and third wave Pentecostalism—seems to have almost thoroughly leavened the loaf of Evangelicalism across the world.

Expansion of Gospel Understanding

At the heart of this merging identity of Evangelicals and Pentecostals today is the theological development of an expanded understanding of the gospel and mission over the past fifty-plus years. Much of the twentieth century was marked by a separation of gospel proclamation and social action in the Protestant world. Liberal Protestants engaged in humanitarian mission while Evangelical Protestants engaged in the spiritual mission of saving souls and planting churches. In between these two extremes, Pentecostalism grew. Theologically, they embraced the Evangelical emphasis on the authority of scripture and the primacy of evangelism. But their praxis emphasized God's desire to transform the whole person, not just the soul and ethics. For Pentecostals, with Roberts becoming the dominant American example, evangelism was accompanied by demonstrations of power through divine healing and miracles. He pressed this further by establishing a university that educated the whole person (mind, body, and spirit) and brought together science and spirituality.

This friendship did not just impact Roberts' life, though; it impacted Graham's as well. Graham watched Roberts pray for the sick in his crusades both in person in 1949 and, likely, on television as they were aired across the country in the 1950s. Members of his family had gone through Robert's prayer line. He witnessed the empathy and compassion that Roberts displayed for people's physical suffering. Graham believed Roberts had the gift of healing. In the context of his Southern Baptist heritage that strongly leaned toward cessationism before the growing influence of the Charismatic and third wave movements, this acceptance of healing was rather remarkable and progressive. During his visit to Oral Roberts University, Graham witnessed the philosophy of whole person education firsthand and endorsed it in his dedication speech.

Humans do not just have a mind and a spirit. They have a body. The three are integrated; all three matter to God, and all three need to be developed. It was not just whole person education that was at the core of the university but healing as well. This was summed up in the culminating and final statement of the university's purpose articulated in 1970: "to enable students to go into every man's world with healing for the totality of human need."[27] Healing for the totality of human needs goes beyond physical ailments and spiritual wellbeing. It includes relational, emotional, economic, organizational, and societal health. Graham's presence on the campus and personal conversations with Roberts regarding the mission and vision of the university would have exposed him to Roberts' holistic perspective that included both theory and practice.

Because of Graham's role at the center of Evangelicalism, Roberts' impact on Graham planted a seed in his heart that influenced all of Evangelical Christianity. Not only did other Evangelical leaders shift their attitudes toward Roberts and his brand of Christianity because of the public friendship of Graham, Graham participated in laying the foundation for the fundamental shift in the Evangelical world in the understanding of mission and evangelism. Just eight years after the Berlin Congress on World Evangelization, Graham and another friend, John Stott, organized an even larger, long-lasting, and impactful congress, the Lausanne Congress of World Evangelization in 1974. The resulting Lausanne Covenant became "one of the most significant documents in modern church history, shaping Evangelical thinking for the rest of the century."[28] A watershed component in the Lausanne Covenant was the inclusion of "Christian Social Responsibility" as one of the fifteen affirmations of the covenant.

Graham alluded to the importance of meeting the social needs of man in his closing address at the Berlin Congress in 1966. In reflecting on the content of the previous ten days, he remarked, "I think, secondly, that we have said that *the social needs of men can be met in the Gospel and only in the Gospel.* A person's basic need is conversion."[29] On the one hand, he recognized the importance of meeting the social needs. However, he still held on to the Evangelical dogma of the day represented in that gathering: that the spiritual takes precedence and it is only through conversion of the individual to Christ that social needs can be met.

Eight years later, at the Lausanne Congress, social responsibility was elevated and elaborated on through the editorial work of Stott in the Lausanne Covenant. The covenant called for "justice...and for the liberation of men and women from every kind of oppression."[30] It went on to repent for not embracing both evangelism and social action. "We express penitence both for our neglect and for having sometimes regarded evangelism and social concern as mutually exclusive."[31] It continued, "We affirm that evangelism and socio-political involvement are both part of our Christian duty."[32] Even the message of salvation is not just for individuals, but it also speaks to societal systems. It read, "The message of salvation implies also a message of judgment upon every form of alienation, oppression, and discrimination, and we should not be afraid to denounce evil and injustice wherever they exist."[33] While Graham was not the architect of this document, his opening address at Lausanne made it clear he valued social action and desired that this congress would flesh out the relationship between evangelism and social action. The fifth affirmation of the covenant was the result of his intention for the conference.

Graham's opening speech entitled "Why Lausanne?" detailed four foundation stones and four hopes for the conference. Embedded in both the foundation stones and the hopes was the issue of social responsibility. The foundation stones were "four basic presuppositions" that he believed "should undergird our labors." He also clarified that these four "have guided our planning and should underlie everything we do at this congress."[34] The fourth foundation stone was that "we reaffirm that our witness must be by both word and deed," to which he was referring to social action. Both verbal witness and social action are essential. In fact, works or social action are the evidence of salvation that comes from grace through faith. He noted that "many today are debating the question of the proper place of social action in the overall program of the Church" and he promised that "much will be said at this Congress concerning the matter."[35] While he did not know if this would all be sorted out during the Congress, "both our words and our deeds must both reflect the Gospel."[36] He also highlighted the great Evangelical tradition of social action wherein "evangelicals have changed society, influencing men everywhere in the battle against slavery and in the quest for social justice."[37] In addition to this fourth cornerstone of Lausanne, Graham expressed a similar hope regarding the outcome of the congress. Graham declared, "I trust we can state what the relationship is between evangelism and social responsibility. Let us rejoice in social action, and yet insist that it alone is not evangelism and cannot be substituted for evangelism. This relationship disturbs many believers. Perhaps Lausanne can help clarify it."[38]

Obviously, Graham had been thinking deeply about meeting the needs of humanity along with sharing the gospel. While there was mention of social action in Berlin eight years earlier, it was completely subjected to the primacy of evangelism. There appears to have been an evolution of thought for him eight years later as he articulated the issue and sought to make it one of the key topics for the Lausanne Congress to hammer out. The fifth article in the Lausanne Covenant was the result of that work. During the eight years between Berlin and Lausanne, Graham visited the ORU campus twice. He affirmed Roberts' philosophy of whole person education and he valued Roberts' healing gift. Although Roberts was not present at Lausanne, his praxis and perspectives aligned with those Graham expressed in his opening speech and the agenda for the congress.

After Lausanne

Lausanne was a watershed moment. The Lausanne Covenant established the legitimacy of social action once again for Evangelicals; there was even repentance for neglecting social action. However, the covenant did not clearly explain the relationship between evangelism and social action. Is evangelism still the primary mission of the church, or is social justice and compassion ministry equal to verbal witness? Evangelicals debated and wrestled with these questions for the rest of the century. Graham and Roberts believed verbal witness held the highest place. But their inclusion of social action opened the door for an eventual new understanding of mission, gospel, and evangelism that Evangelicals of the twenty-first century now embrace.

Roberts' and Graham's gospel centered on individual spiritual salvation appropriated by faith in the atonement of Christ on the cross for the forgiveness of sins. Graham's gospel message was "God loves you, God will forgive you, God can change you, if you repent of your sins and receive Jesus Christ as your savior."[39] Similarly, Roberts' salvation prayer for people in his crusades displayed his understanding of the gospel as the saving of souls. He asked people to raise their hand and then stand if they wanted him to pray for them "that Jesus will come into your heart, that Jesus will forgive your sins, give you peace in your heart and save your soul."[40]

Like Graham, Roberts, too, emphasized the love of God. But he went much further with his revelation and core message that "God is a good

God." Not only did God want to save souls, but he also wanted to heal people. Consequently, in his crusades, the salvation prayer was followed by prayer lines for healing. "This conviction that 'Something Good Is Going to Happen to You' led him to proclaim that believers could expect miracles, good things, prosperity, healing, and overall blessings because God intends for his children to live that way in their journeys through life."[41] Roberts also emphatically emphasized the present reality of God in our lives through the Holy Spirit. In his course called, "The Holy Spirit in the Now," Roberts began his last teaching lesson with this intention: "I want to try to help you understand more fully the part the Holy Spirit (the divine Paraclete) plays in bringing Christ into the NOW of your great needs."[42] Roberts' good news message included both the present and the future. Even his magazine title, *Abundant Life,* reflected his emphasis on the present. He agreed with many of his Evangelical contemporaries that saving souls was primary. However, his emphasis on present daily life needs and his practice of praying for both salvation and for healing in every crusade made evangelism and social concern co-equals in his ministry practice.

After Lausanne, scholars gathered, debated, and theologized on the relationship between evangelism and social action. Practitioners were found at both ends of the spectrum. The burgeoning church growth and church planting movements among Evangelicals championed evangelism measured in numerical growth. Conversely, liberation theology outside Evangelical circles pushed radical social action to liberate the poor through revolution against corrupt systems. Almost ten years after Lausanne, scholars gathered at Wheaton and produced the Wheaton '83 Statement on Transformation. C. Rene Padilla believes "Wheaton '83 completed the process of shaping an evangelical social conscience... It made it evident to evangelicals that evangelism cannot be divorced from meaningful involvement with people with all their needs."[43] The Wheaton '83 Statement emphasized "the biblical vision of the Kingdom of God" and the goal of personal and social transformation in this biblical vision. Padilla points out that "by emphasizing that the Kingdom of God is 'both present and future, both societal and individual, both physical and spiritual,' it laid a sound theological basis for the mission of the church with no dichotomy between evangelism and social responsibility."[44] The kingdom of God came in the incarnation of Christ and the ascension of

Christ. It is coming presently on the earth through the people of Christ empowered by the Spirit. And it will come in fullness in the return of Christ. Al Tizon remarks, "In light of the assured future, the Spirit-filled Church perseveres and hopes as it engages the world in bold holistic mission according to love, justice, righteousness, and peace of the coming kingdom. In light of the End, the Church participates with God to accomplish the *missio Dei*, God's mission."[45] Today, forty years after Wheaton '83, Evangelicals have fully embraced holistic mission. The church is a sent church, it is a "missional church." That mission includes verbal witness, lived example, social justice, signs and wonders, proclamation (evangelism), peacemaking, leaven in every domain of society, creation care, etc.

Rollin Grams rightly observes that Pentecostalism played a contributing role in the rise of holistic gospel. He suggests that the Pentecostal emphasis on divine power contributed to the theology of transformation. Transformation is possible because it comes from God, who has the power to do it. Twentieth-century Pentecostalism "was a movement that had a more holistic theology in the area of miracles."[46] They did not just believe it was possible for God to heal; they pursued it. Signs and wonders performed by "Jesus of the Gospels and the church of Acts presented the paradigm for the Church and missions today... The gradual inclusion of Pentecostals into Evangelical circles meant that more holistic theology was on offer within Fundamentalist Evangelicalism in the West."[47] The friendship between Roberts and Graham sped up that process.

Conclusion

Today, we are benefactors of the friendship between Roberts and Graham. In recent years, however, new fault lines are appearing in the Evangelical world. The relationship between Oral Roberts and Billy Graham illustrates the potential long-term impact of forging friendships across divides of difference. Roberts and Graham were immersed in separate and distinct Evangelical communities, yet their intentional friendship carved channels for the waters of their two streams to flow toward each other. For Roberts, his friendship with Graham had a personal benefit of encouragement and comradeship, but it also opened a door into new Christian circles and into new methods of evangelism. For Graham, his friendship with

Roberts was more than a connection with a fellow evangelist; it provided a window to peer into God's heart to heal more than just man's soul in the present time. Their friendship was intentionally pursued despite lines of demarcation and separation within the Evangelical world at the time. Their public display of friendship and solidarity transformed the attitudes of other Christian leaders and strengthened their witness for Christ in the broader culture. Their fellowship reverberated beyond their lifetimes into subsequent generations. Their influence on each other's thinking sparked an evolution in how we now conceptualize the gospel, evangelism, and mission. Cultivating friendship over decades of time can shape people, influence their work, and even leaven their communities.

Notes

1 Oral Roberts, "Oral Roberts: Legendary Oklahoma Evangelist, Founder of ORU," interview by John Erling, *Voices of Oklahoma*, August 11, 2009, audio chapter 9, 5:57, https://www.voicesofoklahoma.com/interviews/roberts-oral.

2 Hiley H. Ward, "Roberts Says Graham is the Greatest" (Newspaper clipping from 1966 Berlin Congress) in ORU Archives, Oral Roberts University.

3 Oral Roberts, "Oral Roberts," interview by John Erling, *Voices of Oklahoma*.

4 Billy Graham to Oral Roberts, July 1950, Correspondence File, ORU Archives, Oral Roberts University.

5 "Statement from Oral Roberts University on the Passing of Reverend Billy Graham," ORU News Page, February 21, 2018, https://oru.edu/news/oru_news/20180221-billy-graham-statement.php?locale=en.

6 Oral Roberts to Billy Graham, Correspondence File, ORU Archives, Oral Roberts University.

7 The first time was in 1950 in Portland, Oregon. The second time was in 1965 at Graham's crusade in Denver. This second visit came shortly after Graham had sent Roberts a personal congratulatory note on the founding of the university. During Roberts' visit at Graham's Denver crusade, they discussed the university among other things. Billy Graham Interview Oral Roberts Specials – Playlist, OR-116H Oral Roberts On Campus, 1972, https://video.lemoin.com/video_playlist_oru_specials.htm. In 1974, Roberts drove to Oklahoma City where Graham was speaking. After the meeting,

Graham asked Roberts to give him a ride to Tulsa so he could catch an early morning flight out of Tulsa. This time the conversation included praise from Graham regarding the latest primetime television show Roberts had just aired. He said, "Oral, that's the best Christian program I have ever seen on television. I admire your willingness to change your methods when it will get your message across better." *Oral Roberts, Expect a Miracle: My Life and Ministry* (Nashville: Nelson, 1995), 371.

8   Roberts, "Oral Roberts."

9   David Edwin Harrell, Jr., *Oral Roberts: An American Life* (San Francisco: Harper & Row, 1985), 270.

10 Roberts, *Expect a Miracle*, 158.

11 Roberts, *Expect a Miracle*, 159.

12 Billy Graham to Oral Roberts, correspondence file, ORU Archives, Oral Roberts University, April 1965.

13 He mentioned that Jonathan Edwards was one of the founders of Princeton, Charles Finney founded Oberlin, and Dwight L. Moody founded the Norfield Schools and Moody Bible Institute. He then jumped to Oral Roberts establishing this university, but then circled back to spiritual purposes in the founding of Columbia and Dartmouth. Billy Graham, "ORU Dedication," April 2, 1967, https://vimeo.com/210812674.

14 Graham, "ORU Dedication."

15 Roberts, "Meeting Billy Graham."

16 Oral Roberts, "My Personal Impressions of the World Congress on Evangelism," *Abundant Life* (January 1967): 28.

17 Harrell, *Oral Roberts*, 201.

18 Oral Roberts, "We Have Been Conquered by Love," *Abundant Life* (February 1967): 23.

19 Harrell, *Oral Roberts*, 204.

20 Harrell, *Oral Roberts*, 299.

21 Harrell, *Oral Roberts*, 269.

22 Harrell, *Oral Roberts*, 275.

23 Harrell, *Oral Roberts*, 276.

24 Harrell, *Oral Roberts*, 303.

25 Harrell, *Oral Roberts*, 228.

26 Harrell, *Oral Roberts*, 291.

27 Roberts, *Expect a Miracle*, 183–184.

28 "Billy Graham and John Stott," Lausanne Movement Page, accessed on May 31, 2023, https://lausanne.org/billy-graham-and-john-stott.

29 Billy Graham, "Stains on the Altar," *One Race, One Gospel, One Task: World Congress on Evangelism.* Papers and Reports 1, eds. Carl F.H. Henry and W. Stanley Mooneyham (Minneapolis: World Wide Publications, 1967), 151. The emphases are in the original.

30 John Stott, "The Lausanne Covenant," *Let the Earth Hear His Voice, International Congress on World Evangelization Lausanne, Switzerland: Official Reference Volume: Papers and Responses*, ed. J. D. Douglas (Minneapolis: World Wide Publications, 1975), 4.

31 Stott, "The Lausanne Covenant," 4.

32 Stott, "The Lausanne Covenant," 5.

33 Stott, "The Lausanne Covenant," 5.

34 Billy Graham, "Why Lausanne?," *Let the Earth Hear His Voice, International Congress on World Evangelization Lausanne, Switzerland: Official Reference Volume: Papers and Responses*, ed. J. D. Douglas (Minneapolis: World Wide Publications, 1975), 25.

35 Graham, "Why Lausanne?," 29.

36 Graham, "Why Lausanne?," 29.

37 Graham, "Why Lausanne?," 29.

38 Graham, "Why Lausanne?," 34.

39 Billy Graham interview, Oral Roberts Specials – Playlist, OR-116H.

40 Oral Roberts, "Everything God Has is Yours," sermon video, https://www.youtube.com/watch?v=2LAOxyXOfPA.

41 R. Samuel Thorpe, "An Overview of the Theology of Oral Roberts," *Spiritus* 3, no. 2 (2018): 272–273, https://doi.org/10.31380/2573-6345.1089.

42 Oral Roberts, "The Holy Spirit in the Now – I," *The Holy Spirit in the Now* (1974), 71, http://digitalshowcase.oru.edu/holyspiritnow/10.

43 C. Rene Padilla, "Evangelism and Social Responsibility: From Wheaton '66 to Wheaton '83," *Transformation* 2, no. 3 (1985): 31, https://www.jstor.org/stable/43052119.

44 Padilla, "Evangelism and Social Responsibility," 31.

45 Tizon, *Transformation after Lausanne*, 123.

46 Rollin G. Grams, "Transformation Mission Theology: Its History, Theology and Hermeneutics," *Transformation* 24, no. 3-4 (July and October 2007): 204, https://www.jstor.org/stable/43052710.

47 Grams, "Transformation Mission Theology," 205.

19 The T. L. and Daisy Osborn Model for Empowering National Evangelists: Strategies and Implications after Seventy Years of Osborn Ministry

LaDonna Osborn and Daniel King

Abstract

The ministry of T. L. Osborn (1923–2013) and Daisy Washburn Osborn (1924–1995) is known worldwide for mass crusades, miracles, literature distribution, and the placement of Tools for Evangelism in scores of languages. But another significant extension of their ministry was the National Missionary Assistance program. Over a thirty-year period, this evangelism program sponsored over 30,000 national missionaries which led to millions of conversions and to the planting of over 150,000 self-supporting churches. This article explores the long-term commitment of Osborn Ministries International (OMI) to raising up national evangelists in the majority world, including Africa, Asia, and Latin America, thus contributing to significant growth of the body of Christ around the world.

Introduction

With the establishment of OMI (originally incorporated as Voice of Faith Ministry in 1949), the Osborns embarked on a mission to propagate the gospel of Christ worldwide, encapsulated by their motto: "One Way—Jesus; One Job—Evangelism." For nearly seven decades, they personally reached millions of people in over one hundred nations through massive gospel crusades, with audiences ranging from twenty thousand to over 300 thousand attendees. Their dedication to spreading the message of Christ is underscored by the publication of literature in 132 languages and the production of multimedia resources, including DocuMiracle crusade films, audio and video materials, and audio sermons, all designed to facilitate public evangelism. Beyond their direct evangelistic efforts, the Osborns have been instrumental in equipping others for ministry. They have authored a substantial library of Bible and ministry training courses, empowering individuals to engage in the work of evangelism. Their commitment to supporting Christian workers worldwide is evident in their provision of essential tools, such as vehicles equipped with film projectors, screens, generators, and literature, all tailored for effective evangelism. This article explores the impact of their method of supporting national missionaries and provides a possible roadmap for contemporary evangelism.

The National Missionary Assistance Program

The Osborn's National Missionary Assistance program had a profound impact on world missions. OMI's sponsorship of over thirty thousand qualified national preachers, both men and women, as full-time missionaries to unreached areas, has significantly expanded the reach of the gospel. In the beginning, the program was launched under the name "Native Evangelism." Later, however, the Osborns stopped referring to local people and local missionaries as "natives" or "native evangelists" because of the demeaning tone of that word. Today more common terms include "national evangelists" or "national missionaries," which is what will be used here.[1]

According to a handwritten note in T. L. Osborn's diary, the Osborn program for *Native Evangelism* was birthed on February 25, 1953.[2] Later, Osborn explained that the idea came to him at an Oswald J. Smith missionary convention in Toronto, Canada.[3] In the introductory issue of a new magazine called Native Evangelism, Osborn writes, "Previously, we had never thought of native preachers serving in a capacity as missionaries; we had thought of them only as native pastors, teachers, helpers, etc., but the idea of utilizing their resources as missionaries opened vast new opportunities before us."[4] By July of 1953, Osborn was telling people about the vision to raise up national missionaries.[5]

The Osborns saw the need for more evangelists firsthand as they conducted large crusades in several countries around the world. Osborn wrote, "Everywhere the challenge is the same, 'the harvest is plenteous, but the laborers are few.'" He told his partners, "The population of the world is...increasing at the rate of 44 million each year...there are 400 million more unevangelized souls in the world today than a generation ago.... During the last generation alone, a tragic 750 million souls went into eternity who were never touched by the Gospel of Christ...of 2,974 major languages presently spoken in the world, 1,789 have not a single portion of God's Word."[6] This is why he says, "We must send the Native to reach the Native."[7]

When Osborn launched the National Missionary Assistance program, it was revolutionary for several reasons. First, it was envisioned to provide temporary financial assistance for nationals who had completed Bible school training. Osborn believed national missionaries had several advantages over traditional Western missionaries. The nationals spoke the local languages and dialects; they understood the local cultures; they were able to eat the local food; they required less financial resources because they were able to live at the level of the people to whom they ministered; they traveled using local means of transportation; and they never needed to go home for a furlough because they were already at home.[8] As a missionary in Africa wrote, "Several natives can be supported for what one white Missionary requires. Besides this, he can do a much better job than his white brother because there is no language problem, no tribal-custom barrier, no transportation issue, and his clothing and equipment is by far less expensive."[9]

Second, Osborn insisted upon calling the nationals "missionaries." In those days, the title of "missionary" was reserved for the foreigners who came to the country from far away on a special mission from God. By calling the national evangelists "missionaries," Osborn elevated them to the highest ranks of those who could be used by God. The idea that nationals could be missionaries going to their own people was revolutionary.

Third, Osborn gave the national missionaries temporary financial assistance. In the early 1950s, it was uncommon for foreigners to give money to nationals because Western missionaries often assumed that the funds would be misused or create dependence on foreign missions. In contrast, the Osborns believed national missionaries could accomplish great exploits for the kingdom of God if given some financial help. The Osborns trusted nationals to use the money for gospel advancement. Osborns noticed that the Western missionaries used large sums of money to support a few centralized locations, and this resulted in slow gospel advancement.[10] In contrast, the Osborns' program was designed to put a small amount of money into the hands of national missionaries and send them to completely unreached areas to preach the gospel and plant churches. This simple shift in perspective resulted in the spread of the gospel in many thousands of previously unreached areas.

The Osborns' decision to raise up national missionaries gave them greater impact than many of the other evangelists of their day. Edith Prakash writes, "What separated [Osborn] from his American contemporaries was his promotion of ongoing evangelism in the countries he visited. In contrast, his colleagues—William Branham, Billy Graham, A. A. Allen, and others—conducted crusades without planning any long-term projects to sustain the growth of evangelism."[11] Evaluating the impact of Osborn's method of supporting national missionaries in India, Prakash notes that "this strategy made Osborn's ministry different from his contemporaries and impacted India on a larger scale than those of visiting evangelists or missionaries."[12]

How the National Missionary Assistance Program Worked

The administrative strategy for the National Missionary Assistance program was developed by Daisy Osborn. This structure for the ethical administration of funds included the approval of a missionary supervisor (foreign or national), a method for sending money to the field monthly, written policies for the use of the funds, a requirement for monthly reports from each national missionary, and the submission of an annual report for each national missionary from the missionary supervisor. These policies and procedures were vital for the oversight of the program, the recruitment of financial sponsors, and the overall success of the program in the work of evangelism.

By November of 1956, there were thirty-nine different Full Gospel missionary organizations and agencies that were represented by missionary supervisors.[13] These were church leaders who operated a Bible school. These Bible schools were graduating an army of trained nationals who were zealous about carrying the gospel to their people. The missionary supervisors selected qualified graduates and recommended them to the Osborns to receive support. Daisy Osborn explains, "For a native to qualify for assistance, he [or she] MUST give up all secular employment to devote full time to Gospel ministry; and he [or she] must go to an area or village where no Full Gospel work exists."[14] The missionary supervisors submitted official applications, which were personally reviewed and approved by Daisy Osborn.[15]

The National Missionary Assistance program committed to support each national missionary for one year. In a nation such as the Philippines, this amount could be as low as fifteen dollars each month, and in Brazil, a sum of forty dollars per month would have been enough to fully support the evangelist and family at the level of the people to whom he or she was ministering. Each national missionary would lead people to Jesus, teach the new converts to tithe and plant a church. When ten converts were tithing, the missionary could begin living on the economic level of the people in which he or she was ministering. In most cases, the national missionary would begin planting branch churches in the surrounding areas during their guaranteed one year of financial assistance. It was not unusual for six or eight branch works to be established from the one central self-supporting work. While the financial assistance was usually only needed for one year, in some cases, because of local hardships, the assistance was extended beyond. The goal of the program was to establish a self-supporting church within twelve months. On many occasions, the national missionary was a gifted evangelist who would turn the new church over to another Bible school graduate who was a gifted pastor. These evangelists would go on to establish more churches in additional unreached areas. These new churches were numbered among those of the missionary supervisor's denomination; none carried the Osborn name. During the decades that this program was needed, at least thirty thousand completely self-supporting churches were established in formerly unreached areas.[16]

The success of this program challenged the mentality of many twentieth-century missionaries. It was assumed that giving money to native preachers would harm them. As the Osborns explain, "Missionary tradition has held for years that financial assistance would injure the native's faith."[17] But the Osborns emphasized that the financial help was meant to be temporary and was to be focused on sending evangelists to preach in unreached areas. By clearly explaining these constraints upfront, the Osborns were able to help national missionaries get started in ministry without running the risk of the missionaries becoming financially dependent on foreigners. "As soon as the native can be supported by the Native population, this assistance is discontinued."[18] The purpose of the program was to give national missionaries a chance to become self-sufficient. Without financial assistance, a Bible school graduate would usually be forced to find secular employment in order to provide for the family. The financial assistance from the Osborns, allowed the new graduate to launch into ministry, establish a new church in a formerly unreached area, and relinquish the temporary assistance.

To introduce the National Missionary Assistance program, the Osborns personally visited the leaders and mission boards of most of the major Pentecostal denominations in the United States including the Assemblies of God, the Pentecostal Church of God, Pentecostal Holiness, the Church of God of Prophecy, the Church of God, and others. The denominational leaders were excited to learn of this financial assistance program to accelerate the growth of their mission programs overseas. The Osborns recruited Christian sponsors for each national missionary. The funds would reach the national missionary through the hands of the appropriate missionary supervisor. By November 1956, the Osborns were sponsoring nationals of many denominations including the Apostolic Faith Mission, American Assemblies of God, Canadian Assemblies of God, Church of God, Finnish Foreign Mission, Swedish Mission, Pentecostal Holiness, Foursquare, Norwegian Evangelistic Mission, Open Bible Standard, Mongolia Evangelistic Mission, Bethel Full Gospel, Congregational Holiness, South American Inland Mission, Japan Evangelistic Fellowship, and others.[19] By May 1957, they were supporting missionaries through over forty-three different denominations and organizations.[20]

The Osborns solicited donations directly from believers in the United States. At the time, there were few opportunities for people to directly support missionary activities beyond their own denominational churches, so Christians were happy to have this channel through which to support global evangelism through the efforts of specific national missionaries. The Osborns would connect a sponsor directly with a national missionary. When the sponsor was assigned, a certificate with a photograph of the national missionary and details about the village or area where he or she was ministering were sent to the sponsor.[21] Every month, the Osborns would receive a report from each national missionary that would then be forwarded to the sponsor. Once each year, the missionary supervisors would submit an annual report on everything God had done that year through the missionaries under their supervision.[22] In July 1956, the Osborns raised $15,000 to support 1,043 national missionaries,[23] and by May 1957, $23,000 was received to support 1,400 national missionaries.[24] These pictures and reports became the content of their monthly magazine known as *Native Evangelism*, which continued to attract sponsors to the National Missionary Assistance program.

A unique feature of the National Missionary Assistance program was that 100 percent of the money donated by sponsors was passed directly to the field for the support of the national missionaries. No funds were used for administrative or fundraising expenses. When a sponsor gave twenty-five dollars, they could be confident that the full twenty-five dollars would reach the national missionary. Daisy Osborn said, "One hundred percent of the funds contributed by sponsors of native preachers goes for the assistance of the natives assigned. Not even postage money is withheld from these Sponsor Funds."[25]

The Impact of the National Missionary Assistance Program

Testimonies from the national missionaries rolled in and were shared in the monthly magazine with headlines like, "Native Missionary Reaches Filipino Village, Preaches Gospel with Miracles,"[26] "Dead Child Raised Under Pioneer Ministry of Native Missionary,"[27] "40,000 Hear the Gospel Through Native Missionary,"[28] "Native Missionaries Invade Interior Indonesian Islands,"[29] "Former Witch Doctor Become Native Missionary,"[30] and "Another Witch Doctor Saved."[31]

By 1966, the program was producing impressive results.[32] Osborn reported that the ministry had assisted a total of 9,930 pioneer missionaries to the unreached. These missionaries represented eighty different mission organizations, had traveled to 29,700 unreached areas, and had built 1,481 church buildings. The missionaries supported in 1965 reported 252 new church buildings, 241 self-supporting works established, 88,411 public decisions for Christ, 52,550 confirmed healings, and 18,367 people filled with the Holy Spirit. Each month during 1965, an average of eighty-six new national missionaries began receiving assistance and OMI fully supported a total of 2,300 national preachers.

Many of the national missionaries who were supported by the Osborns' National Missionary Assistance program went on to become great leaders in their nations. They planted churches, built Bible schools, and some even founded significant denominations. For example, David Yonggi Cho (1936–2021) of Seoul, South Korea, went on to pastor the world's largest church.[33] Benson Idahosa (1938–1998) founded a thriving and multi-faceted ministry, Church of God Mission International, that now has over six thousand churches, schools, a university, a hospital and multiple clinics. Wirachai Kowae went on to establish the Assemblies of God in Thailand.[34] Many lesser-known names are among the gifted evangelists who were assisted by the Osborns, enabling them to give their full time to gospel ministry in unreached areas of our world.

Moses Muguro is an example of the impact of the Osborn ministries. He is currently a pastor with the Pentecostal Evangelistic Fellowship of Africa (PEFA) in Nairobi, Kenya. His father was led to Jesus by a man who was saved at an Osborn crusade and who became a pastor. In the words of Muguro:

> My dad came from a polygamous family...my twin brother and I had a strange rare disease...my parents took my brother and me to many hospitals and for treatment, but unfortunately there seemed to be no hope for our healing... tired and hopeless, my dad decided to visit a local church after his sister encouraged him to try Jesus. The local pastor in that church had given his life to Jesus through an Osborn Crusade in Mombasa, Kenya, and when the preacher called out for the alter call, my dad showed up to the altar.... The preacher led my dad in the sinners' prayers.... When he came back home, my dad decided to try the newfound faith in Jesus on his twin boys. He laid his hands on George and me, and as my dad narrates, he heard some strange sounds depart from his sons, and we were instantly healed—completely healed. My dad then joined the PEFA Church, where the Osborns were supporting many local pastors, and he later became one of the local PEFA pastors in Muranga, Kenya. Though retired by now, his three sons; George, Steven, and I are pastors of some growing PEFA Churches, and my brother George is also the principal of a famous PEFA Bible school, Manna Bible College in Nairobi, Kenya.[35]

The Osborns supported many national missionaries that were affiliated with PEFA. In the Osborn offices are three full boxes of approved national missionary applications from PEFA missionary Bud Sickler that were supported by the Osborns. Today PEFA has over seven thousand churches in Kenya, and thousands of churches in the Democratic Republic of the Congo, Burundi, Tanzania, and Rwanda. Muguro's church continues to use the soul-winning teaching of the Osborns. In 2023, Muguro's All Nations PEFA Church sponsored a football tournament for twenty-four teams. At the end of the tournament, they shared the gospel with all the participants. This soul-winning effort is fully funded by their church of Kenyan believers.

Historical Context of the National Missionary Assistance Program

The Colonial Mindset

The Osborns' program to support native evangelists was launched near the end of the colonial era. This was a time of great change in many nations. Between the end of World War II and 1960, thirty-six nations in Africa and Asia "achieved autonomy or outright independence from their European colonial rulers."[36] For example, in 1947, India gained its independence from Great Britain after one hundred years of colonial rule. It was time for a new mentality concerning the potential of nationals. The entire world was in the throes of dramatic change. As new independent nations were shaking off the chains of colonial rule and establishing their own governments of self-rule, it was time for the church to rethink their paradigm of foreign missions. For the gospel to be proclaimed globally, national soul winners and evangelists, both men and women, were needed.

During the colonial era, many missionaries were sent out by Great Britain, as part of the missionary movement inspired by the William Carey (1761–1834). Under colonialism, there was a perception that Western nations advanced their interests by sending the three M's: the military, merchants, and missionaries. These colonial missionaries were supported by churches in the West and often lived on mission compounds.[37] Local believers were allowed to clean the missionaries' houses, cook their meals, and do the menial tasks. However, they were not usually allowed to preach at a pulpit or to plant a church of their own. At that time, many in the Western church world looked upon local believers as uneducated, inferior, unprepared, and unsophisticated. As Finley points out, "By 1900, the foreign missionary presence was generally looked upon by native peoples as part and parcel of the colonial establishment" and "the European rulers assumed an attitude of superiority toward the peoples they had conquered."[38] Colonial missionaries often arrived in foreign lands with an imperialistic mindset, viewing themselves as cultural and religious superiors to the indigenous populations they encountered. This perspective often led to the imposition of Western values, practices, and beliefs, which sometimes alienated and marginalized local cultures.

The Osborns' vision to support indigenous evangelists represents a significant departure from the approach of colonial missionaries, marking a welcome change in the attitude, methodology, and results of evangelistic actions. The support of indigenous evangelists recognizes the inherent value of every believer. It acknowledges that individuals in each nation are best equipped to understand their own cultures and connect with their fellow countrymen and women on a deep, personal level. This shift towards indigenous leadership fostered an inclusive, respectful, and culturally sensitive form of evangelism that recognized the Holy Spirit empowerment of every believer, not just believers from the West.

The Tactics of the Communists

Another significant post-World War II influence was the spread of communism. In many nations (known at that time as third-world countries), young people were recruited by communists. They were trained, equipped, and were given money by the Soviet Union to spread communist propaganda through the printed page, recorded messages, and movies. These recruits were often not from the big cities, but from villages and remote regions. These trained nationals were known as "Sons of the Soil." The Osborns witnessed the methods of the communists advance firsthand, and they asked, "Why can't the church use the same methods? If these methods are working for the communists, why wouldn't they work for the church for the sake of evangelism?"[39] The Osborns believed that, if trained, national missionaries could be supported, then "entire nations can be saved from the awful, Anti-God, Red siege."[40]

The Idea Spreads

The Osborns were innovative evangelistic thinkers, and their ideas have influenced several generations of both foreign and national church leaders. For example, T. L. Osborn was the first evangelist in modern times to pray a mass healing prayer. Now his methodology has been adopted by almost all healing evangelists.[41] In a similar way, his emphasis on supporting national missionaries has been influential. The idea of empowering indigenous evangelists has spread throughout the body of Christ. Now, some of the largest national denominations are sending their own trained evangelists into remote regions of their own nations and to other nations. The global works of Redeemed Church, founded by Bishop

Adeoye; Christ's Chapel, founded by Bishop Oyedepo; and Church of God Mission, International, founded by Archbishop Benson Idahosa (now led by Archbishop Margaret Idahosa) have sent missionaries from Nigeria to nations around the world. Voice of Salvation and Healing, founded by Archbishop Silas Owiti of Kenya, has sent trained evangelists and church planters across Kenya and East Africa. Wherever the church is growing at exponential rates, you will see leaders training, supporting, and sending their own to the ends of the earth to proclaim the gospel of Jesus Christ. According to a recent mission report, 47 percent of missionaries today are being sent from churches in the Global South.[42]

> The Pentecostal/Charismatic movement is one of the fastest-growing trends in World Christianity today, and it has been for some time. This movement grew from 58 million in 1970 to 656 million in 2021. The Global South is home to 86 percent of all Pentecostals/Charismatics in the world.[43]

In 1972, Bob Finley, an Evangelical evangelist who was friends with Billy Graham and Dawson Trotman, became the president of Christian Aid Mission. His organization focuses exclusively on funding indigenous evangelists. He advocates for eliminating all Western missionaries and only supporting national leaders (a view the authors of this article think is too extreme). In 1985, he published a book entitled "Reformation in Foreign Missions." In it he defines a colony as "a territory under the rule or influence of a foreign power" and missionary colonialism as "when church denominations or independent mission boards establish and perpetuate branches in countries outside the one where they are based."[44] He defines indigenous as "native to the land."[45] Finley believes the vast majority of Western missionaries are ineffective and actually harm the body of Christ. He thinks the church should stop sending all Western missionaries and only send support to indigenous missionaries.

A significant reason behind Finley's methodology is that indigenous missionaries typically require fewer financial resources to sustain their work compared to foreign missionaries who must adapt to a different lifestyle and culture.[46] By supporting national leaders, Christian Aid Mission believes they can maximize the impact of each dollar donated, ensuring that more resources go directly toward spreading the message of Jesus.

K. P. Yohannan is the founder of Gospel for Asia, which as of 2008 had supported over 16,500 national missionaries in the heart of the 10/40

Window. In his book, *Revolution in World Missions* (first published in 1986), he points out that after World War II many nations broke free from their colonial overlords and that "with their new freedom, most decided Western missionaries would be among the first symbols of the West to go." But he goes on to write, "Far from slowing the spread of the Gospel, the withdrawal of foreign missionaries has freed the Gospel from the Western traditions that foreign missionaries had unwittingly added to it."[47] Yohannan's perspective comes from his understanding of the cultural and linguistic diversity of India, as well as the unique challenges faced by foreign missionaries attempting to connect with local communities. He argues that indigenous preachers, being intimately familiar with their own people's customs, languages, and traditions, possess a significant advantage in effectively communicating the gospel. They can bridge the gap between Western Christianity and Indian culture, making the message more accessible and relatable to the local population. Yohannan believes that empowering native leaders ensures long-term sustainability as they can continue the work of evangelism and discipleship within their communities, ultimately leading to a more impactful and enduring transformation in the spiritual landscape of India and the Majority World.[48]

John Osteen (1921–1999), founding pastor of Lakewood Church in Houston, Texas, gave a significant financial gift to P.G. Vargis, who founded the Indian Evangelical Team. Vargis used the money to plant seven thousand churches in India by sending Bible school graduates out into unreached areas of India. His pastors are supported for a time, then they become self-sufficient and eventually send money back to the home organization to support new pastors. Thus, Vargis's work in India has become largely supported from within India.[49] Osborn preached several times for Osteen, so it is likely that Osborn's methodology influenced Osteen's commitment to train up indigenous pastors in India.

David Shibley (whose father, Warren Shibley, served on the Osborns' board of directors) founded Global Advance. Their focus is on training front-line shepherds."[50] Shibley writes,

> I believe the single greatest key to world evangelization lies in the empowering of indigenous leaders. As national church leaders receive relevant training, effective tools, and the touch of God's Spirit, they are then enabled to reach

their nations and nearby unreached peoples, strengthen existing churches and plant new ones.[51]

Shibley opines,

There is still a place for career missionaries from America and other Western nations. But there is no place for any America missionary who wears the grave clothes of colonialism, provincialism, or paternalism. The new role of American missionaries is as the junior partner, strengthening the hands and affirming the vision of the church in developing nations and partnering with our brothers and sisters worldwide to ensure "a church for every people and the gospel for every person."[52]

Indigenous Leadership in the Early Church

The Book of Acts provides an example of how indigenous leadership played a central role in the expansion of the early church. In Acts 13:1–3, Barnabas, and Saul (later, Paul) are set apart by the church in Antioch for the work of evangelism. This event marks a critical turning point in the missionary endeavors of the early church, as it exemplifies the practice of recognizing and empowering local leaders for cross-cultural ministry.

Acts 13:2 emphasizes that it was the Holy Spirit who initiated this commissioning, underlining the divine affirmation of indigenous leadership in missions. The church in Antioch recognized the unique cultural and contextual insights that Barnabas and Saul possessed, making them effective communicators of the gospel in regions beyond their own. This scriptural precedent underscores the theological principle that indigenous leaders are not just valuable but essential in the task of spreading the gospel effectively.

The Bible consistently highlights the importance of indigenous believers as agents of God's mission. In Romans 10:14–15, the apostle Paul poses a series of rhetorical questions that emphasize the role of indigenous evangelists: "How then shall they call on Him in whom they have not believed? And how shall they believe in Him of whom they have not heard? And how shall they hear without a preacher? And how shall they preach unless they are sent?" (NKJV). These questions serve as a theological reflection on the necessity of sending those who are intimately acquainted with the cultural and linguistic nuances of their target audience.

Paul's own missionary journeys further exemplify this principle. Paul often began his work in new regions by engaging with the local Jewish synagogues, leveraging his own cultural background as a Pharisee to connect with the Jewish community. But, in Athens, he adapted his message when addressing Gentile audiences, recognizing the need for contextualized ministry (Acts 17:22–23). This biblical model underscores the theological significance of indigenous leaders who can bridge cultural gaps and effectively communicate the gospel within their own contexts.

A foundational theological principle that emerges from the biblical narrative is that of contextualization—the process of presenting the unchanging message of the gospel in culturally relevant ways. The apostle Paul exemplified this principle when he declared, "I have become all things to all people, that I might by all means save some" (1 Cor 9:22).[53] Paul's approach reflects an understanding of the importance of adapting the message, methods, and cultural expressions of the gospel to resonate with diverse audiences.

Lessons Learned from the Osborns

Every Believer is Valuable

Far too often, ministers are placed on a pedestal. The average Christian is told that the minister is special and has a special anointing. They might start to think the minister's prayers are more effective. But the Osborns always valued individuals and emphasized the worth of every human being. T. L. Osborn was known for lifting people up. For example, when T. L. and his daughter LaDonna Osborn ministered in Russia in 1996, one of the attendees at their conference commented, "We have had great preachers come to Russia, and when they left, we knew they were great. But when the Osborns came to Russia, when they left, we knew that we were great."[54]

Every Believer is a Soul Winner

In the book, Soul Winning, T. L. Osborn makes a case for the importance of soul winning. First, he points out that "non-Christians do not go to church." Then he emphasizes that our commission is to preach the gospel to every creature (Mark 16:15). Finally, he says, "Because unbelievers do not go to church, Christians must take the Gospel to them wherever they are, outside the walls of the church."[55] The Osborns support national missionaries because they are convinced that these missionaries can be used by God to reach people for Jesus outside the walls of the traditional church building.

Women Make Great Evangelists

T. L. and Daisy Osborn were a team and they each contributed significantly to the success of their global ministry. They emphasized that God could use women in ministry just as he uses men. The Osborns saw no distinction in the spiritual gifts and callings between men and women, citing passages from the Bible that highlighted women's crucial roles in spreading the gospel; they believed that God's anointing and power were not limited by gender. "We had always believed that in redemption 'there is neither male nor female: that we are all one in Christ Jesus' (Gal 3:28). We consistently shared all aspects of life, ministry, and business as equals."[56] Because of their belief that God uses women, they eagerly supported many female national missionaries whose ministries proved to be just as effective in evangelism and church planting as the men who were supported.

National Missionaries Are Effective

Indigenous national missionaries are often better equipped to reach their own people. Not only are they more effective at ministering within their own culture, but they are also less expensive than their foreign counterparts. The results of the National Missionary Assistance program testify to this fact. The long-term impact of the Osborns' ministries and global missions are in no small measure the result of their pioneering National Missionary Assistance program.

The Future for National Missionaries

At the Amsterdam2023 EveryONE conference, Dr. Billy Wilson, the president of Oral Roberts University and chairman of Empowered21 (E21), announced a focused effort to reach every person on earth with the gospel of Jesus Christ. This three-day event drew over 7,500 missionaries, pastors, and evangelists from more than 125 nations, with an additional online presence representing 150 countries. Wilson announced a vision for every person on earth to have an authentic encounter with Jesus through the power and presence of the Holy Spirit by the year 2033, the two thousandth anniversary of the crucifixion, burial, resurrection of Jesus, and the descent of the Holy Spirit on the Day of Pentecost.

If this vision is to be realized, the effort must involve national leaders, who must train, equip, and sponsor their people as national missionaries who will go as missionaries to their own nations. Under E21, the Global Evangelist Alliance (GEA) is comprised of evangelists who are committed to training up a new generation of evangelists and missionaries to help facilitate the vision of reaching "EveryONE." The GEA is developing plans for training, mentoring, and supporting evangelism. Perhaps the Osborns' proven method of supporting national missionaries can be adapted for a new generation of evangelists. The Osborn model has also been effective in engaging ordinary Christians in the West in the biblical priority of world evangelism. Christ's commission was addressed to all of his Spirit-empowered followers. As Christians are taught this mandate and given an opportunity to be personally involved through their financial contributions, the sponsor, the national missionary, and the kingdom of God are all increased.

There are several reasons why national missionaries are needed for a new era of evangelism:

1) Cultural Relevance: National missionaries are familiar with their own cultures, languages, and religious influences. They understand the nuances of local customs and traditions, making it easier to communicate the gospel in a way that resonates with the people they are trying to reach. This cultural relevance helps break down barriers to acceptance.

2) Cost-Effectiveness: Supporting national missionaries is cost-effective. They often require fewer financial resources than foreign missionaries, who might need extensive training, language acquisition, and lifestyle adjustments. More of the donated funds can directly support evangelism.

3) Long-Term Sustainability: National missionaries are committed to their communities for the long term. They are less likely to leave, ensuring continuity in spreading the gospel, discipleship, and church planting initiatives. This approach helps build a strong foundation for lasting fruit, impacting nations.

4) Multiplication Effect: National missionaries can disciple new converts, train soul winners, and support new evangelists,

creating a compounding effect. As new believers are trained to understand their responsibility to evangelize their own communities, empowered by the Holy Spirit, they can become evangelists and ultimately leaders themselves, further expanding the reach of the gospel. This cycle of gospel harvest is effective and continues into future generations.

5) Respect for Local Autonomy: Supporting indigenous evangelists respects the autonomy and self-determination of national organizations, local churches, and communities. This strategy avoids imposing foreign beliefs or practices and encourages local expressions of Christianity, fostering a sense of ownership, which leads to greater impact.

6) Global Collaboration: The body of Christ is a global community, and supporting national missionaries encourages collaboration among believers from different parts of the world. The GEA, E21, and Spirit-empowered churches from around the world can work together to provide training, equipping, financial and other resources, prayer support, and leadership for the work of evangelism within each nation of the world.

The T. L. and Daisy Osborn model for empowering national evangelists will work today. In this new era of evangelism, national evangelists will play a vital role in reaching their communities effectively. Their cultural understanding, cost-efficiency, long-term commitment, and ability to multiply leaders make them uniquely equipped for long-term gospel impact. By respecting local leadership and encouraging global collaboration, the Spirit-empowered movement can equip national evangelists to lead a powerful, Spirit-driven movement that has the ability to reach everyone for Jesus.

Notes

1   Editor's note: while both the author and the publisher endeavor to be sensitive to preferred terminology as much as possible, please be aware that the word "native" will still appear in the names of several historical references and direct quotes in this chapter.

2   T. L. Osborn and Daisy Osborn, "February 25, 1953," in *Faith Library in 23 Volumes,* vol. 1 (Tulsa: OSFO International, 1997), 659.

3 T. L. Osborn and Daisy Osborn, "What is Native Evangelism?" in *Faith Library in 23 Volumes*, vol. 3 (Tulsa: OSFO International, 1997), 266.

4 T. L. Osborn and D. Osborn, "What is Native Evangelism?," 266.

5 *Voice of Healing Magazine*, July 1953 according to Prakash, 112.

6 T. L. Osborn and Daisy Osborn, "We Must Reach the Heathen Now," in *Faith Library in 23 Volumes*, vol. 3 (Tulsa: OSFO International, 1997), 386–387.

7 T. L. Osborn and D. Osborn, "We Must Reach the Heathen Now," 386–387.

8 T. L. Osborn and D. Osborn, "We Must Reach the Heathen Now," 388–389.

9 T. L. Osborn and Daisy Osborn, "The Mounting Controversy Among Missions!" in *Faith Library in 23 Volumes*, vol. 3 (Tulsa: OSFO International, 1997), 211.

10 T. L. Osborn and Daisy Osborn, "The Challenge as I See It," in *Faith Library in 23 Volumes*, vol. 3 (Tulsa: OSFO International, 1997), 335.

11 Edith Prakash, *Yesterday, Today, and Forever: The Extraordinary Life and Ministry of Tommy Lee Osborn* (Lanham, MD; Seymour Press, 2018), 99.

12 Prakash, *Yesterday, Today, and Forever*, 110.

13 T. L. Osborn, "Questions Answered," in *Faith Library in 23 Volumes*, vol.3 (Tulsa: OSFO International, 1997), 459.

14 T. L. Osborn and Daisy Osborn, "Mrs. Osborn Shares a Secret," in *Faith Library in 23 Volumes*, vol. 3 (Tulsa: OSFO International, 1997), 268.

15 T. L. Osborn and D. Osborn, "Mrs. Osborn Shares a Secret," 268.

16 T. L. Osborn and LaDonna Osborn, *Soul Winning* (Shippensburg, PA: Harrison House Publishers, 2020), 331.

17 T. L. Osborn and D. Osborn, "The Mounting Controversy Among Missions," 210.

18 T. L. Osborn, "Questions Answered," 458.

19 T. L. Osborn, "Questions Answered," 469.

20 T. L. Osborn and Daisy Osborn, "And This Gospel Must First be Published Among All Nations," in *Faith Library in 23 Volumes*, vol. 3 (Tulsa: OSFO International, 1997), 798–799.

21 T. L. Osborn and D. Osborn, "Mrs. Osborn Shares a Secret," 268.

22 T. L. Osborn and Daisy Osborn, "How Sponsor Funds are Handled!," in *Faith Library in 23 Volumes*, vol. 3 (Tulsa: OSFO International, 1997), 435.

23 T. L. Osborn and D. Osborn, "What is Native Evangelism?" 266.

24 T. L. Osborn and Daisy Osborn, "And This Gospel Must First be Published Among All Nations," 798.

25 Daisy Osborn, "Native Evangelism Marches On," in *Faith Library in 23 Volumes*, vol. 3 (Tulsa: OSFO International, 1997), 429.

26 T. L. Osborn and Daisy Osborn, "Native Missionary Reaches Filipino Village, Preaches Gospel with Miracles," in *Faith Library in 23 Volumes*, vol. 3 (Tulsa: OSFO International, 1997), 270.

27 T. L. Osborn and Daisy Osborn, "Dead Child Raised Under Pioneer Ministry of Native," in *Faith Library in 23 Volumes*, vol. 3 (Tulsa: OSFO International, 1997), 271.

28 T. L. Osborn and Daisy Osborn, "40,000 Hear the Gospel Through Native Missionary," in *Faith Library in 23 Volumes*, vol. 3 (Tulsa: OSFO International, 1997), 390–391.

29 T. L. Osborn and Daisy Osborn, "Native Missionaries Invade Interior Indonesia Islands," in *Faith Library in 23 Volumes*, vol. 3 (Tulsa: OSFO International, 1997), 432.

30 T. L. Osborn and Daisy Osborn, "Former Witch Doctor Become Native Missionary," in *Faith Library in 23 Volumes*, vol. 3 (Tulsa: OSFO International, 1997), 433.

31 T. L. Osborn and Daisy Osborn, "Another Witch Doctor Saved," in *Faith Library in 23 Volumes*, vol. 3 (Tulsa: OSFO International, 1997), 470.

32 T. L. Osborn, board meeting minutes, March 14, 1966.

33 LaDonna Osborn, "Korea for Jesus," https://osborn.org/korea-for-jesus-may-2023.

34 "With Our Sympathy," Asia Evangelical Alliance, published January 1, 2018, https://asiaevangelicals.org/2019/01/28/with-our-sympathy.

35 Moses Muguro, email to Daniel King, September 8, 2023.

36 "Decolonization of Asia and Africa, 1945–1960," United States Department of State, https://history.state.gov/milestones/1945-1952/asia-and-africa, last modified April 8, 2018.

37 Bob Finley, *Reformation in Foreign Missions* (Charlottesville, VA: Christian Aid Mission, 2010), 36.

38 Finley, *Reformation in Foreign Missions*, 60.

39 LaDonna Osborn, Interview with Daniel King, September 5, 2023.

40 T. L. Osborn and Daisy Osborn, "The Mounting Controversy Among Missions," 211.

41 Daniel King, "Healing En Masse: Examining the Unique Contribution of the Spirit-Empowered Movement to the Practice of Mass Evangelism," *Spiritus: ORU Journal of Theology 4*, no. 2, article 10 (2019).

42 Gina A. Zurlo, Todd M. Johnson, and Peter F. Crossing, "World Christianity and Mission 2021: Questions about the Future," *International Bulletin of Mission Research* 45, no. 1 (2021): 17.

43 Zurlo, Johnson, and Crossing, "World Christianity and Mission 2021," 18.

44 Finley, *Reformation in Foreign Missions*, 278.

45 Finley, *Reformation in Foreign Missions*, 281.

46 Finley, *Reformation in Foreign Missions*, 260.

47 K. P. Yohannan, *Revolution in World Missions* (Carrollton, TX: Gospel for Asia, 2004), 154.

48 Yohannan, *Revolution in World Missions*, 79.

49 History shared with Daniel King on mission trip to India, 2002.

50 Daniel King, "David Shibley | Global Advance," The Evangelism Podcast,

https://kingministries.com/podcast-episodes/david-shibley-global-advance.

51 David Shibley, *The Missions Addiction* (Lake Mary, Florida: Charisma House, 2001), 161–162.

52 Shibley, *The Missions Addiction*, 38.

53 Unless otherwise stated, all scripture references are taken from the New Revised Standard Version (NRSV).

54 Kevin McNulty, *God's Gold* (Daytona Beach, FL: Christian Adventures International, 2020), 3.

55 T. L. Osborn and L. Osborn, *Soul Winning*, 23.

56 T. L. Osborn, *Why: Tragedy Trauma Triumph* (Tulsa: OSFO International, 1998), 133.

20 Spirit-Empowered Internet Evangelism in an Age of Global Individuality

Mark Flattery

Abstract

This chapter presents internet evangelism as a contextual strategy for twenty-first century ministry. In order to fulfill the remaining task of Great Commission, Spirit-empowered believers can leverage the internet as an evangelistic tool and interact with individuals on a global scale. This necessitates the understanding of the opportunities in the virtual world and requires a strategy to journey online with individuals and connect them with communities of faith in the physical world. This paper explores both the challenges and opportunities for evangelism presented by the virtual world.

Introduction

As followers of Jesus Christ, we take the Great Commission as our marching orders. It is our desire to "go and make disciples of all nations" (Matt 28:18–20) and to "Go into all the world and preach the gospel to all creation" (Mark 16:15).[1] As internet usage has exploded and is now woven into the fabric of societies worldwide, the church has an unprecedented opportunity go to all nations to speak truth into the lives of individuals in every nation, tribe, people, and language (Rev 7:9). An outcome of the global expansion of the internet is the creation of a new persona that I call "global individuality." Global individuality is a mindset that empowers the individual in the global marketplace. Individuals are equipped to express opinions, join groups that were previously unreachable, participate in the global economy, and interact with anyone, anywhere. It enables individuals to develop a personal sense of "self" and empowers them to exist far beyond the limitations of the physical world. Spirit-empowered believers can leverage the internet as an evangelistic tool and interact with other individuals on a global scale. This necessitates the understanding of the opportunities in the virtual world and requires a strategy to journey online with individuals and connect them with communities of faith in the physical world.

A New World Paradigm Created by the Internet

The Impact and Usage of the Internet

We can begin our journey by considering the internet and its impact on individuals and nations. First, Statista reported that "As of 2024, the estimated number of internet users worldwide as 5.5 billion, up from 5.3 billion in the previous year. This share represents 68 percent of the global population." This would put the global population at approximately 8.0 billion people.[2] Second, the impact and reach of the internet is immense and growing. It is reported that China has the highest amount of internet users in the world with 854 million individuals. It is estimated that the internet has over 1.8 billion websites (as of 2021), 359.3 million domain name registrations (as of 2023), and that revenues from ecommerce retailed reach a projects $5.7 trillion in 2022.[3] Third, it is estimated that, of the world's 7.75 billion people, over 5.19 billion use a mobile phone, 4.54 billion people are internet users, and 3.8 billion individuals are "active social media users."[4] Fourth, the United Nations (UN) saw the importance of the internet on a global scale and acted. The UN's draft resolution entitled, "The Promotion, Protection, and Enjoyment of Human Rights on the Internet," condemned internet access disruption as a human rights violation.[5] In the United States, life, liberty, and the pursuit of happiness are valued as unalienable rights. Now, internet access is valued as a human right.

The fact is that the internet is impacting the lives of individuals in both the physical world and in the virtual world. It is so significant that the lines between the physical and virtual worlds are increasingly blurred and becoming ever more indistinguishable. This gives Spirit-empowered believers an open door to fulfill the Great Commission within the virtual world. It provides opportunities to engage people in almost every nation in the world as well as those who are not reachable in the physical world due to their beliefs or who are living in a location where Christianity is discouraged or where Christians are persecuted.

The Internet as a Mission Field

The internet is becoming so woven into the fabric of society that a new phrase has been created: "the internet of things." This is when almost anything electronic can be operated in an existing internet structure. Televisions, refrigerators, vehicles, and lights can all intersect via the internet. People around the world are embracing the internet and discovering ways to embed it into their lifestyle. Soon, the internet will be available for everyone on the planet. Some companies are working diligently to get power wirelessly to every location on the globe. Others are working to lower the cost of handheld devices so they will be affordable even to the poorest of the poor. Competitors are attempting to be the first to bring artificial intelligence to everyone, everywhere, and will take internet usage to a whole new level. The internet is not a passing fad but is becoming a necessity of life.

As technology advances, people around the world are gaining increasingly more access. The internet goes beyond being a one-way communications medium. It goes to the next level because it creates a community in which people live, interact, and have a choice as to what content they will consume. Online, people can redefine their identity, persona, and brand so much so that they can be a completely different person than they are in physical reality.

Like the marketplace of old, the *agora* of antiquity, the internet is a place of commerce, interaction, and exchanging of ideas. Individuals from every continent, nation, economic status, religious belief, gender, political viewpoint, language group, marital status, parental status, and ethnicity go online for many of the same reasons: business, news, entertainment, social networking, and education. But they are also searching for answers to the dilemmas of life that trouble them. People with varied religious affiliations, political views, and motives are available to provide answers to these questions. Most are ready and willing to voice their opinions and interact with others.

We, as the church, must also be online to tell those who are searching about Jesus. The church has an unprecedented opportunity to present the gospel, interact with individuals at their point of need, offer discipleship, and direct people to local churches around the world. The harvest fields of the internet are plentiful (Matt 9:35–38). Thus, the internet is a mission field.

"Internet Users" as a People Group

Since the internet is a mission field, it follows that "internet users" is a people group. The 1982 Lausanne Committee Chicago meeting statement defines a people group this way:

> A significantly large sociological grouping of individuals who perceive themselves to have a common affinity with one another. For evangelization

> purposes, a people group is the largest group within which the gospel can spread as a church-planting movement without encountering barriers of understanding or acceptance.[6]

Of course, when this statement was written, we in the general public were unaware of the concept of the internet and of its ability to empower individuals. Internet users is a group of individuals who gather online and have a "common affinity with one another." The common affinities include using the internet for many reasons such as business, news, entertainment, social networking, education, and even church services. On the internet, you can find like-minded people, do business, find and build relationships, download and upload news and opinions, find entertainment, and learn from others about life, love, and languages. Individuals go online to meet their needs and find what they are seeking.

Another common affinity for internet users is that they go online as individuals who have a choice as to what content they will consume. They may or may not allow that which defines them in their physical life to impact their online activity. For example, a Muslim seeking an understanding of who Jesus is, may not feel safe in asking people in his offline reality but will do so online with the anonymity and security that the virtual world affords. A devout Christian man would never visit a brothel and yet is tempted to delve into the depths of pornography online. Regardless of what they do, they have a choice, and the presence of this choice is a common affinity.

In one sense, the concept of "people group" has directed mission agencies and missionaries to focus on reaching people as groups, neglecting the fact that we can also minister to individuals. Ministry opportunities online offer believers the ability to minister on an individual basis rather than projecting their evangelistic message to crowds or to train others to minister. As people migrate to other nations and are forced to adapt, the concept of defining them by their languages, tribal affiliation, and geography becomes increasingly difficult. Also, when they become believers in Christ, their identity in the family of God trumps all other designations. However, an increasing number of these same people go online to join the internet culture and are empowered to express their voice, engage others, and find solutions to their life issues. Thus, we must add to the conversation about people groups the mission field of the internet and internet users as a people group.

Globalism as a World System

As people around the world join together online, "globalism" as a world system has developed, forcing us not to be limited by geography or language but to consider how people can interact on a global scale. Globalism is a world system that influences everyone. Our world is becoming increasing smaller as people move from one nation to another and as economics have brought nations together in working relationships. For example, some people in the US want to buy vehicles that are "made in America." However, the fact is that most cars have parts that were created in other nations and shipped to the US to be assembled. In fact, there are a significant number of vehicles assembled in the US with none of the parts being manufactured in the States. It may be that to buy a new car made entirely in the US, or any other single country, is impossible. The world comes together to manufacture, assemble, and ship vehicles in the global marketplace.

Internet users are now able to engage others around the world as global citizens. Online, you are in the cyber world and can communicate with anyone on the globe. You can play video games with someone in Russia. You can FaceTime family in Argentina. You can watch a video posted on Facebook by the missionary from a sensitive nation who you support. You can receive emails from friends in Japan just as easily as you can from your friends in Florida. You can order online from China, South Africa, or Los Angeles and have your purchases delivered to your front door within days. You can watch videos of church services from the International English Church in Jakarta, Indonesia, or from James River in Ozark, MO. You can follow your favorite sports team, whether they're a professional football team in the US or a professional *futbol* team in the English Premier League. The world is just a click away. Access to everyone everywhere is as easy as using your handheld device. In the physical world, we are limited by time, space, and finances. In the virtual world, we are global citizens interacting with others in our internet users people group.

Globalism, Global Individuality, and Implications to Evangelization

Globalism as a world system presents the church with an opportunity to present the gospel. God's anointing is on believers around the world and thus, ministry can be networked on a global scale and is not limited to only one people group, denomination, or nation. The church can engage the internet to learn more about individuals and their beliefs as they migrate from their country of origin to a new nation. Globalism should empower the church to eschew the limits of geographic boundaries and to seek to impact individuals no matter their location, economic status, or religion.

With the common use of the internet, ministers of the gospel have the opportunity to proclaim truth to the people in the global marketplace. A worship leader in Australia, a pastor in Kenya, an evangelist from Brazil, or a teacher from France can all have a powerfully effective ministry to the nations, via the internet. People are no longer limited to receiving truth from only what is available in their local town or media market. Globalism is uniting the world and bringing people together.

"Global Individuality" as a Mindset

I submit that members of the internet users people group have developed a new mindset, a new manner of looking at themselves and how they fit into society. I call this new identity "global individuality." While individuals participating in the mission field of the internet will not recognize this label, once they learn of it, they will have to admit that it applies to them on some level. Individuals worldwide, like you and me, engage the internet to meet their needs, become global citizens, and experience empowerment as individuals. Global individuality is the mindset that empowers the individual in the global marketplace. Individuals worldwide can now declare, "I am in control of my life. I can do anything, with anyone, and be anyone I want to be in a virtual, on-demand world. I am not limited by geography, nationality, religion, economic status, culture, gender, or language. I am looking for communities to join so that I can grow in my areas of interest, interact with like-minded people, and have a sense of belonging."

Individuals around the world are using the internet daily for many of the same reasons: to fulfill a need, including searching the internet to discover answers to life's issues that trouble them. The issues range from the practical, like how to change a light bulb, to the profound, such as how to discover true meaning in life. Some use the internet for personal improvement, such as learning how to play a musical instrument or learning another language, while others will feed the desires of their flesh, which leads to their spiritual demise.

Internet users can participate in the virtual world as well and be active as global citizens of the internet mission field. Online, one can read current events from news agencies from nations around the world, as well as uploading their own video, podcast, or article, thus creating news for other global citizens to consume. Social media provides access to people from other nations at the click of a mouse, both to strangers and friends, even from decades past. In this sense, there are no longer any limitations of geography or accessibility.

Global individuality empowers individuals to express their views in the global marketplace. Blogs, chat rooms, and comment sections on websites are examples of how the internet provides anyone with the opportunity to voice their opinions. Previously, only those with appropriate credentials, name recognition, or status of some nature had their comments made public. Today, everyone has a voice, to the extent that those who consume the opinion no longer care about the qualifications of the one presenting the views but take the comments at face value. A benign example of empowering the individual is seen when someone has a negative experience at a hotel, restaurant, or place of business. Previously, a disgruntled customer would proclaim, "I will sue!" or "I am contacting the Better Business Bureau!" The contemporary response is "I'm writing a terrible review on your website!" or "I'm telling my friends on social media and warning them about you!" Grave and tragic examples include the man in Egypt who was photographed after being beaten to death[7] and the man in Tunisia whose self-immolation sparked uprisings that went viral and led to the Arab Spring.[8] The internet empowers individuals to deliver their message to their nation and to challenge the people of the world to respond.

Global individuality empowers the individual to seek answers and address their quest for learning. Among their friends, people might be afraid to investigate issues of life that interest them or cause them to question. In voicing their doubts and questions, they risk shame, rejection, or reprisal. Instead, they go online looking to interact on subjects such as religious views, health issues, or relationship matters. Online, there is a sense of anonymity and security that empowers individuals to delve into issues that matter to them and connect them to those who are in the same situation.

I use the word "individuality" because it emphasizes the individual, the person. To me, "individualism" implies that I can stand out among others and be unique in the context of my group. "Individuality" means that I can be whomever I want regardless of my context. In fact, I choose which contexts I want to belong to. No longer am I limited by the realities of my physical life, such as nationality, language, social status, or economic status. If I choose, I can present an identity online in one community that is vastly different from my identity in a different community.

It should be noted that not everyone who is active online as an internet user will create a new persona or be someone in the virtual world that they are not in the physical world. It seems that most people will be the same person online that they are in physical reality. However, their participation as an internet user activates the global individuality mindset. They are empowered with the opportunity to open their hearts and minds online and find answers. While a Muslim woman in Algeria, an atheist man in France, and a Kenyan teenager in Nairobi contemplating suicide may not seek answers from a religious person, go to a church, or seek spiritual answers, they will go online looking for help, hope, and even a reason to live. The global individuality mindset empowers them to look beyond their physical world and the limitations of their personal reality and engage in conversation with people they could encounter in no other manner. For this reason, we must be online to tell them about Jesus.

Implications of Global Individuality

We will now consider three specific outcomes of global individuality. First, an outcome of global individuality is that individuals are so active online, and it captures so much of their time, that their presence in the virtual world has become their reality. A significant number of adults in first-world nations are constantly online. The stereotype for younger people is that they spend multiple hours daily playing online video games. Others are very active on social media channels, such as Facebook, Instagram, and X/Groc. While some may not consider the virtual world to be their reality, they use the internet regularly to the point that they would not want to live life without it. Imagine if, today, you went through your day without internet access, without using your computer, handheld device, or cell phone. How would you feel, and how productive would you be? What if businesses were forced to operate without technology? Your experiences in the grocery store, at your bank, and at the airport would be vastly different, frustratingly and painstakingly so. Without internet access, your involvement as a global citizen and empowerment to control aspects of your life in an on-demand world would be altered severely.

The second outcome of global individuality is that many are empowered now to be self-focused in both the real and virtual worlds. Individuals are enabled to be whomever he or she desires to be without regard for others or the rules of society. Thus, the focus shifts from the community to the individual. Individualism means that I could be all that I can be within the context of a group, and ultimately, it will benefit the community. Global individuality means that I can be whoever I want regardless of my external communities, and thus, it mandates that either my community changes to accommodate me or I will go and find like-minded people, and we will form our own community.

Third, in spiritual matters, the huge positive implication of global individuality is that people are searching online for answers to the dilemmas of life. As previously mentioned, this presents an amazing open door into their hearts and lives so that we can help them "discover and grow in their journey with God."[9] The negative aspect of global individuality is that people have such an overabundance of information from which they can pick and choose biblical teaching and curate their own personal theology. Global individuality presents an opportunity for the church to proclaim Jesus Christ to all the world on a one-to-one basis. Individuals are empowered online to go beyond the physical world that defines them to seek answers to issues that concern them and heartfelt needs that matter most to them. They are encouraged online to interact with others, to listen to alternative views, and to state their personal opinions. While the internet is a tool and neutral in and of itself, when evaluated in the light of morality, the users of the internet are empowered to utilize it as a community in which they can interact with others.

The internet is a mission field, internet users is a people group, globalism is a world system, and global individuality is the mindset that empowers individuals in the global marketplace. Over five billion people are online. Internet users are enabled to participate online as individuals and participate without the limitations of the physical world. The global individuality mindset presents an open door for the church to connect with them on a personal level, present the love of Christ, and fulfill the

Great Commission. We must continually seek to better understand the opportunities in the virtual world while simultaneously utilizing an effective strategy to journey with individuals online and connect them with communities of faith in the physical world.

The Network211: A Case

Network211 Strategy

An impactful strategy to reach individuals through the virtual world can be exemplified by an online ministry called Network211.[10] Dr. George M. Flattery founded Network211, which became incorporated in December 1996. The original intent was to use twenty-first-century technology to communicate the first-century gospel. Dr. Flattery aimed to make gospel presentations to ten million individuals in ten years. The plan became a reality when Network211 launched Project 10Million on October 15, 2008. Project 10Million was completed in five years and then expanded to become Project 100Million.

The vision of Network211 is to proclaim Christ to all people, build a global community of believers, and work with our partners in ministry. The mission is still to use twenty-first-century technology to communicate the first-century gospel by helping people discover and grow in their journey with God. The strategy is to join individuals in their journey: together, they search, view a Network211 gospel presentation online, connect to Network211 by writing, grow as they receive further Network211 content online, and are directed to belong to a local church. In summary: search, present, connect, grow, and belong. The Network211 motto is that they journey with individuals, "from searches to churches." As of April 30, 2025, Network211 has made over 62.9 million gospel presentations to individuals in 242 countries and territories. Over 3.9 million individuals made an evangelism response and over 582 thousand have written to Network211 to begin a discipleship connection. Network211 offers JourneyOnline. org, an online interactive community that includes JourneyAnswers and WhoJesusIs websites, and provides discipleship content called "The Jesus Path." It also offers JourneyPrayer, JourneyWorship, and JourneyTalks, as well as over four thousand articles that help individuals apply God's truth to daily life.

The key reason that Network211 has been able to connect individuals online to their content is that they focused on the "commonality of human nature."[11] Many missiologists believed that every culture and people group are different and that they must be addressed specifically; Dr. Flattery agreed, but with one distinction. He believed that people share a commonality of human nature with life issues that are relevant in most cultures. For example, while people may laugh and cry for different reasons, they all laugh and cry.

As the global individuality persona empowers individuals to express themselves on a virtual platform and participate in a global system, the commonalities of human nature bring people into a common affinity. Network211's primary online interactive evangelism feature is called JourneyAnswers. This identifies thirteen life issues that are relevant in most cultures. They are anxiety, brokenness, confusion, death, depression, emptiness, fear, guilt, hopelessness, insignificance, illness, love, and shame. Whether individuals are in Japan, Nigeria, Brazil, the United States, or any other country, they encounter depression on some level. The answer to this common affinity is Jesus Christ, as he will journey with them to discover freedom, wholeness, and transformation. Network211 offers JourneyAnswers in sixteen languages through JourneyOnline.org. Network211 presents Jesus as the answer and directs individuals to write to them for further conversation. Network211 has teams located in many nations of the world who answer these individuals with a personalized response, direct them to further online content at JourneyOnline.org, and connect them to a local church. This connection brings individuals from the anonymity of an online search in the virtual world into a community of faith in the physical world.

A second main online interactive community is Network211's WhoJesusIs.com. People worldwide search for "Who is Jesus?" or "who Jesus is" in an effort to find an answer to a question that they may hesitate to ask in person or that they are unsure of who could provide an adequate answer.

Focal Points for an Effective Strategy

As we seek to create an effective online strategy, we must remember that we are ministering to individuals. While the internet is global, we are interacting with an individual with a specific need. This necessitates that our endeavors are focused on the opportunities that the venue provides. Here are ten focal points for an effective strategy that can be considered for online evangelism.

First, the persona of those we are attempting to reach is that of global individuality. Individuals are being empowered online in the global marketplace. They are moving beyond their physical realities and are empowered to interact online as a global citizen.

Second, our presentations must speak to the individual. As most internet access is viewed on a handheld device, we are presenting the good news to individuals who have searched online for an answer to a life dilemma. Thus, our content and approach must go beyond uploading a church service but be designed to speak into the life of that one person accessing it at the time and encourage interaction.

Third, we meet individuals at their point of need. Individuals go online searching for answers to life's dilemmas. They will engage with anyone online who presents what they consider a viable answer. While these seekers may not darken the door of a church, they are open online to hearing alternative views. We should avoid a cold call mentality where we attempt to convince them to buy what we are selling; instead, we meet them at their point of need and allow the Holy Spirit to use the truth of the gospel to penetrate their hearts and transform their lives.

Fourth, as we engage on the internet, we must be clear as to what is our desired outcome. The Great Commission reveals that our goal is to make disciples. We journey with individuals from discovering who Jesus is to developing them into followers of Christ who walk in Christian maturity (Matt 28:18–20 and Eph 4:11–13).

Fifth, we must be prepared to journey with individuals. We want to go with them from where they are to where they need to be in Christ. The start of our journey with people often begins at their point of need. We engage them online and then, with a personal response, we direct them to develop their relationship with Jesus and to apply God's truth to their daily lives. Content for the various aspects of their life journey must be available online to continually empower and exhort them to become disciples and to mature in their faith.

Sixth, we must define our terms. Network211 defines a "visit" as individuals who actually visit their page. They do not count "impressions" or visits by bots. An "evangelism response" for Network211 is when a visitor responds to the evangelism presentation by clicking a button such as "I prayed the prayer," "I still have questions," or "prayer request." Network211 terms someone who writes to them as a "discipleship connection." We must be clear as to our terminology and true to what the analytics reveal.

Seventh, we must determine what is a win. Once our terms are defined, we must state what we value in an effort to obtain our desired outcome. Is a visit a win? Are evangelism responses or discipleship connections wins? Is there a combination of responses that formulate a win? Network211 views each aspect of ministry as a win, yet the ultimate goal is to see people go from "searches to churches."

Eighth, we must be kingdom-minded rather than locally fixated. A local church that offers interactive communities online cannot assume that all who view their content will attend their specific church. The goal for fulfilling the Great Commission must be to see people come to Christ and be disciples. We are not to limit the goal by wanting people to attend only a specific local church.

Ninth, partnerships must be formed to fulfill the Great Commission. Network211 partners with Spirit-empowered believers who serve as "1-2-1 Connectors" (response teams), content providers (written, audio, and video), and prayer and financial partners, from local churches around the world. We can do more together than if we attempt to fulfill the Great Commission alone.

Tenth, we must view the internet as its own ministry opportunity for evangelism and discipleship. As mentioned earlier, it is a new wine that must not be forced into old wineskins (Luke 5:36–38). Online activity is a venue in its own right and offers new opportunities to journey with individuals to a transformed life.

Conclusion

The fields of the internet are white unto harvest. Individuals are empowered with a global individuality mindset to participate in the global marketplace. This necessitates the understanding of the opportunities in the virtual world and requires a strategy to journey online with individuals and connect them with communities of faith in the physical world. May the Lord give us wisdom as Spirit-empowered believers to use the internet as a tool of evangelism in an age of global individuality for the purpose of fulfilling the Great Commission and for the glory of God.

Notes

1   Unless otherwise noted, all scripture references taken from the New International Version (NIV).

2   Ani Petrosyan, "Global number of internet users 2005–2024," Statista, May 6, 2025, https://www.statista.com/statistics/273018/number-of-internet-users-worldwide, accessed on May 12, 2025.

3   Ying Lin, "10 Internet Statistics Any Marketer Should Know in 2024," Oberlo, December 11, 2023, https://www.oberlo.com/blog/internet-statistics, accessed May 12, 2025.

4   Simon Kemp, "Digital Trends 2020: Every Single Stat You Need to Know About the Internet," The Next Web, January 30, 2020, https://thenextweb.com/news/digital-trends-2020-every-single-stat-you-need-to-know-about-the-internet, accessed June 1, 2022.

5   United Nations, "The Promotion, Protection, and Enjoyment of Human Rights on the Internet: Draft Resolution," Geneva, June 27, 2016, https://digitallibrary.un.org/record/845728?ln=en.

6   Dan Scribner, "A Simple Guide to People Group Lists for World Mission," Lausanne World Pulse Archives, 2010, https://lausanneworldpulse.com/perspectives-php/1320/09-2010.

7   Lara Logan, "The Deadly Beating that Sparked Egypt Revolution," CBS Evening News, February 2, 2011, https://www.cbsnews.com/news/the-deadly-beating-that-sparked-egypt-revolution/.

8   Thessa Lageman, "Remembering Mohamed Bouazzi: The Man Who Sparked the Arab Spring," Al Jazeera, December 17, 2020, https://www.aljazeera.com/features/2020/12/17/remembering-mohamed-bouazizi-his-death-triggered-the-arab.

9   This is the tag phrase for Network211's JourneyOnline.org.

10 See Network211.com.

11 George M. Flattery, "Cooperative Multinationalism: An Emerging Philosophy of Missions," unpublished paper, 1969.

Postscript: The Difference the Gift Makes

Jaime L. Riddle

> Repent and be baptized, every one of you, in the name of Jesus Christ for the forgiveness of your sins, and you will receive the gift of the Holy Spirit. This promise belongs to you and your children and to all who are far off—to all whom the Lord our God will call to Himself (Acts 2:38-39).[1]

The Cross Made the Gift Possible

When God poured out his Spirit on Pentecost, Peter proclaimed the fulfillment of Joel 2:28–32, that the Spirit was to indwell old and young, male and female, rich and poor, and near and far. Wonsuk Ma contends that this was the hinge of human history: that since the Fall, all things had led up to this point, the return of God's Spirit back into human beings.[2] With the divine breath now inhabiting humanity's chest, the Holy Spirit who had been promised was ready to commence worldwide restoration.

The cross had made the Gift possible! For the apostles, this meant no more waiting. Though they had been saved, washed, trained, and commissioned, Jesus explicitly commanded them to wait (Acts 1:4–8). It wasn't until his own breath from heaven anointed them that it empowered the mission he'd walked in through the Spirit. Notably, his resurrected ministry had been a mix of Spirit-empowered moments and ordinary ones. He had taught them, eaten with them, walked with them, and instructed them. But he had also walked through walls, vanished, ascended before their eyes, and spoken from the sky! Having broken the power of death embedded in the earth, Jesus appeared in many ways, in surprising places, as if to illustrate that the Spirit within him was no longer limited by any human conception or endeavor.

Thus, when he poured out his Spirit to anoint his followers, that ministry continued: tongues of fire appeared, Paul grew cataracts, jail cells opened, and Philip was caught up by the Spirit. It was clear that the same Spirit that animated Jesus was now animating his disciples. Scripture describes the baton pass this way: the authorities took note that these men had been with Jesus (Acts 4:13).

The first generation of Spirit-empowered evangelists entered the commission and God inaugurated a history of *Spiritus receptus* in each nation. Each would have their own people, revivals, and transformation history bearing witness of his ways being planted among them by the Spirit. This volume captures just a sample of that history and the present reflects this long work. Spirit-empowered evangelists in each chapter are described as interrupting the natural course of events to bring in more of Jesus. And while each nation or people group has its own journey of encounter, what unites the global Spirit-empowered movement is a desire to partner consciously with the Holy Spirit and be a vessel of that encounter for others. With this in mind, a few closing thoughts are offered on the difference the Gift has made.

Spirit-Empowered Evangelism Through Healing

A common thread in many chapters is divine healing as a hallmark of Spirit-empowered evangelism. Jun Kim explores why this is so and connects the ubiquity of healing to its significance as a type of wordless gospel. Without being bound to time, place, or language, healings demonstrate that God has conquered death and all the things that lead to it. This indicates that his will is "individual, communal, and cosmic wholeness."[3] Scott Adams locates the source of healing in Christ's ascension over the powers of darkness that hold people in bondage. The giving of the Spirit for mission thus entails spiritual warfare. Spirit-empowered evangelists enter this fray and, through divine healing, aid the process of all things coming under Christ's feet through the church (Eph 3:10).[4]

While this theology is intellectually acknowledged in the West, Charles Obara notes that "power evangelism is indispensable in the Majority World, where an awareness of the spirit world is acute." Accordingly, Obara observes that Reinhard Bonnke's "pnuema-centric" mission style fit Africa better than historic Western missionary styles. Bonnke's evangelism featured distinctive Spirit-empowered elements, including its teams of intercessors, prayer against territorial spirits, and intentional Spirit-baptism opportunities. Although Bonnke did not consider himself a healing evangelist, Vinson Synan confirmed physical healings and deliverance by the thousands from Bonnke's gatherings.[5]

Likewise, LaDonna Osborn and Daniel King share how important healing and miracles were in T. L. and Daisy Osborn's mission work. Their motto, "One way—Jesus; One job—evangelism" left no doubt about their focus.[6] But the Holy Spirit empowered healing so that many would encounter the true Lord Jesus Christ. The Spirit also inspired conviction about, and strategies for, elevating indigenous evangelists to continue working with strength and support.

Spirit-empowered strategies were similarly part of Oral Roberts' healing evangelism, as noted by John Paul Thompson. Roberts' style was different from that of America's most famous evangelist, Billy Graham. Yet, Graham rejoiced in Roberts' prayer lines and obedience to the Spirit in constructing a university to connect evangelism with "the totality of human need."[7] Arguably, their friendship with one another might have been distinctly Spirit-empowered for modeling a rare kind of bridge-building that bore considerable fruit.

Spirit-Empowered Ministry Leaders

The difference the Spirit makes is also evident in the lives of evangelists whose ministries were graced by the Spirit's presence and transformation. In Finland, evangelist Niilo Yli-Vainio was completely changed by his encounter with the Holy Spirit. According to Arto Hämäläinen, before his baptism in the Spirit, Yli-Vainio was famous for describing "the horrors of hell in dramatic colors" out of an urgency to "frighten people into faith." But after receiving the Spirit, he was enveloped in a gentle, unfolding peace and filled with compassion for people that "burst out through him as loving words." He ministered only a few more years before passing away, but his radical joy, surrender, and fasting led to significant revivals in Latin America, Eastern Europe, and the Soviet Union.[8]

Yoriko Yabuki tells of similar impact made through Kyoko Funatsu, whose distinctly Spirit-empowered ministry as a female pastor in the Japan Assemblies of God has been appreciated even more since her passing in 2024. Funatsu was known for local evangelistic meetings where she led roadside teams whose intercessory prayers were heard "dozens of meters away." She spoke in tongues, discerned spirits, fasted to cast out demons, and laid hands on people for healing and Spirit-baptism within very hostile environments. She was a vessel for Spirit-empowered fullness that current disciples in Japan testify as being instrumental to their own encounters with the living Christ.[9]

The restorative ministry of Jesus was also the one encountered through evangelist Newton Emmanuel Singh. David Singh recounts that N. E. Singh was not signs-and-wonders-focused, but Spirit-empowered songs, Bible lessons, and love poured out through him and his sitar in the heartland of northern India. His gentle manner found favor among rural communities and also Indira Ghandi.[10] The fruit of the Spirit he exhibited and the legacy he left among Hindus and Muslims testify that his gifts were not "ordinary" in any way. While his style appears less sensational than that of Cindy Jacobs—whose bold, prophetic evangelism for decades has brought people into healing, salvation, and wholeness[11]— it is not lesser in its touch of the Spirit. Jacobs and Singh demonstrate that a life poured out in Spirit-empowered witness is what defines Spirit-empowered evangelism and cannot be caricatured.

Churches Mobilized for Spirit-Empowered Evangelism

Spirit-empowered ministers across the globe have changed history, but the power of the Spirit also moves through empowered churches. Because church-based evangelistic ministry does not depend on one specific gifted person, it may be an even greater force for global witness. Testimonies of collective empowerment suggest that what Ma calls the "democratization of the Spirit," described in Joel 2:28,[12] is coming in greater measure, perfectly timed for a burgeoning world population and the deeper transformative work that so many yearn to see.

Younghoon Lee, for example, explains how promoting female cell group leaders in Yoido Full Gospel Church has helped change the perspective of women in broader Korean society. In the context of "Jesus as Healer," following his predecessor David Yonggi Cho's lead on holistic salvation, Lee describes the healing Spirit on a long march through areas impacted by sin and the Fall.[13] Personal salvation leads to ripple effects through the church, making God's desire for relational wholeness discernible. As a result, many Yoido women who have been changed now change others. They pray, they fast, they pastor, and they organize outreach. A coworker recently told me how many young mothers and children come to church or get saved as a result of the way the older women love them. Female leaders' diligence in evangelism and outreach has fueled revival and a larger redemptive mission in their socio-historical context.

Alfred Cooper maintains that this is what church should be about. His concept of "pneuma plasticity" describes the Spirit responding to a desire and motivation for re-empowerment. "The Spirit is given to the church for mission," he claims, so it "may be withdrawn in part when the church stops spreading the kingdom." What a sobering thought! The idea that a congregation's dedication to evangelism could promote or depress the Spirit? Or, as Dongsoo Kim explains it, that Spirit-baptism is about immersing God's people in a consecrated experience that fuels their going?[14] Tying empowerment to mission or purity in these ways is not popular but elicits a heart-level referendum on the question: "What kind of church do we want? Our kind, or the Spirit-filled kind?"[15]

Cooper's honest probing and Lee's warning that a church must officially prioritize evangelism—"We will make it what we do"—has tested Stavros Ignatiou's Greek congregation significantly. His study describes changing his entire church to welcome Muslim refugees, despite the language barrier, logistical load, and culture gap. Ultimately, his Spirit-empowered laity rose to the challenge through an unlikely strategy: "We liked them." "Liking" as a Spirit-empowered gift? Yes, because "[t]hey came to the conclusion that if we liked them, then our God must also like them." Ignatiou summarizes the messy and stretching path of Spirit-led listening, accepting, and adapting. But the fruit was moving from "frozen" to "incarnational," and discovering the power of an Isaiah 61 posture of love, even without words.[16]

Finally, the testimony provided by Sabina Cappello Lee about two Malaysian sisters finding their call as revivalists and missionaries exemplifies the "democratization of the Spirit" occurring in the Catholic church. Since Vatican II and the Catholic Charismatic Renewal initiated new perspectives of laity, mission is no longer "activities of the Church in certain territories" carried out by specially appointed clergy. Now, lay Spirit-filled believers are holding global conferences, uniting with like-minded Protestants, and—in the case of the Antoine family and their two daughters—starting their own ministry that preaches the gospel, prays for Spirit-baptism, and disciples others in the Spirit-empowered life.[17]

In these studies, empowerment of laity begins within the church and extends outward. It starts with perceiving the democratization of the Spirit, that "they have received the Holy Spirit just as we have" (Acts 10:47). The Osborns, for example, built their National Assistance program to promote nationals to "missionaries" and resource them.[18] Bonnke, likewise, crafted Fire Conferences for local leaders to receive the Spirit and formulate their vision for the next phase of ministry.[19] These founders had true faith for their "Timothies," who were called to reach the next generation. The humility required to support their successors and then vacate without name recognition came from a conviction that, in Al Tizon's words, "the church participates with God to accomplish the *missio Dei*"—*God's* mission, not our own.[20]

This provides context for Onyinah's affirmation that "the giving of the Spirit at Pentecost is unintelligible without the calling of the nations."[21] In addition to the gift of tongues uniting people through prophetic declaration of the gospel, the power that was given was meant to do battle. It had an objective: to restore, globally, what had been lost in Eden. Our job, Onyinah continues, is to partner with God in this. Evangelization is a massive, collective effort because the world has to be continually re-evangelized as time passes. No-one has enough resources, authority, or anointing to achieve it on their own, and each nation is in different parts of the process with unique contextual factors in play. Fortunately, God has foreknown and designed the commission so that it can only be done in partnership with him and each other. Relying on the Spirit therefore has the effect of increasing our inward desire to partner—changing us who are on the mission, along with those we reach.

It Takes Everyone to Reach EveryONE

Moving forward, Daniel King lays out the facts bluntly: "Jesus died for every one of the eight billion people on earth. And it is going to take every one of us to reach them with the gospel."[22] Jay Gary adds that 28 percent of the world's population still has no access to the gospel from a church in their language or culture—a number that sounds small but signifies 2.3 billion people![23] J. Kim reinforces this urgency in Asia, the most densely populated but least evangelized continent.[24]

In addition to how fast evangelism needs to accelerate just to keep up with world population growth, King states another central problem: that while 65 percent of young Christians report believing in being a witness for Jesus, nearly half (47 percent) say it is wrong to evangelize. This dissonance clearly needs to be resolved for the expansion of the faith. Christians also report that it is the church's responsibility to evangelize, not theirs personally.[25] A pressing priority is therefore shifting churchgoers' negative perceptions of evangelism. But also, William M. Wilson says it is time to re-personalize the Great Commission and embrace reaching everyone, one person at a time.[26]

Stewarding this as a word from the Lord, Wilson chairs Empowered21 and frames its mission as giving every person on earth a real chance to receive the gospel prior to 2033, the second millennial anniversary of Pentecost. Joining hands with other groups pursuing global evangelization, Empowered21 connects more than 650 million Spirit-empowered Christians seeking to help the world encounter Jesus Christ through the power of the Spirit.[27] Gary chronicles the history of this initiative, joining with Wilson and King in the call to reach every one, as well as affirming the power of one to reach.[28] The Global Evangelist Alliance, led by King, seeks to mobilize and resource as many Spirit-empowered groups as possible.[29] The Global Prayer Alliance, advised by Jacobs, aims to pray for every person by name by 2033. The Global Network of Spirit-Empowered Scholars (GNSES), led by Onyinah and Ma, convene global scholars who aid evangelism, shape the church, and shift thought patterns by analyzing systems, values, theologies, and trends defining their contexts.[30] The synergy of global Spirit-filled voices being invited into the task of God reaching every person's world is encouraging for evangelization but also for the role of God's people in holistic mission until he returns.

New Frontiers of Spirit-Empowered Ministry

With the extent of this task in mind, a key issue is whether we can broaden the definition of Spirit-empowered evangelism to embrace frontiers of contemporary society where the Spirit desires to go—AI and digital technology, for example. Mark Flattery and Lydia Wonget bring this to the forefront in their studies on digital evangelism. Flattery asserts, "The harvest fields of the internet are plentiful. Thus, the internet is a mission field." He then explains how almost all demographics can be found online, with many expressing openness to truth or facing life's troubles.[31] With the most remote places now reachable by technology, and the ability to connect instantly, cross-culturally, with ministers, churches, and resources, there is now an unsurpassed opportunity for the Holy Spirit to move.

Wonget frames the challenge saying, "It is time to unlearn the fact that missionaries can only be found or sent to a physical place." Her study on online missionaries who are trained technologically and sent out into the digital world to start "faith conversations" illustrates the almost unbounded potential of remote ministry. Although there are new challenges, including how to protect new believers, ministers in closed countries, and sending organizations from cyberattacks,[32] Wonget and Flattery contend that the digital landscape (including social media, AI, VR, and the metaverse) is the newest application of the apostle Paul's paradigm: becoming "all things to all people so that by all possible means, I might save some" (1 Cor 9:22b).

Of course, the digital world is a different application, and Pentecostals have been known at times to resist modernization. Yet, Spirit-empowered people have always put the Holy Spirit at the forefront of every medium to get their message out: newspapers since A. J. Dowie's era, microphones in the big tents of the 1920s–60s, television, cassettes, prayer cloths, tracts dropped by prop planes, radio Bibles, and the Jesus Movie, just to name a few. Today, it is YouTube, Facebook, and apps that carry music, messages, and ministries all around the world. While non-Spirit-empowered Christians are also part of the ecosphere, it is Pentecostal-Charismatic theology that supports moving beyond the rational and conventional that makes the Spirit-empowered movement so strong and versatile evangelistically. Holiness concerns may (and arguably should) at times act as "brake pedals," but as Wonget elegantly puts it, "The Holy Spirit uses anything and any means to capture people unto Himself."[33] Ultimately, we trust the Spirit to provide prophetic vision of what lies downfield and how more people can be encountered with the power and love of Christ.

I end this section with an anecdote about personal humility toward these new frontiers. This year, my college-aged son asked to skip spring break to go on a "digital mission trip." I had no idea what this meant but learned that a dozen computer science students were to ride eighteen hours in a van to code (for free) a multilingual website that displayed gospel content for a missions organization. The leader of the trip was from the Center for Missions Computing, which develops software for mission efforts around the world and recruits on Christian college campuses. Now, if I'm being honest, because the idea of a digital mission was completely new to me, I was slightly embarrassed when he sent out his support letter—but he raised more than enough funds in just one week! Hearing of the tremendous blessing they brought afterwards humbled me considerably—as did the time I learned that my friend with a Christian cosmetology TikTok channel had led more people to Christ on it than I have ever personally witnessed to.

Being challenged by these things, I am confronted with the realization that ministries prioritizing technology and creativity are no longer on the fringes of mission but on the frontlines of it. Some evangelistic methods will continue to be distinctly and recognizably Spirit-empowered, but others may appear less distinctive and still be. Without fail, new methods will arise that require suspended judgment. Whether or not I can personally make the shift into what the Spirit may be doing in the digital sphere, I support it because of how much global missions and cultural "salting" are already facilitated by the internet. Who knows what may be possible in the decades ahead? Who is to say that "the God of technology"[34] will not be as evangelistically effective as the God of healing?

Conclusion

In the end, the Holy Spirit is the source of all impetus to come closer to God. The Spirit surrounds the entire evangelistic endeavor, inspiring the body of Christ to go, to create, to love, to suffer. He can use anything to reach someone: a prayer, an act of kindness, a song, a book, a healing, a video clip—it doesn't have to explicitly acknowledge the Spirit to be used by the Spirit.

But while all evangelism is imbued with the Spirit, Spirit-empowered evangelism is distinctive for being Spirit-conscious and Spirit-centric. Jesus himself lived this way. He spoke by the Spirit (John 3:34), acted by the Spirit (Luke 4:18), and partnered with the Holy Spirit, doing nothing on his own (John 5:30a). Then he died to send us the Spirit (John 16:7)—

his Spirit, the Spirit of God. This is a weighty realization. A humility and awe sets in as we recognize the call to walk in Christ's steps and destroy the works of the devil so others may experience renewal and restoration (John 10:10, 1 John 3:8). We stand squarely in that transcendent reality, praying for the difference the Gift makes, and anticipating, in Onyinah's words, "the satisfaction that goes with the fulfillment of the King's assignment."[35]

Notes

1 All scriptures are taken from the Berean Standard Bible (BSB).

2 Wonsuk Ma, "The Spirit and Leadership: Where It All Began…," *Malaysian Pentecostal Journal* 2 (2024): 25–42.

3 J. Kim, chapter 13.

4 Adams, chapter 4.

5 Obara, chapter 8.

6 Osborn and King, chapter 19.

7 Thompson, chapter 18.

8 Hämäläinen, chapter 16.

9 Yabuki, chapter 14.

10 Singh, chapter 11.

11 Jacobs, chapter 7.

12 Ma, "The Spirit and Leadership: Where it All Began…," 29.

13 Y. Lee, chapter 12.

14 D. Kim, chapter 3.

15 Cooper, chapter 17.

16 Ignatiou, chapter 15.

17 H. J. C. Lee, chapter 10.

18 Osborn and King, chapter 19.

19 Obara, chapter 8.

20 Tizon, quoted by Thompson, chapter 18.

21 Onyinah, chapter 2.

22 King, chapter 6.

23 Gary, chapter 5.

24 J. Kim, chapter 13.

25 King, chapter 6.

26 Wilson, chapter 1.

27 Gary, chapter 5.

28 Gary, chapter 5.

29 King, chapter 6.

30 Onyinah, Introduction.

31 Flattery, chapter 20.

32 Wonget, chapter 9.

33 Wonget, chapter 9.

34 Wonget, chapter 9.

35 Onyinah, chapter 2.

Contributors

Scott Adams serves as the Dean of Our Savior's College in Lafayette, Louisiana, where he resides with his wife of twenty-one years and their four children. He also serves as an assistant professor at Regent University School of Divinity and an associate professor at Oral Roberts University. In addition to his academic interests, Adams' passion involves equipping leaders for gospel-centered, Spirit-empowered pastoral ministry.

Alfred Cooper, an Anglo-Chilean bishop, was born in Valdivia and sent to the Oratory School in Reading, then later attended Bristol University to study modern languages. While traveling through Spain in 1969, he encountered Christ in a way that drew him out of Marxism and existentialism. He returned to Chile in 1974, married Hilary Barratt, and has been rector of La Trinidad Anglican Church for forty years. From there, he continues to plant churches. He recently concluded his doctoral thesis on the Chilean Pentecostal Revival of 1909 at Oxford Centre of Mission Studies.

Mark Flattery is a lifelong missionary who has served in Europe, Africa, and Pacific Oceania and has ministered on six continents. He is president of Network211, an internet ministry focused on global evangelism and discipleship.

Jay Gary is an associate professor and director of the Doctor of Strategic Leadership program at Oral Roberts University, Tulsa, OK. He was the lead developer of the Perspectives Study Program and the AD 2000 Movement. In looking toward the year 2000, he authored *The Star of 2000: Our Journey Toward Hope* (1994). He serves on task forces of the International Leadership Association and the World Futures Studies Federation.

Arto Hämäläinen is chairman of the Advisory Committee of the Africa Peak Mission – Africa Pentecostal Mission (APM), and founding chairman of the World Missions Commission of the Pentecostal World Fellowship (PWF), the Pentecostal European Mission (PEM) and the Asia Pentecostal Mission (PAM). He is a member of the Global Council of the Empowered21 movement and Executive Director Emeritus of the Fida International (Finnish Pentecostal Mission), which he served for 27 years. He has authored several missiological books and articles and served in his teaching and training ministry in around sixty countries. He is married to Sirkka and has two daughters and three grandchildren.

Stavros Ignatiou is currently a director of Created Equal, a non-governmental organization committed to supporting refugees and vulnerable communities through holistic programs. Under his leadership, Created Equal has implemented a range of services, including the distribution of dry food parcels, provision of hot meals, laundry services, medical clinics and structured integration programs—particularly for women and children. He has more than thirty-five years of experience in the field.

Cindy Jacobs is an author, speaker, and teacher with a heart for discipling nations in the areas of prayer and prophetic gifts. She and her husband Mike co-founded Generals International in 1985. That small seed has sprouted and grown into an international ministry, taking Cindy to more than one hundred nations of the world where she has spoken before hundreds of thousands on Spirit-empowered topics and ministered prophetically. She also serves in the Empowered21 cabinet as Senior Advisor to the Global Prayer Alliance.

Dongsoo Kim is an ordained minister with the Korean Assemblies of God and has served as a professor of New Testament at Pyeongtaek University in Korea since 2003. From 2017 to 2019, he was president of the New Testament Society of Korea. He holds a Ph.D. from the University of Cambridge and a Master of Theology from Harvard Divinity School.

Jun Kim is a Korean Pentecostal scholar who currently serves as the academic dean and Vice President at Asia Pacific Theological Seminary and President of the Asia Pentecostal Society (2024-2026). Since 2004, he and his wife Jane C. Kim have been missionaries in the Philippines.

Daniel King is a missionary evangelist who has traveled to over seventy nations in his quest for souls. He is the founder of King Ministries International (kingministries.com) and is a board member of the Global Evangelists Alliance for Empowered21. He lives in Tulsa, Oklahoma with his wife, Jessica.

Hyeon Ju (Sabina) Cappello Lee was born in South Korea and was the first in her family to encounter Jesus and embrace the Catholic faith. Her missionary call has taken her across continents, serving in evangelization, formation, and leadership. She currently serves as the International

Coordinator of WINS, a Global2033 initiative mobilizing women for Spirit-empowered evangelism with the vision of helping fulfill the Great Commission by 2033.

Younghoon Lee is senior pastor of Yoido Full Gospel Church in Seoul, South Korea. He previously served as president of Bethesda Christian University in Anaheim, California; professor of theology at Hansei University, Korea; senior pastor of Tokyo Full Gospel Church and Los Angeles Full Gospel Church; and chairman of the Theological Committee at National Council of Churches of Korea.

Wonsuk Ma, a Korean Pentecostal, is executive director of the Center for Spirit-Empowered Research and Distinguished Professor of Global Christianity at Oral Roberts University, Tulsa, Oklahoma. He also serves as co-chair of Empowered21's Global Network of Spirit-Empowered Scholars (GNSES). Previously, he served as dean of the College of Theology and Ministry at Oral Roberts University as well as executive director of the Oxford Centre for Mission Studies in the UK.

Charles Obara is the senior pastor of Christ is the Answer Ministries, a classical Pentecostal church based in Nairobi, Kenya. He is currently pursuing doctoral studies at Oral Roberts University, Tulsa, Oklahoma, researching the Spirit-empowered movement in Africa.

Opoku Onyinah serves as co-chair of Empowered21's Global Network of Spirit-Empowered Scholars (GNSES). He is also the immediate past president of the Ghana Pentecostal and Charismatic Council, as well as immediate past chairman of the Church of Pentecost, Ghana. He was the first international mission director of the Church of Pentecost and founding rector of Pentecost University in Accra.

LaDonna C. Osborn is President and CEO of Osborn Ministries International, a world missionary organization founded by her parents in 1949. She is Founder and Overseer of the International Gospel Fellowship, which includes more than fifty ministries and one thousand churches, in more than fifty nations globally.

Jaime L. Riddle serves as the administrative assistant to the Director of the Center of Spirit-Empowered Research at Oral Roberts University. She is a managing editor of multiple titles and has spent twenty years in lay ministry focused on biblical education and young adults.

David Emmanuel Singh is a senior research tutor at the Oxford Centre for Mission Studies.

John P. Thompson is Professor of Global Leadership in the College of Theology and Ministry at Oral Roberts University, Tulsa, Oklahoma.

William M. Wilson serves as president of Oral Roberts University, Tulsa, Oklahoma, while leading Empowered21 and Pentecostal World Fellowship as chair. With over four decades of executive leadership, Wilson is instrumental in developing Spirit-empowered leaders through whole person education to impact the world.

Lydia Wonget serves as National Coordinator for Children's Ministry in Cameroon, and as training coordinator with the strategy team of OneHope International. She is also chair of the Africa Assemblies of God Alliance Children's Ministry Commission (AAGACMC). Currently, she is training a new generation of pastoral and educational leaders as an adjunct professor at multiple Assemblies of God Bible schools across Africa.

Yoriko Yabuki is an ordained minister in the Japan Assemblies of God, currently serving as a church planter in Mitaka City, Tokyo, Japan, with her husband, Reverend Daisuke Yabuki, at Revive International Church. She has been serving at Asia Pacific Theological Seminary teaching "Biblical Theology of Women in Ministry" as an adjunct professor since 2021 and also teaches missiology as an adjunct lecturer for Central Bible College in Tokyo, Japan. Previously vice president (2015–2017) and director of Women in Ministry (2012–2019), she has worked to empower Japanese people in the United States.

Select Bibliography

Ahonen, Lauri. "Finland." *In International Dictionary of Pentecostal and Charismatic Movements*, edited by Stanley S. Burgess with Eduard M. van der Maas. Grand Rapids: Zondervan, 2002.

Alvarez, S. J., D. Francis, and Todd M. Johnson. *Christianity in East and Southeast Asia*. Edinburgh: Edinburgh University Press, 2020.

Anderson, Allan. *Introduction to Pentecostalism: Global Charismatic Christianity*. Second edition. New York: Cambridge University Press, 2014.

________. *Spreading Fires: The Missionary Nature of Early Pentecostalism*, 1st ed. New York: Orbis, 2007.

________. *To the Ends of the Earth*. Oxford: Oxford University Press, 2013.

Antturi, Eero J. "Helluntaiherätys tänään." In *Helluntaiherätys tänään*, edited by Kai Antturi, Juhani Kuosmanen, and Valtter Luoto. Vantaa: Ristin Voitto, 1996.

Arnold, Clinton E. *Ephesians*. Zondervan Exegetical Commentary on the New Testament. Grand Rapids: Zondervan Academic, 2010. Kindle.

Barna Report. Produced in Partnership with OneHope. *Guiding Children to Discover the Bible, Navigate Technology, and Follow Jesus*. Barna Group, 2020.

Beougher, Timothy K. "Revival, Revivals." *Evangelical Dictionary of World Missions*, edited by A. Scott Moreau with Harold Netland, and Charles van Engen. Grand Rapids: Baker Books, 2000.

Bonnke, Reinhard. *Evangelism by Fire*. Lake Mary, FL: Charisma House, 2011.

________. *Even Greater-Real Life Stories that Inspire You to Do Greater Things For God*. E-R Productions LLC, 2005.

Burge, Gary M. *The Anointed Community: The Holy Spirit in the Johannine Tradition*. Grand Rapids: Eerdmans, 1987.

Bush, Luis. "Catalysts of World Evangelization." Ph.D. diss. School of World Mission. Fuller Theological Seminary, 2002.

Calvin, John. *Commentaries on the Epistles of Paul to the Galatians and Ephesians*. Trans. William Pringle. Grand Rapids: Baker Books, 2003.

Clark, Clifton. *Pentecostalism: Insights from Africa and the African Diaspora*. Eugene: Wipf and Stock Publishers, 2018.

Clinton, J. Robert. *The Making of a Leader: Recognizing the Lessons and Stages or Leadership Development*. Colorado Springs, CO: NavPress, 1988.

Clowney, Edmund P. *The Church: Contours of Christian Theology*. Leicester, UK: Inter Varsity Press, 1995.

Detrick, Jodi. *The Jesus-Hearted Woman: 10 Leadership Qualities for Enduring and Endearing Influence*. Springfield, MO: Influence Resources, 2013.

Douglas, J.D., ed. *Let the Earth Hear His Voice, International Congress on World Evangelization Lausanne, Switzerland: Official Reference Volume: Papers and Responses*. Minneapolis: World Wide Publications, 1975.

Global Evangelists Alliance. *The Spirit-Empowered Evangelist*. Tulsa, OK: Empowered21, 2023.

________. *Spirit-Empowered Witnessing*. Tulsa, OK: Empowered21, 2023.

Gordon, Jon and Mike Smith. *You Win in the Locker Room First: The C's to Building a Winning Team in Business, Sports, and Life*. Hoboken, NJ: John Willey & Sons, Inc., 2015.

Grey, Jacqueline N. "Women Leaders in the Old Testament." In *Women & Men: One in Christ, Christians for Biblical Equality*, edited by D. Cooper-Clarke and K. Giles. (2016): 1–13.

Hall, Ian R. *Times of Renewal: A History and Theology of Revival and Spiritual Awakenings*. Oradea: Metanoia, 2023.

Harrell, David Edwin, Jr. *Oral Roberts: An American Life*. San Francisco: Harper & Row, 1985.

Hiebert, Paul G. "Healing and the Kingdom." In *Wonders and the Word*, edited by James R. Coggins and Paul G. Hiebert. Winnipeg: Kindred, 1989.

Hirsch, Alan. *The Forgotten Ways: Reactivating Apostolic Movements*. Grand Rapids, Michigan: Brazos Press, 2016.

________. *The Forgotten Ways: Reactivating the Missional Church*. Grand Rapids, Michigan: Brazos Press, 2006.

Hollenweger, Walter. *Pentecostalismo*. Buenos Aires: Editorial Aurora, 1976.

Keener, Craig S. *The Spirit in the Gospels and the Acts: Divine Purity and Power*. Peabody, MA: Hendrickson, 1997.

________. *Paul, Women & Wives: Marriage and Women's Ministry in the Letters of Paul*. Peabody, Massachusetts: Hendrickson Publishers, 1992.

Kessler, John. *A Study of the Older Protestant Missions and Churches in Perú and Chile*. Goes, The Netherlands: Oosterbaan & Le Contre N.V., 1967.

Kotter, John P. *Leading Change.* Boston, MA: Harvard Business Review Press, 2012.

Ma, Wonsuk, Opoku Onyinah, and Rebekah Bled, eds. *The Remaining Task of the Great Commission & the Spirit-Empowered Movement.* Tulsa, OK: ORU Press, 2023.

Menzies, Robert P. "John's Place in the Development of Early Christian Pneumatology." In *The Spirit and Spirituality: Essays in Honor of Russel P. Spittler.* London: T & T Clark, 2004.

Onyinah, Opoku. *Apostles and Prophets: The Ministry of Apostles and Prophets Throughout the Generations.* Eugene, OR: Wipf & Stock Publishers, 2022.

Orellana, Luis. *El Fuego y la Nieve* 1. Hualpén, Chile: CEEP Ediciones, 2006.

________ . "El Futuro del Pentecostalismo en América Latina," edited by Daniel and Luis Orellana Luis. Red Latinoamérica de Estudios Pentecostales (RELEP). *Voces del Pentecostalismo Latinoamericano* 4 (2011): 141–56;

Osborn, Tommy Lee and Daisy Osborn. *Faith Library in 23 Volumes: 20th Century Legacy of Apostolic Evangelism.* 23 vols. Tulsa: OSFO International, 1997.

________ . *The Message that Works.* Tulsa, OK: T.L. Osborn Ministries, 1955.

________ . *Soul Winning.* Tulsa, OK: OSFO Publishing, 1963.

________ . *Soul Winning Out Where the Sinners Are.* Tulsa, OK: Harrison House, 1980.

Paulus, Michael J. Jr. and Michael D. Langford. *AI, Faith, and the Future: An Interdisciplinary Approach.* Eugene, OR: Pickwick Publications, 2022.

Phiri, Desmond, ed. *Digital Discipleship in Africa: The Church's New Frontier.* Nairobi: Hippo Books, 2024.

Roberts, Oral. "Oral Roberts: Legendary Oklahoma Evangelist, Founder of ORU." Interview by John Erling. *Voices of Oklahoma,* August 11, 2009. Audio chapter 9, 5:57. https://www.voicesofoklahoma.com/interviews/roberts-oral.

Ross, Kenneth, Kwabena Asamoah-Gyadu, and Todd M. Johnson. *Christianity in Sub-Saharan Africa.* Edinburgh: Edinburgh University Press, 2017.

Roxburgh, Alan J. *An Introduction to the Missional Church Conversation.* Eagle, ID: Allelon Publishing, 2008.

Saari, Mauno. *Saarnaaja: Niilo Yli-Vainion taistelu, testamentti ja päiväkirjat.* Porvoo-Helsinki-Juva: WSOY, 1983.

Snyder, Howard A. and Daniel V. Runyon V. *Decoding the Church: Mapping the DNA of Christ's Body.* Eugene, OR: Wipf and Stock, 2002.

Stetzer, Ed. *Planting New Churches in a Postmodern Age.* Nashville: Broadman and Holman, 2004.

Stoll, David. *Is Latin America Turning Protestant?* California: UCC Press, 1991.

Stott, John. "The Lausanne Covenant." Lausanne Movement. https://lausanne.org/content/covenant/lausanne-covenant#cov/.

Synan, Vinson and Billy Wilson. *As the Waters Cover the Sea: The Story of Empowered21 and the Movement It Serves.* Tulsa, OK: ORU Press, 2020.

Tizon, Al. *Transformation after Lausanne: Radical Evangelical Mission in Global-Local Perspective.* Eugene: Wipf & Stock, 2008.

Toffler, Alvin. *Future Shock.* New York: Random House, 1970.

Toukola, Marja, ed. *Suomen herättäjä – Niilo Yli-Vainion syntymästä sata vuotta, 1920–2020.* Virrat: KKJMK, 2020.

Turner, M. *The Holy Spirit and Spiritual Gifts: In the New Testament Church and Today.* Peabody, MA: Hendrickson, 1998.

van Rossum, Joost. "The 'Johannine Penecost': John 20:22 in Modern Exegesis and in Orthodox Theology." *St. Vladimir's Theological Quarterly* 35 (1991): 149–67.

Wairimu, Teresia and Anne Jackson. *A Cactus in The Desert: An Autobiography.* Nairobi: Revival Springs Media, 2011.

Wilson, Billy. *The Power of One.* Tulsa, OK: Empowered Books, 2023.

Zurlo, Gina A. and Johnson, Todd M. *World Christian Encyclopedia,* 3rd edition. Edinburgh: Edinburgh University Press, 2019.